THE
WORLD'S MOST
EVIL PEOPLE

THE WORLD'S MOST EVIL PEOPLE

by
RODNEY CASTLEDEN

timewarner
paperbacks

A Time Warner Book

This first edition published in 2005

ISBN 0 7515 3666 0

Produced by Omnipress, Eastbourne

Printed in the EU

Time Warner Books
Brettenham House
Lancaster Place
London WC2E 7EN

Photo credits: Corbis
Front cover images: *Henry VIII,*
Adolf Hitler and *Harold Shipman*

Dedication: For Les, Shirley and Charlie Berry

The views expressed in this publication are those of the author. The information and the interpretation of that information are presented in good faith. Readers are advised that where ethical issues are involved, and often highly controversial ethical issues at that, they have a personal responsibility for making their own assessments and their own ethical judgements.

CONTENTS

Introduction 7

Introduction

THERE ARE OVER 18 million websites on the internet relating to evil. Many of them are facetious or relate to games of various kinds. We are all afraid of evil, yet we make jokes about it and it is easy to see why. When we encounter evil, whether it is in a lurid newspaper piece reporting the trial of a serial killer or when we are betrayed by someone we thought we could trust, we are at a loss to understand. Evil goes against the grain – for most of us – yet it is part of the warp and weft not only of history but of the everyday world that we live in. Evil acts are shocking, yet common. Laughing them off and making jokes about them is sometimes the only way we can cope with them. But the very fact that evil is commonplace makes it essential that we look at it hard and steadily, and try to understand it, not least so that we can defend ourselves as best we may.

There is a point of view that there are no evil people at all, only misguided actions. No bad people, only bad acts. After writing this book, I cannot agree with that. As a result of a misjudgement or a mistake, any one of us can commit an evil act; we all have the capacity to do something wrong inadvertently. But most of the people featured in this book deliberately and systematically committed evil acts, and they often committed them over and over again. We should not try to make excuses for what these people did. On the other hand, it is in all our interests to try to understand why they did what they did, so that we can avoid creating the situations in which evil is born, and so that we can detect the early signs of evil in the making, so that we can bring up our young in a way that makes them least likely to tread the downward path towards evil.

Evil depends partly on the zeitgeist, the spirit of the age. Looking back across the centuries there seem to have been more evil people about at certain times than at others. The twentieth century was one of those times, possibly because technology and in particular the industrialization of warfare made it possible, using weapons of mass destruction, to kill very large numbers of people with relative ease. Evil sometimes appears or disappears according to your viewpoint. It is possible to see the dropping of the atomic bomb on Hiroshima as a good act, because it brought the Second World War quickly to an end, or as a necessary evil, because it did that but also killed a lot of people, or as an act of unqualified evil, because the people killed were civilians, slaughtered in cold blood, and they should never have been considered as military targets. The American decision to drop the bomb on Hiroshima is a classic moral paradox.

The twentieth century saw an outbreak of evil that was completely unprecedented. There was a blood-letting on a scale that had never been seen before in human history. The 20 worst bloodlettings of the twentieth century each involved a million deaths or more; they were:

1.	Second World War	50 million
2.	Mao Zedong's regime in China	48 million
3.	Stalin's regime in the Soviet Union	20 million
4.	First World War, including Armenian massacres	15 million
5.	Russian Civil War	8.8 million
6.	Warlord and Nationalist era in China	4 million
7.	Congo under King Leopold	3 million
8.	Korean War	2.8 million
9.	Second Indo-China War	2.7 million
10.	Chinese Civil War	2.5 million
11.	German expulsions after Second World War	2.1 million
12.	Second Sudanese Civil War	1.9 million
13.	Congolese Civil War	1.7 million
14.	Cambodia Khmer Rouge regime	1.7 million
15.	Afghanistan Civil War	1.4 million
16.	Ethiopian Civil Wars	1.4 million
17.	Mexican Revolution	1.3 million
18.	East Pakistan massacres	1.2 million
19.	Iran-Iraq War	1 million
20.	Nigeria: Biafran War	1 million

This list implies a lot of separate events but many of them are closely linked. They form part of a single, complex and appalling upheaval which some have described as the Haemoclysm, the 'Blood Flood', which swept 155 million human lives away. The Western Haemoclysm started with the Balkan Wars, led on through two World Wars to the establishment of Communism in Eastern Europe. By the end of the Western Haemoclysm, marked by the death of Stalin, 80 million lives had been swept away.

The processes of political and social change play a great part. There was a great socio-political spasm in which monarchy imploded and republicanism exploded, imperialism collapsed and self-government became paramount, traditional religions (apart from Islam) seriously weakened, and Communism and the personality cults of dictators strengthened. These and many other changes have generated the violence. And there are always evil people waiting to seize opportunities to take power for themselves – and abuse it.

Necessarily, however long we make this book some people are going to be included and some left out. Napoleon and Charles Manson were left out, though they were on the draft list. A decision has to be made about who is more evil and who is less evil. We can ask ourselves hypothetical questions, 'Who would I least like to meet in a dark alley at night?' or 'Who would I least like to be in a room with?' The historian Professor Sir Alan Bullock, who wrote knowledgeably about both Hitler and Stalin, was once asked which of the two monsters he would have preferred to spend time with. He chose Hitler. Although an afternoon with Hitler would have been less exciting than an afternoon with Stalin – boring, even, according to Bullock – there was a better chance of getting through it alive. That makes Stalin easily the more evil of the two. Who would you least like to meet? My guess is that if you are a woman you will probably most fear a nightmare figure like Jack the Ripper. If you are a man, the choice is more open-ended. Probably all of us fear encountering Dr Harold Shipman, the GP from Hell – superficially ordinary, yet lethal.

There are different kinds of evil. There is the expert pediatrician who falsely accuses parents of abusing or even killing their children – evil by expertise. There is the lynch mob who throws stones through the window of a pediatrician, not understanding the difference between the words 'pediatrician' and 'paedophile' – evil through ignorance (not that there would be a right window for stone-throwing).

Inevitably, various writers have attempted to identify the 'Top Ten' or 'Top Twenty' most evil people. One list I came across was a 'Top Twelve', a short enough list to quote in full: Torquemada, Vlad the Impaler, Hitler, Stalin, Amin, Ivan the Terrible, Eichmann, Pol Pot, Mao, Genghis Khan, H. H. Holmes and Gilles de Rais. It is easy to see how each of those names qualifies for the top twelve, and they all find their place in this book, because they were all killers, but how many deaths did they cause? Gilles de Rais was a horrible man, but he didn't cause nearly as many deaths (800) as Stalin (20 million) – or does the fact that de Rais committed the murders with his own hands and Stalin simply gave the orders to kill make de Rais's killing more evil? It is not, after all, quite as easy to rank evil as we might have thought. I was glad that I was able to make this

11

book a much longer exploration of evil. I have had the luxury of choosing from over 90, and that is rather easier to do, though still not easy. The structure of the book shows that there are different kinds of evil, and I have grouped people according to the type of evil they perpetrated. The last type is probably the most controversial – Evil by Doing Nothing. I describe one classic example in detail but you, the reader, will probably be able to think of many others.

Evil reputation is not always the best guide to evil actuality. Rasputin, Richard III and Lucrezia Borgia have evil reputations they don't deserve. History is kind to some people, unkind to others. It is useful to take another look and ask whether this historical figure was really as evil (or, indeed, as good) as they have been made out to be. In this book I try to rectify a few of the unfairnesses of the past.

So – fame or infamy may not be the best guide to goodness or evil. Political agenda often influences people in identifying evil. While researching this book I found one alarming 'Top 25' Most Evil People of the Millennium. It included some fairly predictable names – Hitler, Stalin, Ivan the Terrible and Genghis Khan – but also two surprise entries in the shape of Bill and Hillary Clinton!

It may be that the most evil people in the world don't get found out; history doesn't notice them. The serial killer Dr Harold Shipman got very nearly to the end of his career as a GP without being detected; once he had retired, there would

THE WORLD'S MOST EVIL PEOPLE

have been no reason for anyone to investigate any of his patients' deaths. He very nearly got away with it. All of it. How many others, and not just in Britain, have got away with mass murder? In the days before forensic science it was much easier to poison people without detection. In the nature of things, there is no way of knowing how many of these 'successful' evil people there may have been. We can never know. We do know that large numbers of people have been executed for crimes they did not commit. Timothy Evans was one. Even in some high-profile cases, like that of Mary Queen of Scots, it may be that the convicted and executed 'criminal' was not only innocent but the terribly wronged victim of an even greater evil, framing by the authorities; was Mary the evil conspirator, or Walsingham?

What we can know with a terrible certainty is that the evil continues. There are still people committing terrible crimes against other people and who have yet to be brought to justice. There are several alleged 'war criminals' who have yet to stand trial for the atrocities they committed in Bosnia at the end of the twentieth century. There is an Iraqi ex-head of state who has, at the time of writing, yet to answer for his crimes. There are the leaders of Al-Qaeda and their successors who look as though they will go on committing atrocities – on and on into the future. There is no foreseeable end to evil. It is therefore all the more important that we face up to it, recognize it and do whatever we can to limit its impact on our lives.

PART ONE

ANCIENT EVIL

Alexander the Great
(356–323 BC)

IT MAY SEEM odd to launch a list of evil people with an individual who has been held up for centuries in many different countries as a role model, an icon of virtue and valour - as the ultimate hero. But history is what people say about the past, and that is always selective. Have we been selecting the good things about Alexander and ignoring or overlooking the bad?

Alexander 'the Great' was born at Pella in Macedonia in 356 BC. He was the son of King Philip of Macedon, who was a first-rate general and administrator, and Queen Olympias, who was brilliant, impulsive and hot-tempered. Alexander inherited to a high degree the qualities of both his parents. The most striking difference was that Alexander was far more ambitious than his father; he was in fact one of the most ambitious people of all time. His mother Olympias taught him that Achilles was his ancestor, and he became so fixated with this idea that his tutor, Aristotle actually called him Achilles. As part of this obsession, Alexander learnt the Iliad by heart, always carried a copy of Homer's epic poem with him, and consciously acted out the dangerous fantasy that he was one of Homer's heroes.

As a boy, Alexander was strong and fearless. He famously succeeded in taming Bucephalus, a spirited horse that nobody else dared to mount. It was when he was 13 that Alexander became Aristotle's pupil, and Aristotle imbued him with a great love of literature, geography and ethnology, all of which fed and informed his military career. When he was 18, Alexander commanded a section of his father's cavalry at the Battle of Chaeronea. He was also entrusted with acting as his father's ambassador to Athens. He was a youth carefully groomed for kingship.

Then, when Alexander was 20, Philip of Macedon was assassinated. It is still unclear whether Alexander connived in the conspiracy to kill his father, but the assassination looks like a well-orchestrated palace coup, and the timing suited Alexander perfectly. There is a suspicion that his mother Olympias played a part in it. While Alexander was away making war on a barbarian tribe in the north, the people of Thebes, to the south, heard a rumour that he was dead and revolted against Macedonian domination, inviting Athens to join them in a rebellion. Alexander swiftly rode to Thebes with his army, stormed the city and destroyed every building except the temples and the house of the poet Pindar. The incident shows several aspects of the nature of Alexander well: the well-judged reverence for certain things, the poignant sentimentality, the grand gesture, the brutality, the wanton destructiveness. Fans of Alexander weaken at the knees at the thought that he spared the house of the poet, and gloss over the fact that he sold 30,000 captive Thebans into slavery. Clearly, a case can be made for Alexander as a war criminal.

Alexander turned then to Persia. The father had dreamed of conquering Persia; now the son wanted to outdo the father by achieving it. In 334 BC, he crossed the Hellespont with an army 35,000 strong. He was met by the Persian army on the banks of the Granicus River. He was victorious, and all Asia Minor opened before him. Halicarnassus withstood a siege, but the other towns gave in easily. In 333 BC, after a serious bout of illness, he marched along the south coast of Anatolia into Syria. Darius III, the Persian king, raised a huge army to stop him, but Alexander captured Darius's camp, taking Darius's wife and mother prisoner. Once again, Alexander won credit by behaving gallantly towards them.

He turned south to capture Tyre, after a seven-month siege, by building a causeway out to the island. He killed 8,000 citizens of Tyre, selling 30,000 more into slavery. This operation is considered Alexander's greatest military achievement. He went on to do the same to Gaza. After that came Egypt, where Alexander was welcomed as a deliverer; the Egyptians hated their harsh Persian rulers. On the Nile Delta, Alexander founded a new city, egotistically naming it after himself – Alexandria.

In 331 BC, Alexander turned back to deal with the Persian army. Darius had gathered an enormous host, including the heavy cavalry of the Persian steppe, and many chariots with scythe-like blades protruding from the wheel-axles. The Persians cleared and smoothed a huge level plain at Arbela, east of the River Tigris, to make an arena where their chariots could be effectively deployed. In the Battle of Arbela which followed, Alexander's army routed Darius's and the Persian army retreated. It was one of the most decisive battles in history. Babylon surrendered, and Alexander took the Persian cities of Susa and Persepolis, which yielded vast treasures in gold and silver.

At Persepolis, Alexander committed some of his worst atrocities. All the inhabitants of the city were either killed or sold as slaves, and finally the great and beautiful city was burned to the ground. It was a terrible act of vandalism.

Alexander crossed the Zagros Mountains in 330 BC, to reach Media. Darius had fled there, and he was shortly afterwards killed by his own nobles. With Darius dead, Alexander effectively became king of the entire region, from Greece, right across Anatolia and the Near and Middle East. Not content with this, Alexander took his army on to the southern shore of the Caspian Sea, hammering local tribes as he went, and setting up Persian nobles as local governors, though many of these rebelled against his overlordship after he had moved on. The march continued through Bactria and Sogdiana, where Alexander married Roxane, the daughter of a Sogdian lord. It was in Sogdiana that the violence in Alexander broke out on a personal level. He lost his temper when drunk and killed a close friend, Clitus. For this single act, amongst all the acts of mass cruelty, his Macedonian troops never forgave him.

They remembered him as the murderer of Clitus.

In 326 BC, Alexander reached northern Pakistan, where he defeated Porus, one of the local princes. He had planned to go on to conquer the Ganges valley, but his army mutinied. They were getting too far from home. It is interesting to speculate just how far Alexander would have gone if the troops had been willing. Would he have gone on to China? The huge sprawling military campaign had reached its furthest point though, and he turned to sail down the Indus River to its mouth, then led the army west in a terrible march across the desert of southern Iran. The army and the fleet returned to Susa.

Alexander then busied himself with an insane plan to turn Europe and Asia, or at least as much of Asia as he had conquered, into a single country. Babylon would be its capital. Intermarriage would be one of the means by which the different regions would be bonded together, and this was why he married a Persian princess himself. He placed soldiers from all the provinces of this empire in his army. He introduced a common currency system throughout the empire. He encouraged the spread of Greek ideas, customs and laws into Asia, regarding them as more enlightened than the existing local laws. Thus far, it all sounds very modern and progressive – not unlike the European Union. But the scale was hopelessly grandiose, given the communications systems of the time, and there was underlying all of it the megalomania of the mad dictator. Naturally, to gain recognition as the supreme ruler everywhere in his empire, Alexander required all the provinces to acknowledge him as a god. It came back, in the end, to this ultimate ego-trip.

Alexander's plan simmered, steamed and expanded, and at the time of his death he was planning a new expedition to Arabia. He was taken ill with what may have been malaria in Babylon. He died on 13 June, 323 BC. His body was put into a gold coffin and transported to Memphis in Egypt, and from there to Alexandria where it was placed in a beautiful tomb. The tomb of Alexander has, rather surprisingly, been lost. Alexander left no successor either, and a successor was essential for the survival of his empire. For all the brilliance and dash of Alexander's career, much of it was to do with personal vanity and egotism, and the manner of his conquest was invariably cruel. As always, too many people had to die to fulfil one man's dream.

There are today, just as there always have been, varying views of Alexander. He was very conscious of his image, and worked hard to project an image of himself as a reckless, energetic, romantic super-hero ready to take on the world. He even got his architect Deinocrates to prepare a plan to sculpt the Greek peninsula of Mount Athos into a vast sculpture of himself, Alexander the Great, reclining; this astonishingly egotistical scheme was revived in the seventeenth century, when the idealized (sanitized) image of Alexander seemed to represent a great human ideal. The idea was presented to his namesake Pope Alexander VII in about 1655, but fortunately came to nothing.

Alexander very deliberately followed his role models, the warrior-heroes of Homer's Iliad, and it was not at all by chance that he crossed the Hellespont to visit Achilles's tomb at Troy before going to meet the Persian army. He needed his army and his biographers to see him doing that. He was a brilliantly successful propagandist for his own self-image, but his murderous actions speak far louder than the propaganda. His actions were those of the mass-killer, and whatever glamour the distance of history may lend, the misery and suffering he caused thousands of his contemporaries, across a swathe of Eurasia from Greece to the Indus valley, were on an incalculably grand scale.

Herod the Great
(74 BC–4 BC)

BECAUSE OF THE Bible story, most of us have grown up feeling that we know King Herod all too well. Herod is one of the great archetypes of evil. He was the king who was visited by the wise men from the East when they were trying to find their way to the infant Messiah. He was the king who tried to kill Jesus by having all the male babies in Bethlehem massacred. But how evil was Herod, really? How great could that so-called 'Massacre of the Innocents' have been?

The Christian Church has been eager to inflate the Massacre of the Innocents, at different times claiming that 60,000 or 100,000 male infants were slaughtered by this anti-Christ. But if we look at the reality of the situation, Bethlehem was only a village, and even if there were a thousand people living in that village there can only have been a score of male babies. It could not have been much of a massacre after all. Will a closer look at Herod perhaps reveal a very different historical figure?

Herod was the son of Antipater, the procurator of Judaea under Rome. When he was 25, Herod's father appointed him ruler of Galilee. He immediately arrested Hezekiah, the arch-brigand, and executed him. He was summoned to appear before the Sanhedrin, charged with overriding their rights in executing Hezekiah. When he appeared with his bodyguard in full strength, the Sanhedrin was overawed and naturally reluctant to find him guilty. The governor of Syria, where Hezekiah had been a problem, sent a demand for Herod's acquittal, which let the Sanhedrin off the hook. The trial was adjourned and Herod was informally encouraged to abscond. Herod was humiliated and angry. He was ready to return later with an army to wreak vengeance, but his father dissuaded him from massacring the Sanhedrin.

In 43 BC, Antipater was poisoned at the instigation of Malichus, who seems to have been a Jewish freedom-fighter. Herod had Malichus assassinated in Syria, which was by now in a state of anarchy. Mark Antony, who was Master of the East after the Battle of Philippi, wanted to support the son of his friend Antipater, but he was away in Egypt when the Parthians invaded Palestine and put Antigonus on the throne in 40 BC. Herod escaped to Rome, where Antony made him and his elder brother tetrarchs; Antony persuaded the Roman Senate to proclaim Herod the rightful King of Judaea.

In 39 BC, Herod returned to Palestine and, with Antony's Roman troops at his disposal, he was able to lay siege to Jerusalem. Jerusalem was taken by storm. Antigonus, the usurper king, was beheaded at Antioch. In 37 BC, Herod was King of Judaea in fact, but still as a Roman client-king sponsored by Mark Antony. The Pharisees were resigned to accepting Herod's harsh rule as a judgement of God. Herod's marriage to Mariamne brought enemies into his household. Herod had ten wives, by whom he had 14 children. He tried to annihilate the rival Hasmonean faction by killing 45 members of the Sanhedrin and confiscating their possessions, but while there were members of the Hasmonean family still living there would always be a rival claimant to his throne. Mariamne's unscrupulous mother Alexandra used her position to try to overthrow her son-in-law. She found an unexpected ally in Queen Cleopatra, who bore a grudge against Herod because he had spurned her advances. Alexandra's plot nevertheless ensured that her name was added to Herod's death list.

Herod's reign was a battleground of different factions and interest groups. His Babylonian high priest was deposed so that Mariamne's brother, Aristobulus, might hold the post. Cleopatra acquired grants of territory next to Herod's and she demanded that Herod should collect arrears of tribute from these lands for her.

After the Battle of Actium in 31 BC, and the consequent suicides of Mark Antony and Cleopatra, Herod somehow managed to remain untainted by his association with both Antony and Cleopatra, and gained favour with Augustus, the victor. It was an extremely dangerous time for him, as he could easily have found himself deposed by Augustus. Herod took the initiative and went straight to Augustus in person to declare his loyalty. Augustus was impressed and confirmed Herod's position as a client-king.

Herod was uncertain about the outcome of his

meeting with Augustus, and left orders that if he did not return his wife Mariamne should be killed also. When he got back, he discovered that Mariamne knew all about this plan. She was furious, gave him a piece of her mind and refused to sleep with him any more. It had always been a turbulent marriage, though Herod genuinely loved her. In retaliation, he had her accused of adultery. At the trial, which Herod himself heard as judge, Mariamne's mother Alexandra came forward to give evidence that Marimane was indeed an adulteress. Alexandra was evidently trying to get her name removed from Herod's death list, and did not mind conniving at her daughter's death in order to do it. Mariamne was duly sentenced to death and executed.

Herod also successfully eliminated one potential rival claimant to the throne after another, however innocent and unthreatening, until by 25 BC they were all dead. Then, in the way of great dictators, he was free to do some spectacular building work. This he needed to do in order to win round the Jewish people. They absolutely detested him, partly for not having been born a Jew, and partly for consolidating Roman control over their country; they saw him as a fake, a quisling, a traitor. In an heroic effort to win the Jewish people over and gain personal popularity, Herod rebuilt the Temple in Jerusalem in lavish style, making it one of the wonders of the world. But it was a futile effort. The Jews still hated him. Perhaps they knew his efforts were shallow, insincere and vainglorious. His next

venture was to build a new city on the coast.
Foolishly, he dedicated the city and a temple in it
to the Roman Emperor, naming it Caesarea. There
were arenas for gladiatorial games, which were
also offensive to the Jews.

Herod became intermittently ill. Some said he
was deranged and should be deposed, but few
dared to act on this thought. Alexandra decided to
take the risk. She declared Herod unfit to rule and
herself queen in his place. This was just what
Herod needed to stir him from his sickbed. He got
up and staggered out to order Alexandra's summary execution. She was executed immediately,
without trial.

Still he had enemies in his household. His
brother Pheroras and sister Salome plotted against
the two sons of Mariamne. On his deathbed,
Herod learnt that his eldest son, Antipater, had
been plotting against him. He accused him formally before the governor of Syria and obtained
permission from the Emperor Augustus to put his
son to death. Herod had his son and heir Antipater
executed, just five days before his own death. It
was another son, Herod Antipas, who succeeded
him – and this Herod too was a monster. This new
Herod was the Herod who had a hand in the
executions of both John the Baptist and Jesus.

Herod the Great's reign was stained with
cruelties and atrocities. Sooner or later, every
member of the rival Hasmonean family fell victim
to his suspicions and fears; all were to die on the
slightest pretext. In the Bible he is blamed for the
slaughter of the innocents. This was the organized

killing of all male babies under the age of two, just in case one of them proved to be the king who would supplant him, the prophesied Messiah. This remarkable atrocity is not mentioned by the historian Josephus, but Josephus was much more interested in great events and important people and although he may have known about it a village massacre would not have seemed important to him. The killing becomes important in the Gospel of Matthew because the massacre, however small in scale, was intended to ensure the death of the infant Jesus, and was therefore profoundly relevant to the story. The Greek word used in Matthew in any case means 'killing' not 'massacre'. Some historians think the killing of the firstborn didn't happen at all, but appears in the Gospel because of an elision of two events. The wise men may well have arrived in the court of King Herod at a time when the firstborn were slaughtered – but it was Herod's own firstborn, the two sons he had executed round about the time that Jesus was born.

Whether it happened or not, the killing of the firstborn in Bethlehem would have been entirely in character; it was very much the kind of thing Herod did, especially in the later years of his reign. His ordering the death of his wife Mariamne and his two sons by her were atrocities in the same style. It is now generally believed that Jesus was born in 5 or 7 BC, and both of these dates would have fallen in the final years of Herod the Great's reign, when his paranoia reached fever pitch. He was completely unhinged, and justifiably hated by his family, his courtiers, his rivals and the great mass of Jewish people who were his subjects. He had his wife's brother, Aristobulus, drowned in his swimming pool during a party. The network of fortresses he built across the land were not built to defend his kingdom against foreign enemies, but to defend himself against his own people.

Yet, in a perverse way, Herod caused something else to happen. Herod nurtured and intensified the Roman occupation of Judaea and therefore helped to create the climate of despair and rebellion that allowed Christianity to flourish. It was because of Herod that the Jews wanted a Messiah.

Tiberius
(42 BC–AD 37)

TIBERIUS CLAUDIUS NERO was born on 16
November, 42 BC. His father, who had the same
name, was one of Julius Caesar's officers. His
mother was Livia, who had been handed on to
Octavian, the future emperor Augustus, in 38 BC.
Three months after her second marriage,
Tiberius's brother Drusus was born. Livia was to
have no children by Augustus, and she devoted
all her efforts towards the advancement of her
sons. As a prince, Tiberius passed through all the
appropriate state offices. At 21 he became a
quaestor; at 29 he became a consul. He learnt the
tasks associated with each role and proved to be
a conscientious administrator

Tiberius's main milieu was the army camp.
From 22 to 6 BC and again from AD 4 to 10 he
spent most of his time with the army. In 20 BC
Augustus sent Tiberius with an army to seat
Tigranes of Armenia as a Roman client king. In 15
BC he went to help his brother subjugate two
German tribes in the Black Forest.

A great unhappiness befell Tiberius when Agrippa
died in 12 BC. This left Julia, the emperor's only
child, a widow. Livia persuaded Augustus to force
Tiberius to marry Julia. Tiberius was already

married to Vipsania, whom he loved, and did not want to divorce. In 9 BC Drusus died. Tiberius had always been eclipsed by his brilliant younger brother, but now he, Tiberius, was the first soldier of the Roman Empire. The soldiers under his command did not especially like Tiberius – he was not a man they could warm to – but they respected and trusted him and he always made their safety his first consideration. Tiberius returned from his Rhine campaign in triumph and was rewarded with the title 'imperator'. He was also made consul again, and tribune. Tiberius was in this way closely associated with the emperor in the civil government of the empire, and it was thought at the time that this marked him out as the heir to the throne.

Tiberius had a dark side. He suddenly asked for permission to retire to Rhodes in order to study. He refused to give any reason for this retreat. It emerged years afterwards that his reason was to give the young princes Gaius and Lucius, the sons of Agrippa and Julia, their chance to shine – at least that was the reason he gave. It may rather be that he had no wish to become the servant of the two boys whom Augustus had adopted and evidently saw as joint heirs. Possibly Tiberius had no ambition to be emperor, and he wanted to get away from his mother's endless scheming on his behalf. Possibly he wanted to get away from his wife Julia's scandalous behaviour and it was safer to be nowhere near her when her sexual exploits were discovered by Augustus. When Augustus did indeed find out and exploded with anger, inflicting terrible punishment on Julia, Tiberius interceded on her behalf and did what he could to reduce her suffering. Possibly there were attractions on Rhodes that we know nothing of, but he did indeed pass time there with scholars, with whom he discoursed intelligently.

After five years, he asked for leave to return, and Augustus angrily refused. Livia managed to persuade Augustus to make him a legate, which to an extent legitimized his absence from Rome. Augustus then relented and allowed Tiberius to return on condition that he held no public office. The moment he returned, in AD 2, Lucius died, and about a year later Gaius died. They may have died naturally, but there is reason to suspect that Livia arranged their deaths to clear the way for her son to become emperor. Evil was done on Tiberius's behalf, rather than by him; he was the beneficiary of evil.

The emperor was left with only one male descendant now, Agrippa Postumus, Julia's son, and he was only a boy. Augustus adopted both Postumus and Tiberius as his sons, and indicated that he expected Tiberius to be his successor. Now Tiberius resumed his military career, returning in triumph to Rome once more in AD 11. From this time until Augustus's death in AD 14, Tiberius was in effect joint emperor. When Augustus died, Tiberius was no longer young: he was 56.

Possibly because of the overriding ambitions of his mother, he had learnt to hide his feelings, ambitions and motives. What struck everyone was how impenetrable he was. Throughout his career as a military commander, he is only known once to have discussed anything, and that was after the catastrophic annihilation of Varus's legions in Germany. He was stern and totally inscrutable, and therefore almost totally dislikable. The men of his own legions mutinied when they heard that he had become emperor and it was only the skill of Germanicus that prevented a mutinous march on Rome to unseat Tiberius. He was not a brilliant man, so he brooded over problems for a long time to get at the solution. Silent, gloomy men are never popular.

He was held in check for much of his life by his mother and the necessity of keeping the right side of Augustus. Once he became emperor, his true nature came increasingly out into the open. He cut himself off from his controlling mother by setting up court on the island of Capri, where he indulged in all kinds of perverted pastimes, which involved the sexual abuse of slaves and children. He became a monster of wickedness.

When Germanicus was in the East, Tiberius set Piso in place there to spy on him. Piso and his wife poisoned Germanicus, and it would seem likely that this was on Tiberius's orders. Tiberius had Piso brought to Rome for a show trial; Piso was forced to commit suicide. Tiberius named two of the sons of Agrippina, Germanicus's widow, as his heirs. In Rome, Tiberius maintained control through his minister, Sejanus. Sejanus in turn maintained his own position by feeding the emperor's suspicions about Agrippina and her household. Then, after brooding on the situation on Capri for a while, Tiberius launched a purge. In his own memoirs, Tiberius claimed that he killed Sejanus because Sejanus entertained an insane rage against the sons of Germanicus. This cannot be true, because the destruction of Sejanus was a bloodbath, a Roman purge that consumed Agrippina and her two sons as well. It was Agrippina's third son, the awful Caligula, who was to become Tiberius's heir.

Tiberius was remembered in Rome as a dangerous emperor who could not be trusted. Under his rule, scores of people were prosecuted for treason on the slightest of pretexts and a climate of terror was created in which informers flourished as they provided Sejanus with the perjured evidence required to commit one judicial murder after another. Much of this evil may have been carried out by Sejanus while Tiberius was away, frolicking on Capri, but Tiberius was nevertheless responsible for delegating power to Sejanus. It was all the more terrible as an experience for Rome because of the contrast with the way Augustus ran things. Under Augustus there was no doctrine of constructive treason. Under Tiberius, more and more people were put to the sword and their property confiscated under trumped-up treason charges. As time passed, Tiberius seems to have become more and more indifferent to the shedding of civilian blood, so that Rome looked increasingly like one of his battlefields.

Caligula
(AD 12–41)

WHEN THE 25-year-old Gaius Caesar became third Emperor of Rome on the death of Tiberius, there was general rejoicing. Tiberius was old, corrupt, depraved and had shut himself away on Capri while his critics were cruelly executed in Rome. He had done Rome a favour by nominating little Gaius, great-grandson of the great Augustus and son of the military hero Germanicus, as his successor. As a child, Gaius had been taken on campaigns by his father. The soldiers had adopted him as a mascot, dressing him in a miniature uniform, complete with little boots, 'caligulae' – hence his nickname, Little Boot, Caligula.

But in four short years the nickname would turn into a by-word for capricious cruelty far worse than any of Tiberius's. Caligula was wild, extravagant, with a penchant for sexual adventures. What started as youthful excesses resulting from too much power too young turned into insane excess.

Things started well, with Caligula declaring amnesties for all Romans imprisoned or exiled under Tiberius and stopping the treason trials. He gave away much of Tiberius's wealth in tax rebates and cash bonuses for the garrison in Rome. He lavished huge amounts of money on the German mercenaries of his personal body-guard. Senators who warned that he would bankrupt himself if he carried on like this were disregarded as he organized lavish circuses for the people. Exotic menageries of animals from all over the Roman Empire were collected for mock hunts in the arenas. Pay for gladiators doubled and trebled.

Behind the scenes things began to develop in an even more unsettling way. He had made his three sisters leave their husbands, and move into his palace so that he could sleep with them. At night, Caligula wandered round the city with his guards, joining in orgies with prostitutes.

After reigning for only seven months, Caligula fell seriously ill with a 'brain fever'. After a month he recovered physically, though he was clearly mentally ill. He thought he had turned into a god. The programme of circuses accelerated, with more and more public holidays, and Caligula began to run out of money. The pay for gladiators fell, and only fat old gladiators lured out of retirement turned up in the arenas; the quality of the shows dropped and the people of Rome disliked what they saw. The crowd in the amphitheatre rose and booed. Caligula had those who had led the jeering rounded up. They were dragged off into the cellars, where their tongues were cut out; then they were forced out into the arena to do battle with the wild animals themselves. The spectators were shocked into silence by what they saw, but the Emperor shouted, laughed and clapped until the last of the jeerers had been killed. As he left,

Caligula said, 'I wish Rome had but one neck, so that I could cut off all their heads with one blow!' Few Romans appreciated the Emperor's strange sense of humour.

From then on, Caligula had to make economies. His idea of economies was to feed criminals from the prisons to the lions to fatten them up and launch a series of treason charges against wealthy citizens. Evidence was bought from perjurers, just as in Tiberius's time, and entire estates and fortunes were taken as 'fines'.

Finally, in the time-honoured way of political leaders then and now, Caligula resorted to foreign adventures as a means of acquiring wealth and distracting subjects from misery and mismanagement at home. He looked to Gaul and Spain, but spent the last of his imperial wealth on a strange event in the Bay of Naples. He moored 4,000 boats to make a floating bridge across the bay and rode across on horseback – to give the lie to an old prophecy that he had no more chance of becoming Emperor than of riding across the bay. When the bridge was destroyed in a storm, Caligula swore he would take revenge on Neptune, the Sea-god.

He also threw a party for his horse Incitatus, giving him presents of paintings to hang on his marble bedroom walls. Caligula threatened to make Incitatus a senator.

The prefect of the Praetorian Guard, Macro, had helped Caligula gain the throne, but now Caligula felt he owed him too much. Caligula tricked Macro into thinking he was to become prefect of Egypt, then had him arrested and executed.

Now desperate for cash, Caligula sank to sending his guards round the city, demanding cash from ordinary citizens in the street. The guards reported that they had extorted money even from the prostitutes, which gave Caligula another sick idea. He announced that his palace was to open as a brothel, with his sisters as prostitutes. Senators were obliged to turn up at the orgies, each paying an entrance fee of a thousand gold pieces; their humiliation was doubled when they were ordered to return with their wives and daughters. They were all obliged to join in the fun.

Caligula's popularity was over, as he alienated one social class after another. In Gaul, he behaved equally madly, organizing a mock-auction in which French noblemen were forced to outbid one another for what turned out to be bundles of rubbish. In Germany, a thousand prisoners were captured. He decided that he only needed 300 prisoners to make an impressive triumphal return to Rome, so the rest were killed. His last great campaign was to be the conquest of Britain, but he lost his nerve when he reached the Channel, remembering that Neptune was his great enemy. Camping near Boulogne, he ordered his bewildered and unnerved soldiers to line up on the beach. Archers formed up at the water's edge. Cavalry waited on the flanks. All looked out to sea as if waiting for the enemy to appear. Then Caligula rode into the sea, slashing at the water with his sword and swearing revenge on Neptune for wrecking his ships at Naples. Catapults were fired into the sea. Archers fired into the waves. Then Caligula ordered his men to gather seashells in their helmets – the plunder after the victory.

His was a weak, quirky personality totally corrupted by power, and now no-one found him funny. The army had been humiliated and he would not be forgiven for that. During the long march back to Rome, the conspiracy to get rid of him was hatched. For a month after his return home he was allowed to celebrate his imaginary victories – the celebration included plans to replace the heads of all the statues of gods in Rome with his own. Then Caligula pushed one of his veterans too far. He forced Cassius Chaerea to torture a young girl. Cassius wept at the girl's innocent anguish. When Caligula got to hear about it, he ridiculed Cassius mercilessly.

In January AD 41, when Caligula was in his private theatre, Cassius waited for him in a covered walkway. He sent word in that a troupe of young Greek dancing boys was waiting to perform for him. This brought Caligula out into the passage. Cassius drew his sword, felled Caligula and killed him with ten thrusts of his sword. Cassius strode straight into the theatre and announced, 'The show is over. The Emperor is dead.'. After a moment's silence there was a roar of applause.

Attila the Hun
(AD 406–453)

THE ROMAN EMPIRE was carved out of other people's territories and interests; all round the Mediterranean the Romans encroached on the lands and possessions of others. Inevitably, there was resistance and counter-attack, though the Romans often seem to have been surprised by this. The people of central and northern Europe were seen as 'barbarians', people who represented a continual threat and who needed subjugation. These people, who were on the whole simply trying to defend their homelands, repeatedly attacked Rome. Often they were demonized by the Romans for doing so, and it is sometimes hard to evaluate the Roman accounts of what happened.

The Greek historian Herodotus, writing in around 480 BC, was in the same mindset when he described the Scythians skinning their enemies to make coats. There were, even so, several tribes who were astonishingly aggressive and bloodthirsty, and who relentlessly harried the Romans, to the extent that within a few decades they caused the Roman Empire to collapse under the strain.

The Goths from Sweden moved south and reached Rome in AD 410. The city was sacked in a week-long orgy of killing and destruction. A few decades later, the Vandals arrived from Germany, after raiding Gaul, Spain and North Africa, leaving a trail of destruction behind them. The third group to harry Rome was the Huns.

The Huns came originally from the windswept steppes of central Asia. They had been driven westwards out of their homeland by the Chinese in the second century. This push from the Far East had a domino effect, displacing people westwards until they impacted on Rome. The Huns massacred their way through, eventually settling north of the Danube, where they came to an arrangement with Rome, buying acceptance by agreeing to subdue troublesome neighbours. Rome paid an annual tribute of 350 pounds of gold to King Ruas, but also took hostages as a guarantee of loyalty. King Ruas had a nephew called Attila, who went to Rome as one such hostage. It was a useful experience, as it enabled him to learn the customs and geography of Italy.

King Ruas died when Attila was 27 years old. Attila inherited the Hun throne jointly with his brother Bleda, and worked to strengthen their kingdom by fighting neighbouring Teutonic tribes like the Gepidae and the Ostrogoths. By AD 444 Attila had consolidated his control over the lands that are today Romania and Hungary. He had also made himself sole ruler by the simple, age-old technique of murdering his brother. Now he was ready to take on Rome.

He soon found a pretext. Honoria, the sister of the Roman Emperor Valentinian III, had a scandalous affair with a courtier. She became pregnant.

Valentinian had her removed to Constantinople, where she was kept a virtual prisoner. Bored and frustrated by events, she smuggled a plea for help to Attila, who was at Budapest, offering to marry him if he would rescue her. Attila already had many wives and did not need another, but saw this invitation as a major political opportunity. He wrote to Valentinian asking for permission to marry Honoria – and as a dowry half the Roman Empire. It was a very cheeky request, and he knew it would be refused, but the snub gave him his excuse to release a ferocious attack on the Empire.

In AD 447 Attila led his warriors south into Macedonia (northern Greece) to Constantinople. The Romans bought him off with a massively increased annual tribute and paid a huge indemnity for Attila's withdrawal. Attila went home with his plunder.

Four years later, Attila led a huge army of Franks, Vandals and Huns westwards across the Rhine into Gaul. Several Gaulish towns were ruthlessly destroyed. As Attila was about to attack and destroy Orleans in the same way, Roman legions arrived together with a Visigoth army. Attila withdrew to the plain near Chalons-sur-Marne, ready to fight. The battle lasted all day, with huge loss of life on both sides. One person who was there described the fighting as 'ruthless, immense and obstinate'. Among the thousands who died that day was the king of the Visigoths. Attila was forced to retreat, back across the Rhine. The battle was crucial in European history. Had Attila, with his Mongol background, won, not only would subsequent history have been different, but the ethnicity of Europe would have been different.

But the defeat at Chalons did not deter Attila from trying again. The next year he led his warriors south into Italy, completely destroying Aquileia, the main city in Venetia, and inflicting appalling atrocities on its inhabitants. The Huns went on to the Adriatic Sea, killing the innocent citizens of the towns of Altinum, Concordia and Padua and burning their houses. Refugees fled to islands in the coastal lagoon, where they founded a new settlement that would one day become the city of Venice. As the Huns rampaged across the Plain of Lombardy, Rome itself was clearly in danger. Pope Leo I made the incredibly brave decision to travel to meet Attila, who was so struck by the Pope's boldness that he agreed to end the blood-letting and take his men home, though he still talked of coming back if Honoria was not treated better. But he did not return.

On 15 March, AD 453, Attila gave a great banquet to celebrate his marriage to yet another wife, the beautiful Ildico. In bed with Ildico that night, Attila burst an artery and died of the resulting haemorrhage.

Genghis Khan
(1162–1227)

IT WAS ALMOST a millennium after the time of Attila that a very similar Mongol war-leader emerged. Temuchin, or Temujin, as he was called, after a tribal chief his father Yesukai had recently defeated, was born in 1162 at Deligun Bulduk on the River Onon, the son of a Mongol chief. Thirteen years later, Yesukai was killed in an ambush, leaving the boy Temuchin deep in tribal in-fighting. He had to fight for years against hostile tribes. He proved more than equal to the dangerous situation he found himself in, killing one of his brothers in a petty dispute over a fish, and massacring an entire tribe who dared to kidnap his wife.

He spent six years subjugating the Naiman tribe, between Lake Balkhash and the Irtysh, and conquering the land of Tangut, which lay to the south of the Gobi Desert. The Turkish Uigurs surrendered to Temuchin's overlordship without fighting, and it was from them that the Mongols developed most of their culture, including an alphabet and laws.

Temuchin was cruel and ruthless, but it could be argued that he needed to be as he was fighting for survival in a cruel and ruthless world. One of his rivals boiled 70 of his followers alive in cooking pots. But by being more cruel and more ruthless than any of them, he rose to supremacy. By 1206 Temuchin was strong enough to impose his will on all of the Mongol tribes. He courageously called together the leaders of many warring factions to a gathering by the River Onon, where he proclaimed himself their overlord. He took a new name, Genghis Khan, 'Universal Ruler'.

The Chinese were the first to feel Temuchin's new power. In 1211, the Mongol hordes poured across the Great Wall, sacking cities, trampling down and setting fire to the crops. By 1214, Genghis Khan had control of most of China north of the Yellow River. In 1217, he conquered and annexed the Kara-Khitai Khanate, which stretched from Lake Balkhash to Tibet.

Next, in 1218, he looked to the south-west, to the lands of the Khwarizms (Turkestan, Iran, Iraq, Afghanistan, Pakistan, northern India). Genghis Khan sent messengers to Shah Mohammed promising peace and suggesting a trading treaty. This met with a favourable reply, but the first caravan of Mongol traders was massacred by the local governor, Inaljuk, at the border town of Otrar. Genghis understandably demanded the extradition of the governor. Mohammed responded by beheading the leading envoy and sending the others home without their beards. This dangerous insult resulted in a ferociously bloodthirsty response from Genghis Khan.

400,000 Khwarizm warriors posted along the border river, the Syr Daria, were not enough to stop the invasion of the Mongol hordes. Inaljuk was captured and executed by having molten metal poured into his eyes and ears. The Shah fled, leaving his subjects to be raped or slaughtered. One technique Genghis Khan used on this campaign was the human shield. He herded crowds of prisoners in front of his army, as many as 30,000 at a time, as he moved into the new territory. A terrible catalogue of cruelty unfolded as one town after another was taken. At one, all the women were raped in front of their families. At another, the inhabitants were tied up and shot with arrows. At another, the poor were decapitated, while the rich were tortured to find out where their treasure was. And all this happened at great speed.

Shah Mohammed fled to a village on the Caspian Sea, where he died of pleurisy. Meanwhile Genghis Khan followed his son and successor, Jelaleddin, in the conquest of the huge new territory. At Herat, where the governor he had installed was deposed, Genghis Khan put the city under siege for six months. When Herat fell, it took a week for all the inhabitants to be killed.

Remarkably, and undeservedly, Genghis Khan died of natural causes at the age of 65. He set out to chastise the king of Tangut, and thoroughly subdued the territory in the usual way. It was while laying siege to the Tangut capital of Ninghsia in 1227 that he fell ill and died. He has been described as the 'mightiest and most bloodthirsty conqueror of all time'. The final victims were in a way the most pitiful of all. They were innocent bystanders who accidentally saw the funeral procession making its way to the burial ground in the valley of Kilien. They were all killed. They had seen too much.

Tamerlane the Great
(1336–1405)

TAMERLANE WAS THE great-great-grandson of Genghis Khan. He was born at Kesh, near Samarkand, and given the name Timur. As a young man he nursed the pipe-dream of rebuilding his ancestor's empire, which had subsequently fallen apart and been divided into a large number of small principalities. It seemed unlikely that he would be able to fulfil this dream, as he was disabled. The locals nicknamed him Timur i Leng, Timur the Lame. Yet in spite of walking with a limp, he is remembered as Tamerlane the Great, a ruthless and sadistic warmonger just like his great-great-grandfather.

He was 33 when he seized the Transoxian throne at Samarkand, acquiring the power base he needed for his scheme of conquest. He was an expert military strategist and this skill enabled him to conquer Turkestan, Iran, the Ukraine, Crimea, Georgia, Armenia and Mesopotamia. Tamerlane did not reward those loyal to him with support. Governors who appealed to him often found they were betrayed once he had taken control of their kingdoms.

Tamerlane invaded India, leaving a trail of destruction across the north all the way to Delhi, which he totally destroyed, massacring the 100,000 inhabitants.

Tamerlane looked extraordinary. Apart from the limp, he was tall, with a huge head. He was also white-haired even from childhood. He was altogether a frightening figure, and he relied on fear above all to ensure the allegiance of his subjects. Even so, revolts were common, and cruel and brutal reprisals equally common. Cities were destroyed out of revenge. Whole populations were slaughtered. Huge towers made from his enemies' skulls were built for Tamerlane to look at with gratification. On two occasions he ordered thousands of his enemies to be walled up to die slowly of suffocation. On another occasion he had his enemies thrown over a cliff.

Following the India campaign, Tamerlane turned his attention to Syria to exact revenge on those who had failed to assist him in his earlier campaigns. He seized Aleppo and sacked it. He occupied Damascus in 1400. He sacked Baghdad, still reeling from the atrocities inflicted by Halagu a hundred years before, and set it on fire, killing 20,000 people. By 1402, he had moved on into Turkey, where he beheaded 5,000 Ottoman soldiers at the end of a siege; their Sultan was captured, put in an iron cage and killed.

The reign of Tamerlane was a nightmare revisitation of an earlier era - just as he had hoped it would be. It came to an end with Tamerlane's death. He was on his way, with his army, to attack China, when he fell ill at a campsite beside the Syr Daria river. It was there that he died, like Genghis Khan before him, of natural causes. By chance, he died at Otrar, whose governor had triggered the violent anger of Genghis Khan three centuries before. Along with his bloodthirsty forebear, Tamerlane died with the blood of hundreds of thousands of people on his hands.

PART TWO

MEDIEVAL & RENAISSANCE MONARCHS

Vlad the Impaler
(1431–1476)

IF DRACULA HAD any real-life existence outside the fiction of Bram Stoker's novel, then it was in the form of Vlad Tepes or Vlad III – or Vlad the Impaler.

Vlad was born late in 1431, in the fortress of Sighisoara, in Transylvania. Vlad the Impaler's mother was called Barbara. His father, Vlad II Dracul, was given the nickname 'Dracul' (Dragon), because he was a member of a crusading Catholic order of chivalry with that title. Vlad II had been admitted to the Order of the Dragon a year before the young Impaler was born. 'Dracul' was the nickname the Romanian boyars (noblemen) decided to call him. 'Draculea' means 'son of Dracul', and was often used by Vlad III to describe himself, which brings us to the familiar name Dracula. Vlad III supplied another element of Bram Stoker's story with his habit of drinking the blood of his victims, of whom there were many. Stoker borrowed another element in the form of the Order of the Dragon's official uniform, a black cloak over a red robe.

His terrible reputation sprang from the horrible methods he used for killing his enemies. He sat down to dinner on one occasion, surrounded by a crowd of slowly dying victims. His dinner guests were nauseated by the screaming and the stench. One of them made the mistake of objecting and was himself impaled.

It was late in 1436 that Vlad became Prince of Wallachia, one of three Romanian provinces, the others being Moldavia and Transylvania. He took up residence at the palace in Targoviste, the capital. In 1442, Vlad III and his brother Radu were taken hostage by Sultan Murad II; he was held in Turkey until 1448, though Radu was kept until 1462. This period of Turkish captivity played a key role in the development of Vlad's black personality. He became profoundly pessimistic. The Turks set him free only when news broke that his father had been assassinated, at the orders of Vladislav II, who wanted the Wallachian throne for himself. He also then learned of the death of his older brother Mircea. Vlad was 17 and, supported by a force of Turkish cavalry, he made a move to seize the throne of Wallachia, but Vladislav was defeated only two months later. Then, in August 1456, Vlad was able to kill Vladislav and begin his longest reign (6 years). During this time he committed many cruel atrocities.

His first major atrocity was, inevitably, an act of revenge aimed at the boyars of Targoviste who had conspired to kill his father and his brother Mircea. On Easter Day 1459, he invited all the boyar families who were involved to a feast. He impaled the older ones and forced the rest to march 50 miles to the town of Poenari, where they were made to build a fortress overlooking the

Arges River; many died during this ordeal. This building is what is today known as Castle Dracula.

This sick sadistic monster was, even so, regarded as a hero. He was a gifted general, and he succeeded in ending decades of feuding within his country. He also fended off the Turks who were constantly trying to encroach on his lands.

In 1462, Vlad launched a campaign against the Turks along the Danube, killing over 38,000 people. The Turks sent envoys to agree a peace settlement but, when the envoys refused to remove their turbans in his presence, Vlad had their turbans nailed onto their heads. This was risky, as the Sultan's army was three times larger than Vlad's, and the Sultan pushed his huge army forward. Vlad was forced to retreat to his capital. As he did so, he burned his own villages and poisoned the wells, so that there was nothing for the Turks to eat or drink. When the Sultan reached the capital, he was met by an appalling sight, the impaled bodies of 20,000 Turkish captives – the Forest of the Impaled. This tactic had the desired effect. The Sultan admitted defeat.

Vlad's favourite method of execution was impaling his victims on stakes. This was an exceptionally slow and painful way to die, and Vlad usually insisted that the stakes should not be too sharp, so that it would take longer. His preference for impaling led to his nickname, 'The Impaler', first recorded in 1550; even the Turks, who were frequently his victims, called him 'Kaziglu Bey', 'The Impaler Prince'. But he used other techniques too.

After the Forest of the Impaled, Vlad's support

dwindled, and his brother Radu, with his own Turkish-supported army, pursued Vlad to Poenari Castle. According to legend, Vlad's wife committed suicide by throwing herself from the battlements. Vlad escaped the siege by using a secret passage. He made his way to Transylvania, where he met the new King of Hungary, Matthias Corvinus. Instead of offering help, Matthias arrested and imprisoned him at the Hungarian capital of Visegrad.

He was able to return as Prince of Wallachia again in 1475, but this third reign was brief. He was assassinated in December 1476. His head was cut off and sent to the Sultan, who mounted it on a stake as proof that the Impaler was dead.

Some dictators have used the death penalty as a means of getting rid of enemies, and as a deterrent to potential opponents. But what Vlad did went beyond this. He was a sadist who derived deep pleasure from watching other people's sufferings. We can only speculate that the extraordinary experiences of his boyhood must have played a great part in generating feelings of intense and violent rage towards others. One good effect of his brutal regime was that it was designed to enforce honesty and order, which to a great extent it did. Vlad placed a golden cup in the central square of Targoviste, for the use of thirsty travellers. It seems that it was never removed, that no attempt was made to steal it. Vlad was also concerned that everyone should be productive; vagrants and beggars were treated as thieves, because they were unproductive parasites. This sounds good, but Vlad took it to a surreal extreme. He invited all the poor and sick of Wallachia to a hall in Targoviste for a feast. Afterwards, he asked them if they would like never to be poor again. Naturally they said yes, so Vlad had the hall locked and set on fire. None of them survived.

Vlad is supposed to have been buried at the Snagov monastery, which is located on an island near Bucharest, but his tomb contains only the bones – of a horse. No-one knows where the Impaler's body is.

Richard III
(1452–1485)

RICHARD III IS another great icon of evil. We know the nature of this evil man all too well from Shakespeare's presentation of him. But playwrights often bend history to make a better play. Just how evil was Richard III?

Richard III, King of England, was born on 2 October, 1452 at Fotheringhay Castle in the Nene Valley not far from Peterborough. He was officially the fourth son of Richard Duke of York (who himself had a strong claim to the throne of Henry VI) and his wife, Cecily Neville. The young Richard spent much of his childhood at Middleham Castle, which he later made his home when he married.

Richard's father was killed at the Battle of Wakefield when Richard was still a boy, and after that he was taken into the care of Richard Neville, Earl of Warwick, 'Warwick the Kingmaker'. It was relatively common in the middle ages for young noblemen to be farmed out and brought up in the households of other princes; it was the precursor of the English public school system. Warwick the Kingmaker was closely involved in turning Henry VI off the throne and replacing him with Richard's oldest brother, Edward, as Edward IV. At

Edward's coronation, Richard was made Duke of Gloucester.

However, when Edward decided to marry Elizabeth Woodville, Warwick disagreed strongly. She was a commoner and he could not allow the marriage to go ahead. He therefore drove Edward out of England. Warwick proclaimed Henry VI King again in 1470, but within a year Edward returned, fought back and reclaimed the throne in 1471.

As a boy, Richard was of no consequence until this event, when he supported his brother against Warwick, shared his exile and took part in his triumphant return. He fought loyally and effectively on his family's behalf, the Yorkist cause, in several battles in the Wars of the Roses.

During his brother's reign, Richard worked with steadfast loyalty, using his great skills as a military commander to support the king, and was rewarded with huge estates in the north of England and the title of Duke of Gloucester. He thus became the richest and most powerful nobleman in England. The other surviving brother, George Duke of Clarence, was by contrast disloyal to Edward IV, who had him executed for treason.

After the Battle of Tewkesbury, which the Yorkists won, Richard married Anne Neville - the widow of Henry VI's son, Prince Edward, and the daughter of Warwick the Kingmaker. It was in fact Richard and his brother George who in cold blood had stabbed Prince Edward to death after the battle. Richard was also present in the Tower of London shortly afterwards, on the night of 21 May, 1471, when Henry VI was murdered, and may have been responsible for that assassination too. Richard and Anne had one son, Edward Plantagenet, who died aged 11 in 1484, just before his father. Anne also died before her husband.

Edward IV died suddenly and unexpectedly in April 1483. The king's sons (Richard's nephews), the 12-year-old Prince Edward and the nine-year-old Prince Richard, were apparently next in the order of succession. In view of Richard's conscientious loyalty to his brother's cause, it seems remarkable that he moved to claim the throne for himself. Richard arranged for the young boy-king, Edward V, to be escorted to Stony Stratford, where he met him and his younger brother. He took personal charge of the two boys, accompanied them to London and lodged them in the Tower, then more a royal residence than a prison.

Richard appointed himself Lord Protector and Chief Councillor (in effect Prime Minister). Something even more extraordinary followed. At a meeting of the Royal Council in the Tower on 13 June, 1483, Lord Hastings was arrested for treason. He was the king's chamberlain and had regularly visited the king; he was also a known anti-Ricardian. A few minutes later, he was executed by beheading outside. Three other alleged conspirators, Lord Rivers, Richard Grey and Sir Thomas Vaughan, were executed elsewhere.

After ruthlessly removing all possible opposition at court, Richard had a statement read out, outside St Paul's Cathedral, declaring that he was the rightful king, that his brother Edward IV had been illegitimate and that therefore the two princes were excluded from the line of succession. The declaration was startling for many reasons – not least that Richard was not just denouncing the boy-king as illegitimate but his elder brother as well, the brother he had served with unswerving loyalty. Why had Richard shifted his ground? Was it that he was incredibly devious and ambitious?

A few days later, some evidence was produced, probably by the Bishop of Bath and Wells, to show that Edward IV's marriage to Elizabeth Woodville had been bigamous, and therefore all their children were bastards. If Edward's two sons were illegitimate they could have no right to the throne. The children of George Duke of Clarence had lost their right on account of their father's treason. That left Richard. He was crowned King Richard III at Westminster Abbey on 6 July, 1483.

The two princes were seen a few more times in the Tower shortly after that, then never again. Eventually their skeletons were discovered, hidden under a stone staircase in the Tower. When they were murdered – by whom and on whose orders – is still not known, though it has usually been assumed that Richard III was responsible for ordering their murder. Richard had most to gain by their death and it does seem more likely than not that he gave the order for their assassination. It is nevertheless possible that they survived Richard's short reign – he was only in power for two years – and were removed by

Henry VII, who would equally have wanted rival claimants out of the way.

Because of the way he had removed potential opposition, Richard was left with too few friends to govern safely. His was a very short and very troubled reign. His own loyal supporter, Henry Duke of Buckingham, turned against him and was promptly executed. Richard's enemies finally united against him on the battlefield at Bosworth on 22 August, 1485. He was killed fighting bravely in the battle, famously unhorsed, and his body was carted naked through the streets of Leicester before being buried at Greyfriars Church.

Richard III has become one of the most controversial English kings. Shakespeare was a mouthpiece for Tudor propaganda, and his play *Richard III* is in effect a justification for Henry VII's usurpation of the throne; but Henry VII's right to the throne was not as strong as Richard's. Shakespeare blames Richard for the murder of his brother, the innocent George Duke of Clarence, but history records a very different story – that Clarence did indeed plot against Edward IV and it was Edward IV himself who had him executed. Nothing to do with Richard at all.

Some have excused the (alleged) murder of the two princes on the grounds that England needed to be governed by a man, that the safety of the realm demanded that they should go. As for the accusation that Prince Edward (the boy-king) had no right to the throne, that turns out to have been doubly true. Edward IV was a bigamist, so Edward V was illegitimate. Edward IV was himself illegitimate. His mother was Cecily, but she conceived Edward while her husband was away and she had an affair with an archer called Blaybourne. The fact that Edward's baptism was a very low-key event compared with the baptisms of George and Richard indicates that the Duke and Duchess knew perfectly well that he was illegitimate. It was also a matter of general comment that Richard and George were slightly built like the Duke of York, yet Edward IV was huge. His body was exhumed in modern times and the skeleton measured 6 foot 4 inches. Richard would certainly have known this, but kept quiet for safety's sake, during Edward IV's lifetime. George was unwise enough to challenge his brother – perhaps he even dared to mention the unutterable and now treasonable family secret, the matter of Edward IV's parenthood – and was executed for it. Once Edward IV was dead, it was not only safe for Richard to expose the illegitimacy of Edward IV's sons, but it was his family duty to the purity of the bloodline, and his patriotic duty to the integrity of the Crown. History reveals a very different Richard III from the crook-backed villain of Shakespeare's play.

Context and zeitgeist are important. Richard III did stab Prince Edward to death at Tewkesbury, he did have Lord Hastings summarily executed, and he may have killed Henry VI and the Princes in the Tower, but he turns out not to have been such an overwhelmingly evil man, as medieval kings went.

Cesare Borgia
(1476–1507)

CESARE BORGIA WAS born with distinct advantages. He was born into one of the most corrupt, ruthless and self-seeking families that ever lived - and his father was Pope. When Pope Innocent VIII died in 1492, the year of the first Columbus voyage to America, Rodrigo Borgia was one of the three possible successors. Borgia handed out huge bribes, promising highly-paid positions and palaces to delegates if they voted for him. Naturally, he won the election, and became Pope Alexander VI. He used his position to advance his illegitimate children in every way possible. He gave them high-status positions. He made them rich.

In 1470, Rodrigo Borgia had begun an affair with Vanozza deo Catanei, a 28-year-old beauty. By Vanozza, he had three sons, Giovanni, Cesare and Goffredo, and a daughter, Lucrezia. Cesare, the second son, was born in 1476.

Cesare was just 16 when he was appointed Archbishop of Valencia by his father; he was 17 when his father made him a cardinal. But these were nowhere near enough for this spoilt rich boy. He was envious of his older brother, who had been given command of the Papal Army. Cesare had to content himself with riding arrogantly through the streets of Rome, fully armed, with one beautiful mistress after another at his side. His flirtation in public with his sister Lucrezia made it plain to everyone who saw it that they had an incestuous relationship. Cesare seems to have inherited (or imitated) his father's philandering streak. When Sanchia, the notoriously promiscuous daughter of the King of Naples, arrived in Rome to be vetted as a prospective bride for Goffredo, both Rodrigo and Cesare gave her a test drive before giving their approval.

The new Pope's reign was beset by political problems. When Sanchia's father, King Ferrante of Naples, died, Rodrigo recognized Ferrante's son Alphonso as his successor. Unfortunately the French King, Charles VIII, thought he had a superior claim and invaded Rome to enforce it. Rodrigo was obliged to cave in, allowing Charles to take Cesare to Naples as a hostage to guarantee safe conduct. Cesare managed to escape, return to Rome and with his father form an anti-French alliance with Venice, Spain and Milan. Charles realised he was in danger of being cut off by an offensive alliance, and quickly returned to France, leaving Naples to Alphonso.

The Borgias then took their revenge on those who had helped Charles VIII to humiliate them. Cesare Borgia arrested the Swiss mercenaries who had broken into his mother's house while the French had occupied Rome and subjected them to merciless torture. Rodrigo ordered the people of Florence to arrest Savonarola, the ascetic monk who had denounced corruption in the Church and had publicly welcomed Charles as the champion of old Catholic values. The Florentines responded to this with enthusiasm, as they too had suffered many a lashing from Savonarola's tongue; he had put a stop to their carnivals. They were glad to have an excuse to be rid of him. He was racked no less than 14 times in one day during a campaign of weeks of torture before he was finally hanged.

Rodrigo sent his elder son Giovanni to attack the fortresses of the Orsini family, who had collaborated with the French. Giovanni proved to be a hopeless military leader, and he returned in 1497 after losing the battle that was supposed to punish the Orsinis; he was regarded as a family disgrace, adding to rather than avenging its humiliation. A few months later, on 14 June, he dined with his mother and Cesare. He and his brother afterwards left on horseback, taking different routes. The next morning, Giovanni's body was pulled from the River Tiber. He had been stabbed nine times. Giovanni's murderer was never found, but the gossip was that Cesare had done it. He had long resented and envied his brother's position as military commander, and may have seen it as essential to family honour that Giovanni should be seen to be punished for the Orsini fiasco.

Rodrigo was content to send Cesare away on business to calm the gossip, and it was possibly a relief to both men that Cesare could give up the ecclesiastical offices that suited him so poorly, and take up the military role he really wanted. Cesare was even so becoming an embarrassment. His sex life was a public scandal – the mistresses, the continuing incest with his sister, the relationships with boys – so a more active military life taking Cesare outside Rome suited Rodrigo. Lucrezia was placed in a convent after her husband fled, rightly fearing Cesare's sexual jealousy.

Cesare's duties took him to Naples and France. The French King, Charles VIII's successor, Louis XII, wanted an annulment of his marriage so that he could marry his mistress. Cesare negotiated. Rodrigo agreed. Cesare was made Duke of Valentinois and given a bride, the 16-year-old sister of the King of Navarre. He was also offered French troops to subdue rebel nobles in northern Italy and create a kingdom for himself south of Venice, in Romagna. This invasion was launched in 1499. Cesare Borgia proved to be ruthless and unscrupulous in both sex and war. When he captured the castle of Caterina Sforza at Forli, he insisted that she surrender herself to him. He wrote to his father, describing in gloating terms how he had made love to her before confining her to a convent. He took Faenza. The well-liked master of Faenza, the 18-year-old Astorre Manfredi, surrendered on condition that his life should be spared. Cesare dishonourably sent him to Rome, where he was tortured and killed.

Cesare quickly acquired a well-deserved reputation for being cruel and untrustworthy. Even his lieutenants were put off by the fear that Cesare spread everywhere. He was moody, given to bouts of anger, and did not inspire unswerving loyalty – except through fear. Some of his men began plotting against him with nobles he had deposed.

Cesare lured the plotters to a banquet, where they were seized; two were instantly strangled.

The expensive campaigns Cesare mounted were paid for by the Pope, who funded them by selling cardinals' hats to those who wanted them. Some of these new cardinals died in mysterious circumstances not long afterwards, conveniently leaving their estates to the Vatican.

Whenever Cesare Borgia returned to Rome, the body count rose alarmingly. Any insult, real or imagined, was answered with murder. Many of his homosexual partners were found dead in the streets of Rome or in the Tiber, poisoned, stabbed or drowned. The Venetian ambassador reported, 'Every night four or five murdered men are discovered . . . All Rome is trembling for fear of being destroyed by the Duke Cesare.'

In 1500, Cesare's incestuous love for Lucrezia led to another spectacular murder. After Lucrezia was abandoned by her first husband, who very understandably ran off in fear of his life, Rodrigo annulled the marriage. Rodrigo then married her off to Alphonso, Duke of Bisceglie and King of France (Sanchia's brother). Lucrezia fell in love with Alphonso, and this Cesare could not tolerate. One summer night, after dining with the Pope, Alphonso was walking across St Peter's Square when a gang of thugs attacked him. Stabbed and seriously injured, Alphonso was taken to a room in the Vatican for safety. Lucrezia nursed him there. One night, after leaving him for a short time, she came back to find him strangled. Cesare admitted to the murder, claiming that Alphonso had earlier tried to kill him with a crossbow. Naturally, no action was taken. Cesare Borgia was entirely above the law. Within a fortnight, Cesare was once again forcing his attentions on his sister. This continued until Rodrigo found another husband for her, the son of the Duke of Ferrara.

In August 1503, Rodrigo and Cesare fell ill with malaria just outside Rome. The 72-year-old Pope was dead within the week, and Cesare was too ill to protect his own interests. For a time he was safe, as Rodrigo's successor was an ineffectual old man with no reason to come after Cesare. But he died a month later and the new Pope was Giuliano della Rovere, one of the candidates shouldered aside by Rodrigo's bribes in 1492. Cesare was arrested, removed from his kingdom of Romagna, and obliged to withdraw to Naples. As Naples was now under Spanish rule, he hoped to make a new power base there, but he was re-arrested for disturbing the peace and had to go to the King of Navarre for sanctuary. In March 1507 he was wounded and captured while leading a siege at Viana. His captors stripped him and left him to die of thirst.

The individual acts of evil committed by Cesare Borgia and his family are too many to list. They add up to something quite distinct, and can be seen as foreshadowing the activities of the Mafia, the Family whose financial, political and social interests come before anything else. Such ethics and codes of conduct as exist are entirely governed by the Family's interests.

Henry VIII
(1491–1547)

HENRY VIII OF England was born at Greenwich, the second son of Henry VII, who won the Wars of the Roses by defeating Richard III at the Battle of Bosworth. Henry VII consolidated his rather shaky claim to the throne by marrying Elizabeth of York, whose claim was, if anything, stronger than his own.

The young Prince Henry was brought up in a disciplined, scholarly way, developing interests in poetry, music and religious thought. As a young king, in 1521, he wrote a religious tract, which was in effect a reply to Martin Luther and a defence of the Roman Catholic Church, and for this work he was awarded the title Defender of the Faith by the Pope. No irony was intended, but subsequent events took both Henry and the English Church in exactly the direction indicated by Luther. Henry was much admired as the most handsome and most accomplished prince of his time. His accession to the throne of England was widely hailed by men of distinction – Thomas More, Colet and Erasmus.

From the beginning there were hints, for those who were well-informed enough to read them, that Henry was going to be a ruthless dynast.

Henry was well aware of the weakness of his father's claim to the throne, and he doubtless knew of the superior claims of others. There was, in spite of the death of Richard III, still a Plantagenet line that could become a problem to him. Pretenders had, after all, popped up more than once during his father's reign. In 1521, he had the Duke of Buckingham executed on a trumped-up treason charge; in reality his only crime was that he was a descendant of Edward III.

To play his part in international affairs, Henry needed money, and he looked to unscrupulous courtiers like Cardinal Wolsey to find it for him. Wolsey took on himself all the loathing of the nation as he increased the burden of taxation. Wolsey attracted even more detestation when he shut down all small religious houses, those with fewer than seven inmates, and took their revenues. By 1525, Henry VIII's foreign policy was costing so much that Wolsey had to introduce a new levy, the entirely illegal Amicable Loan. This time there was so much opposition that he had to drop it.

Seven weeks after his accession, Henry married Katherine of Aragon, his brother's widow. This marriage, and subsequent marriages, proved to be a great problem to the king, who desperately needed a son and heir to consolidate the Tudor dynasty. It became clear that Katherine was not going to bear him a son. She had given birth several times, and all but one child had died in infancy; the only survivor was a girl, Mary Tudor. Henry saw a way out. Katherine had been his elder brother's wife first and marrying his brother's wife was against church law. The lack of sons was divine retribution for the invalidity of the marriage, which had been, in reality, no marriage at all in the eyes of God. Initially the Pope was inclined to agree to nullify the marriage and in 1528 sent Cardinal Campeggio to London to explore its validity. The visit was inconclusive, and the Pope referred the case to the Curia. This ruined Wolsey, who had staked his political future on achieving the royal divorce. He now had no friends in England or abroad. In 1529, Henry stripped him of his goods and honours and dismissed him for failing. In 1530, Henry summoned him to London to stand trial for treason, but Wolsey died on the journey at Market Harborough. The adroit Wolsey had failed, and the Pope refused to co-operate, yet Henry was still determined to have his marriage annulled – the more so since he was now infatuated with Anne Boleyn. Anne was no great beauty, but she had a bright, flirtatious manner and Henry was besotted with her breasts – 'those pritty duckys I trust shortly to kysse', he wrote. Anne was not bowled over by her royal suitor. She had seen from close quarters how he had seduced her sister Mary and then dropped her when he lost interest in her. She was determined that would not happen to her. No sex before marriage for her.

In 1531 Henry VIII tried to bully the Pope into agreeing to the annulment by humiliating the entire English clergy; he accused them all of treason, but gave them the option of paying fines. He also extorted recognition as 'protector and supreme head of the clergy and church of England'. The English church, and by implication the English, were no longer bound by what the Pope agreed or did not agree. Henry accordingly went ahead, divorced Katherine and married Anne Boleyn, though he at least was circumspect enough to do so in private (in 1533). John Fisher, Bishop of Rochester, and Sir Thomas More, who had been his chancellor, were both beheaded for refusing to support the new marriage.

The Dissolution of the Monasteries was in part a gesture against the old 'Catholic' order, to prove that the English Church was independent. It was also to a great extent a way of acquiring a huge reservoir of wealth. In 1535, a commission was set up under Thomas Cromwell, to report on the state of the monasteries. The report was a catalogue of corrupt and unfair practices in monasteries and abbeys up and down the country, based on evidence that was often suspect. In some cases, malicious complaints about abbots were brought by criminals who had scores to settle. Cromwell's commissioners eagerly recorded all this groundless scandal as, true or untrue, it justified closing the monasteries. They were indeed closed in 1536. The bulk of the revenues passed to the Crown.

In 1536, Katherine of Aragon died and Henry had Anne Boleyn executed for alleged treason. She was accused of infidelity, but the evidence was procured under torture and cannot be believed; the real reason seems to be that Anne had failed to produce a son. Henry had also shifted his affections to Jane Seymour, a surprisingly straight-laced woman to whom Henry was betrothed the day after Anne Boleyn's execution. Jane, in spite of looking unpromisingly puritanical, supplied Henry with the necessary son, Edward VI in October 1537, but died immediately afterwards.

Cromwell botched the arrangements for the next marriage. Henry expressed interest in the current troupe of princesses at the French court and proposed a beauty contest in Calais (still an English possession). The French ambassador, who obviously thought the idea preposterously tasteless, made the counter-suggestion that if the princesses were to be run round a ring like ponies why not mount them one by one to see which gave the best ride? The idea was dropped, though it might have worked better than Cromwell's botch-up. He supplied a Holbein portrait of Anne of Cleves that was far too flattering. Henry rashly agreed to marry Anne on the strength of the portrait, but found the reality unattractive. She was 'not as reported', he said; her breasts sagged, and she seemed generally in poor physical condition. Cromwell had made many enemies while in office, and those enemies were only too glad to exploit the king's indignation at having to marry an ugly woman. This was the opportunity they had been waiting for. The Duke of Norfolk accused Thomas Cromwell of high treason and Cromwell was executed without trial in 1540.

Henry then divorced Anne, and next married Katherine Howard, who unwisely had affairs during her short marriage to the King, was found out and duly executed. In 1543, Henry married for the sixth time. Catherine Parr was lucky to survive Henry.

In Henry VIII, we have a different kind of figure, someone who was regarded by many of his contemporaries, the ordinary people of Tudor England, as an admirable king. He certainly looked the part. He was a fine big regal-looking man, who knew how to behave in public, and knew how to dress. We have inherited a view of Henry as a jolly, merry monarch with an eye for the ladies. He was scandalous certainly, but in a roguish, raffish, forgivable sort of way. The occasional beheadings we shrug off as lapses, and the monasteries – well, they were dens of corruption anyway and it was high time they went. The Hollywood and TV treatments of Henry have laundered his image several times over to give us the ultimate colourful costume drama king.

But Henry VIII was a very expensive king, extorting a great deal from his people in the form of taxes. He was also an asset-stripper of the worst kind. The elaborate infrastructure of the Church with its religious houses, hospitals, abbeys and priories had been built up and developed over a period of a thousand years. It had been a major force for good, in effect supplying social services for the poor and needy, offering many kinds of work, offering education for all, offering a route out of the poverty trap for aspiring young men and women, however low-born, and maintaining some sort of order even through major civil wars like the Stephen and Matilda War and the Wars of the Roses. Henry ripped all that apart for the sake of the wealth invested in it, and replaced it with – nothing. It is hard to imagine the distress that many ordinary people must have felt when they heard that the Pope was no longer the head of their Church, and when they saw the great and beautiful abbeys, like Glastonbury, Tintern and Rievaulx, torn down. Because of his pre-occupations with his foreign policy, his marriages, his acquisition of wealth, he also turned a blind eye to what was happening in the country, where unscrupulous 'improving' landowners turned people off the land by the thousand, disinheriting them and turning them into 'vagabonds' who could be disowned by any village they came to. With all this needless cruelty – evil by negligence – came the drift of country people into the towns hoping to find work. Henry knew these things were happening but did nothing at all to stop the landowners who were behind them.

As for the fat, jovial, lovable image – it is worth remembering that as he lay dying the news came that his life-long rival, the strikingly similar Francis I of France, was dead. And Henry VIII's reaction to this news was – peals of laughter.

Suleiman the Magnificent
(1494–1466)

SULEIMAN I (OR Soliman I) was the son of Selim I, and he became Sultan of the Ottoman Empire on his father's death in 1520.

Suleiman the Magnificent, who ruled from 1520 until his death in 1566, was the last great Sultan. In an age that produced many great and spectacular absolute monarchs in Europe and Asia, he was among the greatest. He was lucky to inherit a well-organized country, with full coffers and a well-disciplined army. To these advantages he added his own personal qualities, among which was the ability to identify talented generals, admirals and viziers and exploit their abilities to the full. Suleiman was able to take the Ottoman Empire to the zenith of its power, but it goes almost without saying that this was achieved by unscrupulousness, bloodthirstiness and carnage on a huge scale. Some historians have fallen for the glitz of his military glory and praised Suleiman for his 'achievements'. He has even been praised for his justice, wisdom and courtesy. To later Turks he was 'The Lawgiver', because of his organization of the learned class; he set the mufti of Constantinople at the head of this body.

In 1526, he invaded and annexed part of Hungary – some of Hungary was already in his domain – and he organized a massacre of 200,000 Hungarians. Two thousand of these were killed for his pleasure, as he watched from a throne. He also took 100,000 slaves back with him to Constantinople.

Three years later, in 1529, when he laid siege to Vienna and that city refused to surrender, he ransacked the surrounding countryside for good-looking young women to stock the Turkish harems. Then he piled hundreds of Austrian peasants that he did not want onto a huge bonfire, close to the city so that the citizens of Vienna could see what was happening. This display of military strength is not only evil but insane by any modern standards, but it was not exceptional – except in scale – in the sixteenth century. Cruelty, and cruelty towards the innocent and powerless, was a normal way of demonstrating political strength.

Suleiman the Magnificent died in September 1566 at the age of 72, while engaged in yet more mayhem, the siege of Szigetvar. He was buried in Constantinople in the precincts of the mosque that bears his name.

Ivan the Terrible
(1530–1584)

IVAN WAS BORN in 1530, the son of Vasily, Grand Duke of Moscow. He was orphaned at an early age; his father died when he was only three and his mother, then acting as Regent, was poisoned by political enemies when he was eight. After that, Ivan claimed he had 'no human care from any quarter'.

Naturally, in the power vacuum that followed his father's death, a struggle for power went on among the leading Muscovite families, and Ivan was a pawn in the midst of this struggle. One of Ivan's uncles was seized and murdered by a Moscow mob during an uprising.

Ivan quickly learnt by example how to survive in this environment. He was 13 when he organized his own first political murder. He threw his victim's body, a troublesome prince, to his dogs. In 1547, Ivan proclaimed himself Tsar and at a specially arranged beauty contest he selected himself a bride, a 15-year-old girl called Anastasia. She gave birth to six children, though four had died by the time she herself died in 1560. It is possible that the loss of the children followed by the loss of his wife, who had been a steadying influence on him, caused him to topple over into bloodthirsty megalomania after that date.

In his grief, he accused his chaplain, Father Silvestr, and another close adviser, Alexei Adashev, of plotting to kill Anastasia, and banished them both. Then he went into retreat, leaving Moscow in order to go into seclusion in the provinces. He was begged by every level of Moscow society to return, for fear of another power vacuum in his absence, something they must later have regretted. Ivan agreed, but on one terrible condition – that he would be free to govern without hindrance. He was in effect assuming dictatorial powers, and he used them. He re-organized the country into huge administrative units; he would be absolute ruler in one, while the others were governed on his behalf by teams of bureaucrats.

This is when the terror began. He created a force of oprichniki, black-cloaked assassins riding black horses. In their saddles they each carried their emblems of office, a broom and a dog's head. The black riders descended like Furies on anyone who was suspected of opposing Ivan and slaughtered them. Ivan used them, among other things, to settle scores dating back to his childhood. Anyone he could remember thwarting him during his early years was marked for a visit by the black riders. More than 4,000 aristocrats were murdered in this way, including the entire Staritsky family; they were relatives of Ivan's, but because of this they were potential rivals too. When the leader of the Orthodox Church, Metropolitan Philip, condemned the oprichniki attacks and withheld his blessing from the Tsar, with ruthless inevitability the black riders came for him and executed him.

Throughout history, dictators have behaved in this way, getting underlings to commit their murders for them. Ivan was unusual in wanting to take part himself. He joined in orgies of rape, torture and killing.

The peak of Ivan the Terrible's terrible reign came when he was informed that the city leaders of Novgorod, at that time the second city of Russia, were planning to rebel. Ivan's rage knew no bounds. He did not bother to check whether his informant was telling him the truth, which he probably was not, but summoned the black riders and rode to Novgorod with them. First they pillaged the monasteries and homes of the aristocracy of the area, laying waste to the lands within 50 miles of the city. Then he built a wooden wall round Novgorod to prevent anyone from escaping. For the five weeks that followed, he and his men systematically slaughtered everyone inside the wall. Nor was the killing quick and merciful. Sometimes families were forced to watch while fathers, husbands or wives were tortured. Women were roasted alive on spits. Ivan joined in with relish. He mounted a horse, took a spear and rode about, running people through as if it were a sport.

Russian historians have been keen to keep alive the memory of a great king, and have put the death toll at Novgorod at 2,000, but historians in the West put it at 60,000. Ivan's savagery at Novgorod, and his similar treatment of Pskov on a similar pretext, had the effect of suppressing opposition. Many who knew they had become suspects killed themselves rather than risk the unimaginably horrible death that Ivan would inflict on them. When Ivan invaded the adjacent state of Livonia, one doomed garrison that was under siege blew itself up rather than risk falling into Ivan's hands.

In 1572, Ivan suddenly disbanded the black riders, and forbade any future mention of their existence. Unpredictability and capriciousness are hallmarks of the dictator. No-one is wholly evil. Most ordinary people keep their shadow side well hidden most of the time, and it only occasionally appears. With dictators it is the shadow side that is on show much of the time, and just occasionally the other side, the light, shines through. Ivan was probably a manic depressive, with bouts of frenzied sadism alternating with periods of static religious depression. During these religious phases, he would wear sackcloth and publicly confess his sins. Perhaps it was real, deep-seated shame that brought the six-year reign of terror to an end. Perhaps there was no need to go on because all Ivan's enemies were dead; but that had not stopped him killing thousands of imaginary enemies. Perhaps there was a more political reason. Perhaps it was an attack from outside Russia that caused him to call off the debilitating internal revenge attacks; the Turks were advancing from the south.

It is hard to see how a state can survive such destructive leadership. Ivan survived partly because he had the Orthodox Church's support.

While Western Europe was going through the challenge of Protestantism, and the trauma of the Reformation was in full swing, Ivan was allowing no protest of any kind in Russia, and would maintain the status quo. Ivan took a predictably tough line on religious dissent, with the depressingly familiar burnings for heresy, and in this way he bought the support of the Church. In return, the Church acted as a propaganda machine for the Tsar. When peasant revolts were crushed with brutal cruelty, it was never the Tsar who was behind it. The atrocities were always blamed on the excessive zeal of underlings.

The English ambassador in Moscow, Giles Fletcher, reported when safely back in London that 'the desperate state of things at home maketh the people for the most part to wish for some foreign invasion, which they suppose to be the only means to rid them of the heavy yoke of this tyrannous government'.

Ivan died before that could happen. In 1581, he murdered his son and heir with a spear during a quarrel. His licentious sex life had left him riddled with disease. A British trader reported that Ivan 'began grievously to swell in his cods, with which he had most horribly offended above fifty years, boasting of a thousand virgins he had deflowered.'. Ivan was about to play a game of chess when he collapsed and died. But even Ivan's legacy was terrible. He had recently killed his heir, the young Ivan, and left his imbecile son Theodore on the throne. Russia was plunged again into decades of chaos, with invasions by both Poles and Swedes.

It is by no means clear whether Ivan was consciously evil, deciding to do bad things, or unconsciously evil because he was insane. On balance, we can explain a lot of his behaviour by interpreting his personality as manic depressive. The characteristics of both sides of his personality were exaggerated by the personal freedom that came with absolute power. As with Caligula, his existing personality traits became accentuated because there was nothing to hold him back.

Murad IV
(1612–1640)

SULEIMAN THE MAGNIFICENT was succeeded as Sultan by his son Selim II, who was a drunkard, in spite of the Koran's ban on alcohol. Selim II died in 1574 when he lost his footing climbing into the bath after a drinking bout, and died of a fractured skull. Selim's son Mahomet III was the next Sultan. He killed his 19 younger brothers to ensure his own safety. Mahomet III was succeeded by his son Ahmed I, then by his imbecile brother Mustafa I, then by his grandson Osman II.

Osman II ruled for less than a year before he was murdered in 1618. He loved archery, so long as the targets were page-boys or prisoners. During these lax and undisciplined reigns, the Ottoman Empire weakened perceptibly.

After Osman II, the imbecile Mustafa I was briefly dragged to the throne again. Murad IV, the son of Ahmed I, succeeded as Ottoman sultan on the forced abdication of his uncle, Mustafa I. It was in 1623, at a time of widespread rebellion, defeat and instability throughout the empire, that Murad IV took over as Sultan. In the first ten years of his reign, Murad got through as many as seven viziers. The Janissaries, the special army of the

Sultan, were the real power in the empire when Murad acceded. In fact it was they who had forced the previous sultan to abdicate. The Janissaries also forced Murad to dismiss his chief minister and many other officials. The last time they were able to do this was in 1632, when they entered the palace, demanding the heads of the grand vizier Hafiz Pasha and 16 other officials. The young sultan could do nothing to save them. Later, when he was stronger, Murad was able to take his revenge by having 500 of the leading Janissaries strangled in their barracks.

This was Murad's simple technique. Anyone who came under the slightest suspicion was executed. In one year, 1637, Murad had 25,000 of his subjects executed. He executed many of them himself. He beheaded his chief musician for playing a Persian tune. He walked the streets at night, visiting taverns. If he caught anyone smoking, he revealed who he was and executed them on the spot. On one occasion he caught one of his gardeners and his wife smoking; he had their legs amputated and showed them off in public while they bled to death. Murad spent hours exercising his royal prerogative of taking ten innocent lives a day by shooting passers-by with an arquebus, people he deemed to be too near the palace walls. He came upon a group of women in a meadow and took exception to the amount of noise they were making, so he had them drowned.

Murad's heavy hand produced the desired effect. A turbulent and unstable empire stabilized, though at a terrible cost in human lives.

Sultan Murad IV took his cruelty abroad with him too. In 1638 he led an expedition to Baghdad, then the capital of Persia. He laid siege to the city. During this siege he engaged in single combat a Persian champion, slicing the man's head in half. When Baghdad finally fell, he pitilessly massacred the 30,000 defenders.

But at least Murad IV was the last of the all-powerful tyrannical Ottoman despots. He died in 1640. At 28 he was worn out by habitual self-indulgence.

Peter the Great
(1672–1725)

PETER THE GREAT, Tsar of Russia from 1682, was the fourth son of Tsar Alexei I Mikhailovitch, by his second wife, Natalia Naruishkina. He was born on 30 May 1672. He was made co-tsar jointly with his half-brother Ivan V, when their elder brother Fedor III died; the boys ruled under the regency of their sister, the Grand Duchess Sophia. His election as tsar seems to have been a signal for general rebellion. He saw one of his uncles dragged from the palace and butchered by a savage mob. He saw Artamon Matvyeev, his mother's mentor and his own best friend, pulled away and cut to pieces. These awful childhood experiences made Peter a twitchy and anxious boy, and it is thought that the convulsions he experienced in later years had their roots in these early traumas.

During the regency of his sister, Peter was free to indulge himself. His new friend, a Swiss adventurer called Francois Lefort, introduced Peter to all the delights of a dissolute lifestyle in a special house, which was built at Peter's own expense. Peter's mother was understandably alarmed at her son's antics, and hastily arranged his marriage to the beautiful but stupid Eudoxia Lopukhina, the pious daughter of a nobleman, when he 'came of age' in 1689. The marriage was a disaster, and Peter virtually abandoned Eudoxia only a year later. He also had his sister, the Grand Duchess, arrested and immured in a convent, where she died in 1704, so that he could rule on his own with his feeble-minded brother as a figurehead. In 1690, Eudoxia had a son, the Tsarevich Alexis.

Peter's strength and failing lay in his boundless energy and curiosity. This gave him a great capacity for work, but also an appetite for roistering. He had a coarse contempt for religious ceremony and political formality.

In 1695, after six years of preparation, Peter moved his army against the Turks. Peter characteristically served in this army as a humble bombardier. The following year, he captured the crucial Black Sea port of Azov.

In 1697, Peter the Great set off incognito on a Grand Tour. This 'Grand Embassy' of Europe had the ostensible purpose of winning allies for Russia against the Turks. Peter spent a year and a half touring Holland, Germany, England and Austria, even working as a shipwright in shipyards in Holland and at Deptford on the Thames. Peter's private mission, his personal agenda, was to gather a comprehensive knowledge of western technology so that he could modernize Russia. He hired thousands of specialist craftsmen and military personnel to return to Russia with him to instruct the Russian people in western methods.

Peter had to return to Russia in a hurry in 1698 to deal with a rebellion of the musketeer regiments (streltsy). This he suppressed with great savagery with the help of a Scottish general, Patrick Gordon. The Tsarina Eudoxia was accused of conspiracy, divorced and sent to a convent. He then started introducing many western customs, by force, and caused a great deal of unnecessary offence by doing so. He ordered all beards to be shaved off at court. He insisted that 'German' dress must be worn. Houses were to be built in western style. Peter's son Alexis was put in the charge of a German tutor.

In 1700, he launched the Great Northern War against Sweden, but Karl XII of Sweden marched his troops on a pre-emptive strike, routing the Russian army at Narva in Estonia. Peter ordered the church bells of Moscow to be melted down to make extra cannon. He refused to allow a new patriarch to be elected, enabling him to take all ecclesiastical revenues for the war effort. In 1703, Peter founded the new city and port of St Petersburg, which became the new capital of the empire.

Possibly appalled at his father's example, the Tsarevich Alexis decided that he never wanted to become Tsar. Peter's rage has been described as cyclonic, and rarely stopping short of extermination. Now he was cyclonically and dangerously angry with his son and heir. In 1718, when the Tsarevich Alexis insisted on renouncing the succession, Peter had him imprisoned and gradually and mercilessly tortured to death. Alexis himself had a son, the Grand Duke Peter, but he was only six years old and the Tsar did not want him to succeed. Peter's next step was to denounce primogeniture in the male line as the normal title to succession to the throne. With the 1722 ustav or ordinance (an Act of Succession) Peter assumed the right to choose his own successor, and the following year he took the precaution of issuing a second manifesto in November 1723 to explain at length why he was nominating his new wife Catherine as his heir. It was extremely unpopular, a scandalous innovation, and doubly so because of his new wife Catherine's low birth, but on Peter's death she succeeded him without any opposition. She was crowned empress in May 1724.

Peter the Great had more convulsions and died in agony on 28 January 1725.

Peter the Great achieved an extraordinary cultural revolution in Russia, forcing it, with undue harshness, into line with developments in western Europe and making it a major power. The war with Sweden was unnecessary, except in that dictators seem frequently to need foreign adventures to rally support at home. The unnatural, brutal and murderous treatment of his son was incredible, and an indication of the conflicting elements in Peter's personality. He was the great modernizer and westernizer, yet he sometimes behaved like Ivan the Terrible. He was the self-effacing shipyard worker and bombardier, yet he was also a tyrant who could not be gainsaid.

Catherine the Great
(1726–1796)

CATHERINE THE GREAT, Empress of Russia, was born at Stettin in Germany. She was no Russian, nor was her name Catherine. Her given name was Sophie. She was the daughter of Prince Christian Augustus of Anhalt-Zerbst, Commandant at Stettin, and Princess Johanna, who showed no affection to her daughter and considered her life provincial and dull. The daughter's life was to be far from provincial or dull.

Sophie rose to her remarkable position as Empress of Russia in a remarkable way. At 15 she was singled out as a possible bride for Grand Duke Peter of Russia, probably because (as the courtiers might have thought) her relatively low status would make her less ambitious, easier to control. Peter himself was no great catch; he was deformed, with an ugly thick-lipped face and an unstable personality. She took the name Catherine in 1744, on entering the Orthodox faith, and she and Peter were married. The marriage, which took place in 1745, was still unconsummated after eight years of marriage.

Catherine took a lover, one of the Chamberlains, Serge Saltykov. In 1754 Catherine became pregnant; the baby boy was called Grand Duke Paul, and Saltykov was advised to travel for the sake of his health. The baby was taken away from Catherine too. The whole awful experience hardened Catherine's personality. Next she fixed her attention on Count Stanislas Poniatowsky, who was nervous about having an affair with so dangerous a lady, but she was determined. He was found out, and called before the Grand Duke, who liked to know what was going on. Poniatowsky confessed, the Grand Duke summoned his mistress and his wife and the four of them played cards together. Poniatowsky was drawn into the web of court intrigue and eventually driven from Moscow. Long afterwards, when Catherine was Empress, she exacted a peculiar revenge on him for betraying her to the Grand Duke by making him King of Poland one day and forcing him to abdicate the next. The humiliation was too much to bear and Poniatowsky died shortly afterwards.

In December 1761 the Empress Elizabeth died and the Grand Duke became Tsar Peter III. He went wild with his new-found freedom, mocking the Empress's coffin and fooling about in the funeral procession. By contrast, Catherine dressed in black from head to foot and showed respect to the hated Empress. She was by now pregnant again, this time to a handsome Tartar called Gregory Orlov. The new son was sent out to be brought up by foster parents, while the Tsar shouted, 'God knows where she gets her children from!'. This attempt to humiliate Catherine was the last straw. She decided to depose him. With the help of Orlov and his four brothers, and the army firmly behind her, Catherine rode into St Petersburg on 30 June 1762 as Empress. Dressed in military uniform, she took control of the 20,000 strong army in a well-organized bloodless coup. The Tsar was bundled into a carriage and taken to the Schlusselberg Castle, a place associated with torture and which she would have known he dreaded. He asked Catherine to be allowed to keep his mistress, his dog, his negro and his violin. She commented, 'Fearing scandal, I only granted him the last three.'. Within three weeks he was dead. Catherine said he died of apoplexy, but it was known that he died violently on 17 July 1762. It was believed at the time that he was poisoned with a glass of wine, but when that took too long one of the Orlovs strangled him with a table napkin. It was also believed that Catherine had been behind the murder.

Catherine then visited another prisoner in his cell. He was a thin, pale-faced 22-year-old. He was significantly known as Prisoner Number One. He was the rightful ruler of Russia, Tsar Ivan VI, and he had been shut away at the age of six by the hated Empress Elizabeth. His mind wandered, but the one thing that he could remember was that he was the Tsar. Catherine gave him a lethal stare and left, ordering a doubling of the guard. If any attempt was made to rescue him, he was to be killed. In due course he was stabbed to death by Lieutenant Morovitch.

Her own son, Paul, remained as a potential rival,

and she made sure that he remained a nonentity.

Gregory Orlov remained the court favourite, and he became increasingly powerful. He even proposed marriage. When she refused him, he behaved badly, and she saw that it was time for him too to be removed. She gave him the title of Prince and sent him off on a tour of Europe. He was tremendous to look at, with his fine good looks and magnificent uniforms, but had no intellect. One observer commented, 'He is like an ever-boiling pan of water which never cooks anything'. When he returned to St Petersburg, Catherine gave him a marble palace and an enormous jewel which became known as the Orlov Diamond. By this time, Catherine had a new lover, Vasilchikov, soon to be replaced by Prince Potemkin, the most celebrated of her many lovers. She wrote to him, 'Every cell in my body reaches towards you, oh, barbarian!'. Unlike Orlov, Potemkin had a brain, and Catherine could discuss strategy with him. She fainted when she heard he was dead.

She was what today would be called a control freak. She had to be obeyed. Her main purpose was, like her dead husband's, to make Russia great. This was a worthy enough goal, but she treated the serfs as less than human. A serf could be bought for one-seventh the price of a pedigree dog. On one level, it would be possible to write off the sex scandals, the endless appetite for young men, as mere 'private life'. But the relationships cost a great deal, considered in terms of cash alone. It has been estimated that she spent 100 million roubles, just in cash, on her lovers. The relationships also distorted political events. Her last lover, Plato Zubov, outlived her to assassinate her son, the new Tsar.

One thing that can be said in Catherine's favour is that she at least showed gratitude to the Orlov brothers. Gregory and his brothers were given seven million roubles, palaces, estates and other gifts for their loyal services. She could never be directly accused of murder, but the assassinations of her husband, Tsar Peter III, and his brother, Tsar Ivan VI, were very likely carried out at her instigation. As a head of state, she greatly inflated the territories of Russia by warfare, but at great human cost.

PART THREE

WICKED WOMEN

Jezebel
(about 880 BC – 842 BC)

JEZEBEL IS ONE of those unfortunate women of history – or proto-history – whose names have become a by-word for evil. But just how evil was she? Was she really evil at all? Or was she someone who represented a principle that obstructed the grand march of Israelite history, and therefore just the wrong person in the wrong place at the wrong time?

Jezebel was a Phoenician princess, the daughter of Ethbaal, the king of Tyre and Sidon who also doubled as the priest of Astarte. She married King Ahab of Israel, who acceded to the Israelite throne in 869 BC. As a Phoenician princess, it was natural that she should want to introduce her own Phoenician customs to the Israelite capital, Samaria, and as the daughter of a priest it was equally understandable for her to attempt to introduce her own religion too.

She was a vigorous and strong-minded woman, which in itself provoked hostility. She tried to bring in the autocratic model for monarchy, then common in the east, and this too provoked hostility. But it was her attempt to introduce her foreign religion that sealed her doom. She attempted to replace the worship of Yahweh with the worship of the Tyrian Baal, Melkart, and she persecuted the prophets of Yahweh. Her political position as an absolute monarchist and her religious position as a Baal-worshipper inevitably roused national feeling against her and attracted the fury and hatred of the Hebrew prophet Elijah – and his successors.

Elijah successfully challenged the authority of the god Baal in the high places (peak sanctuaries) on Mount Carmel, and this resulted in the destruction of the Tyrian prophets. Elijah launched a terrible curse against Ahab and Jezebel. King Ahab died in 850 BC, and Queen Jezebel for a time remained the power behind the throne of her sons. Then the usurper Jehu seized power in an army coup. Jehu had Queen Jezebel thrown to the ground from a palace window; then he rode over her body with his chariot. The curse of Elijah was fulfilled in the massacre of the house of Ahab.

Standing back from the highly-coloured version of events offered in the Bible, it looks as if Jezebel's main crimes were that she belonged to the wrong religion and subscribed to the wrong political party as far as the writers of the Old Testament were concerned. As a result, rightly or wrongly, her name has become a by-word for a wilful, wild, uncontrollable hussy.

Empress Livia
(58 BC – AD 29)

DRUSILLA LIVIA WAS the famously ambitious wife of the Roman Emperor Augustus. When Augustus first noticed Livia, she was married to Tiberius Claudius Nero. Augustus was on his second wife, Scribonia, and she was a taciturn and unappealing woman; Augustus asked Tiberius to give him Livia. Livia was already pregnant with young Tiberius, the future emperor, when she divorced Tiberius Senior and Augustus married her in 39 BC.

Augustus won two famous battles, one in which he defeated the great Roman general Pompey, the other, the Battle of Actium, in which Mark Antony was defeated. Suddenly Augustus was self-evidently the right choice, and Livia basked in his reflected glory. A town called Liviada was named after her. Her sons by her previous marriage, Nero Claudius Drusus and Tiberius, were given commands in the Roman army, and she saw to it that every victory they had was treated as a triumph. Tiberius was cruel, arrogant and depraved and Augustus said that if he ever came to power he would cause the greatest suffering. Drusus on the other hand was a model heir and Augustus would have liked to name him as his successor, though he held back from this, thinking that it would imply that Drusus was his own son born out of wedlock. Instead he chose Marcellus, his nephew and adoptive son. Livia had her own plan, which was to remove anything or anyone who stood in the way of Tiberius's succession.

At first it looked as though little could stand in the way of one or other of her sons by her first marriage inheriting. She had no children by Augustus.

Drusus died as a result of a fall from a horse while returning from battle. Livia was grief-stricken, but all the more determined to make Tiberius emperor. Marcellus had been poisoned by Livia, but then Marcellus's widow Julia was married to Agrippa, and she gave birth to two sons, Lucius and Gaius, and both boys would succeed before Tiberius. But both boys died suddenly, one in Lycia, the other in Marseilles.

Augustus depended on Livia's advice in most things. He also complained bitterly of the cruelty of his destiny, in losing so many members of his family one after another. He made up his mind to visit young Agrippa, the grandson he had exiled to an island prison. He kept his visit secret, as he was beginning to be suspicious of Livia's hand in the deaths. Livia was so angry that he should act without her knowledge, that she decided to kill both Augustus and Agrippa. At his palace at Nola, the remains of which have only recently been discovered, Augustus was given a dish of poisoned figs by Livia. His death was kept secret for a time, because Tiberius was away. As soon as he returned, the death of Augustus and Tiberius's succession were announced. Livia secretly sent assassins to the island to kill Agrippa.

On the death of Augustus in AD 14, Livia changed her name to Julia Augusta.

Rome now feared Livia, and lavished honours and titles on her. She revelled in the status of mother of the Emperor. She continued to persecute all the remaining members of Augustus's family. There was still Germanicus, her own grandson, Drusus's son; him she had poisoned in Syria by her agents. Tiberius grew to hate Livia and her endless ambition and relations between mother and son became increasingly strained as she tried to influence political decisions. To escape her endless interference, he left Rome and spent most of his time on the island Capri, leading a dissolute but by no means carefree existence. Meanwhile courtiers squabbled for power in Rome, and Livia effectively governed in his absence.

When Livia finally died aged 80, she was laid to rest in a mausoleum with Augustus. Caligula gave the funeral oration. She had wanted to be made a goddess, but Tiberius, determined to thwart her last wish, refused to allow it and refused to execute her will.

Alice Kyteler
(about 1280–about 1340)

LADY ALICE KYTELER lived in the town of Kilkenny in Ireland, where she married four husbands, one after the other. She was unpopular in Kilkenny because she was both wealthy and arrogant. Rumours circulated that Lady Alice was involved in witchcraft.

Her first husband was William Outlawe, a banker and money lender who died before 1302. Her second was Adam le Blund of Callan, who died before 1311. Her third was Richard de Valle, who also died relatively soon after. The assumption was made that 'three is murder', but the death rate was relatively high in the middle ages, and the three deaths could have been coincidences.

Two of the men were widowers who left everything to Alice when they died, leaving their children nothing; these children made no complaint at the time, suspecting nothing. But when the fourth husband, Sir John le Poer, fell ill in 1324, people began to suspect that something was seriously wrong. He began to waste away. His fingernails and toenails fell out. His hair started to fall out. He began to show all the same symptoms that the earlier husbands had developed. Sir John's children raised the alarm, but Sir John loved his wife and would not listen. Then one of the servants talked to him and he decided he must act. He confronted Alice and demanded the key to her room. She refused to hand it over, so he seized it. In the room he found several locked boxes and chests and when he forced them open he found the evidence that his wife was a poisoner – and a witch.

Sir John gathered up the collection of potions, powders and wafers inscribed with the name of Satan, and sent them, with two monks, to the Bishop of Ossory. The Bishop, a Franciscan called Richard De Ledrede, was a fanatical witch-finder, greedy for funds. If Lady Alice could be found guilty her wealth would be forfeit. After investigating the evidence, the Bishop levelled seven charges against Lady Alice. She went out at night, it emerged, to hold meetings in churches with her accomplices; there they held ceremonies and sacrificed animals, whose limbs they left at crossroads. She had made charms from a wide variety of awful ingredients, including the hair of hanged criminals and the flesh of unbaptized babies. These elements were boiled up in the skull of a beheaded robber. The indictments continued. Lady Alice had an unholy association with a demon called Robert Artisson, who would sometimes appear in the shape of a huge cat, sometimes as a black prince with two tall attendants. Lady Alice was said (by her maid) to have sex with this demon.

The Bishop clearly believed that the demon or

'apparition' was a living person, perhaps from another town. He tried to catch him, but failed.

It soon emerged that Lady Alice had used her potions to kill her first three husbands and that her motive was money. Her one other concern was for her favourite son, William Outlawe. She would take a broom into the street at sunset, rake all the dirt towards her son's door, and chant, 'To the house of William my son, Hie all the wealth of Kilkenny town.'.

The Bishop ordered Lady Alice's arrest, but he found it hard to take her in. Sorcery was at this time a secular crime, not under Church jurisdiction, so the Bishop needed a writ from the Lord Chancellor before she could be arrested. The Lord Chancellor was Roger Outlawe, a relative of Lady Alice's by her first marriage, and he supported her. The Bishop decided to take the law into his own hands, sent two representatives to summon her to his Church court, but she refused. The court sat without her and sentenced her to excommunication. Lady Alice's supporters retaliated by locking the Bishop up in Kilkenny Castle for over a fortnight, while they issued a writ against him for defamation of character.

The Bishop went on trying to bring the sorceress to court, and went on failing. With the help of her friends, Lady Alice gathered her belongings and escaped to England, where she lived out the rest of her life.

Ironically, others suffered far worse fates. Lady Alice's maid, Petronilla, was eventually brought to trial with other accomplices, and became the first witch to be burned in Ireland. It was blatantly unjust. Petronilla was just a novice; on her own account, she had been taught everything by Lady Alice and there was no more powerful witch in the world than Lady Alice. Poor Petronilla went to the stake on 3 November, 1324. Lady Alice was tried in her absence, but was safe so long as she never returned to Irish soil. The Kyteler case was extraordinary in many ways, not least because it was the first of its kind in Ireland.

Lucrezia Borgia
(1480–1519)

LUCREZIA BORGIA WAS born in 1480, the daughter of Rodrigo Borgia, Pope Alexander VI. Equally important in her biography is the fact that she was unlucky enough to be the sister of Cesare Borgia.

Lucrezia has acquired a bad reputation as a member of a sinister and repulsive family, but it is not entirely clear whether she ever deserved her bad reputation. For one thing, she lived in a Renaissance world where morals and standards of behaviour were very different from ours. The fact that her father, Rodrigo Borgia, could bribe his way into being elected Pope, in spite of leading an openly dissolute life, shows how different things were. Once he was Pope, Rodrigo took it for granted, and so did everyone else, that he could do as he liked. He thought nothing of making his 16-year-old son, a boy with absolutely no interest whatsoever in the Church, an Archbishop and then a year later a Cardinal. It was all to do with status and displaying personal power.

Lucrezia was probably not in a position to make many decisions, and it seems fairer to see her as a victim of her father's and brother's evil, rather than as an evil-doer herself.

She was the daughter of Rodrigo Borgia and his

mistress Vanozza. She was brought up in her mother's house on the Piazza Pizzo do Merlo. Rodrigo, a Cardinal, could not and did not acknowledge Lucrezia or her siblings until he was sure it was safe to do so – when he was Pope. She was a beautiful girl and there were several suitors. She was married, at 13, to the Lord of Pesare, Giovanni Sforza. The marriage was brief, partly because of Cesare's incestuous passion for Lucrezia, which naturally unnerved the bridegroom, partly because the Borgias realised they could have caught someone much bigger and more important with the bait. They announced publicly that Sforza was impotent and that Lucrezia was still a virgin. Sforza put up a spirited defence, swearing that he had had sex with his wife 'on countless occasions'. But the Borgias wanted their daughter back and he was obliged, under threat, to sign a confession of impotence. He left Rome before they could do anything worse to him.

Lucrezia was put into a convent to restore her virginal image, ready for the next husband. In 1498, news spread that Lucrezia was pregnant and that the lover was a Spaniard called Pedro Calderon. It seems that Calderon did indeed fancy Lucrezia, and he may have been the father. Cesare Borgia had him thrown in prison and shortly afterwards his body was found in the Tiber; this happened a lot to people who crossed Cesare Borgia. Cesare certainly loved his sister to an unnatural degree, but there is nothing to suggest that this unnatural affection was returned. If he did have sex with Lucrezia, it is likely that she complied out of fear. No-one crossed Cesare Borgia and lived. Her survival depended absolutely on compliance. Sforza, still smarting from the terrible public insults he had received, got his own back by accusing Lucrezia of having sex not only with her brother but with her father too.

Lucrezia gave birth to a boy called Giovanni, who was probably, though not certainly, Calderon's, in March 1498. She always referred to him as her little brother; others referred to him enigmatically as 'The Roman Prince'. No-one really knew who he was.

The next husband was to be Alphonso, son of the King of Naples. The Borgias were hoping to gain a dynastic link to the House of Aragon. Alphonso promised to stay with Lucrezia in Rome for a year before taking her home. Cesare once again became a major threat to the husband, arranging for him to be mugged in St Peter's Square. Alphonso survived this brutal attack and was kept in a place of safety in the Vatican, but Cesare managed to reach him – and strangled him.

Lucrezia was grief-stricken at the loss of the husband she genuinely loved, but she braced herself for the next marriage. The Borgias chose Alfonso d'Esta, the son of the Duke of Ferrara, but he was understandably nervous, and had to be coerced by his father. She went off to live in the huge medieval castle at Vecchio, where she lived out her life with charm, grace and modesty. There were still scandalous speculations surrounding her, though as we have seen, Lucrezia's reputation was to a great extent created by those around her. She was friendly with a young poet called Ercole Strozzi, who was obviously in love with her. Scandal broke out afresh when Strozzi's body was found in the street, peppered with stab wounds. Those who hated the Borgias said that Lucrezia had had Strozzi killed out of jealousy, because he had been about to get married to someone else. It is possible but the truth is that no-one knows who killed Strozzi, or why.

As time passed, Lucrezia became the model for another image of womankind. She became miraculously transformed from Jezebel to the Virgin Mary. The new Lucrezia was outstandingly virtuous, perfect, a veritable angel of mercy. It was almost certainly no truer than the old image.

Mary Tudor
(1516–1558)

MARY TUDOR WAS born at Greenwich in February 1516, the daughter of Henry VIII and Katherine of Aragon. This should have been a great start in life, but it was not. Her father desperately wanted a son to continue the Tudor dynasty, and the fact that she was a girl was a great disappointment. The King seems to have been fond of her, even so, and saw to it that she was well educated, just as her half-sister, the yet unborn Elizabeth, would be. Mary's long unhappiness began when her father tired of waiting for her mother to produce a male heir and became infatuated with Anne Boleyn.

In the long struggle to have his first marriage annulled, Henry VIII pushed both Katherine and Mary to one side. When he finally married Anne Boleyn in 1533, Henry ordered that Mary should no longer use the title Princess, and that she should give precedence to the new Queen's daughter. The point Henry was trying to make was that the first marriage had been an illegal one and that therefore Mary was illegitimate; any children of the new Queen's would therefore take precedence over her. The old Queen was sent away to Kimbolton, while Mary was lodged with

Anne Boleyn's sister at Hatfield. The severity of the King's treatment of Queen Katherine and her daughter aroused a great deal of sympathy in the country, especially when Katherine died, in 1536, without being allowed a visit from her daughter. Mary's only ally through this difficult time was Charles V of Spain, her mother's nephew. The Spanish king's ambassador, Chapuys, frequently tried to act on Mary's behalf when he thought her interests were threatened. At the same time, Chapuys had to advise Mary to behave a little more diplomatically; she was proud, hot-tempered and outspoken. Many believed that it was only the concern of the King of Spain that prevented Henry from permanently disposing of Mary, who was becoming a nuisance.

Suddenly things started to improve for Mary. Queen Anne was beheaded and Henry married Jane Seymour, who was far more compassionate towards Mary. Jane advised Mary to show humility towards her father, agree to acknowledge the divorce and beg the King's forgiveness for her obduracy. Thanks to Chapuys's and the new Queen's persuasion, Mary signed the papers accepting her parents' divorce. After a few months, she was allowed back to Greenwich.

In 1537, Jane Seymour gave birth to a son, the prince who would shortly be Edward VI, and Mary wisely recognized that Edward would take precedence over her. The fact that he was a boy was decisive, but by now Henry had (for the time being) declared both Mary and Elizabeth bastards, so they were (for the time being) both out of the line of succession.

In 1547, Henry VIII died and was succeeded by Edward VI. He had tuberculosis and would not live long. Because of his illness and his youth, the real power lay in the hands of Edward Seymour, his uncle and the brother of the late queen. Seymour, a Protestant, became Lord Protector and together with Cranmer they attempted to establish a Protestant England. Once again Mary was in difficulties. She was a staunch, unswerving Catholic, and so found it increasingly difficult to remain at court, even though she was very fond of her brother, the King. She withdrew to the country and was allowed to say mass in private.

In 1553, Edward VI lay dying and Mary prepared to succeed, as Henry VIII had intended that she would. Her brother's death approached and Mary prepared to return to London. Meanwhile a rebellion was mounted by a group of Protestant nobles, who feared a return to Catholicism if Mary took the throne, not least because it would greatly reduce their own power and influence. The rebellion was led by the Duke of Northumberland, who supported the candidacy of Lady Jane Grey. She was Edward VI's cousin. She had no ambition to become Queen, but this did not deter Northumberland, who married her to his son, Lord Guildford Dudley. Northumberland made the dying King sign a new will, bequeathing the crown to Lady Jane Grey and confirming, once again, that both Mary and Elizabeth were illegitimate.

Lady Jane Grey was Queen for only nine days. A counter-rebellion to put Mary on the throne gathered momentum; most of the great barons wanted to be on the winning side. In July 1553 Mary was proclaimed Queen in London, to great rejoicing, and she entered the city in triumph. It was the high point of her reign.

Queen Mary set about getting rid of those who had acted against her. She was endangering her popularity, and her advisers proposed that she should marry in order to consolidate her position. After all, another Protestant candidate could quickly be found. Her old supporter Charles V of Spain offered her his son, Prince Philip, as a suitor. There were several problems looming. The prospective bridegroom was only 26, 11 years younger than Mary, and reported to be very virile. Mary disliked the idea of sex. She was naturally very reluctant, and feared marriage almost as much as her half-sister Elizabeth, and probably for a similar reason – the appalling example of their father's catastrophic marriages. She finally forced herself to accept the marriage, only to find that it was extremely unpopular with the English people. The Spaniards were, after all, 'the enemy'. There were riots. There were revolts, the most serious revolt being that of Sir Thomas Wyatt, a 23-year-old Catholic, who led an army of 15,000 to London before it was stamped out.

This experience hardened Mary's heart, and she now moved against all of those involved in the rebellions against her. Even Lady Jane Grey was executed; although she was entirely innocent she would continue to be a focus for Protestant hopes if she remained alive.

Prince Philip of Spain arrived for the wedding in July 1554. Mary fell in love with him immediately, but he found her unattractive. He was courteous and attentive towards her in public, but privately she was a great disappointment to him, as her aversion to sex was all too apparent. Twice during their marriage Mary claimed that she was pregnant, but it turned out that she was swelling up because she had a diseased womb instead.

It was in the midst of this unhappiness that the persecution of Protestants began. A tribunal was set up in Southwark to question suspected heretics. The Bishop of London, Edmund Bonner, led a procession through London to celebrate the triumph of Rome. Bonner was quickly to gain an evil reputation as an inquisitor. He had suspected heretics to stay at his house, where he perfected the 'nice-and-nasty' style of interrogation. An invitation to stay at Bishop Bonner's house was no treat.

The first victim of the persecutions was John Rogers, who was a married priest. He was burned at Smithfield in February 1555. The Bishop of Gloucester soon followed, a great surprise to everyone, as he had been loyal to Mary in spite of their difference in religion. Many Protestant bishops and theologians fled abroad. Those that remained went one by one to the stake. Hugh Latimer, Bishop of Worcester, who had helped establish the Protestant Church in England, was an obvious target. Ridley, the Bishop of London who had supported Lady Jane Grey, was another.

The pair of them were taken to Oxford and burnt together in the town ditch (now Broad Street). Archbishop Cranmer was burnt shortly afterwards.

These were great men, who had taken an active part in public life. They had taken calculated risks and lost. But most of Mary's victims were ordinary people who had played no part in state politics and represented no threat to her at all. It was generally assumed, because of the Inquisition in Spain, that Prince Philip of Spain was egging her on, but in fact the opposite was the case. He urged her to stop it and practise more moderate policies. He had, meanwhile become disenchanted with Mary in every way. She had not yet reached 40, yet her face was heavily lined and she looked much older. She was carrying out pointlessly cruel persecutions of her subjects. He spent as much time overseas as possible, and whenever he left Mary wept.

Still the persecutions went on. People who saw the burnings came to regard those who were punished in this way as saints. Mary became very angry at the sympathy shown to the heretics, and demanded that anyone who voiced compassion for them should be punished too. In Norwich, a man who protested against the cruelty was given a flogging for it.

In 1558 Mary fell ill. It may have been dropsy. It may have been a malignant growth in her womb. She gave in to self-pity, weeping for Philip, weeping for the loss of Calais, England's last possession in France. Protestantism flourished everywhere, with secret prayer meetings and increasingly open demonstrations against the burnings – but still the burnings went on.

On 10 November, she signed the death warrants for five Protestants to be burnt in Canterbury, bringing the total number of Protestant 'martyrs' to 238. On 13 November, she mercilessly signed away the lives of two more men in London. On 17 November, she died herself, just in time for the last two to be saved; they were set free at once. Mary's half-sister Elizabeth became Queen. She generously laid on a lavish Catholic funeral for Mary, but the dead Queen was to be remembered by the people of England, for ever after, as 'Bloody Mary'.

Elizabeth Bathory
(1561–1614)

ELIZABETH BATHORY WAS a countess who lived in the Carpathian Mountains. It was said that she was a real vampire, a drinker of human blood, and one of the inspirations for Bram Stoker's novel about Dracula. The countess was born in Hungary in 1561. She was a beautiful girl with a good complexion and fair hair. At the age of fifteen she was married to an aristocrat and became the mistress of the Castle of Csejthe in the Carpathian Mountains.

Elizabeth's husband was a soldier. He was often away on campaigns, and Elizabeth became very bored with life alone in the gloomy castle. She wanted excitement. This took the form of witchcraft, and she gathered around her a gang of alchemists, sorcerers and witches who were ready to teach her about witchcraft. She armed herself with a special pair of flesh-ripping silver pincers and a manual of torture that her husband had used when fighting the Turks.

Elizabeth's husband died in 1604, when she was 43. She longed for a lover, but the mirror told her that too many years had passed and her good looks had gone. When one day she slapped the face of a servant girl and drew blood, she noticed, or fancied she noticed, that where the girl's blood had spattered her the skin was much fresher and younger than before. She became convinced that bathing in the blood of young girls, and drinking it, would restore her beauty and preserve it for ever.

At night, Elizabeth and her deadly witch-band rode about the countryside looking for girls. When they found one, they took her back to the castle and drained off her blood for the countess to drink and bathe in. The countess carried on like this for five years before she realised that the blood cure was not working. She assumed it was because the blood was from peasant girls. What she needed was blood from virgins of her own class. In order to gain access to the girls she wanted, she opened a finishing school and took in 25 girls at a time to teach them the social graces. She treated her aristocratic pupils with the same ruthless cruelty that she had dealt out to the peasant girls before, but now she grew careless. The bodies of four of the girls were thrown over the castle walls. The villagers took them away for identification, and Elizabeth Bathory's secret was a secret no more.

Once the authorities knew what had been happening, the Hungarian Emperor, Matthias II, was informed. He ordered that the countess must be made to stand trial for her crimes. As the law then stood, she could not be arrested because she was an aristocrat, so a new law had to be passed to enable her to be arrested. At her trial in 1610 it was alleged that she had killed as many as 600 girls. Dorotta Szentes, known as Dorka, was the procuress who had supplied first the peasant girls, then the girls of higher class. She was sentenced to be burnt at the stake along with the whole band of witches.

The countess herself could not be sentenced to death because of her class. She was, even so, sentenced to be imprisoned in a small room in her own castle and fed only on scraps. She died four years later.

La Voisin
(about 1620–1680)

CATHERINE DESHAYES VOISIN, Madame Deshayes, who was better known as La Voisin, was the Queen of the witches in France at the time of Louis XIV. It was known, even at the time, that many of the most famous women in France sought her out for help. She was supremely confident of her abilities. 'Nothing is impossible to me,' she boasted to her clients. She only came to grief when it seemed that her evil-doing might harm the King himself. Then she was brought to justice.

La Voisin was a small, dumpy woman. She was not unattractive, apart from the disconcertingly piercing eyes. Her abilities as a witch were apparently inherited or learnt from her mother, who was also a famous sorceress, consulted by kings. She lived in the St Denis district of Paris with her husband, her daughter and their lodger, an executioner called Levasseur. She officially claimed that she was a practitioner of chiromancy and a student of physiognomy. She was a gifted fortune teller, not least because she relied on a network of informants in French high society. She was also able to crystal gaze, read Tarot cards, read palms and read faces. She said that reading the lines in a person's face was easier than reading the lines in their hand; passion and anxiety were easy to read there.

La Voisin made happiness powders and love potions, selling them in silk pouches. She also supplied aphrodisiacs and herbs for ending pregnancies. She visited the Sorbonne to discuss astrology with some of the academics there and made sure, for form's sake, that she was seen regularly at Mass at her parish church.

She was, nevertheless, queen of a coven of witches that was the most powerful coven in Paris. To begin with, she had sought clients where she could get them, people of any class. But as she became better known as a sorceress, she became more and more ambitious and cultivated her court contacts. Morality fell away as people became richer and more powerful, and she found that rich people would pay almost anything to get rid of an unwanted wife, husband or rival.

La Voisin specialized in poison. She sub-contracted the manufacture of the poisons to two women who were experts. They were able to provide her with over 50 different sorts of poison. By varying the doses, La Voisin could be sure the symptoms would be different each time and therefore unrecognizable. No patterns could ever be established. Nothing could be traced back to her. She made several attempts to get rid of her own husband, a bankrupt merchant, but each time she tried she failed. Her husband had an ally in Margot, the maid, who on one occasion saved him in the nick of time by jogging his elbow as he was about to drink some poisoned soup. On another occasion, Margot administered an antidote, though it left the man with incurable hiccups. It was a running joke among La Voisin's friends, who would greet her with the polite enquiry, 'How is your husband? Not dead yet?'

At her house La Voisin took part in the Black Mass, for which she supplied the altar (a naked woman), a priest (the Abbe Guibourg), and vestments (an alb with black phalluses embroidered on it). She herself wore a huge cloak of crimson velvet. She admitted at her trial that in a furnace in her garden she disposed of the bodies of hundreds of babies and embryos that she had used in her Black Masses.

In the end, in 1673, information supplied by two monks reached the King that there was gossip that Madame de Vivonne and Madame de la Mothe were employing La Voisin to dispose of their husbands. There was talk of 'succession powders' being used, so-called because the powders ensured the succession of the poisoner. Louis XIV ordered that there must be an enquiry to get to the bottom of it. One of the ladies concerned was a member of his inner circle at court.

At first, a fortune-teller called Marie Bosse was suspected. The police chief, de la Reynie, sent an agent to consult the fortune-teller on the best way to deal with her difficult husband. Marie Bosse sold her some arsenic and was promptly arrested. Under torture, Madame Bosse named several prominent courtiers among her clients. Under Louis's instructions, de la Reynie widened his enquiries in La Commission de l'Arsenic, which became known to those who were summoned for interrogation as La Chambre Ardente. Marie Bosse admitted to being part of a satanic cult presided over by La Voisin.

La Voisin was arrested along with her accomplices. Her ex-lover, LeSage, revealed all of her secrets. Many distinguished names came out, but La Voisin kept quiet about Francoise Arthenais de Mortmart, Madame de Montespan, who was the King's mistress for twelve years, producing seven children whom Louis had legitimized; they formed the backbone of a new aristocracy. It was LeSage who mentioned her name during interrogation; de Montespan had gone to La Voisin when she thought the 18-year-old Duchesse de Fontages came to court to seduce the King, and she, de Montespan, understandably feared he was losing interest in her. The young duchess gave birth to a son who died after a month, then she herself was taken ill and poisoning was suspected.

The Chief of Police, Nicolas de la Reynie, reported back to the King, who asked for any documents relating to Madame de Montespan to be handed to him. Louis burnt the incriminating evidence himself, but afterwards hardly ever spoke to his former mistress.

De la Reynie collected some damning evidence against La Voisin, including the testimony of her own daughter, Marie-Marguerite. She admitted to having seen animals being sacrificed. Under pressure, she admitted to having seen human sacrifices too. The presiding priest had dedicated a child to Astaroth and Asmodeus, holding it upside down and slitting its throat. The blood had spurted into a chalice on the stomach of the naked woman functioning as an altar. The priest has smeared the blood on his penis and had sex with the naked woman. And one of the worshippers had been Madame de Montespan.

In the end, La Voisin gave way to panic, trying to retract much of what had already come out. The poisons were mere purgatives for family use. The oven in the garden was for making pate. But when the police raided her property, they found plenty of evidence of satanic activities, stocks of black candles, wax figures bristling with pins and needles. She was trapped by the huge weight of evidence against her. She confessed to killing hundreds of children over a thirteen year period of devil-worship. In 1680, she was sentenced to be burnt alive. As she was burnt, she turned her face from the crucifix held in front of her. In the purge that followed de la Reynie's report, about 150 courtiers were arrested for poisoning and given a variety of sentences, from death to slavery and banishment.

Madeleine Smith
(about 1837–1928)

THE SENSATIONAL TRIAL of Madeleine Smith took place in Glasgow in July 1857. Was she a cold-hearted killer, or the victim of circumstances? She was on trial for the murder of her lover Emile L'Angelier, who died an agonizing death by arsenic poisoning.

Madeleine was the eldest daughter of a successful Glaswegian architect, James Smith. He kept a comfortable household with six servants, but ruled that household with a rod of iron. Often in the evening there was a social function for her to attend, but for much of the time there was nothing at all to do, so Madeleine was expected to occupy herself with lady-like pursuits such as painting or making collages with seaweed. Madeleine, in short, was bored stiff and ready for an adventure.

She first saw Emile L'Angelier, a packing clerk, in the street, when their eyes met by chance. He later found an opportunity to send her a flowery message of love. She rather foolishly replied that she had worn it next to her heart. A correspondence started that would prove very damaging to her in court. She tried to break off the relationship, but Emile was obsessed. In July 1855 he wrote her a menacing note: 'Think what your father would say if I sent him your letters for perusal.'. Given the stern character of Mr Smith, Madeleine must have been very frightened by the threat. She was already virtually a prisoner in the family home, and her father would be deeply shocked at the content of her letters. They were full of barely suppressed sexuality, and this at a time when women in her class were supposed to put up with sex, not enjoy it. When L'Angelier lay dead and his lodgings were searched, over 500 of these steamy letters were found.

It was obvious from the letters that they had had sex together. 'If we did wrong last night, it must have been in the excitement of our love. I suppose we should have waited until we were married.'.

When they moved out to their country house at Row in the summer of 1856, Madeleine asked for a ground floor room. Then she could just step out of the window to meet Emile. They met again and again at night without Madeleine's parents knowing. But then a middle class suitor appeared on the scene, William Minnoch. He was a businessman in his thirties, and began 'calling on' Madeleine. She received these calls, 'without finding Minnoch attractive', she told Emile.

When the Smiths returned to their town house in India Street in Glasgow at the end of that summer, secret meetings were made more difficult. Madeleine's bedroom was in the basement, with the window at pavement level covered by bars. Here there was no chance of her slipping out to have sex with Emile. Emile would come at night for a whispered conversation through the window, but it was scarcely enough. Emile went into a depression. Worse still, Madeleine's letters began to talk of their love as if it was in the past. She was seen in public with Minnoch and her letters to Emile were getting shorter. On 28 January she agreed to marry Minnoch. This was a decisive moment. She now had to end the affair with Emile. She wrote him a letter that was cold-hearted in tone. 'We had better for the future consider ourselves as strangers. I trust to your honour as a gentleman that you will not reveal anything that has passed between us.' And she asked him to return the deadly letters.

Emile became hysterical. He would not give her up. He would show her father the letters. If he couldn't have her, no other man would either. He raved to his work-mate Tom Kennedy, 'Tom, it's an infatuation. She shall be the death of me.' Madeleine in her turn became frantic when she realised that Emile was not going to return the letters. 'Hate me, despise me – but do not expose me.' She asked him to come to the house so that she could talk to him through the window. He kept that appointment, on 11 February 1857. It seems she was playing a game with L'Angelier now, playing for time, keeping his hopes alive so that he would not show her father the letters. She seems to have agreed to marry him in the autumn, which she really cannot have intended to do.

On 20 February, Mrs Jenkins, Emile's landlady went to his room to call him for breakfast, and found him very ill. During the night he had been very sick after feeling violent stomach pains on the way home. Four days later Mrs Jenkins was awakened by Emile's groans. He had the same symptoms as before. The symptoms were those of arsenic poisoning. It emerged at her trial that Madeleine had been shopping for arsenic at exactly this time. The chemist gave it to her mixed with soot according to the law, and he was surprised that Madeleine was concerned about the colour of it; why would it matter if she was giving it to rats, as she said?

Emile said to his friend and trusted go-between, Miss Perry, that he couldn't understand why he was so ill after taking coffee and chocolate from Madeleine. He even said he thought the drinks might have been poisoned. On 22 March he arrived at his lodgings very late, presumably because he had been to see Madeleine again. This time he was doubled up with pain. A doctor was fetched, but Emile died the next morning.

The post mortem showed that Emile had enough arsenic in his stomach to kill 40 men, and the presence of arsenic throughout his body showed that he had taken several doses.

At her trial, Madeleine pleaded Not Guilty and changed her explanation about the arsenic; she had bought it for cosmetic reasons. The prosecution explored the idea that she had used the sooty arsenic to lace the coffee and chocolate and fed them to Emile L'Angelier through the bars. She had got herself into such a difficult position that murder seemed the only way out. But the defending advocate argued that Emile was vain, unable to accept rejection, and boasted of being an arsenic eater. It is possible that Emile, in his depressed and desperate state, took the arsenic hoping to incriminate Madeleine; if he couldn't have Madeleine, no other man would have her either. If he could commit suicide in a way that reflected badly on Madeleine, so much the better. If he could make it look as if she had murdered him, best of all.

But the coldness of Madeleine Smith at her trial was incriminating in itself. She showed no feeling when the sufferings of Emile L'Angelier were described. She showed the same indifference to William Minnoch's sufferings. The whole affair had made him ill. Yet when asked about the man she had planned to marry, she said, 'My friend I know nothing of. I hear he has been ill, which I don't much care.'. The jury in Glasgow in 1857 could not decide – they gave a verdict of 'Not Proven' – and it is no easier for us to decide now. Could she possibly have committed that cold-blooded murder? If she did, she was indeed evil. It was noted at the trial that her defending advocate, normally a courteous man, left the courtroom after the verdict without a glance at his client, implying that he thought her guilty.

But Madeleine was free. She moved to London, married an artist and led an interesting and fulfilled life. She spent her later years in America, where she died, of natural causes, at the age of 91. A photograph of Madeleine Smith, taken when she was an old lady in America shows her to be fastidiously and beautifully dressed, giving the camera a sunny, direct and guilelessly innocent smile, and with her arms round two children. She looks happy, untroubled and innocent. But appearances often deceive.

Lizzie Borden
(1860–1927)

LIZZIE BORDEN WAS born on 19 July, 1860 in Fall
River, Massachusetts, into a family that was at
odds with itself almost from the start. When Lizzie
was only two, her mother Sarah died, leaving her
father Andrew to care for Lizzie and her elder
sister Emma. When Lizzie was five, Andrew Borden
remarried.

The new wife, Abby Durfee, was a short, heavy
and rather withdrawn and reclusive woman. Local
rumour had it that this was a marriage of
convenience, and that all Andrew wanted from
Abby was the services of a maid and child-
minder; nevertheless, Andrew Borden seems to
have cared for his new wife, who was one of life's
non-starters.

The problems arose from the poor relationship
that developed between the two girls and their
new stepmother. The 32-year-old Emma despised
Abby, seeing her as likely to rob her of her
inheritance. As the two girls grew older, things
got steadily worse and they refused to eat meals
with Abby, pointedly calling her 'Mrs Borden'.
Lizzie decapitated Abby's cat after it annoyed her.
Andrew Borden, now 70, had become wealthy as
a result of his investments but, in spite of being

one of the richest men in town, he and his family lived frugally in a small house in an unfashionable district of Fall River.

Another problem was the narrow focus of Lizzie's life. At the age of 32, she still had no job, no husband, no love life, nothing to distract her from the long-simmering grievance against her father and his second wife. She did some voluntary work and taught Sunday school, but those were not enough to distract her from the frustrations that were intensifying in her mind. Then, in 1891, her feud with her parents erupted into physical action. On one occasion when Andrew returned from an outing, Lizzie reported that Abby's bedroom had been broken into and ransacked by a thief who had stolen a watch and jewellery. Mr Borden called the police, then dismissed them halfway through their investigation, once it was obvious that Lizzie herself was the culprit. Again, later in the same year, the Borden's barn was broken into – twice. Andrew Borden again assumed that Lizzie was behind the petty crime. He retaliated by cutting the heads off Lizzie's pigeons, probably as a reminder of what Lizzie had done to Abby's cat. It is not known what Lizzie's reaction was to this act. Probably she sat around, as the Bordens tended to, and fumed in silent malevolence for days afterwards. Probably Andrew Borden's fate was already sealed, but the double murder of Lizzie's parents did not come until the following summer.

Lizzie Borden was known to have 'funny spells'. There were days when she behaved totally unpredictably, and those days became more frequent during the unusually hot year of 1892, when all New England steamed and suffocated. The local drugstore noticed that Lizzie was regularly buying small doses of prussic acid, well known as a lethal poison. By the end of July the entire Borden household was afflicted with stomach upsets. These were probably nothing to do with the prussic acid, but more likely to do with the fact that fresh food was going off faster than normal in the high temperatures.

Abby Borden was nevertheless convinced that she had been poisoned after she had suffered a long bout of vomiting. She made one of her rare trips out, to see the doctor who lived over the road. When she returned she was told off by her husband for her nonsensical behaviour. The doctor pointed out that the whole family was retching, including the maid. Lizzie's hate grew, Abby's apprehension grew, Andrew's irritation grew.

The day of 4 August, 1892 began like any other, only rather hotter. It was the hottest day of the whole summer. By mid-morning Andrew and Abby Borden were dead. Exactly what happened in between is still not known. It is uncertain whether Lizzie committed the murders – and some investigators have suggested other culprits, such as a discontented employee, or the maid, Bridget – but such evidence as there is points directly to Lizzie.

Luckily for her, Lizzie's sister Emma was out of town. Uncle John Morse, who had been invited to stay for a few days, was up early. The maid,

Bridget Sullivan followed him down to start her chores, but she had to stop to be sick. By 7.30 a.m. Abby and Andrew were dressed and sitting at breakfast with Uncle John. Just over an hour later, Uncle John went into town. Lizzie came down for a light breakfast, Bridget went outside to clean the windows and Abby got on with some dusting. At about 9 a.m. a youth called with a note and Andrew Borden went into town. He waited outside the bank and then decided to return home, where he arrived at about 10.30.

While Andrew Borden was out, a second young man arrived and hung about outside the Borden house. He was noticed by the neighbours. He seemed agitated, then he disappeared. He was never identified.

Inside No. 92 Second Street nasty things had started to happen. Someone had crept up behind Abby Borden while she was dusting the guest room and brought a hatchet crashing down on her head. She was killed instantly, but the attacker, whoever he or she was, carried on raining blows on her. There was no noise, at least not enough to alert anyone else in the house that anything untoward was happening. It was then, at 10.30 a.m., that Andrew Borden turned the key in the lock on the front door, hot and tired after his walk back from town. Lizzie helped her father settle himself for a rest on the sofa in the sitting room, then went to the outbuilding. She was, according to her own testimony, away for 20 minutes before returning.

At 11.10 a.m. Lizzie 'found' the body of her

father sprawled on the sofa in the sitting room. Half of his head was shorn away by blows from an axe, and blood was still trickling from his wounds. Lizzie's composure during the next few hours was a matter of comment. Lizzie summoned the maid, Bridget Sullivan, and went to a neighbour to tell her what had happened. 'Oh, Mrs Churchill, do come. Someone has killed Father!' is what the neighbour remembered her saying. She also called the family doctor and the police. Lizzie said her mother had had a note asking her to go and visit a sick person, so she did not know where Mrs Borden was. That was odd, because Abby virtually never went out – and where was the note?

Even when the police and the doctor arrived, the body of Abby Borden still lay undetected upstairs. Then Lizzie 'remembered that she thought she had heard Abby coming back from town' and a curious neighbour went upstairs to look. It was only then that the body of Abby Borden was found on the floor beside the bed in the guest room. Dr Bowen found that Andrew Borden had been killed, probably with a hatchet, where he lay on the sofa; he had suffered 11 axe-blows to the head, delivered from above and behind. The weather had been oppressively hot for days, so it was understandable that Mr Borden should have reclined on the sofa in the middle of the morning. Abby had similarly been attacked from behind as she cleaned the bedroom. The much-hated Abby received 18 blows to the head. She had probably died at about 9.30 a.m., Andrew at 11 a.m.

In spite of the heat, a crowd was gathering in the street outside the Borden house. Then a man came walking up the street. It was Uncle John. It was his behaviour that now seemed remarkable. Instead of seeing the crowd and hurrying to see what was wrong at the Borden house, which would have been most people's response, he slowed right down. When he at last reached the house, he went round to the back garden, picked some fruit from a tree and ate it. Even with the evidence of some domestic disaster round him, Uncle John was in no hurry to find out what it was. Did he perhaps already know?

Once he was inside the house, Uncle John was a changed man. His story of the morning's events cascaded out of him. His alibi was so watertight that he became the principal suspect. When he emerged, the crowd had already decided it was him, and they chased him back inside.

Emma was out of town, visiting friends, and Lizzie and Bridget were the only people left alive in the house. Bridget told the police she had been washing windows most of the morning, and then gone up to her room to lie down. Her story never changed, but Lizzie kept on contradicting herself and giving versions of events that could not have been true. She said she was in the barn loft for 20 minutes before discovering her father's body, but when the investigators went up to the loft they saw that the floor was covered with an undisturbed layer of dust: nobody had been up there recently. In the cellar they found four hatchets. One of them had no handle and was covered in ash; this was the murder weapon that would be presented at Lizzie's trial.

The next day, Emma hired a lawyer. The District Attorney Hosea Knowlton, resisted the pleas from the police to arrest Lizzie but, as he said, 'You don't have any evidence against her'. Five days later, after an inquest had been held, Lizzie Borden was arrested, charged and taken to Taunton Jail. If it had been someone outside the family circle, an intruder, that intruder would have been incredibly lucky to hit a moment when Bridget was outside cleaning windows, and Emma and Uncle John just happened to be out.

The Grand Jury trial, a preliminary hearing, opened on 7 November. One of the Bordens' friends, Alice Russell, gave evidence; she had seen Lizzie burning a dress she said was stained with paint three days after the murders. On 2 December, Lizzie was formally charged on three counts of murder, one for the murder of Andrew, one for the murder of Abby, one for the murder of them both.

The main trial opened on 5 June, 1893 and lasted 14 days. Witnesses for the prosecution testified that Andrew Borden was drawing up a new will. He intended to leave half his estate to Abby, and the rest to be divided between his daughters. Another witness testified that Lizzie had tried to buy prussic acid from a drug store, which she could have used to poison her parents. The defence took only two days to present its case, calling witnesses who said that they had seen a mysterious man near the Borden house.

Emma Borden – not the most impartial of witnesses, since she had hated Abby as much as Lizzie – confirmed that Lizzie had no motive for killing their parents. Was Emma protecting not only Lizzie but herself? Did she perhaps know that Lizzie was planning the murders?

A leading question related to Lizzie's visit to the outbuilding during the 20 minutes when her father was being murdered. What was she doing in the outhouse? 'To look for a piece of metal with which to mend a window screen, also to get some lead suitable for fishing weights.' Detectives searching the house found no broken screens and no lead that could be used for fishing weights. She also claimed that she had eaten three pears while she was in the outbuilding, even though it had been stifling and she had a queasy stomach. None of this sounded true.

In her favour was the lack of bloodstained clothing. If she had done the killings, she would have been soaked in blood, twice in the space of 90 minutes, yet when the house was searched all of Lizzie's clothes were found to be spotless. Alice Russell told a slightly different story. Before the second police search was carried out, Lizzie had torn up an old dress and burnt it in the kitchen stove. She asked Lizzie why she was doing it. Lizzie said, 'Because it was all faded and paint-stained'. Alice said, 'I wouldn't let anybody see me do that, Lizzie, if I were you.'. Alice couldn't see any paint on the dress and obviously suspected that the dress was stained in some other way.

The court gave two rulings on points of order,

which proved decisive as far as the jury was concerned. This is unusual, in that the points of order were technical rather than substantive. Lizzie's inquest testimony was disallowed as trial evidence on the grounds that when she made the statement she had not at that stage been formally charged. The evidence of the drug store assistant was also disallowed because the matter of the poison was irrelevant to the case. No poison had been involved in the murders. These rulings evidently impressed the jury, who were no doubt left feeling that the case for the prosecution had been heavy-handed, illegal and unfair. It took only half an hour for the jury's sense of fair play to prevail. They found Lizzie Borden not guilty on all three counts of murder. The court room reverberated with applause. That night she was guest of honour at a celebration party. She laughed over the collection of newspaper cuttings of the trial that her supporters had kept for her.

If Lizzie was innocent, then who had committed the murders? Was it the agitated young man seen by the neighbour outside the house? And who was he? If it was the agitated young man, how would he have got through the locked front door?

Lizzie Borden was released, but the suspicion that in spite of the acquittal she had killed her parents hung in the air at Fall River. Lizzie and Emma had to leave the neighbourhood, though surprisingly they did not leave Fall River. Five weeks after the trial, the sisters moved to a house in a more fashionable neighbourhood, and called the house Maplecroft. Lizzie took to calling herself Lizbeth which, in a similar way, was a sort of break with the past but not really enough to make any difference.

Lizzie's underlying criminality, which seems to have been there all along, emerged in a small way again in 1897, when she was accused of shoplifting. The matter of a hundred dollars was settled out of court. Or if we do not want to call it criminality, perhaps, as one writer has proposed, Lizzie suffered from temporal epilepsy, which could account for what the family called her 'peculiar turns'.

Lizzie's lifestyle underwent a transformation when she met a young actress called Nance O'Neill. Nance moved into Maplecroft and Lizzie started throwing parties for Nance and her new-found theatrical friends. Emma did not like any of these new developments and moved out; she never spoke to her sister again. Lizzie Borden died at the age of 66 on 1 June 1927, after gall bladder surgery. Just a week later, her sister Emma died falling down stairs.

The Borden murders remain officially unsolved. The maid, the doctor, an illegitimate brother demanding money, Uncle John – all have been blamed by various authors, but Lizzie still looks like the obvious culprit. The Borden family was a profoundly dysfunctional family, and it is clear that both the daughters had a strong financial motive for resenting Abby's intrusion and their father's intention to draw up a new will in her favour. Abby could have been killed out of hatred; Andrew because he would have avenged Abby's murder; Andrew had to die before he could sign the new will. There is no need to look outside the immediate family for suspects or motives. We also know enough about Lizzie's criminal tendencies (the faked burglaries and the shoplifting) and her violence (the beheading of Abby's cat) to sense that she was capable of murder and criminal deception. It is also possible that someone else, a nameless stranger, or a disaffected neighbour, was guilty of the break-ins, and that Lizzie was incensed that her father should blame her for them. Anger at her father's unjust accusations could easily have fuelled her frenzied attack on him.

But there was something else that happened that morning. Uncle John was there for a particular purpose. Andrew Borden had already transferred a piece of property to Abby's name and it had led to a massive row, with Lizzie protesting that she was being disinherited. Uncle John was there to assist in the transfer of another property to Abby Borden. A young man called at about 9 a.m. with a note. He may have left the note just before or just after Andrew Borden left for the bank. Neither Andrew nor Uncle John would have wanted to upset things by telling Lizzie, but supposing the note arrived at 9 a.m. just after Andrew left. Lizzie could have read it and realised its significance. She could easily have flown into a rage and gone upstairs and killed Abby within the half-hour. That makes more sense than the temporal epilepsy. If it had been temporal epilepsy, Lizzie would have been quite certain she hadn't committed the murders and would probably have gone on living in Second Street.

Lizzie Borden was guilty, beyond all reasonable doubt. This was the general perception in America at the time, and America delivered its own sentence on Lizzie Borden by turning her into folklore. She became, like the Big Bad Wolf, a nursery rhyme hate figure, this girl who 'gave her mother forty whacks. When she saw what she had done, she gave her father forty-one.'. She was pilloried in sneering ballads, where she became a jolly cautionary tale. Lizzie Borden quickly turned into a kind of joke-evil which still persists and is in a strange way far worse than the guilty verdict that comes from a court of law.

Mata Hari
(1876–1917)

MATA HARI, THE most famous woman spy of all time, was said to have used her seductive beauty to win strategic secrets from men. She was born as Margaretha Zelle in the Dutch town of Leeuwarden in 1876. As a girl she was unexceptional. It was an ordinary childhood and she developed into the most ordinary of students. Her idea, then, of a more exciting life was to take herself off to a teacher training college at the age of 18. She quickly became bored with teacher training, married an army officer and went off to Java.

It was in Java that Margaretha first heard the name Mata Hari, which there meant 'eye of the day'. But for the next seven years, she continued to live the life of an upper-class colonial wife. She was even so very aware of her own beauty, and aware that she could charm any man she chose. She started a string of affairs. Her husband found out, but turned a blind eye, tolerating her infidelity. It was only when the couple returned to Holland that they decided to divorce.

In 1902, Margaretha found herself with no means of support, and decided to take up dancing, something she had always wanted to do. There was a significant audience in Paris for the provocative sort of dancing she wanted to do, so in 1905 she moved there, and she took the name of Mata Hari. In Paris, now that there was no husband to hold her back at all, she took a string of lovers, most of them army officers. When the First World War broke out, this lifestyle was to prove her undoing. She stayed in Paris at first, but in 1916 she decided to move back to neutral Holland. It was there, in The Hague, that she slid effortlessly into espionage. She slept with a German diplomat, who asked her for details of the disposition of the French army in two locations. One was the Somme, where the Germans were expecting an Anglo-French offensive. The other was Verdun, which had been strongly fortified. The German diplomat promised her money in exchange for the information.

The French later claimed that Mata Hari wheedled secret information about the French army when she was in bed with lovers in the French army. It seems unlikely now that she did. But the fact is that she was betrayed to the French authorities in 1917 when she travelled back to Paris to pass on some information about French strategy to a German officer. She was arrested, tried, sentenced to death and executed by firing squad on 15 October 1917. She faced the firing squad with considerable dignity and courage.

There are several odd features of Mata Hari's case. Certainly information about French strategy could have damaged the prospects of success for France, but how likely is it that Mata Hari would have had any information that could have been damaging? And who betrayed her? Questions hover round the French government's refusal to release papers sealed in 1917 that related to Mata Hari. In 1985, some of the papers came to light at the Chateau de Vincennes, where Mata Hari was executed. It seems Mata Hari did indeed sleep with a German military attaché and may have taken money for information, but the information she passed on was from newspapers, much of it already in the public domain.

The truth seems to be that the French were reeling from terrible losses in the war, and there were strong xenophobic feelings. Probably the incompetent generals were really to blame for the huge body counts at the front, but it was easier to look for a lone foreigner who could be turned into a scapegoat. The Germans in their turn believed that Mata Hari had cheated them by acting as a double agent. Some have speculated that she was a French spy, others that she was a German spy, still others that she was a double agent. She probably passed on harmless bits of gossip and seems to have thrived on the 'dangerous lady' image that she acquired as a result of these antics. She cannot have realised how dangerous a game she was playing.

Wallis Simpson
(1897–1986)

ANOTHER FEMME FATALE who was demonized by an entire nation was Wallis Simpson. Edward Prince of Wales allowed himself to fall in love with a woman that his impending position as King would never allow him to marry.

He tried to keep his affair with Wallis secret, and the British press colluded with him to keep the British people in the dark. Abroad, there was no such restraint and there the newspapers were full of scandalous stories about the affair.

It was in 1931 that the Prince of Wales met Wallis. She was an amusing, but sharp-tongued and rather plain woman of 34. She was the daughter of a Maryland businessman who had died while she was still a baby. She was brought up in Baltimore by her mother, marrying a naval pilot called Earl Winfield Spencer in 1916. The marriage did not last long, and they were divorced in 1922. Four years later she married Ernest Simpson, who was half-American, half-British; he ran the London office of a shipping company. It was his arrival in London in 1929 that brought Wallis Simpson onto the London high society scene. Both Wallis and her mother wanted her to be a big social success, and she worked hard at being a competent and amusing hostess. She was dazzled to find herself entertaining lords and ladies. At the same time she found her husband increasingly dull and boring.

Late in 1930, an American diplomat, Benjamin Thaw, went to dinner with the Simpsons, together with his wife and her sister Thelma, Viscountess Furness. Lady Furness's starlet good looks had attracted the most eligible man in England, and she confided in Wallis that she was having an affair with the Prince of Wales. It was not long before this collusion led to the Simpsons dining with the Prince and Thelma. In January 1934, Thelma told Wallis she was going on a trip to the States, and asked her to look after the Prince while she was away, 'to make sure he isn't lonely'. Wallis seized her opportunity. By the time Thelma returned a couple of months later, Wallis and the Prince were already lovers.

The press kept their respectful distance in a way that they would not in later decades. The only pressure on the Prince was the growing knowledge that he was falling in love with a woman he would not be able to have as a wife when he was King. His father, George V, was dying, and he was the heir to the throne. He would have to choose.

It was an unusual relationship. Although the Prince and Wallis were similar in age, he wanted something close to a mother-son relationship with her. He constantly needed reassurance, guidance, dominance, as his letters to her show. Her letters by contrast are sensible, stern, reproving. He was immature, dependent. She was worldly, manipulative, scheming, dominant. Those in the know were alarmed that this woman was having such a strong influence over the man who would shortly be King of England.

The foreign press was full of details of their stays in foreign hotels, their holidays in Turkey, Yugoslavia and Greece. The British press barons, Rothermere and Beaverbrook, saw it as their duty to save the face of the British monarchy, and were silent about the affair.

Even when the Prince became King Edward VIII in December 1935, the press remained silent. The love letters from the King to Wallis became more infantile than ever. The British establishment went on supporting the King while the affair was secret. The moment it was out, and the King's indiscretion was revealed for all to see, that establishment closed ranks against him. A few weeks before, Wallis had received a divorce from her husband, though Prime Minister Stanley Baldwin had tried to persuade the King to stop her from doing this. But the King refused and Wallis had gone ahead, deliberately freeing herself to marry the King; that was obviously her intention, and his too. But he was not free to marry her. The King had imagined that he would be able to marry Wallis just before his coronation.

The Bishop of Bradford was the first to utter public criticism of the King. He rebuked the King for his incongruously carefree lifestyle. The press report of this coded rebuke was interpreted as a condemnation of the King's affair, and it opened the floodgates. Public opinion was vehemently against Mrs Simpson. The King was taken by surprise. He assumed he was popular and that people would be sympathetic to his wish to marry Wallis. His mother, Queen Mary, was outraged and sent for Baldwin. The King still believed his popularity would carry him through and that people would accept the marriage. Baldwin told him roundly, 'We will not have it, sir.' He told the King that he had had nasty letters from people who said how much they respected his father and how much they condemned the way he was carrying on with 'this American woman'. Somehow the fact that she was American was decisive.

Badly shaken and unnerved that his plan to marry Wallis before she became a constitutional problem was failing, the King decided he had to abdicate. Wallis wept; she was going to get the man, but not the status she hoped for. Instead of being a queen, or something very close to it, she was going to be an exile and a pariah. Edward made his famous radio broadcast, saying that he could not rule without the woman he loved.

He hoped he would be able to live quietly in Britain somewhere, but it was made very clear that he was now a huge embarrassment to his younger brother, the new King, George VI, who didn't want the job at all, and to the country as a whole. He would have to go abroad. He and Wallis left England, she not to return for a very long time, he never to return at all. They lived in a fine mansion in the outskirts of Paris, they married, but they were now at a complete loose end, cut off from the social life they both loved. They were ostracized by the British royal family –

and not just because of the marriage and the abdication. The ex-King, now called the Duke of Windsor, made overtures to the Germans and was evidently viewed by Hitler as a potential puppet-king if and when Britain was successfully invaded.

The entirely disgraced Duke of Windsor died in 1972 aged 77. A sad and lonely figure, Wallis died 14 years later. In the end the Queen, Elizabeth II, relented. When Edward's funeral was held at St George's Chapel, Windsor, the Queen not only invited the Duchess of Windsor to attend, but gave her hospitality, for one night, at Buckingham Palace before she returned to Paris. It was her one brief taste of what she had pursued the Prince of Wales for.

The British public might have accepted the marriage – if only she hadn't been American. Then there was the problem that she was divorced, and not only divorced but twice divorced. By the standards of the time in Britain, that made Wallis Simpson look like a libertine – and a fortune hunter, which she most certainly was. But behind all that was the growing knowledge within the establishment, and Baldwin was well aware of it, that Edward VIII was going to make a very bad King indeed. The Windsors' foolish liaisons with Nazis following the abdication emphatically confirmed just how terrible his judgement was. So perhaps the twice-divorced Wallis Simpson, 'this American woman', did Britain a favour after all. And perhaps the British establishment was secretly relieved to have her as a pretext to get rid of someone who would have made a very bad king.

Jiang Qing
(1914–1991)

JIANG QING WAS born at Zhucheng in Shadong province in 1912 or 1914, as Li Yunhe. She was the daughter of a concubine. She and her mother were badly treated by her father, and she went through her life resenting men.

By the age of 19 she had already been married twice and was earning herself a dubious reputation as a promiscuous young film starlet in Shanghai, under the name Lan Ping. With this background it is very strange that she should have become the fourth wife of the Chinese Communist leader, Mao Zedong.

There was in fact strong opposition to her marriage to Mao Zedong within Mao's party, with very good reason as it later turned out, and it could only go ahead so long as Jiang Qing gave an undertaking that she would play no part in politics. This was an undertaking that, eventually, she would fail to keep – with disastrous consequences. Mao's colleagues were right to be alarmed at the prospect of Jiang Qing acquiring influence over China's future.

To begin with, Madame Mao toed the party line. It was in the early 1960s that she decided to initiate a radical reform of China's cultural life.

She wanted traditional Chinese opera to adapt to the twentieth century and make it explore revolutionary themes. In 1966, the Great Proletarian Cultural Revolution erupted. It was officially launched by Mao to combat traditional Chinese bureaucracy and attitudes, which had been gradually re-establishing themselves since the formation of the People's Republic in 1949. Young men and women were mobilized as Red Guards; it was their job to re-activate the old revolutionary zeal. Universities were closed, and many university teachers were hounded out of work in disgrace. Some prominent figures in Chinese public life were humiliated in public for alleged 'back-sliding'.

Thousands of young Chinese were caught up in the Cultural Revolution, which fed on the personality cult surrounding Chairman Mao and the Little Red Book containing his thoughts. The Cultural Revolution and all the destruction that it engendered went on for a full decade, ending with Mao's death in 1976. All the way through, Jiang Qing was right at the centre of things, directing the mayhem. Mao himself was old and probably by that stage just a figurehead.

With Mao's death came a power struggle between the extreme leftists who were behind the Cultural Revolution and the more moderate Communists. Four extreme leftists, Jiang Qing, Yao Wenyuan, Zhang Chunqiao and Wang Hong Wen, tried to seize power in a coup. They failed and were arrested in October 1976. The new vice-premier, Deng Xiao-ping, had been disgraced twice during the Cultural Revolution and savoured his opportunity to exact revenge. The Gang of Four were held awaiting trial for four years. Mao's widow, he said, 'was so evil, not enough evil can be said about her'.

The trial opened in Beijing in November 1980. The Gang of Four were subjected to a barrage of accusations, which amounted to holding them personally responsible for the persecution of 729,511 people during the Cultural Revolution. They were held responsible for the deaths of 34,800 people. Three out of the four looked pale and defeated as they stood trial. Only Jiang Qing held herself with confidence and pride. She was vehement and aggressively defiant. At some moments during the trial, when evidence was being presented against her, the 67-year-old pointedly pulled out her hearing aid.

One damning accusation related to the framing of President Liu Shao-qi, who was condemned as a reactionary during the Cultural Revolution and died under mysterious circumstances in prison. It seems Jiang Qing was jealous of Liu's beautiful American-born wife, who was in consequence made to spend 11 years in prison. Jiang Qing claimed in court to know nothing about ordering her arrest on trumped-up charges, but when the document ordering the arrest was produced in court she admitted that the signature on it was hers. Liu's cook had been arrested on the grounds that the excellence of his cooking had been a corrupting influence.

The main prop of her defence was that she did everything with Mao's consent. She was only obeying orders. This was tricky, as Mao's personality cult was still very strong, and the prosecutors did not want Chairman Mao posthumously dragged into the dock.

Jiang Qing's trial was intensely dramatic, because of the assertive, sneering and abusive tone she frequently adopted. Finally, the chief prosecutor called for the death sentence, which would have been carried out by shooting in the back of the head. She and her co-defendants were found guilty, which was a foregone conclusion. The sentence was delayed for a month. Then Jiang Qing was given a suspended death sentence. This entailed a two-year prison sentence, followed by execution if there was no repentance. Zhang Chunqiao had the same sentence; the other two received lighter sentences of life and 20 years. Jiang Qing was dragged off, shouting slogans. Two years later, the death sentence was lifted and a life sentence substituted. She lived a further eight years. Apparently she spent her time making dolls.

Ulrike Meinhof
(1934–1976)

ULRIKE MEINHOF WAS born in 1934 in Oldenburg in Lower Saxony. Her parents were middle class professionals, both art historians, but both died during her childhood, her father when she was five, her mother when she was fourteen. After that she was fostered by one of her mother's friends, Professor Renate Riemack, who held strong radical views. It seems that Ulrike picked up many of her radical socialist ideas from Renate Riemack, including refusing to accept authority without question.

Ulrike was a bright student. In 1957, she went to Munster University to read philosophy and sociology. As a student, she joined campaigns against the atom bomb, the American intervention in Vietnam and the whole range of causes that socialist, and many moderate liberal, students were concerned about. She met Klaus Roehl, who ran Konkret, a left-wing magazine, and she joined the staff, quickly gaining a reputation as an effective radical journalist. She began to be talked about further afield, especially when she started asking questions about the German economy and the misery of those who had been by-passed by the alleged 'Economic Miracle'.

She became Roehl's editor – and his wife. The magazine was fairly successful, but then, when the Roehls decided to add sex to politics, it became very successful indeed. They were able to buy an expensive house, and drive a big white Mercedes. Outwardly, Ulrike was very successful, but inwardly she was unhappy and dissatisfied. Her husband had affairs and after seven years their marriage ended. Her job ended with her marriage, and Ulrike moved to Berlin, putting her two daughters into boarding school.

Then Ulrike started mixing with a new set of radical young people who saw violence as the only way of changing society. Some of this was strictly personal, and she launched a campaign against her ex-husband and his magazine, vandalizing the house that had once been hers. She heard about an arsonist called Andreas Baader who was in prison for burning down a shop in Frankfurt. Through Baader's girlfriend, she learnt that Baader was allowed out of prison from time to time to work in a library. In May 1970, Ulrike Meinhof led an armed raid on the library, leaving the librarian and several prison guards wounded.

Andreas Baader and Ulrike Meinhof decided to form a group with about two dozen other committed anarchists. They called themselves the Baader-Meinhof Gang. Baader was good-looking and charismatic, but indolent; Meinhof supplied the drive. After the library raid, the four leaders of the gang went to the Middle East to train with the Palestine National Liberation Front, but there was little tolerance on either side and it was not long before the Palestinians realised the Baader-Meinhof had no particular cause – and asked them to go. In spite of this, Ulrike remained committed to the Palestinian cause. She even planned to send her two daughters to a Palestinian refugee camp in Jordan to become fighters against Israel. Luckily for the two little girls, Roehl was tipped off by private detectives in time to rescue them from a hideout in Palermo. The girls hated his interference initially, as their mother had brainwashed them.

The Baader-Meinhof gang grew until it was about 150 strong. They organized a series of bank raids to raise money for guns and grenades. One raid was particularly nasty. They attacked a bank in the small town of Kaiserslautern, west of Heidelberg, killing a policeman in cold blood. One girl who took part in this raid was so horrified by what happened that she phoned her parents in Berlin. After that, she was summoned by Ulrike, then taken to be executed near some gravel pits. The violence escalated. Ulrike Meinhof showed no concern for human life at all.

The German police force made a determined effort to catch the gang. Eventually in 1972 in Frankfurt, the police trapped several gang members in a short siege, arresting Carl Raspe, who was Ulrike Meinhof's lover, Holger Meins, another gang member, and Andreas Baader, who was shot and wounded. Ulrike remained at large. Wondering where to go, she turned up at the Hanover flat of a left-wing teacher she had known some time before, hoping to stay there. But the teacher's career had developed and he did not want anything to do with Ulrike now. He decided to phone the police and wisely stayed clear of his flat for a while. The police moved in and arrested her.

The trial of the Baader-Meinhof gang was potentially dangerous in itself, and might attract a terrorist raid. A special fortified courtroom was built at the top-security prison at Stammheim in Stuttgart. As the trial wore on, the lack of solidarity among the gang members became evident. Ulrike Meinhof lost heart. On 9 May, 1976 she hanged herself in her cell.

Remarkably, as many as 4,000 people marched behind Ulrike Meinhof's coffin at her funeral. It was hard then and equally hard now to understand why such a negative and destructive woman should have inspired such loyalty. She certainly did not deserve it.

Aileen Wuornos
(about 1962–2002)

AILEEN WUORNOS IS sometimes wrongly described as the first woman serial killer in America. It is true that female serial killers are very rare, but she did have her predecessors. Wuornos was different in murdering strangers, which makes her more like the classic predatory type of male serial killer. Her use of a gun is also unusual. Women have, historically, preferred indirect methods such as poison.

The police first became aware of her activities in December 1989. An abandoned car was found in Florida, near Daytona Beach. There was blood on the seats. It emerged that the car had belonged to Richard Mallory, who was known to pick up prostitutes. Two weeks later, Mallory's body was found in woodland. He had been shot four times. On the day of the murder, Wuornos had returned to the motel room where she was staying with her lover, Tyria Moore, and blurted out that she had just killed a man. Tyria told the court this at Wuornos's trial.

This seems to have been the first murder Aileen Wuornos committed, but the desire to kill men must have been developing for a long time. Her schizophrenic father was imprisoned for raping a seven-year-old girl; then he had hanged himself. A friend of her grandfather's had made her pregnant at the age of 14. She was made to have the baby then give it up to be adopted. After that she was thrown out and had to make her living by prostitution. During the course of her life as a prostitute she had been raped and beaten several times. Her life predisposed her to take revenge on men.

She met Tyria Moore in Florida. Then she got herself a gun, perhaps initially so that she could defend herself if she were threatened with a beating. What Richard Mallory did to provoke Wuornos to shoot him is not known, but he had a history of sexual offences and may well have tried something violent that made her reach for the gun. It was several months before she killed again. A truck was found beside a main road in Florida. The registered owner was David Spears, and his body was found 60 miles away. Like Mallory, he was shot in the chest with a .22. The police found no fingerprints in the vehicle, but they did find a blonde hair. At this stage, the police made no connection between the two murders.

An odd incident was reported, though, which gave the police an important lead. Two women were seen driving a car off a road, changing its number plates, then running off into a wood. The car, it turned out, belonged to a missionary who had gone missing. After the bodies of three more men were found, all killed in the same way, sketches of the two women were circulated. Progress in solving the crimes was slow because they were committed in five different counties. In the end a special task force was formed.

The major breakthrough came when several people identified the two women in the sketches as a lesbian couple, Tyria Moore and 'Lee', who was Aileen Wuornos. The police were able to take Wuornos in for questioning as she was guilty of a parole violation. Tyria Moore was pressed to tell everything she knew. Then the police discovered items belonging to the dead men, locked in storage by Wuornos. Moore was the weak link. She told what she knew and agreed to try to get Wuornos to confess. Finally, in January 1991, Aileen Wuornos went to the police and confessed to the murder of seven men. Even when she was told that one of the men had been a missionary, she insisted that all the murders had been in self-defence. She had been hitch-hiking, they had picked her up, propositioned her and then got violent. And then she had shot them.

The self-defence plea was unconvincing, because it did not tally with what Tyria Moore had said in evidence; she had said nothing at all about self-defence. In January 1992, the jury recommended the death penalty and Aileen Wuornos was sentenced to the death penalty six times over. It was emerging that she had killed at least 11 men. In 2001, she went to court to dismiss her lawyers, and the judge told her she was heading for the electric chair. He was right. Aileen Wuornos was executed in 2002.

PART FOUR
THE NAZIS

Kitty Schmidt
(1883–1954)
Walter Schellenberg and Salon Kitty

KITTY SCHMIDT IS not the first name that would spring to mind when anyone turns their thoughts to the evils of the Nazi regime. In fact it is not even among the first ten names that anyone would think of. Kitty is here as a representative of the many thousands of people who were not in themselves evil but somehow, through circumstances they themselves were powerless to control, got entangled in evil. It happens all the time. Evil regimes breed many different kinds of evil. The Nazi regime in Germany led to the Holocaust. It led to a million deaths in battle. It led to a million smaller acts of treachery too.

Kitty Schmidt owned the Pension Schmidt, in Giesebrechtstrasse, Berlin. On the surface it was a respectable guest-house. In fact it was a very unusual brothel. During the 1930s Kitty's clientele had gradually changed. The Jewish industrialists and bankers disappeared and were replaced by members of the Schutzstaffel (SS). She began to have trouble from the police, and started to salt away her takings in Britain, mainly through Jewish refugees she had helped to escape from Berlin. In June 1938 she decided to follow her money, but was arrested at the Dutch border and taken back to Berlin for questioning. After several weeks of intimidation, Kitty Schmidt was interviewed by the head of the Sicherheitsdienst (SD), the Nazi Security Organization, Walter Schellenberg. He accused her of helping Jews to escape, illegal currency dealing and attempting to leave Germany without permission. He left her in no doubt that she faced the death penalty and asked her to do him a favour. Naturally she would have agreed to anything.

Schellenberg's proposition was to turn the Pension Schmidt into an SD brothel. The girls were to be intelligence agents and all the rooms were to be bugged, with wires leading down to the basement where conversations could be recorded on tape or disc. It would be a place where information would be gathered and the loyalty of SD members could be tested. The outline plan came from Heydrich; Schellenberg added his own ideas, developing the brothel into an SD branch.

Berlin was combed for girls who were attractive, trustworthy and emotionally stable enough to cope with the unusual demands of this espionage exercise. Twenty girls were finally recruited. The cellar was rebuilt, bricked off and fitted with recording equipment. The brothel reopened, apparently as before but redecorated. The old customers were welcomed back, and they were entertained by Kitty's previous 'staff'. But when a client arrived announcing he was 'from Rothenburg', (a code he had been given which he thought meant he was in for special treatment, but which in reality meant that he had been singled out by the authorities for the special security vetting), Kitty showed them a different photo album so that they could select a girl. Kitty made a phone call and the girl arrived within 10 minutes; she was an agent.

The new set-up immediately demonstrated how indiscreet some of the officers were. One man, obviously loyal, revealed that the Fuhrer planned to invade Sweden. He was heading for a court-martial. On another occasion, the system caught the German Foreign Minister, Joachim von Ribbentrop, and a small party that included the Spanish Foreign Minister. Heydrich was delighted to have collected some scandal on Ribbentrop. Heydrich himself was a man of great sexual appetite, and decided on an occasional tour of inspection; naturally he ordered Schellenberg to have the listening apparatus switched off.

The wiring needed overhauling and it happened that, while soldiers were furtively re-routing the wires from the basement out on the pavement, a British agent called Wilson was passing in the street. He knew that Salon Kitty was upstairs and understood at once exactly what was going on. He reported back to London, and he was ordered to pose as a client. In his disguise as Kolchev, Wilson got into Salon Kitty and managed to change the wiring. Now some of the bugs had bugs and for a few months in 1940 London was supplied with some unusual insights into the German Security Service.

A stray bomb hit Salon Kitty in July 1942, severely damaging the upper floors. So important was the information coming from the brothel that teams of men worked on it continuously so that it could re-open – two days later. Early in 1943, Schellenberg decided that it was time to wind the surveillance up and hand the premises back to Kitty. Most of the 'Rothenburg' girls had grown to like the place and agreed to carry on. Within two years, the Russians were there. The incriminating discs, carefully stored at the Gestapo headquarters, vanished like so much else of interest and value in Berlin.

In 1954, Kitty Schmidt died, without ever revealing the secret of No 11 Giesebrechtstrasse. For many years, researcher Peter Norden tried to find the lost tapes. In 1963, he gained access to a secret strong-room in Communist East Berlin, and there were the missing discs – 25,000 of them.

Adolf Hitler
(1889–1945)

PROBABLY THE MOST infamous man of the twentieth century, Adolf Hitler was born in the Austrian town of Braunau, close to the Bavarian border, on 20 April, 1889. His father, Alois Hitler, was a lower middle class customs official, a hard disciplinarian, and the young Adolf had little affection for him.

Alois had been married three times. Little is known of the first wife, but the second, Franziska Matzelberger, is known to have died of tuberculosis after bearing two children. The third wife, Klara, bore two children who died in infancy; Adolf was the third. Adolf was to have a younger brother, Edmund, who died at the age of six, and a sister, Paula. The loss of the brother left a mark on young Adolf, as did the claim, often repeated by his enemies in the 1930s and '40s, that he was illegitimate and that his real name was Schickelgruber. It was in fact Adolf's father who had been born out of wedlock, to Maria Schickelgruber, and Alois's parents had subsequently married in any case and legitimized him. Adolf Hitler was never called Schickelgruber; although there are plenty of legitimate accusations that can be levelled against Hitler, that is not one of them.

There was a great deal of tension between Adolf and his father. Adolf thought his father boorish and unkind to his mother, to whom he was very protective. Adolf had to help his father home after late-night drinking bouts, then hear him abusing his mother. Alois in his turn had no time for his son's high-flown ambitions. He had after all failed twice to get into the high school at Linz.

In 1903, when Adolf was 14 his father died and the family moved to Linz. He decided to become an artist. In 1907, when he was 18, he went to Vienna on a generous allowance from his mother. He approached the Vienna Academy of Art, but was rejected when a sample of his artwork was viewed. He was rejected again a year later. He was turned away by the Academy of Architecture, who told him he had not pursued his school studies at Linz to a high enough level. He was thwarted in the great ambition of his life.

His mother's death from cancer in 1908 left him with an inheritance, which included the proceeds of the sale of her house in Linz. Hitler also claimed part of his mother's pension on the grounds that he was a full-time student, which he certainly was not. The lies, the deception, the myth-making had begun. What Hitler was actually doing was sitting about in cafés, joining in heated arguments about philosophy and politics, visits to the opera, writing a play, painting pictures of street scenes and grand buildings. He earned a little money as an illustrator.

At this stage, Hitler had no close friends, and it may be that the peculiarly unsatisfactory relationship he had with his parents played a part in this. What he did acquire, though, was a relentless hatred of Jews. Anti-semitism was widespread at all levels of society in Germany and Austria, especially in the Catholic south German culture, but with Hitler it was to reach an alarmingly destructive pitch. He was, after all, to become directly responsible for the deaths of millions of Jews. The Jews were a common scapegoat at the time, as large numbers of them were driven west out of Russia and the rest of eastern Europe by persecutions there. It was easy, for Hitler and for others like him, to blame these poor dispossessed people for taking jobs from more deserving local people. Migrants have always had to bear this cross. It was at this time, too, that the ranting tirades started, possibly born out of his frustration at being unable to pursue his chosen career.

In 1912, Hitler's legacy ran out. He had to work on a building site during the day and sleep in a doss-house at night. He made the decision to move in 1913 to Munich. He alleged it was because he wanted to live in the Fatherland; in fact it was to avoid conscription by the Austrian Imperial Army. Hitler was a draft-dodger. The Munich police caught him, returned him to the Austrian authorities. Hitler pleaded to be excused military service, but he was in any case rejected as unfit.

Oddly, when war broke out in 1914, Hitler saw (as Churchill had already seen) that the way forward might be to become a war hero and he succeeded in joining a Bavarian infantry regiment.

He was sent to the front and given one of the most dangerous jobs of all, as a company runner. This exposed him continually to cross-fire in no man's land. He showed surprising courage and acquired a reputation as a man immune to bullets. He was awarded the Iron Cross, first class.

Hitler avoided bullets, but not mustard gas. While he was recovering in hospital, news of Germany's surrender came through. Like most of the rest of Germany, Hitler could not believe it. In military terms, Germany seemed to be winning the war. Hitler blamed the surrender on a Jewish-Communist conspiracy. Certified disabled through gassing, Hitler returned to Munich, where he became the fifth member of the new German Workers Party. He threw himself into the task of recruiting for this new cause, and changed the name of the party to the National Socialist German Workers Party. Its members were often known by the shortened form 'Nazis' to distinguish them from the Social Democrats, or 'Sozis'. The new party adopted the swastika logo and the Roman salute, also used by the Italian Fascists. Hitler himself discovered a hitherto unknown gift for oratory, though often it was a rant against Jews, Communists or Slavs, and a gift for inspiring personal loyalty. It was a remarkable transformation that had taken place, and some have explained it in terms of the psychiatric support he was given to help him overcome the profound depression he felt when in hospital – excessive psychiatric support that gave him excessive self-confidence.

Hitler emerged from the First World a great German patriot, even though he was not actually a German, and he continued to believe that Germany had not really been defeated. Early followers included Rudolf Hess, Hermann Goering, Ernst Rÿhm and Field-Marshal Erich Lüdendorff. Hitler used Lüdendorff as a front in an absurd attempt to seize power on 8 November 1923. In this 'Beer Hall Putsch', the Nazis marched from a beer hall to the Bavarian War Ministry, with the intention of overthrowing the Bavarian government, and then marching on Berlin. They were quickly dispersed by soldiers and Hitler was arrested and tried for treason.

In April 1924 he was sentenced to five years in prison, where he dictated *Mein Kampf* to the loyal Hess. This rambling autobiography contains Hitler's views on race, history and Jews, and includes threats against his enemies if he should win power. It was published in two volumes (1925 and 1926). No-one took any notice, of course, at the time. Considered a harmless crank, Hitler was released early.

Hitler was able to build on a widespread sense of injured national pride, caused by the Treaty of Versailles imposed on Germany. Huge reparations were exacted from Germany to pay for the war. Most Germans bitterly resented having to pay, particularly since they did not consider that they had lost. The second turning point in Hitler's career came when the Depression hit Germany in 1930. The traditional parties were unable to deal with the unprecedented shock of the Depression, and in the September 1930 elections the Nazis won 107 seats in the Reichstag, becoming the second largest party. In the July 1932 elections they won 230 seats, making them the largest party. Behind the scenes, conspirators persuaded Hindenburg to appoint Hitler Chancellor.

Using the pretext of the Reichstag fire, which may actually have been started by Nazis themselves, Hitler issued a decree suppressing civil rights in the interests of national security. The Communist leaders and other opponents of Hitler's regime found themselves in prison.

In the space of a few months, Hitler had achieved authoritarian control over Germany by more or less legal means and without suspending the Weimar constitution. But democracy in Germany was over and the escalation of evil had begun. With Goebbels as his propaganda chief, Hitler was able to persuade most Germans that he was their saviour. Those who were not persuaded were rounded up by the Sturmabteilung (SA), the SS and the Gestapo, the Secret State Police. Thousands were to disappear into concentration camps. Thousands more, including half of Germany's Jewish population, emigrated in order to escape the Holocaust that was clearly coming. Those Jews who had not emigrated soon regretted their decision to stay. Under Hitler's 1935 Nuremberg Laws, they lost their status as citizens and were thrown out of all government employment, the professions and many other jobs too. From 1941 Jews were subjected to the further humiliation of wearing a yellow star in public places. Hitler was the evil behind this, but the Christian Churches, riddled as they were with anti-semitism, stayed silent.

Hitler's foreign policy was to prove astonishingly aggressive. He violated the Versailles Treaty in 1936 by re-occupying the demilitarized Rhineland. Britain and France did nothing. Emboldened by the lack of response, Hitler sent troops to assist Franco in Spain. It was the Luftwaffe that destroyed the town of Guernica in 1937. In 1938, Austria was annexed to Germany (the Anschluss), and Hitler entered Vienna in a triumph that must have had a keen personal edge to it. Vienna after all was the scene of several early humiliations. Hitler's army invaded Czechoslovakia in 1939. At last Britain and France decided to call a halt, but unfortunately they were unable to reach an agreement with Russia to stop Hitler. Hitler managed to outflank them by concluding his own agreement with Stalin, the Molotov-Ribbentrop Pact. After the long period of inaction, Hitler was startled and surprised when Britain and France declared war on him for invading Poland. He had miscalculated.

Even so, Hitler had a run of military successes, invading Denmark, Norway, Holland, Belgium, Luxembourg and France, closely followed by Yugoslavia and Greece. The only major setback was his failure to invade Britain. The Battle of Britain failed because he was unable to use his blitzkrieg technique, which involved sending tanks in as well as planes; Britain was saved from the tanks by the Channel.

The power-crazed land-grabbing went on successfully until Hitler opened up a second front, in the east. Operation Barbarossa, the invasion of the Soviet Union (1941–2), was Hitler's undoing. He was trying to reach the oilfields on the Caspian Sea, but his army was heavily defeated at the Battle of Stalingrad – the first and most decisive major defeat. Then the British army led by Montgomery defeated the German army in North Africa at the Battle of El Alamein, which prevented Hitler from reaching the Suez Canal and the oilfields of the Middle East.

A second motive for invading the Soviet Union was to reach the second largest Jewish population in Europe, after Poland. Hitler's mad intention was to purge eastern Europe of Jews and Slavs, and make room for German settlers. The murder of Jews was going on during and in the wake of each invasion; probably two million Jews were killed as the Germans swept through the newly occupied territories. Then there was the question of disposing of the millions of Jews in Poland. There are no documents to prove it, but it seems that in 1941 Hitler and Himmler agreed on mass murder as the solution, and Hitler must have explicitly ordered Himmler to initiate the Holocaust. The infamous Wannsee Conference held near Berlin in January 1942 was a discussion of the Final Solution, outlining a formal procedure for the Holocaust. Huge numbers of Jews were to die. And so also were large numbers of other minority groups, including homosexuals, gypsies, socialists, communists and others regarded by

Hitler as his enemies. The Wannsee Conference was led by Heydrich and Eichmann, but there can be little doubt that they were working under Hitler's direct orders.

Stalingrad, Hitler's great defeat, unnerved him. His military decisions became more erratic after that. The British considered a plan to assassinate him, but by this stage in the war, he was making such poor decisions that it was better to leave him in charge – the war would be over sooner – and the assassination plan, Operation Foxley, was dropped. The entry of the Americans into the war in 1941 was another major turning-point; now that the British Empire, the Soviet Union and the United States were gathered into a huge coalition against Hitler many German officers could see that Germany must be defeated. This led some courageous officers to try to remove Hitler and bring the war to a quick end. The July 20th Plot of von Stauffenberg almost succeeded in killing Hitler, but not quite; he survived. Hitler responded with characteristic savagery and resistance was stamped out. Mussolini was deposed in 1943, and the Soviet army gradually pushed in from the east.

On 6 June, 1944 (D-Day) Allied armies landed in France; within 6 months they reached the Rhine. Hitler launched a final offensive in the Ardennes, the Battle of the Bulge, but the Allies were now unstoppable. Early in 1945 they were across the Rhine and advancing through Germany towards Berlin.

At the same time Russian troops were

advancing on Berlin from the east, arriving on the outskirts of the city in April. Hitler's advisers wanted him to escape and make a last stand at the Eagle's Nest in Bavaria, but he was set on dying in Berlin. He married Eva Braun, shot her, then shot himself. In his will he ordered that his body should be taken outside and burned, and that Admiral Doenitz should be the new Führer, with Goebbels as the new Chancellor. Hitler's pathetic plans for the future came to nothing. His body was burned, but Doenitz was to be Führer for only a week, and Goebbels glumly bore the burden of the Chancellorship for only a day before killing his entire family and committing suicide. On 8 May, 1945 Germany surrendered.

The war had only been started because of Adolf Hitler's megalomania. It was only drawn out for a final unnecessary year because he had lost touch with reality. The cost in human misery and human life was incalculable. The Second World War was in large part due to the actions of this one man, and that war is estimated to have cost 50 million lives. The only comparable blood-letting in the past century has been Mao Zedong's regime in China, which cost 48 million lives.

Joseph Goebbels
(1897–1945)

JOSEPH GOEBBELS WAS born in October 1897 in
Rheydt, in the German Rhineland. His parents
were working class Roman Catholics. In 1922 he
graduated from Heidelberg University with a
doctorate in literature and philosophy, and began
a career in journalism and writing. In that same
year, he joined the Nazi Party, and began editing
two party periodicals. Three years later, Goebbels
became business manager of the Rühr District
Nazi Party, working in liaison with Gregor
Strasser, leader of the party in north Germany.

In 1926, conflict between Hitler and Strasser
meant that Goebbels had to decide who to back.
He switched his loyalty from Strasser to Hitler and
was rewarded by Hitler with responsibility for the
party in the Berlin-Brandenburg region. Goebbels
also founded the official Nazi periodical *Der
Angriff* (The Attack), designed posters and
organized Nazi demonstrations and spectacles.
The most famous and effective of these were the
great Nuremberg rallies, the first of which was
held in 1927.

Greatly impressed with the way Goebbels had
built the party in Berlin, Hitler gave him the
additional post of Nazi propaganda director for all

of Germany. Goebbels also ran the Nazi election campaigns from 1930 to 1933. He cleverly exploited the suffering caused by the Depression to promote the Nazis, launching an intensive media campaign which promised something for everyone and used a lot of generalizations. Above all, German pride was to be restored. There were enemies and scapegoats. Leftists and Jews were to blame for the country's woes, and Hitler was the country's saviour. It was Goebbels who was responsible for creating the Führer myth round Hitler, accentuating this through public spectacles like the Nuremberg rallies. Goebbels skilfully stage-managed Hitler's public persona as 'the little corporal', surrounding the apparently modest man of the people with power-dressed followers like Goering in spectacularly flashy uniforms. It was a brilliant piece of marketing.

From 1933, Goebbels was able to use his power as head of the National Ministry for Public Enlightenment and Propaganda to develop the Fuhrer myth and the other, equally powerful, myth of the master race. In May, Goebbels staged a book-burning in Berlin; works by Jews, Marxists and other enemies were burnt in huge bonfires.

In 1940, as editor of *Das Reich*, Goebbels was writing regular front-page editorials, praising the successes of the German troops. By 1943, when Germany was losing the war, Goebbels was egging the German people on to fight to the bitter end. 'Are you determined to follow the Führer and fight for victory whatever the cost?'. Well, put like that, yes, of course they were.

Goebbels was responsible for keeping Hitler in power after the Stauffenberg plot to kill him failed. An attempted military coup following the failure of the plot was only thwarted with difficulty, and Goebbels played a key role in suppressing opposition to Hitler. As wartime conditions bit harder, Goebbels introduced an austerity programme and called for even greater sacrifices from civilians, still holding out the promise of eventual victory. He was to a great extent responsible for lengthening the Second World War, greatly adding to the misery of countless thousands of people throughout Europe.

Goebbels and his family were with Hitler in the Berlin bunker when the end came. Hitler committed suicide on 30 April, leaving Goebbels as Chancellor of Germany. On 1 May, as Soviet troops surged into Berlin, Goebbels asked an SS doctor to give each of his six children lethal injections. Then he asked an SS orderly to shoot him and his wife. Goebbels was guilty of complicity in the deaths of the 50 million people who died in the Second World War. As he himself said shortly before his death, when he was clearly beginning to question his own actions, 'We shall go down in history as the greatest statesmen of all time, or as the greatest criminals.'.

The verdict of history on Joseph Goebbels has been unambiguous. Had Goebbels lived and stood trial at Nuremberg there is little doubt that his active involvement in planning the Final Solution would have ensured a death sentence; it seems more likely than not that he would have joined the twelve who were sentenced to hang. Goebbels is often credited with a keen intelligence, but it was the intelligence of the master propagandist. He could find arguments for anything, so lacking in moral scruple was he. Sometimes it has been said that Goebbels never actually lied, only exaggerated. But in fact he embraced Hitler's philosophy that a big lie was often more credible than a small one. Hitler's Germany has gone, but the powerful propaganda continues, still powerful on film – the marching, the banners, the inspiring eloquence of the Fuhrer – and it still has the power to entice. And of course many others since Goebbels have borrowed his methods and modern politics is loaded with carefully worded lies – the sinister legacy of Dr Goebbels.

Heinrich Himmler
(1900–1945)

HEINRICH HIMMLER WAS born in Munich in October 1900, the son of a Roman Catholic schoolmaster who had once tutored the Crown Prince of Bavaria. After secondary school at Landshut, Himmler served as a cadet in the Eleventh Bavarian Regiment at the end of the First World War, and afterwards studied agriculture at the Munich Technical High School. He greatly regretted that he had been just too young to take an active part in the Great War, and idolized the war heroes he saw coming back from the front.

Himmler started his adult life modestly enough, working as a fertilizer salesman, but then joined in the Munich Beer Hall Putsch in 1923 as standard-bearer beside Ernst Roehm. After marrying in 1927, Himmler went into poultry farming for a time, but proved hopelessly unable to make it work as a business. In 1929, he made another sideways step into the twilight world of Nazism when he became head of Hitler's personal bodyguard, the SS (Schutzstaffel), at that time a small group of 280 men; under Himmler's leadership, it would expand enormously and become a major force within the Nazi state.

In 1930, Himmler was elected to the Reichstag,

and concentrated on extending SS membership, which soared to 52,000 by 1933. He also organized a security service, the SD (Sicherheitsdienst), under the leadership of Heydrich, and the two men together tightened the Nazi grip on Bavaria. In 1934, Himmler also became head of the Prussian Police and Gestapo. A major turning-point in Himmler's career was the master-minding of the purge of June 1934, which destroyed the SA (the Sturmabteilung) and ensured the emergence of the SS as a powerful organization, safeguarding Nazi principles – especially racist principles. By June 1937, Himmler had succeeded in making himself supremo of the political and criminal police throughout the Third Reich, becoming head of the Gestapo as well as Reichsfuhrer of the SS.

Himmler was an able organizer and administrator, efficient, hard-working but also power-crazed, as can be seen from the way he collected official posts and titles. If Hitler was a monster, it was Himmler who enabled him to be so. Himmler was largely responsible for organizing and perfecting methods of state terrorism against the regime's enemies, real and imagined. In 1933 he set up the first concentration camp at Dachau. With Hitler's encouragement, he greatly extended the categories of people who qualified for imprisonment in the camps.

Himmler was a very peculiar man, with peculiar obsessions. He thought he was the reincarnation of Henry the Fowler. He was interested in mysticism, mesmerism, the occult, herbal remedies – and there was the major and fanatical obsession with the narrow racialism of Nazism. The mission of the German people was 'the struggle for the extermination of any sub-humans, all over the world, who are in league against Germany, which is the nucleus of the Nordic race.' Himmler's death camps were the negative side of that racism. The dream of a race of blue-eyed, blond heroes bred by selective breeding was the positive side of it. He wanted to rear a new synthetic, racially pure aristocracy that would lead a vast colonization of the East. He accordingly organized a State-registered human stud farm known as Lebensborn, where young, perfectly formed 'Nordic' girls would breed with SS men and their offspring would be cared for.

Himmler looked like a bank clerk, but he was seething with mad and dangerous visions. He appeared to have no emotions, no nerves at all, but he suffered from a variety of severe psycho-somatic disorders, including headaches, intestinal spasms and occasional unpredictable squeamishness. On a visit to the Russian front, he watched a hundred Jews, men and women, being executed by shooting for his benefit. He felt nauseous and almost fainted. After this, he ordered a more humane method of execution; this involved using poison gas in specially built gas chambers disguised as shower rooms. Here was a curious glimpse of 'normal' sensitivity and humanity. But he still wanted the killings to go on, and on other occasions he showed no qualms about the sufferings of others at all.

In 1943, he said to the SS Group Leaders, 'What

happens to the Russians, what happens to the Czechs, is a matter of utter indifference to me. Whether [these] other peoples live in comfort or perish of hunger interests me only in so far as we need them as slaves for our civilization. Whether or not 10,000 Russian women collapse from exhaustion while digging a tank trench interests me only in so far as the tank ditch is completed for Germany. We shall never be rough or heartless where it is not necessary; that is clear. We Germans, who are the only people in the world who have a decent attitude to animals, will also adopt a decent attitude to these human animals.'

As the Second World War began to turn against Germany, Himmler tried to save himself. He sought to win asylum for himself and 200 other leading Nazis in the final days of the war, after the D-Day landings, by offering deals to the Allies behind Hitler's back. This is the same man who had exacted revenge on all those involved in the Stauffenberg plot by having them executed by hanging with piano wire, yet he himself was now betraying the Fuhrer. Himmler offered money and the freedom of 3,500 Jews held in concentration camps. According to documents recently released by British intelligence, the concentration camp victims – and quite a small number of them, really, considering the astonishing deal he was trying to pull off – were to be sent to Switzerland in two trains.

After Hitler's suicide, Himmler was so far detached from the reality of the situation that he deluded himself into believing he could succeed as the new German leader. But Grand Admiral Doenitz was the Führer now, according to Hitler's will, and Doenitz dismissed Himmler from all of his posts as he was considered 'politically questionable'. Doenitz must have realised that Himmler was guilty of a string of monstrous crimes against humanity, not just war crimes but crimes dating right back to the early '30s; Himmler would have to be called to account for those.

It was then that Himmler realised the game was up. He took off his glasses, changed his name to Heinrich Hitzinger, and tried to lose himself in the great milling crowds of soldiers, refugees and displaced people trying to find their way home all over a Germany that was chaotic in defeat. Himmler could have escaped from Germany but gave himself away in the most extraordinary fashion as he joined a long queue of people trudging across a bridge at Meinstedt. Perhaps his bureaucratic punctiliousness got the better of him but, whatever the reason, he offered to show his papers to the British soldiers who, up until that point, had not been paying much attention to the endless column of people. He was instantly suspected because of his odd behaviour in drawing unnecessary attention to himself. He seemed to be trying to tell them something. The soldiers did not immediately recognize him, but his behaviour was certainly suspicious enough to make them arrest him. It was only later that he was recognized. In prison he admitted he was Himmler and asked to be taken to Montgomery. When this request was refused and British intelligence officers arrived to question him, he bit on a cyanide capsule concealed in his teeth and died instantly. His body was taken to the Luneburg Heath and buried unceremoniously in an unmarked grave in the woods. Only the five soldiers who buried him knew the location of the grave of the second most feared man in the Third Reich.

Reinhard Heydrich
(1904–1942)

REINHARD HEYDRICH WAS born in 1904 at Halle in the Teutoburg Forest. His father was a teacher. At 18 he joined the Navy. He was an accomplished fencer and skier, and was also a violinist; he enjoyed weekends of croquet and chamber music at the home of Admiral Canaris. With all of this, he was tall and handsome. Yet at the age of 26 he abruptly spoilt the naval career that was developing so promisingly by getting the daughter of a powerful industrialist pregnant. He said that a woman who agreed to sex before marriage was unworthy of marriage – and he refused to marry her. He was dishonourably discharged from the Navy for this impropriety.

Looking for a new job, he joined Himmler's personal staff in 1931. Heydrich was imaginative, cruel and intelligent, and proved a most useful right-hand man for the plodding Himmler. They became a greatly feared double-act. Once Hitler became Chancellor in 1933, Himmler's SS suddenly became extremely powerful. In just three months, Himmler had founded the first concentration camp, at Dachau, filling it with assorted political opponents of Nazism.

Hitler's distrust of the SA was systematically

whipped up by the SS chiefs. Himmler and Heydrich repeatedly warned that the SA were planning a coup. Eventually Hitler summoned the SA leaders to Bad Wiesse in Bavaria; they were taken to prison and shot. The Bad Wiesse killings were taken as a signal by SS officers throughout Germany to execute leading politicians on lists prepared by Himmler and Heydrich. Hitler reported to the Reichstag that 79 had died; it is more likely that over 500 people perished in the 'Night of the Long Knives'.

The SS became all-powerful, and Himmler and Heydrich were answerable only to Hitler. In 1938, Polish Jews living in Germany were stripped of their Polish citizenship by the Polish government. Shortly afterwards, they were informed by the SS that they were not German citizens either. Heydrich organized a round-up and the stateless Jews were taken by truck to the Polish border and left in the no man's land between the two countries.

When he heard of this pointless cruelty, a 17-year-old youth, himself a Polish Jew, attempted to shoot the German ambassador in Paris. He shot the wrong man, and was arrested. Heydrich used this assassination attempt as an excuse to arrange through local police forces 'spontaneous' demonstrations against the Jews. These 'Kristallnacht' demonstrations led to 35 deaths, the destruction of 180 synagogues and the loss of 7,500 Jewish-run businesses.

Heydrich was responsible for setting up an exclusive brothel in Berlin, Madame Kitty's, where all the rooms were bugged. Here the loyalty of all the Nazi leaders would be tested. Heydrich was also responsible for master-minding one of the biggest Nazi money-making schemes. For very large sums of money, Austrian Jews could buy exit visas instead of risking death in the concentration camps. By the end of 1939, nearly two-thirds of the Jews in Austria had handed over everything they owned to the SS and left the country. A similar Office of Jewish Emigration was opened in Prague after the occupation of Czechoslovakia, and it proved equally profitable.

It was Heydrich who thought of the pretext to invade Poland. A German radio station in the border town of Gleiwitz was attacked by Polish troops; many Germans were killed. The following day, the German tanks rolled across into Poland and the German newspapers were full of righteous indignation about the unprovoked Polish attack. The 'Polish troops' had of course been SS men in disguise. The bodies found on the site of the attack were concentration camp victims.

Heydrich was appointed Reich Protector for Bohemia and Moravia. Within a very short time he had earned the nickname 'Butcher of Prague', as he supervised the annihilation of Czech resistance. The Czech Prime Minister was condemned to death after a show trial. Czech agents formed a vital link between a key spy in the Nazi hierarchy and London. It seemed Heydrich was close to identifying him and the Czech government in exile made the decision to assassinate Heydrich. Two assassins, Jan Kubis and Josef Gabcik, were parachuted in. They set an ambush on a sharp bend in the road between Heydrich's country house and his office in the Hradcany Palace in Prague. On 27 May 1942, Heydrich's Mercedes slowed to take the hairpin bend, and Gabcik stepped into the road and tried to shoot Heydrich, but his gun jammed. The car stopped, Kubis threw a grenade, and Heydrich jumped out of the car with his revolver in his hand. But Heydrich was mortally wounded and he staggered and fell, dying in hospital nine days later.

But the atrocities associated with Heydrich were not yet over. There was the revenge for his assassination yet to come, including one of the worst atrocities of the Second World War, the set-piece destruction of the village of Lidice, which was burnt to the ground; the men and boys in the village, all 1,300 of them, were shot.

Adolf Eichmann
(1906–1962)

ADOLF EICHMANN WAS born in the Rhineland in 1906 and brought up in Austria. As a young adult he was a travelling salesman, a 'rep', but he fell on hard times when he lost his job. Then he joined the SS as a researcher; he studied Freemasonry in particular.

When Heydrich opened the Offices of Jewish Emigration, Eichmann was responsible for streamlining the bureaucratic procedures so that more and more cash streamed into the SS accounts. He was enormously successful at this job in Vienna and Prague, so much so in fact that, when Poland was invaded, he was summoned to Berlin and put in overall charge of the national Centre for Jewish Emigration.

The downward spiral of evil took another twist in 1941, when Heydrich told Eichmann that the policy had changed. Instead of making as much money out of escaping Jews as possible, they were to exterminate them. It would be Eichmann's new job to organize the transport to the death camps of Jews from everywhere in Europe. It would be his job to round the Jews up and lay on the special trains. Conditions on the trains need not be considered, as the passengers were being taken to their deaths anyway. Some people died during these journeys. In fact, one train returning to France from Auschwitz was found to contain the bodies of 25 small children who had died on the previous journey out. The guards at the camp had not even bothered to unload them.

Eichmann, like Himmler, was a cold, calculating man, good at organizing. Hoess, one of the commandants at Auschwitz admitted that about 2,500 people had died in the Auschwitz gas chambers between August 1941 and December 1943, and another 500,000 had died in the camp of starvation or disease. He said Jews had arrived from Holland, France, Belgium, Germany, Czechoslovakia, Greece and Poland. Eichmann's operation had been terrifyingly efficient. Hoess drew comparisons between his camp and the camp at Treblinka. At Treblinka they used monoxide gas, which he considered ineffective; at Auschwitz they used Zyklon-B, which was much more effective. At Treblinka they had chambers that could only take 200 people at a time; at Auschwitz, he boasted, they had chambers big enough to take 2,000. The Zyklon-B chambers were Eichmann's idea. They sped up the process of extermination, made it possible to kill 24,000 people a day. As a result the air at Auschwitz was continuously full of the awful smell of burning bodies.

Eichmann seems to have known that what he was doing was wrong. He went to a lot of trouble to cover his tracks so that he could never be called to account.

Like Himmler, Eichmann was arrested in May 1945, but he was not recognized. When he was stopped by American soldiers he was disguised as a Luftwaffe pilot, and ordinary airmen were of little interest. Eichmann was able to slip away from the Allied soldiers unnoticed.

It was not until 1957 that Israeli agents picked up Eichmann's scent. The German secret service had had a report from a former Dachau inmate living in Argentina. One of his daughter's school friends had been making suspiciously vehement anti-Jewish statements, and the boy's surname was Klement. The girl described the boy's father, and he sounded like Eichmann. The name Klement seemed familiar. One high-ranking Nazi had headed for South America using the name Ricardo Clementi. The Germans were now able to supply an address for the Klement family in Buenos Aires. The Agentinian government allowed Israeli agents to put Klement under surveillance. They took long-range photographs of the suspect and showed them to Holocaust survivors, but unfortunately none could identify him. The Israelis were unable to act. The agents were fairly sure they had the right man, but there was insufficient evidence to attempt an extradition.

It was a bunch of flowers that gave Eichmann away. On 21 March, 1960, Klement left the Mercedes Benz factory where he worked in Buenos Aires, and bought a bunch of flowers for his wife. He was still carrying them when he got off the bus outside his house; he was clearly taking them home for his wife. This unlikely give-away was the final piece of evidence. 21 March was the Eichmanns' wedding anniversary. There was no longer any doubt that the man Klement was in fact Adolf Eichmann. The remaining problem was how to get Eichmann out of Argentina; a formal extradition application might simply warn Eichmann that it was time to slip away and the inevitable bureaucratic delays would make it quite likely that he and his family would vanish again. The Israelis decided on a radical and controversial solution, which was in itself not only an overtly illegal act but one that threw doubt on the ethical basis of the trial that was to follow. In May, Eichmann was kidnapped by Israeli agents, who bundled him into a car, drugged him and put him on a plane with papers saying that he was an Israeli car crash victim. Before long he was in Tel Aviv, and a prisoner of the Israelis.

At his trial, which started in December 1961, Eichmann sat in a box made of bullet-proof glass, facing 15 charges of deporting and causing the deaths of millions of Jews, being party to the murder of 91 children, and so on. Eichmann put up a carefully reasoned defence, that in organizing the Emigration Offices he was only doing what the Zionists wanted, in facilitating the exit of Jews from Europe. He said he had wanted to set up Jewish settlements in Madagascar and Poland, but had been prevented by other Nazi leaders. He said that when Hitler had organized the extermination of the Jews he, Eichmann, had lost all pleasure in his work, and that after that he just obeyed orders. But this did not square with evidence that Himmler had wanted to stop the extermination at the concentration camps as the end of the war approached, and that it was Eichmann who had wanted the killing to continue.

Given the controversy surrounding the abduction, the Israelis had to demonstrate as much fairness as possible at the trial, but the result was a foregone conclusion.and there was considerable comment in Europe that Eichmann could never have had a fair trial in Israel. Even so, the Israelis went through with their revenge, hanging Eichmann just before midday on 31 May 1962 at Ramleh Prison outside Tel Aviv. One of Eichmann's lieutenants remembered Eichmann saying in 1944 that 'he would leap into his grave laughing because the feeling that he had five million Jews on his conscience only filled his heart with gladness.'.

Joseph Mengele
(1911–1985)

ONE OF THE most enduring and terrible images of the Second World War is the archive film of trainloads of Jews arriving at Auschwitz. In the midst of the milling crowds and gangs of soldiers is a lone figure in immaculate uniform and white gloves. He inspects the inmates and directs some one way, some the other.

In one direction lie brutality, starvation and deprivation, but a slender chance of surviving. In the other direction, instant death in the gas chambers awaits. The frighteningly cold and clinical figure making the life and death decisions is one of the camp doctors, Dr Joseph Mengele.

The great Nazi hunter Dr Simon Wiesenthal produced a list of ten names in 1983, at the time of the extradition of Klaus Barbie. These were the Nazis he most wished to bring to justice, in fulfilment of his 'compact with the dead'. Wiesenthal was then 76 and must have realised that his chances of bringing all ten to justice were slim. 'If I could get all ten, it would be an achievement. But if I could get only Joseph Mengele, I think my soul would be at peace.'.

Who was this hated monster, Mengele? Joseph Mengele was born in 1911 into a family of upper middle class industrialists in Gunzburg in Bavaria. The family firm manufactured machine tools. At the age of 20, Mengele joined the Stahlheim, a militant right-wing organization founded by discontented former soldiers unhappy about the outcome of the Great War. In 1934, he moved to the SA and became a member of the NSDAP and SS in 1937.

Mengele's Nazi ideology was already developing while he was at university, in Munich, Bonn, Frankfurt and Vienna. At Munich he was attracted to the racial theories of Alfred Rosenberg, the philosopher of Nazism. At Frankfurt-am-Main he received his medical degree, studying under Otmar von Verschuer, the Director of the Institute for Racial Hygiene at Frankfurt University. He completed a dissertation with a distinctly racist focus on 'The morphology of the lower jaw bone among four racial groups'. He went on to do a similar (and similarly useless) racial study of cleft palates and cleft lips. Mengele was a thorough-going Nazi racist, hating the Jews, but hating the gypsies even more.

As a member of the Institute for Hereditary Biology and Racial Hygiene, Mengele voluntarily joined the Waffen-SS, and began work as a medical officer with several units in the invasion of the Soviet Union. He was awarded four medals but was declared unfit for military service after he was wounded – and that was how he came to get the job at Auschwitz.

It was in 1943 that he went to work at Auschwitz under Eduard Wirths, the chief physician, where he conducted his now-notorious series of medical examinations. One of Mengele's main research interests was on twins, and he was bent on verifying theories of genetic determinism. This involved examining twins both before and after death. Another research interest was dwarfism. One of Mengele's jobs at Auschwitz was to take his turn on the station platform, supervising the selections of incoming transports. Other camp doctors were involved, but of all of them it was Mengele who seemed to enjoy the work, revelling in the overt display of power. He was often on the arrival ramps even when he was not scheduled to be there – the doctors took it in turns to do the selections – using his riding crop to indicate his life-or-death decisions. He often used the riding crop to beat prisoners as well, and it was reported that he used a revolver to kill prisoners who were awkward or unco-operative.

Mengele gloried in his role at Auschwitz, according to the doctors who worked with him there, and was in total accord with the camp's brutal regime. On several occasions Mengele himself murdered inmates, either with his pistol or with fatal injections of phenol. He was technically a doctor, in the sense that he had qualified as a medic, but his behaviour was grotesquely at odds with his training. Instead of saving lives, he killed. Instead of relieving pain, he inflicted it. His ethical standards are vividly shown by his action on arriving at Auschwitz, when he found 600 sick women in the hospital; he immediately ordered all of them off to the gas chambers. Then there were the experiments.

Mengele's twins, his prized collection, were housed in a special block where he and his staff could examine them. He protected them from harsh labour assignments and made sure they were properly fed, but he still treated them as no more than laboratory animals – and, as with laboratory animals, when it suited him to do so he killed them and dissected them.

Another area that interested Mengele was the connection of eye colour with racial type. He began a series of experiments that involved injecting various chemicals into the eyes of his subjects. The experiments caused pain and infections, and at least one child was killed and another blinded. Mengele also collected 'specimens' for Dr Verschuer. It is known, for example, that seven sets of twins with different coloured eyes were killed with phenol injections, and their eyes sent to Verschuer. Verschuer himself wrote about Mengele's assistance to him in supplying specimens in reports that he wrote at the time, mentioning Himmler's support for the project. Mengele's notes on his experiments did not survive the end of the war, but there is no evidence that any of his experiments had any scientific basis or had any practical application whatever. The suffering was entirely for nothing.

Mengele, nicknamed 'the Angel of Death' by the Auschwitz inmates, worked at the concentration camp until the experiments stopped, shortly before the end of the war, and then he returned to Gunzburg. He never attempted to return to any kind of medicine, and it is not clear what earthly use he would have been as a general practitioner, but instead went back to an earlier phase, working towards rebuilding the family manufacturing firm of Carl Mengele and Son.

Mengele somehow escaped notice until ten years after the Second World was over. Then, in the mid-1950s, the author Ernst Schnabel drew attention to Mengele's work at the concentration camp when he was writing about Anne Frank. People then started to ask questions about Mengele and began calling for him to be put on trial for war crimes.

By that time, Mengele had secretly taken his family to South America for safety. He lived as a fugitive in Paraguay from 1973 onwards. The Nazi hunters led by Simon Wiesenthal were on his trail and the net gradually closed in on him. Wiesenthal believed he had traced Mengele to a remote Mennonite community on the border of Paraguay and Bolivia, but as a Paraguayan citizen and a registered refugee he seemed to be immune from extradition. It would be gratifying to think that Joseph Mengele lived in a state of increasing fear of capture and retribution during those final decades, but that may be no more than wishful thinking. Mengele's Nazi friends in Paraguay circulated a story in 1979 that he was dead. They even published a post mortem photograph of a body on a slab, showing a scar on the right arm where his SS tattoo had been surgically removed. But Wiesenthal was not so easily fooled; he found out that the body was that of SS Captain Roschmann, another war criminal, who sent

80,000 Jews to a concentration camp in Riga. A skeleton was eventually exhumed that is believed, from forensic examination, to have been Mengele's; and it seems that the old man died of a stroke while swimming in 1985.

Klaus Barbie
(1913–1991)

WARTIME FRANCE WAS divided in two. German troops occupied and were in direct control in the north. The collaborator government of Marshal Pétain in the south did the Germans' work for them there. The SS and the Gestapo were in control throughout France.

French Jews went in fear of being recognized, and many who were identified were transported east to the death camps. In southern France, Jewish families sent their children off to discreet refugee homes in the rural areas. The local German commanders tended to turn a blind eye to this practice, especially as the war neared its end and Germany appeared to be losing. There was one notable exception, and that was Klaus Barbie, 'the Butcher of Lyons'.

Barbie identified a refuge for Jewish children in the village of Izieu, close to the Swiss border. On 6 April 1944 Barbie ordered some trucks to go up to the village to collect the children and the staff. He proudly sent a message to the Gestapo headquarters in Paris, to say that he had captured 41 children and ten Jewish staff, and was arranging their transport to Drancy, which was a holding camp near Paris. Two months later all the children were sent in cattle trucks to Auschwitz, where they all died. The names of the 41 children are recorded on a commemorative plaque on the wall of the house in Izzieu that had been their home.

Barbie was extradited from Bolivia in February 1983, and flown back to France to stand trial for his war crimes.

Barbie was born at Bad Gödesberg not far from Bonn in 1913. He joined the Hitler Youth and at the age of 22, when he joined the SS, he was posted to Dortmund to work in the SS security branch. At 24 he was promoted to Obersturmfuhrer and posted to Lyons as head of the Gestapo there. He discovered that clearing the region of Jews was quite easy. There were plenty of informers and collaborators; indeed the Pétain administration seemed to be enforcing Nazi policy more zealously than the Germans. There were even French paramilitary units who carried out many executions.

At his headquarters in Lyons, Barbie installed torture chambers equipped with chains, whips, spiked clubs, welding torches and electric shock equipment. Barbie also installed two baths, one to be filled with ice-cold water, the other with near-boiling water; prisoners were ducked, first in one, then the other, until they talked. The methods Barbie ordered his men to use were barbaric in the extreme. Many died under 'interrogation'.

But Barbie made one big mistake. He employed Gottlieb Fuchs as his interpreter. Fuchs was a double-agent, working ultimately for the

Allies; he fed information gleaned from Barbie to the Swiss secret service. While other German officers were keeping one eye on the reckoning that would surely come once Germany lost the war, and behaving with a certain amount of circumspection, Barbie's torture sessions and atrocities continued relentlessly. On one occasion he took 110 men and women from Montluc prison, had them driven to an old fort and machine-gunned.

Allied troops reached Lyons on 3 September 1944. Barbie had vanished, after a reign of terror lasting just under two years. In that time, he had been responsible for executing over 4,000 people. Barbie went next to Frankfurt, where he made a living of sorts from the black market. His luck nearly ran out in August 1946, when he was arrested by Americans and driven off towards their base for questioning in the back of a jeep. He jumped out. In the confusion that followed, the jeep was driven into a tree, and Barbie escaped.

Barbie adopted the name Altmann in Augsburg until 1951, when he and his family set off for South America. They settled in La Paz, where Barbie became a successful businessman and he seemed to have 'got away with it'. In the 1980s, though, things began to go wrong. His son was killed in a hang-glider accident. His wife died of cancer. A new liberal president, Siles Zuazo, came to power, promising to purge Bolivia of the Nazis taking refuge in his country. The French author-ities knew where Barbie was and pressed for his extradition. He was arrested on 4 February 1983 and told he would be sent abroad. At first he was unconcerned. But that changed when he realised the crew on the plane were French, and he realised where he was being taken.

PART FIVE

EVIL BY INCOMPETENCE

Charles I of England and Scotland
(1600–1649)

CHARLES I SHOULD never have been King of England. He was the second son of James I and Anne of Denmark, and a backward child, so weak that he could hardly walk and very slow in starting to talk. During his boyhood he grew a little stronger, and became quite a good horseman and walker, but the stammer stayed with him all his life.

Charles I's elder brother, Henry, Prince of Wales, was the Heir Apparent, but Henry died and Charles became Prince of Wales in November 1616. Two years later there was a further misfortune when he fell under the malign influence of the Duke of Buckingham, one of his father's favourites, who dominated the King's royal councils. The first major wrong cause he espoused was that of his sister Elizabeth. He felt very keenly for his sister's humiliation when her husband, Frederick V, was driven from the throne of Bohemia and also lost the electorate of the Palatinate. Family honour was suddenly at stake, though it is hard to see how England gained or lost anything by this episode in the Thirty Years'

War. James I and Prince Charles both believed that an alliance with Spain was essential to reinstate Frederick, and it was with this in view that Charles took part in the arrangements for a marriage between himself and the Spanish Infanta Maria.

This led to what might have been a romantic adventure, but turned out to be a comic caper, an incognito visit to Spain with the Duke of Buckingham in 1623. The pair arrived in Madrid, with Charles (wearing a false beard, apparently being incapable of growing one of his own) promising to repeal the penal laws against Catholics within three years, but he was also adamant that the Palatinate had to be returned to his brother-in-law Frederick. The Spanish were not at all interested in helping Frederick, so Charles called the visit off and returned to England piqued. The episode shows that Charles's traits of ineptitude, poor diplomacy and lack of imagination were in place from the start. He was supposed to be playing the gallant lover, and yet he made stubborn stand on the interests of his brother-in-law. It almost goes without saying that the Infanta was underwhelmed at the prospect of marrying this puny, pettish and foolish little man. The prince's false beard can have done nothing to reassure her of his manliness.

In a curious way, though, the trip turned into an unexpected success when he returned to England without the Spanish princess. The Spanish bride would have been very unpopular with the English people, who remembered the

Armada and thought of Spain as an enemy country. Charles made capital of this by trying to initiate a war with Spain in retaliation for his treatment there. This was a further folly, showing how he could only think of one issue at a time. A parliament in 1624 supported a diplomatic breach with Spain. One councillor, Lord Middlesex, disagreed, and Charles's intolerance of disagreement led him to seek the impeachment of Lord Middlesex.

Charles then pursued a marriage with a French princess and tried to get his father to agree to a European war to help his sister and recover the Palatinate. The cost meant nothing to Charles, and there was every prospect that Parliament would need to raise £1 million. Then, in March 1625, James I died. Charles married his French princess, Henrietta Maria, the daughter of the French King Henry IV.

The new King sent a disastrously organized expedition against Cadiz. It was set up by the incompetent Buckingham, but Charles would hear no criticism of his favourite. Parliament tried to impeach Buckingham, so Charles intervened and dissolved it. 'Parliaments are altogether in my power for their calling, sitting and dissolution; therefore, as I find the fruits of them good or evil they are to continue, or not to be.' Unfortunately, without Parliament he found it difficult to raise money, so he tried a forced loan. From this point on the relationship between King and Parliament deteriorated, with the Parliament intellectually emancipated by the Renaissance and the King playing the part of a medieval absolute monarch. He was doomed. The assassination of the Duke of Buckingham in August 1628 removed one source of friction between King and Parliament, but the improvement in relations was only temporary.

A point of law seemed to work in Charles's favour. The notorious Ship Money which Charles levied to promote his foreign adventures was held by English judges to be legal, because the King could levy money in the interests of national safety.

Increasingly, in the power struggle between King and Parliament, the army took the side of Parliament and civil war became inevitable. Charles's visit to Scotland in 1641 in an attempt to raise a Scottish army to settle the English problem was yet another error in diplomacy. He dallied with the idea of promising the Irish leniency in return for their support. But he never considered the overall picture, the synergy of his monarchy. Nearly everything he did undermined his own position.

Once the military phase of the Civil War was under way, Charles I revealed one unexpected quality; he was something of a strategist. He could see, for example, that London was at the heart of the Parliamentary cause. On the other hand he could not devise a practical way of attacking London effectively. He was eventually defeated and kept under 'house arrest', but he refused to accept that he was defeated and began secret negotiations with the Scots, encouraging them to invade England and secure his restoration. His captors rightly construed this as a treasonable act and were left with little choice but to kill him. A treason trial was mounted and Charles put up a dignified if futile defence. There was a moment of particular ill-omen during his trial, when he accidentally beheaded his own walking stick. When the broken off knob rolled across the floor and no-one picked it up for him he must have known that things were going badly against him. They were. On 30 January 1649 he too was beheaded in Whitehall.

It is true that Charles I's private life was exemplary. He was a loyal, loving and dutiful husband and father. He was also devout, sober, polite, moderate and clean-living. He had a keen interest in paintings and built up a great art collection. It is nevertheless the inescapable verdict of history that he was the most unsuitable person to become king at that time. It is significant that he rarely if ever read anything; a wider base of knowledge about the world around him might have helped him towards more sensible actions. With his ideas of absolutism and his dismissive view of Parliament he just might have been a more successful monarch in the medieval period. But he was certainly not the man for the times in which he lived. He was disarmingly clear about his position, saying that he 'did not believe the happiness of the people lay in sharing government, subject and sovereign being clean different.'. His heedless military adventures cost an enormous number of lives, set families and communities against one another, caused brothers to kill brothers, and fathers to kill sons. The large-scale destruction of life and property and the dislocation of English society were entirely avoidable, and entirely due to the King's bad judgement. He was stubborn, yet he could not be trusted to honour his word and be resolute when it counted. He promised his faithful servant the Earl of Strafford that he would be safe, but when he thought his wife, the Queen, might be in danger, he let that promise go and sacrificed Strafford. As Strafford said shortly before his own execution, 'Put not your trust in princes'. After the Earl of Strafford's death, the King repented his action and felt guilty about his own treachery for the rest of his life; at the end, he came to see his own execution as an expiation of his treachery.

Charles I's greatest crime was to be the single cause, by extreme provocation, of the English Civil War. As Sir Walter Raleigh observed when he was a prisoner in the Tower in 1603, several decades before these events, "The greatest and most grievous calamity that can come to any state is civil war, a misery more lamentable than can be described.'. Raleigh had in mind the terrible religious war he had himself witnessed in France when young, but what he said was just as true of the English Civil War, at that stage not even imagined.

Charles I did nothing to improve the lot of ordinary people in England during his reign, nothing to enhance the country's reputation abroad, nothing to strengthen England economically or socially, but everything to destroy it. He ranks as one the most incompetent monarchs England has ever had. Under incompetent leaders there is mayhem, and miseries and injustices multiply.

Jack Ketch
(about 1630-1686)

JACK KETCH WAS an infamous English executioner in the seventeenth century. One of his predecessors, Derrick, was a celebrated figure who in the early seventeenth century invented a huge gantry like a crane, which could hang as many as 23 people at once.

After Derrick, Gregory Brandon became the public hangman, then his son Richard Brandon inherited the post. It was Richard Brandon who executed Charles I. 'Squire' Dun followed. Then came the notorious Jack Ketch. His real name was Richard Jacquet, but the surname became his whole name, and that became so well known that it was used as a nickname for his successors for nearly 200 years. He was appointed public hangman in about 1663, in the reign of Charles II.

Jack Ketch was a well-known public figure by 1672, when a broadside was published entitled *The Plotters Ballad, being Jack Ketch's incomparable Receipt for the Cure of Traytorous Recusants and Wholesome Physick for a Popish Contagion*. These were certainly not Ketch's own words, but words put into his mouth by the anonymous author. It was quite common for 'Confessions' to be circulated at public executions; these too were 'fake'; although they purported to be by the condemned man or woman, they were not.

Ketch acquired a reputation for being a very incompetent executioner, which is how he finds his way into this book. The high-profile execution of Lord William Russell on 21 July, 1683 was carried out in a very clumsy way. A pamphlet has survived, which in this case may genuinely represent Ketch's words. In this pamphlet he makes his 'Apologie', claiming that the prisoner was to blame for not lying down properly. Lord William did not 'dispose himself as was most suitable'. Ketch also claimed he was interrupted while taking aim, which amounts to owning up to poor concentration.

There were many tracts aimed against Ketch. One was called *The Tyburn Ghost: or, Strange Downfal of the Gallows: a most true relation how the famous Triple Tree, near Paddington, was pluckt up by the roots and demolisht by certain evil Spirits, with Jack Ketch's Lamentation for the loss of his Shop, 1678*. The triple tree was a triangular gallows with three supporting posts. Each beam could carry eight people, so the whole structure could kill 24 at a time.

A hundred years or so later, Ketch had become a character in Punch and Judy shows. As the executioner was nobody's friend, it delighted audiences to see Punch in the end succeeding in hanging the hangman. It was what the real Ketch justly deserved for the unnecessary suffering he inflicted. But the crowds loved to be shocked by this random cruelty: it was all part of the show. At

Newgate in 1820, when the Cato Street conspirator Thistlewood and his companions were executed for treason, the sentence was both hanging and beheading. The sentences were carried out and the executioner held up the heads one by one to show the crowd. He dropped the last one, and in the spirit of the occasion the crowd yelled, 'Oh, butter-fingers!'.

Nicholas II of Russia
(1868–1918)

NICHOLAI ALEKSANDROVICH ROMANOV was born on 6 May, 1868, the son of Tsar Alexander III and the Empress Marie, who was born Princess Dagmar of Denmark. He became Tsar in 1894. At his coronation in Moscow, several thousand people were trampled to death trying to get presents from the new Emperor.

Nicholas was told about the disaster later in the day, but refused to cancel the ball he had arranged for that evening. This was the first of many very bad decisions, showing him as tactless and lacking in imagination. At his coronation ceremony, the imperial chain broke and fell from his neck. He was deeply and fatalistically impressed by the two bad omens of his coronation day; the air of mystic resignation made him a supremely unsuitable head of state for the time.

Nicholas had not been well prepared to rule any country, let alone one that was in social and political turmoil. His father had died relatively young, which meant that he had little training to be head of state. His English tutor, Mr Heath, taught him fluent English and a love of physical exercise, and General Danilovich gave him military training, but he had no education in geography, history, economics or politics. He relied too heavily on his wife, Alix, who fully embraced the old Russian traditions of autocratic rule and religious mysticism. He also relied too heavily on the advice of his wife's cousin, Kaiser Wilhelm; most of this advice was in Cousin Willy's interests and Cousin Willy was more interested in preventing Britain and Russia from getting too close to each other politically or diplomatically than he was in helping Nicholas.

Nicholas had little understanding of his country's domestic problems. His grandfather, Alexander II, had done much to improve the situation, but revolutionaries had assassinated him anyway, because they wanted a different regime altogether. Nicholas could have won the support of liberals, but he instead alienated them by refusing to reduce the weight of autocracy by giving some constitutional guarantees. In the later years of his reign, he allowed Alix to step in to prevent him from making any concessions – concessions that just might have averted revolution. As a result, he ended up with both the liberals and the revolutionary extremists against him.

Nicholas was preoccupied with family problems. The first was the succession; he and Alix had four daughters before their son Alexei was born in 1904. Then Alexei proved to have haemophilia. Because of the fragility of the monarchy, Nicholas decided to keep this secret; no-one outside the royal household was to know about Alexei's illness. This in turn led on to another problem. Alix looked for help from a monk and mystic, Grigori

Rasputin, who seemed to be able to relieve the boy's pain when he suffered from internal bleeding. Alix's increasing dependence on Rasputin gave Nicholas's many enemies a strong propaganda weapon against him.

The outbreak of the First World War in 1914 found Russia seriously unprepared for war with Germany. There were huge Russian losses. Nicholas then made what was probably his biggest mistake, which was to assume responsibility for leading the army himself. He assumed the role of commander-in-chief in September 1915. This decision was a mistake twice over. First, it meant that he was in neither St Petersburg nor Moscow and he had to leave his wife in his place as an unofficial Regent. He had no awareness that Alix was deeply unpopular, because she was believed to be dependent on Rasputin, and because she was German and therefore, it was wrongly believed, on the side of Russia's enemies. Second, it meant that he was taking on himself the responsibility for the outcome of the war. Since the war was going against Russia, it was particularly stupid to associate himself (and the monarchy) with responsibility for losing it. He was setting himself up for what amounted to a court-martial.

After the so-called February Revolution of March 1917, Nicholas was forced to abdicate in both his own name and that of his son in favour of his brother Michael. Michael too abdicated a few hours later. The provisional government confined Nicholas and his family and moved them to Tobolsk to prevent their escape or rescue. To prevent a restoration of the monarchy, the Bolsheviks shot them all at the Ipatiev House in Ekaterinburg in the night of 16-17 July 1918. There were rumours that one or more of the Romanovs had escaped, and a number of people in the 1920s and 1930s claimed to be survivors of the shootings, probably with the idea of inheriting the Romanov fortune. In the 1990s the bodies of the Romanovs were found, exhumed and identified using DNA. Two were missing, Alexei and one of the girls. The remains were reburied in the Romanov family crypt in 1998, on the 80th anniversary of the murders. It was at a time when the Soviet Union had imploded and there was an economic crisis, and the Romanov funeral generated a (short-lived and misplaced) nostalgia for the Russian monarchy.

If the Russian monarchy could have survived the first two decades of the twentieth century, Nicholas II was certainly not the man to see that it did. Much has been made of his goodness and kindness as a family man – as with Charles I – but that does not in any way qualify him as a national leader. It should not be forgotten, either, that it was Nicholas II who gave the order for the Russian army to mobilize, which means that he played a part in precipitating the First World War. And it was in the mayhem of the First World War that the Russian Revolution was hatched. Without the Russian Revolution, there would have been no Stalin. Nicholas II has much to answer for.

Hirohito
(1901–1989)

HIROHITO, THE SHOWA Emperor, was the 124th Emperor of Japan. His reign of 62 years was the longest of all the Japanese emperors and remains one of the most controversial. Hirohito – he had no other name – was head of state when Japan illegally attacked Pearl Harbour.

Hirohito was born in Tokyo, the eldest son of the Crown Prince Yoshihito and Crown Princess Sadako. From 1908 to 1914 he attended the Gakushuin Peers School and then went to a special institute for the Crown Prince. In childhood he was known as Prince Michi, and he was formally invested as Crown Prince himself in 1916. In 1921 he became Prince Regent in place of his sick father. In 1922 he undertook a six-month foreign tour, and became the first Japanese Crown Prince ever to travel abroad.

Hirohito married a cousin, Princess Nagako in 1924. Hirohito became emperor when his father died on 25 December 1926. From then until 1945 Hirohito stood by and watched as Japan became increasingly militaristic. The Army and Navy had held veto power over the formation of cabinets since 1900 and there were numerous acts of political violence, such as the assassination of the moderate Prime Minister Tsuyoshi Inukai in 1932; from then on, the military held almost total power in Japan, driving the country first into the second Sino-Japanese War and then into the Second World War.

The military faction was powerful, but the Emperor was regarded as divine. He was also the most legitimate emperor for hundreds of years, in that his biological mother was the previous emperor's official wife. He had great authority, which he appears never to have used. Hirohito could have stepped in, early on, and put the brakes on the rise of militarism. For some reason he did not.

In the immediate aftermath of the Second World War, many believed that Hirohito was the evil mastermind behind the war, while others maintained that he was completely powerless. Millions of Chinese, Taiwanese, Koreans and others in Southeast Asia still see Hirohito as the Asian equivalent of Adolf Hitler and think he should have been tried as a war criminal. They may be right. Many Asians living in countries that fell victim to Japanese aggression – and Japanese atrocities – are still hostile to the Japanese royal family. When Hirohito visited Britain, Lord Mountbatten, who was well aware of the atrocities committed by the Japanese in Southeast Asia, could not bring himself to meet him.

Hirohito normally kept himself at a distance from decision making. In September 1941, the Japanese Cabinet decided that for 'self-defence and self-preservation' they were 'resolved to go to war with the United States . . . if necessary'. If the US did not agree by 10 October to give Japan a free hand to continue the conquest of China and Southeast Asia, hostilities would commence. On 5 September Prime Minister Konoe showed a draft of this decision to Hirohito, who was deeply concerned that war preparations were put first and diplomatic negotiations second and announced that he would break with a protocol that was hundreds of years old; he would speak at the conference the following day and directly question the chiefs of staff. Konoe persuaded Hirohito to do this in private. Hirohito duly gave the military chiefs a private dressing-down and told them, his face turning red and his voice rising, that a peaceful settlement was to be pursued 'up to the last'. They had never been reprimanded by the Emperor before.

But it was no good. At the Imperial Conference the following day, all the speakers agreed on war not diplomacy. The Emperor then astonished them all by speaking as he had threatened, publicly stressing the need for peaceful resolution of international problems. He read them a poem written by his grandfather, which he said he had read over and over again:

'All men are brothers, like the seas throughout the world; So why do winds and waves clash so fiercely everywhere?'

The Emperor's wishes were very clear, but the war preparations went ahead regardless, and Pearl Harbour was attacked on 7 December, 1941. From this episode it is plain that Hirohito did not want war, but was incapable of stopping it. He had left it too late. He should have intervened ten years earlier.

Once the war was under way, Hirohito shelved his doubts and showed every interest in the progress of events, doing everything he could to boost morale. He became part of the war effort. The information he was given was often false. He received news of an unending stream of victories, though many of the engagements described were actually defeats. The American raids on mainland Japanese cities that began in 1944 were a rude awakening. Early in 1945, Hirohito called a series of individual meetings with ministers to discuss whether they should continue the war or surrender. Only Prime Minister Konoe advised ending the war by negotiated surrender. Hirohito favoured surrender – but after a significant victory, in order to get better terms. This became a vain hope. The Lord Keeper of the Privy Seal, Koichi Kido, produced a document summarizing the hopelessness of Japan's situation and proposing a negotiated peace; Hirohito warmly approved and asked for it to be circulated. The Cabinet approved it in mid-June, but still only after the American attack on the mainland of Japan had been repulsed.

Neither Hirohito nor his Cabinet were prepared to consider 'unconditional surrender', as required by the Allies. During the early months of 1945, Hirohito might have steered his Cabinet towards acceptance of unconditional surrender, but he did not try to do this. Hirohito is therefore to blame for the prolongation of the war by several months and the eventual Allied bombing of Hiroshima and Nagasaki in the summer of 1945. On 15 August, it was Hirohito's voice on the radio that announced Japan's unconditional surrender.

Several leading figures wanted Hirohito tried for war crimes, including President Truman, but the US General MacArthur felt it safer to keep him as a symbol of continuity; it would be more likely that the Japanese people would accept the occupation forces. Hirohito was never tried for his responsibility for the war, or the atrocities committed by his troops. He retained his freedom, his throne and most of his status. He was forced to renounce his claim to divinity, and in 1946 he became a constitutional monarch. Immediately after repudiating his divinity, Hirohito asked the Allied authorities for permission to worship an ancestress; he then worshipped the Sun Goddess. The people of Japan understood that he was reaffirming his descent from the goddess and therefore reaffirming his own divinity in spite of what he had been obliged to say. The Americans did not see what was happening here. As in the rest of his career, Hirohito was having his cake and eating it.

During his long post-war reign, Hirohito was careful to cultivate a new, more Western, image of a constitutional monarch, wearing Western clothes, going on public walkabouts, making public appearances on special occasions. He consciously modelled himself on the 'watered-down' monarchs he had met in Europe. He also made a point of travelling abroad and acting as a diplomatic ambassador for Japan. The Japanese people transferred much of the loyalty once reserved for the Emperor, embracing Western consumerism with great enthusiasm.

To the end he remained a morally ambiguous figure. Whether he could have done anything to prevent the Sino-Japanese War or the Second World War is uncertain. It looks as if he could have done more to create a different climate in Japan in the 1930s, but on the other hand others who had stood in the way of the military faction and its aspirations had not survived, and in spite of his apparent divine power there was always the possibility of assassination. In the end Hirohito was a mortal, and he proved this by dying on 7 January, 1989.

PART SIX

MODERN TYRANTS & WAR CRIMINALS

Leopold II
(1835–1909)

LEOPOLD PHILIPPE MARIE Victor was born in Brussels on 9 April, 1835, the son of Leopold I, King of the Belgians. As a youth he entered the army. He married Marie, Archduchess of Austria in 1853 and succeeded his father as King of the Belgians in 1865.

At home, in Belgium, Leopold II's interests were mainly military. He did what he could to strengthen his country by military reforms and agitated, unsuccessfully for most of his reign, to have conscription introduced. He knew that Belgium was vulnerable to invasion and that its best defence was to have a strong army. He was also interested in developing fortifications. But Leopold is not really remembered for any of these sensible and statesmanlike things. He is remembered for having his own personal colony, the Congo Free State, which from 1884 he treated very much as a private estate where he could do as he pleased. In 1908, shortly before Leopold's death, the Congo Free State was annexed by the Belgian state and renamed Belgian Congo.

The irony was that the only thing that was free about the Congo Free State was the behaviour of King Leopold. It was in 1876 that Leopold organized an international association as a front for his personal plan to 'develop' central Africa. Leopold eagerly commissioned Henry Morton Stanley to survey the area and sign treaties with tribes. In 1879, acting under Leopold's sponsorship, Stanley was aggressively competing with a French explorer to lay claim to the Congo region. For five years after that, Stanley worked frantically to open the lower Congo by building a road to connect with the navigable reach of the river; the idea was that this would open the lower Congo basin to commercial exploitation, which it did, on a nightmare scale. Stanley's behaviour was conspicuously ruthless, earning him the nickname 'rockbreaker' among the Africans. Leopold relied totally on Stanley, who must bear some of the responsibility for what followed.

At the Berlin Conference in 1884–85, Leopold gained formal international recognition as sovereign of most of the Congo Free State – something over a million square miles of land. In 1891 he hired William Stairs, a British soldier, to take control of the copper fields of Katanga.

So far, this is a fairly routine story of part of the scramble for Africa, but it was the way in which Leopold exploited his vast new colony that makes it a story of almost incredible evil. At home, in Belgium, Leopold gave every appearance of being a normal, civilized, if rather brusque and strong-willed, European monarch, ruling within the recognized constraints of a constitutional monarchy. But in the Congo he was the self-anointed sovereign. The Congo was his personal domain and only he made the rules there, and he ruled with a barbaric ferocity and a complete heedlessness for basic human rights. He was Jekyll and Hyde.

The Congo was enormous: 76 times bigger than Belgium itself. It was to be a source of rubber, which had historically never before been mass-produced. Leopold was determined to make the Congo produce masses of rubber, and determined to make money out of it. He let multinational concessionary companies set up the rubber production under his auspices, but that does not absolve him from responsibility for the inhuman treatment handed out to the rubber workers.

The native population was controlled by torture, mutilation and massacre, and Leopold must have known that this was how his estate was being run. The population of the Congo fell from 20 or 30 million at the start of Leopold's enterprise to around 9 million by 1911. Between 1880 and 1920 the population of the Congo halved. It was a nineteenth century African holocaust.

The Africans were unaccustomed to the capitalist ethos of production, and they suffered in many ways, from culture-shock, from exhaustion through over-work, murder, starvation and disease. The punishment for a wide variety of offences, including failure to meet work quotas of sap from rubber trees, was amputation of a hand, or a foot, or an arm, or a leg – sometimes an ear or the nose. Over ten million people died as a result of Leopold II's greed. All round the world the colonial powers were exploiting the local indigenous people in order to extract resources of every kind. It was a time of outstandingly unethical behaviour. But even by the standards of the nineteenth century, the exploitation of the Congo was something exceptional. There were human rights abuses in the Dutch East Indies, French Indo-China, German Southwest Africa, Rhodesia and South Africa, but nothing on the scale of the Congo.

Many in Europe and North America knew about the severity of Leopold's regime in the Congo – and condemned it roundly – among them Arthur Conan Doyle, Booker T. Washington and Joseph Conrad. Conrad's novel *Heart of Darkness* is a portrayal of King Leopold's regime of slave labour, rape and mutilation.

There is no doubt that these atrocities happened. Investigators came back with horrific photographs that tell their own story. It is a great mystery how King Leopold reconciled what he was doing in Africa with what he was doing in Europe. In Europe he was respected as a philanthropist and abolitionist. Meanwhile on his estate in Africa hundreds of thousands worked in servitude, falling victim to capricious beatings and punishment by mutilation. The slave labour conditions made him his fortune, which he could then use for good works. Perhaps that is how he justified it in his own mind.

The atrocities became public knowledge in 1908, by which time the Congo was in the (safer) hands of the Belgian government. By then King Leopold himself had only a year to live, and was impervious to the disgrace that was now gathering round his name.

Leopold's wife died in 1902, but he then had two sons, Lucien Philippe Marie Antoine (born in 1906) and Philippe Henri Marie Francois (born in 1907) by a prostitute called Caroline Lacroix (1883–1948). The two boys were born out of wedlock, but Leopold went through a form of marriage ceremony with their mother on 12 December 1909, at the Pavilion of Palms, Chateau de Laeken. The marriage had no validity in Belgian law, as presumably Leopold would have known. Just five days after this curious, belated non-wedding, Leopold II died, on 17 December, 1909, at Spa, Liege. Caroline Lacroix thought she had been created Baroness de Vaughan. She thought her sons were Lucien the Duke of Tervuren and Philippe the Count of Ravenstein, but no royal decrees to confirm these titles were ever issued. Was she deluded, or had Leopold told her lies? It looks as if the bad King Leopold of the Congo Free State was misbehaving in rather different ways back in Belgium. But what we should really remember him for is not the irregularity of his domestic life but the huge number of people in Africa who were mutilated or killed – between 10 and 20 million of them – just to make him rich.

The American poet Vachel Lindsay wrote:

'Listen to the yell of Leopold's ghost,
Burning in Hell for his hand-maimed host.
Hear how the demons chuckle and yell,
Cutting his hands off, down in Hell.'

Kaiser Wilhelm II
(1859–1941)

FRIEDRICH WILHELM VIKTOR Albrecht von Hohenzollern was the last German Kaiser (Emperor) and the last King of Prussia. He is invariably referred to as 'The Kaiser'; he was one of the most disastrous monarchs of all time.

During the First World War he was universally reviled in Britain as the man who caused the war. He was born on 27 January 1859 in Berlin, the eldest child of Crown Prince Friedrich (later Kaiser Friedrich III) and Victoria, who was also Britain's Princess Royal. The family trees of the European monarchs were closely intertwined, and there were occasional events, such as coronations and funerals, where they all met and were photographed together. The Kaiser's mother, for instance, was the aunt of the Russian Tsarina Alexandra and the sister of Britain's King Edward VII.

Wilhelm was critically damaged at birth by a traumatic breech birth, which left him with a withered left arm. He managed both on public occasions and in photographs to conceal the fact that his left arm was much shorter and thinner than his right. In some photographs, he holds the withered left hand inside the normal right hand, concealing it; in others he carries a pair of white gloves in the left hand to make the arm seem longer. Recent analyses of his birth records in the Imperial Archives suggest that he may have experienced some brain damage at birth as well. If so, there may be an explanation of his frequently aggressive, tactless, headstrong, bullying approach, both in public and personal life. By 1894, some were already referring to him as a megalomaniac. The personality defect, whatever its origin, was disastrous in a head of state. He conspicuously fell out with his first Chancellor, Bismarck, and also from much earlier days had a conspicuously poor relationship with his mother. This was not a man cut out for diplomacy.

Wilhelm was educated at Kassel Gymnasium and the University of Bonn. In 1881, he married Augusta Viktoria, Duchess of Schleswig-Holstein, by whom he had seven children. In 1888 Wilhelm's grandfather, Wilhelm I, died. His father, Crown Prince Friedrich, was crowned Emperor as Friedrich III, but he was already terminally ill with throat cancer, dying shortly afterwards. After only three months, in June 1888, Wilhelm II became Kaiser unexpectedly early, at the age of only 29.

Within two years he had forced the resignation of Chancellor Bismarck and appointed von Bülow. After Bismarck, Wilhelm wanted only civil servants as Chancellors, not politicians. Wilhelm's intention was that the Reichstag should accept whatever policies the Kaiser and the upper classes wanted. His entire mindset was in effect that of an eighteenth century princeling, and entirely inappropriate to the situation in Germany at the end of the nineteenth century.

Bülow's foreign policy included the German Naval Bills of 1897 and 1900, which were designed to challenge British naval domination. The British government was right to be worried by the implications of the massive enlargement of the German navy, and even more so by the Kaiser's tactless posturing, his constant emphasis on Germany's military power. He also wanted 'a place in the sun' for Germany, which was a euphemism for wanting a huge German empire; this too obviously involved treading on the toes of Britain. Bülow was replaced by Theobald von Bethmann Hollweg, who was more conciliatory towards Britain and tried to come to terms. This tactic foundered when the British refused to promise neutrality in the event of a Franco-German war unless there was a significant reduction in the German fleet; the only reason Germany would need a large fleet would be to take on the British fleet. The Kaiser promoted both the arms race and the scramble for Africa; he did everything he could to escalate the tension, though it is still not certain that he actually wanted the First World War.

A major problem was that the Kaiser was personally responsible for appointing top government officials, and he was commander-in-chief of the armed forces. He was therefore the only person who could ensure that diplomatic and military strategies were harmonized. During the First World War, the Kaiser was roundly accused by the British of causing the war. In fact, he could have done a great deal to reduce the friction between the two countries during the previous decade, some of which was inevitable because of Germany's rapid industrialization and consequent economic growth. He could also have exploited his family ties with Britain to reassure the British that his intentions were friendly. Instead of this, he took every opportunity to escalate the tension, posing for photographs in an incredible array of military uniforms, which he loved to wear and swagger about in. Seeing these photographs made many people, in many European countries, wonder whether they should be amused by the Kaiser's antics or be alarmed. It was hard to tell whether he was a megalomaniac or just playing the fool.

After the assassination of Archduke Franz Ferdinand in 1914, the Kaiser encouraged the Austrians to adopt an uncompromising line. When it came to his own country, he lost his nerve and was unable to stop his generals from mobilizing. On paper the Kaiser was commander-in-chief, but the reality of the war must have disappointed him in more ways than one – the defeat at the end must have been the biggest disappointment of all – he found himself excluded from decision-making. As the war progressed his impotence became more and more obvious; his role was reduced to pinning medals on soldiers who were lucky enough to return from the front. As the losses at the front mounted and civilian living conditions in Germany declined, his popularity evaporated.

When the war ended, he was forced to abdicate (9 November 1918). He was exiled to the Netherlands. There was talk of bringing him to trial, but he evaded this by threatening suicide. His bluff should have been called. But in any case Queen Wilhelmina refused to extradite him as a war criminal. The ex-Kaiser continued to live under her protection in the Netherlands for the rest of his life. When his wife died, he remarried; this time his choice was Hermine von Schoenaich. He dropped the wearing of military uniforms now, and instead acted the role of an English country gentleman, trying to appear just a harmless old buffer. During the 1930s, he nursed the futile hope that the Nazis would revive the monarchy. It seems he was deluded enough to think that he might make a come-back.

Kaiser Wilhelm II died at Doorn on 5 June 1941, while the German occupying troops stood guard at his gates. One consequence of his disastrous reign and the unsatisfactory circumstances surrounding his abdication was that there was no possibility of any sort of monarchy in the 1920s. He had an heir, crown Prince Wilhelm (1882—1951) but there was no chance, after the Wilhelm II fiasco, that the German people would have wanted him. A vacuum was left which someone like Adolf Hitler could fill.

Vladimir Ilich Lenin
(1870–1924)

VLADIMIR ILICH ULYANOV was born at Simbirsk on 22 April (according to the modern calendar) 1870, the son of a Russian civil servant called Ilya Nikolaevich Ulyanov. He had a Jewish ancestry through his mother's father, who later converted to Christianity, though he himself was baptized into the Russian Orthodox Church. At school he was particularly good at Latin and Greek. In May 1887 his eldest brother, Alexander, a student, was hanged for taking part in a plot to assassinate the Tsar, Alexander III.

This traumatic event had the effect of electrifying Lenin, making him become extremely radical; it was his brother's execution that turned Vladimir Ilich into a revolutionary. Later in that same year he was arrested and expelled from Kazan University, and from Kazan itself, for taking part in student protests. This did not stop him from continuing his studies, though, at various places on the Volga and by 1892 he had a licence to practise law.

But the earlier events took over now, and he decided to devote more of his time to politics. He involved himself in revolutionary propaganda efforts. He also studied Marxism, mainly in St

Petersburg, and had become an authority on it. On 7 December, 1895 he was arrested as a subversive and held for a ycar, after which he was sent to Siberia. While there, in 1898 he married Nadezhda Krupskaya, a socialist activist. In April 1899 he published a book, *The Development of Capitalism in Russia*. The next year his exile came to an end and he settled for a time in Pskov, not far from St Petersburg, from which he was still banned. He used his freedom to travel in Europe, leaving Russia on 29 July 1900 for more than five years. He travelled to Switzerland, Germany, London, Paris, then back to Switzerland, at the same time publishing tracts about the revolutionary movement. He also founded a newspaper, which he called *Iskra* (the Spark), which was to be published abroad but circulated in Russia.

At the end of 1901, Vladimir Ilich Ulyanov assumed the pseudonym, or *nom de guerre*, of Lenin. As he became more of a public figure, he evidently felt he needed a short name, possibly because it looked and sounded monolithic, possibly because it could be chanted or shouted more effectively. Stalin, of course, was later to do the same.

Lenin was a small man with a Slavonic face. His huge forehead gave his face strength and he had piercing eyes. He worked tirelessly. He was an intellectual, with a love of the arts and sciences, but led a simple frugal personal life. His life towards the end, when he was virtually the dictator of Russia, was not very different from his life when he was an emigré abroad.

Lenin became active in the Russian Social Democratic Labour Party (RSDLP) and from 1903 he became the leader of the Bolshevik faction after a split with the Mensheviks that was in part precipitated by his pamphlet *What is to be Done?* The prevailing Populist/Economist view was that the revolution would happen as a result of the workers' agitation for rights and that then socialism would 'come naturally'. Lenin's paper argued that this was not the case, that workers are not natural socialists at all; left to themselves they rise to the level of trade unionism, but no further. Socialism would only come out of the philosophical, historical, economic theories that were propagated by the educated middle classes. Only a disciplined party of professional middle-class revolutionaries under the command of a central committee could bring socialism to Russia. With such a party, Lenin joked, the whole of Russia might be turned upside down. Lenin's ideas were indeed revolutionary.

The revolution of 1905 fell short of Lenin's expectations. He arrived in St Petersburg in November and stayed for a while, but lived for the next two years in Finland, visiting Stockholm and London. In 1906 he was elected to the Presidium of the RSDLP. As his profile increased, so also did the danger of arrest, so in 1907 he moved to Finland again for safety, but he continued to travel and to participate in socialist meetings. He was unhappy during these years, partly because he was an unwilling migrant, partly because of ongoing faction-fighting between Mensheviks and

Bolsheviks and within the Bolshevik camp itself.

When the March 1917 Revolution broke out, Lenin was in Switzerland, unable to get back to Russia without crossing enemy territory. The Germans provided the facility of a sealed train, in which he and other Russian socialists might travel across Germany. On 16 April, Lenin arrived in St Petersburg, now Petrograd (and one day to be named Leningrad in his honour), to take a leading role in the Bolshevik movement. The Tsar, Nicholas II, had been deposed. A Bolshevik rising in July failed, and Lenin had to withdraw to Finland once more. In October he returned to Russia to lead an armed coup, this time successfully, against the Provisional Government led by Kerensky.

On 8 November, 1917, Lenin was elected Chairman of the Council of People's Commissars by the Russian Soviet Congress. There was a threat of German invasion, and Lenin advised that Russia should sign the proposed peace treaty because, though harsh, it would at least ensure the integrity of the Russian territories. The Russian delegation failed to take Lenin's advice, and the eventual Treaty of Brest-Litovsk in March 1918 did indeed entail the loss of much of the western territory. Sometimes Lenin displayed the wisdom of a great statesman, showing real insight. But sometimes he displayed the instinct of a raw anarchist. In 1906, for instance, he calmly wrote that what he really wished to see was not the confiscation of the landlords in the interests of the peasantry as a result of legislation to that effect, but the seizure of the land by the peasantry. Only a literally lawless rush for land by the peasantry in its scores of millions would shake the fabric of the state of Russia profoundly enough for him to be able to seize power with a hope of retaining it. What he was overlooking was that anarchy is a Pandora's box. Once you have empowered people in that way, it is be difficult to get them to accept restraints and laws. In 1917 the peasantry did indeed rush lawlessly for the land. Lenin came up with a Soviet constitution, better than any constitution so far known, he said, a constitution based on seizures by any and every mob rather than on any central authority. Lenin called this principle 'the dictatorship of the proletariat'. His associates were understandably amazed and alarmed, not least because this new 'Leninism' was very different from the control by central committee that he had been advocating in the past.

On 30 August, 1918, Fanny Kaplan tried to assassinate him, but he survived. The Bolsheviks prevailed and became the Russian Communist Party. In 1921 a New Economic Policy was adopted, allowing a limited amount of private enterprise, in an effort to modernize industry and agriculture.

In May 1922 Lenin had a stroke which left him partially paralyzed on his right side and his role in government contracted. After a second stroke in December and a third in March 1923, Lenin was bedridden and unable to speak. The fourth stroke, in January 1924, killed him. Petrograd was re-named Leningrad in his honour. After his first stroke, Lenin wrote a number of papers. The most famous of these is the *Last Testament*, which criticized Joseph Stalin, the Communist Party's General Secretary since April 1922. Lenin thought he had 'unlimited authority concentrated in his hands' and asked that 'comrades think about a way of removing Stalin from that post'. Naturally, Stalin and his supporters suppressed these papers for decades. Lenin's criticism of Stalin was rich, given that he himself had virtually dictatorial powers; Stalin was simply about to assume them for himself.

Lenin's speeches and writings were highly regarded by his successors. His major contribution to Marxism were his analysis of imperialism (stressing the importance of colonies as breeding grounds for revolution) and his concept of a highly disciplined revolutionary party.

Because of his leading role in instigating the Russian Revolution, Lenin must carry the major responsibility for the blood shed and the crimes against humanity committed during that revolution. He was by far the greatest single driving force: the man who made it happen. He was responsible for the execution of the Tsar and his family; he may not have explicitly ordered it, but he created a climate within which it was bound to happen. He was responsible for unleashing the peasantry in the chaotic grabbing of property; he gave millions of people the freedom to rob thousands of others, with all the misery, unfairness and social and economic dislocation that that was bound to entail. Russia was no better off after the Revolution than it had been before, and thousands died in the process. It was Lenin who adapted Marxism as a practical instrument for socialist revolution in Asia, and therefore he was responsible for all the ills that followed – including the long, cruel, destructive reign of Stalin. It is interesting that, like Robespierre, Lenin was to a remarkable degree changed by power. He became besotted with the idea and the actuality of dictatorship, the very thing the revolution was supposed to remove.

Joseph Stalin
(1879–1953)

STALIN WAS BORN as Joseph Dzhugashvili at Gori in Georgia on 21 December, 1879. His parents were illiterate peasants: in fact, they were serfs at the time of Stalin's birth. He was severely beaten by his father, who was an alcoholic, and this bad treatment in childhood may explain his harshness and the vengeful feelings he had towards anyone who might wield authority over him.

The young Joseph was forced to work with his violent father as a cobbler until he was 11, when his father was killed in a fight. His mother enrolled him in a religious seminary with a view to his becoming a priest.

Joseph Dzhugashvili's time at the seminary brought him into contact with socialists and led to his involvement with the socialist movement. In 1899 he failed to turn up for school examinations and was expelled. For ten years after that, he worked as a political activist in Georgia. From 1902 onwards he was repeatedly arrested and sent to Siberia. He admired Lenin's idea of a strong centralist party of professional revolutionaries, and he would be one of them. His practical experience in Georgia made him useful to the Bolsheviks, and he gained a place on the

Bolshevik Central Committee in 1912. Some historians think that at this time Stalin was not a genuine revolutionary at all but a Tsarist spy infiltrating the Bolshevik movement. Certainly Stalin was capable of playing a double game like that; he was certainly not interested in personal or group loyalty. It was in 1913 that he adopted the name Stalin.

His revolutionary nickname was Koba, the name of a Georgian, Robin Hood-like folk hero. Stalin used a dozen other secret names to ensure his own anonymity before the Russian Revolution. The nickname 'Stalin', combining 'stal' (steel) with Lenin, was one of his *noms de guerre* from revolutionary days, and that was the one that stuck.

In the Russian Revolution of 1917, Stalin was at first opposed to the idea of overthrowing Kerensky's provisional government, and he was only won over to Lenin's position after Lenin returned from exile in April 1917. He played only a minor role in the Bolshevik seizure of power in November. His stand-off at this crucial moment is very peculiar, and would fit in with the idea of a lack of genuine commitment; it would also fit in with the proposition that Stalin was an observing agent rather than a real revolutionary. If so, it would account for the thoroughness of his later purges; he would want anyone who knew what he was really up to during the First World War eliminated. It is probably best to think of Stalin as a personal and political opportunist, not an idealist; like many others, he was able to exploit a chaotic political situation for personal advancement.

Stalin spent the first years after the Revolution in a sequence of senior posts in the government and party. He became General Secretary of the Communist Party in 1922, and built up the post into the most powerful position in the state.

When Lenin died in January 1924, a triumvirate consisting of Stalin, Kamenev and Zinoviev ran the party, putting themselves ideologically between Bukharin (on the right) and Trotsky (on the left). Stalin advanced a policy of building 'Socialism in One Country', in stark opposition to Trotsky's policy of 'Permanent Revolution', which would involve working towards triggering revolution in other countries. Stalin and Bukharin joined forces against Trotsky, Kamenev and Zinoviev. By 1928, Stalin had emerged as supreme leader and the following year Trotsky was exiled. After that, Stalin exercised dictatorial power until his death in 1953.

Russia was at the time of the Revolution the poorest and economically the most backward country in Europe. To modernize its economy, Stalin introduced a system of centrally-organized Five-Year Plans. These involved ambitious programmes of rapid industrialization and collectivization of agriculture. The first two plans were successful in achieving rapid industrialization. This was financed by restraining consumption by ordinary Soviet citizens and the ruthless extraction of wealth from the peasants. It was odd. Stalin came from the peasant class, yet these were the people he treated worst.

The collectivization scheme was a disaster. In

theory the large new mechanized farms would produce more food more efficiently than the small-scale and inefficient peasant farms. But collectivization meant destroying a way of life that had gone on for centuries, taking control over the land and food production away from the peasants, and their consequent loss of motivation. It also meant a drastic fall in living standards for many peasants. Many of them violently resisted the collective movement. Between 1929 and 1933 Stalin introduced shock brigades to go in and force peasants to join the collectives. Many peasants slaughtered their livestock rather than give in, leading to a major drop in food production. Stalin blamed this on the kulaks, rich peasants who were 'capitalist parasites' and therefore enemies of the people. Kulaks who resisted collectivization were to be shot, transported to Gulag labour camps or deported to remote areas.

These measures were the background to thousands of infringements of human rights, thousands of deaths and untold misery throughout the Soviet Union. The disruption caused by collectivization led to major famines and up to five million deaths in 1932–33, especially in the Ukraine and lower Volga valley. Ironically, at this time Stalin was exporting millions of tonnes of grain.

On the good side, Stalin invested heavily in the provision of basic medical services, increasing the number of doctors and launching campaigns against diseases such as typhus, cholera and malaria. Infant mortality rates steadily dropped. Education was another major growth area.

Like many other dictators, Stalin feared opposition. The fear was justified. He robbed, disinherited and killed many and there were many who would have liked to get revenge. On a day-to-day basis, he disliked attending functions where he had to cross rooms full of people; these were places where he might be assassinated, and he feared assassination. He organized a Great Purge designed to get rid of all actual and suspected political and ideological opponents. Some were imprisoned in the labour camps, some were executed after show trials, some were assassinated. Trotsky and Kirov, the Leningrad party chief, were both assassinated. Stalin is said to have personally signed 40,000 death warrants, but many more than this died. During this reign of terror, there were mass arrests, torture and executions without trial. Anyone suspected by the secret police of opposing the regime was rounded up and killed. The word 'troika' acquired a horrible new meaning – a quick trial by a committee of three – it was a euphemism for summary execution. The scale of the atrocities ordered by Stalin is hard to imagine. There were three major purges, in 1935–38, 1942 and 1945–50. During those purges about a million people were shot and millions more were deported to labour camps.

The big show trials in Moscow were intended as examples for local courts to follow across the rest of the Soviet Union. The big show trials included the Trial of the Sixteen in 1936, the Trial of the Seventeen in 1937, the Trial of the Red Army Generals in 1937 and the Trial of the

Twenty-One, which included Stalin's old colleague Bukharin, in 1938. Stalin was never to be known for personal loyalty. He ordered the assassination of Trotsky in 1940, eliminating the last of his opponents from the old Party leadership. Only two men now survived out of Lenin's Politburo, Stalin and Molotov, and Molotov must have felt very lucky to be alive, though not very safe.

Stalin had an endless capacity for evil. In addition to the judicial murders, he uprooted and deported hundreds of thousands of people. During the Second World War, he organized deportations an a massive scale. Over 1.5 million people were sent to Siberia and central Asia. The reasons given were separatist movements, resistance to Soviet rule, and collaboration with the Germans. Underneath this whole programme there seems to have been an unspoken desire for ethnic cleansing. Various ethnic minorities were removed from the Black Sea region: Tatars, Kalmyks, Chechens, Ingush, Karachai, Greeks and Armenians. The conditions under which these deportations took place were appalling. It is estimated that 60 per cent of the 200,000 people deported from the Baltic states died. Half of the Crimean Tatars died of hunger within a year of being deported.

In 1956, three years after Stalin died, Khrushchev condemned Stalin's deportations as contrary to Lenin's principles. He said the Ukrainians escaped deportation by Stalin only because there were too many of them. Not only were the deportations a savage and totally unjustified act, they left a legacy of hatred which lives on. The memory of the deportations still plays a major role in shaping and driving the separatist movements in various parts of the former Soviet Union long after Stalin's death. The Baltic States were among the first to demand independence from a collapsing Soviet Union; Chechnya still hopes for separation.

Overall, the famines, deportations, prisons, labour camps, torture and political purges accounted for around 20 million deaths, maybe more. Stalin himself was responsible for these, in many cases directly responsible by issuing direct orders, in other cases indirectly responsible by creating situations in which he knew people would die. It is said that he had to have a medical team in constant attendance at his reception desk, because people who were summoned to an interview were literally in fear of their lives and often had to be sedated either before or after seeing him. It is also said that he had a button under his desk. If Stalin was not getting the answers he wanted, or he had found out enough to be sure of the interviewee's guilt, he just pressed the button and two or three men came and dragged the interviewee away to be shot. The harshness and cruelty of the man are hard to understand, yet the simplest explanation may be the right one – that he was getting his own back for the unjustified violence he himself experienced in childhood.

Stalin got a well-deserved nasty surprise in June 1941, when Hitler broke the Molotov-Ribbentrop

Pact, which divided Eastern Europe into agreed German and Russian spheres of influence. Hitler surprised Stalin by invading the Soviet Union, with the intention of reaching, and helping himself to, the Baku oilfields on the shores of the Caspian Sea. Stalin had not expected this invasion and was not prepared for it. In fact, he was too stunned to react appropriately to the invasion for several days. The Germans advanced quickly, capturing or killing hundreds of thousands of Soviet soldiers. Stalin had very unwisely executed many of his most experienced Red Army generals. Now he needed them. Stalin addressed the Soviet Union for only the second time in his 30-year reign. On this memorable occasion he told the Russian people two very big lies – that the Germans had lost 4.5 million troops and that Soviet victory was near. Neither of these facts was true. Russian losses were staggeringly high and Russia was losing the war. Stalin had executed his generals. Now he started executing his soldiers. Order 227 (27 July, 1942) dictated that any soldier who retreated or left his position without orders would be summarily shot. He also ordered a scorched earth policy. Infrastructure and food supplies were to be destroyed before German troops could make use of them; this inevitably meant that even greater suffering was inflicted on the civilian population. In the end about 25 million Soviet citizens died in the war between Germany and Russia.

This episode was a traumatic experience for Stalin, and shaped his post-war strategy in

Europe. Communist-led governments were installed in the East European countries occupied by Soviet troops, forming a Communist Bloc. This was to be a buffer zone, protecting Russia from Germany. It was strengthened in 1955 in the Warsaw Pact. So, the freezing of eastern Europe into a Communist zone was the joint posthumous legacy of two evil dictators, Hitler and Stalin.

The knock-on effects were to be global. Many in the West believed that the Soviet Union's encroachment in Eastern Europe was a sign that the Soviet Union intended to spread Communism round the world. But that was Trotsky's aim – it was never Stalin's. Stalin only ever wanted control over the Soviet Union. The misunderstanding nevertheless led to a Cold War, a long period of distrust and tension.

In the post-war period, Stalin promoted himself as the great war-time leader who had defeated the Germans. He also cultivated the image of the wise and genial elder statesman, and the thousands of gigantic posters showed him as affable, kindly 'Uncle Joe'. Many in the West fell for this image; it was not until after his death that the full horror of the purges and the labour camps became known. In the aftermath of Stalin's death, his successors, Malenkov, Bulganin and Khrushchev, launched a programme of destalinization in an attempt to put the record straight about Stalin's period in office. Meanwhile, behind the genial smiling posters, the repression and the executions continued. In 1953, Stalin was apparently preparing a new purge – this time of Jews – but he died before he could put this scheme into action.

The West understandably treated Stalin with circumspection. One young post-war British MP, Alice Bacon, found herself lucky enough to be included in a routine diplomatic mission to Moscow, where she expected to meet British Embassy officials and maybe some Russian bureaucrats. There was a drinks party at the British Embassy in Moscow. Suddenly, without warning, the doors burst open and in walked Stalin with a group of heavies. Alice Bacon instinctively cringed for safety behind someone else as she saw Stalin advance across the room in her direction. But there was no escape. He walked straight up to her, smiling the big 'Uncle Joe' smile of the gigantic posters and asked her who she was. She told him she was a British Member of Parliament. 'Which constituency?' he asked. 'Liverpool East,' she said. 'Ah,' said Stalin, 'there are two constituencies in Liverpool: Liverpool East and Liverpool West. There is a labour dispute going on there at the moment.'. He was interested, friendly, charming. It was as if he were going back to his roots, checking on the fomenting of unrest in Georgia – but his detailed knowledge of what was going on in Britain was more than a little unnerving. How did he know there was a labour dispute in Liverpool West? Was he reading British newspapers or did he have other sources? Alice Bacon didn't ask.

On 1 March 1953, Stalin had a long dinner with Beria, Malenkov, Bulganin and Khrushchev: too long a dinner – he collapsed at the end of it. He was apparently having a stroke, though the cause of death is still uncertain; Molotov later claimed that Beria boasted to him that he had poisoned Stalin. Either way, because of the centralization of power in the person of Stalin himself, none of the others felt they could take any action. That at any rate is the story they later told, but it may instead be that they deliberately did nothing for several hours in order to ensure that he died. They were safer with Stalin dead. Everybody was safer with Stalin dead. He died four days later on 5 March aged 73. Stalin's body was embalmed and displayed, for a time, alongside Lenin's; Lenin, it should be remembered, had disliked Stalin intensely and warned his successors to get rid of him. If only they had taken his advice, Eurasia would have been spared the worst democide the world has ever seen.

Benito Mussolini
(1883–1945)

BENITO MUSSOLINI WAS born at Predappio, near Forli in Italy. His father, Alessandro Mussolini, was a blacksmith and his mother, Rosa Maltoni, was a teacher. His parents named him Benito after the Mexican revolutionary, Benito Juarez. Benito was destined to subject Italy to revolutionary change - but not for the better.

Like his father, Benito became a socialist and later a Marxist, influenced to some extent by the ideas of Friedrich Nietzsche and Georges Sorel. He qualified as an elementary schoolteacher in 1901, but emigrated to Switzerland the following year. He was unable to get work in Switzerland and after being arrested for vagrancy he was thrown out by the Swiss. He returned to Italy, where he was obliged to do his military service. There were further brushes with the police, and then he joined the staff of a newspaper in Trento in Austria in 1908. At around this time he wrote a novel, *The Cardinal's Mistress*.

Mussolini became politicized by the outbreak of the First World War, founding a newspaper, *The Italian People* and a pro-war group called Fasci d'Azione Rivoluzionaria. Mussolini coined the term 'Fascism' from the fasces, the bound bundles of rods of chastisement that symbolized the life-and-death power of the state in ancient Rome. The symbolism showed exactly what Mussolini had in store for Italy – a new and very strict Roman empire, which he said would strengthen the newly unified nation. Some historians and political observers have reflected that Mussolini wanted something quite different; he wanted a collapse of Italian society that would leave a power vacuum for him to fill. Lenin did the same in Russia.

Italy was a member of the Triple Alliance, allied with the Austro-Hungarian Empire and Imperial Germany. Italy did not join the war in 1914, but it did in the following year – as Mussolini wanted – on the side of Britain and France. Mussolini was called up for military service but, on being wounded during grenade practice, he went back to editing his newspaper – not exactly the most glorious of war records. On several occasions, Benito Mussolini comes close to being a farcical figure, but it is unwise to laugh too loud and too long at dictators. Meanwhile, in the spring of 1919, Fascism had formally developed into an organized political movement. Mussolini failed to gain a seat in parliament in the 1919 elections, but in 1921 he succeeded in winning a seat as a right-winger. The Fascisti formed armed squads made up of war veterans to spread terror among communists and socialists – and the government did nothing to stop them. In return for supporting farming landowners and industrialists, Mussolini gave his support to strike-breaking.

A sequence of short-lived liberal governments proved incapable of stopping the anarchy that Mussolini was deliberately promoting. Then the Fascists organized a menacing March on Rome in October 1922, and this had the desired effect. Vittorio Emanuele III invited Benito Mussolini to form a new government. On 31 October 1922 Mussolini became the youngest Prime Minister in the history of Italy.

The Fascist state that Mussolini set up ten years before Hitler's rise to power provided Hitler with a model that he could use in Germany.

To a great extent, Italy's Fascism was a reaction to the failure of a laissez-faire, free-market economy and to the fear of international Bolshevism. This fear was not entirely unfounded, as a Soviet was set up in Bavaria at about this time, though it didn't last very long. Fascism was also able to take over quickly and easily as there was no maturely developed tradition of parliamentary compromise; all public discourse was inflammatory and polarized. The peace treaties drawn up in the aftermath of the First World War were unsatisfactory to Italians, and there was a sense that victory had been somehow mutilated. Italy's influence in the Aegean was disregarded by the greater powers. Italy lacked colonies. As a 'victor' in the recent conflict, Italy had good reason to feel aggrieved. Faced with the alternatives of a collapse into communism or a weak withdrawal into ineffectual liberalism, Mussolini's Fascisti seemed like a viable 'third way'. It was just the right moment, and Mussolini was able to sweep to power with incredible ease.

To begin with, Mussolini was supported to a surprising extent by the Liberals. They helped him introduce censorship and alter the electoral procedures so that in 1926 he was able to assume the powers of a dictator. Then began the familiar process of managing the press to ensure that the right image of the leader was reinforced at all times. The legend of 'Il Duce' grew: the man who never slept, was never wrong, could solve all problems. It was not long before Italy was a police state. The prominent socialist Giacomo Matteotti was assassinated in 1924. This threw Italy into turmoil until Mussolini asserted his personal authority. He was a good propagandist and there was as a result very little opposition to his emergence as Italy's dictator.

After 1922, Mussolini personally managed the various ministries by turns – the interior, foreign affairs, colonial, armed services, public works. Sometimes he held as many as seven ministries at once. He was also head of the Fascist party and the Fascist militias that were responsible for stamping out any budding resistance in the provinces. It was a well-organized power structure that ensured that no rival organization or individual could emerge. Mussolini spent most of his time on propaganda exercises; here his background in journalism was invaluable to him. He made sure that he personally chose newspaper editors, and it was not possible for anyone to work in journalism unless they had been vetted by the Fascist party. Fascism was presented as the doctrine of the twentieth century.

A particularly clever diplomatic coup was the concordat signed with the Vatican in 1929. In this treaty, the Italian state was recognized by the Vatican, and the existence of an autonomous state of the Vatican City was recognized by the Italian government.

The parliamentary system in Italy was virtually abolished, although its forms were preserved. Trade unions lost their independence. All teachers had to swear an oath to support the Fascist regime; as a qualified teacher himself, Mussolini knew all too well how subversive teachers could be. To begin with, Mussolini had to play up to his financial backers to some extent, so a number of industries were transferred from public to private ownership; but this did not last, and by the 1930s he was moving back to the other end of the spectrum, exerting government control on everything possible.

Then came the things that all dictators love, the monuments, the great public works, the emphasis on heavy industry with a view to arming. He tried to make Italy self-supporting. Unfortunately, Italy was not naturally suited to be self-sufficient and the natural resources did not exist within her borders to support heavy industry. Dictators also love the idea of conquest and empire. As a young man, he had favoured pacifism and anti-imperialism. Now that he had reinvented himself as a Great Dictator, he moved towards a very aggressive nationalism. As early as 1923 he ordered the bombardment of Corfu. Then shortly afterwards he set up a kind of puppet regime in

Albania and consolidated Italy's control over Libya, which had technically been an Italian colony since 1912.

Mussolini's relationship with Germany was the most peculiar aspect of his political career. In the First World War he had supported Italy's alliance with Britain against Germany. As late as 1935 he was opposing German expansionism, helping to form an anti-Hitler front to ensure the independence of Austria. His invasion (conquest) of Abyssinia (now Ethiopia) in 1935–36 was in itself successful, but when it became clear that it was opposed by the League of Nations he changed his mind about Hitler and sought to do a deal with him; he knew Hitler had withdrawn Germany from the League in 1933. It is an extraordinary thought that, but for the need for support over Abyssinia, Mussolini might have joined in the Second World War on the side of Britain and France. As so often with dictatorships, decisions are more to do with opportunities than with principles. Once Mussolini had thrown in his lot with Hitler, and in effect backed the wrong horse, there was nowhere else he could go except the same way as Hitler. By joining Hitler in supporting Franco in 1936–39 in the Spanish Civil War, he was signing his own death warrant. After that there was no chance of a reconciliation with Britain and France.

In 1938, at the Munich Conference, Mussolini was trying to pose as a peacemaker, but his Pact of Steel with Hitler the following year confirmed Fascist Italy and Nazi Germany as the Axis powers. Mussolini's position weakened and dimmed in the shadow of the far more evil and powerful figure of Hitler. Hitler adopted a notoriously strenuous and ambitious racial policy that involved the genocide of the Jews in Europe. Mussolini lamely tagged along with this in a half-hearted way, with a desultory persecution of Jews in Italy and an apartheid policy in the Italian 'empire'. Until this time, Jews had not been persecuted by the Fascists; the important thing to Mussolini was that the leaders of all groups in Italian society had to be members of the Fascist party. Later, he was to refuse to deport Italian Jews to concentration camps, and that policy was only overridden when German troops overran Italy – in effect once Mussolini had lost power. So, from this point of view at least, Mussolini was not nearly as evil as Hitler.

As the Second World War approached, Mussolini made it plain that he intended to enlarge the Italian empire. He would take Malta, Tunis and Corsica; he spoke of this as the first phase of a New Roman Empire that would stretch from Palestine in the east to Libya in the west, from Kenya in the south to Egypt in the north. But these ambitions were wildly at variance with Italy's military and organizational capacity. Although aggressors can never be jesters and it is unwise to treat them as such, there was something almost comic about the grotesquely puffed-up dictator and his grotesquely puffed-up ambitions. Even the annexation of Albania in April 1939, a relatively small-scale enterprise, overstrained the resources of the Italian army, which was also seriously under-trained. When Germany invaded Poland it was a very different matter, and Mussolini knew it. Because his army was under-prepared, he decided to play a waiting game. He decided to remain non-belligerent until he was sure which side was going to win. This was not only totally dishonourable – it was too late. He had signed the Pact of Steel, he had supported General Franco, he had in the eyes of the world thrown in his lot with Hitler and would certainly share his fate.

In June 1940, when the German army reached the English Channel, Mussolini decided that the fall of Britain was about to take place, thanks to a German invasion, and that it was safe to declare war on Britain and France. He ordered a disastrous attack on Greece in the autumn of 1940. Undeterred, and fully confident that his much stronger ally, Germany, would defeat the Soviet Union, Mussolini declared war on the Soviet Union in June 1941.

It was obvious to most people that Mussolini was taking Italy further and further out of her depth. Italian troops were being defeated on all sides. When British and American troops landed in Sicily in 1943, most of Mussolini's associates turned against him. The turning point was a meeting of the Fascist Grand Council on 25 July 1943. Count Galeazzo Ciano, Mussolini's foreign minister, was one of the most powerful voices raised against Mussolini. This major political defeat marked the end for Il Duce. The king was able to dismiss him and order his arrest. The ex-dictator was sent to Gran Sasso, a mountain refuge in central Italy.

Mussolini was replaced by Marshal Pietro Badoglio, who declared that Italy continued to fight at Germany's side, but now the main purpose was to negotiate a surrender. On 8 September, Badoglio signed an armistice with the British-American forces in Italy.

The Germans saved Mussolini in a daring rescue that was more than he deserved, given his devious and half-hearted support for Germany. The raid was led by Otto Skorzeny. It gave Mussolini one more chance. He set up the Italian Social Republic, a Fascist mini-state in northern Italy, but he was no more than a puppet in the hands of the German army. In this strange twilight of his career, Mussolini retraced his steps back to the socialist ideas of his youth, including collectivization. He wrote his memoirs, entitled with startling and disarming honesty *My Rise and Fall*. He also – before we start to feel sorry for him – took the opportunity to get his revenge on some of the Fascist leaders who had abandoned him; he had several of them executed, including his son-in-law and ex-foreign minister, Galeazzo Ciano.

But the Allied troops were advancing inexorably northwards through Italy. They were already in the North Italian Plain. Mussolini knew now that he had to leave Italy. With his mistress Claretta Petacci, he headed for Chiavenna to board a plane for Switzerland. They were intercepted by Italian partisans, who recognized them and shot them immediately. The next day their bodies were hung, upside down, from a lamp post in the Piazzale Loreto in Milan.

Hitler was by this stage trapped in his bunker in Berlin, caught in a pincer movement by American and Soviet troops. He was deeply shaken when he heard the news. He knew the game was up for him too.

Mussolini may not have been quite as evil as Hitler, but that doesn't say much. Ineffectual though Mussolini appears on the European stage by comparison with Hitler, he played his part in encouraging Franco and Hitler, tying up Allied troops, directly causing the loss of many lives, and indirectly causing more by delaying the ending of the war. Within Italy, he was responsible for denying people the freedom of speech and freedom of information – for 20 years. He was also responsible for doing incalculable damage to the fragile new democracy that had been evolving for only a few decades. Mussolini was in effect a major setback to Italy's political and cultural development. Mussolini condemned himself several times over in his speeches. 'Blood alone moves the wheels of history. . . To make a people great it is necessary to send them to battle even if you have to kick them in the pants.' And most telling of all, 'We have buried the putrid corpse of liberty.'.

Tojo Hideki
(1884–1948)

TOJO BELONGED TO the military clique that drove Japan into the Second World War. For taking that initiative alone, Tojo must be held responsible for the loss of millions of lives. As War Minister in 1940, he led Japan into the Axis alliance with Germany and Italy. By 1941 he was Prime Minister of Japan and commander-in-chief of the entire Japanese armed forces. Given that the military dominated Japan, and Tojo controlled the military, he had acquired virtually dictatorial powers.

At the height of the Second World War, Tojo held the posts of Home Minister and Foreign Minister, as well as those of War Minister and Prime Minister. Blame for the Second World War therefore falls squarely on Hitler, Mussolini – and Tojo.

Born in Tokyo on 30 December, 1884, Tojo Hideki joined the Japanese army. His military experience included spells in Germany and Switzerland. Reaching the rank of major general in 1933, he became head of the Kwantung Army's military police in 1935 and chief of staff to the army itself two years later. In 1938 Fumimaro Kondoye made Tojo his Deputy War Minister, though Tojo was to return after only a few months in that post to take command of the army's aviation.

Tojo held extreme right-wing political views and was a natural supporter of Hitler's Germany, a natural partner in crime, though his personality was more like Himmler's than Hitler's. He also feared Russia and Stalin's long-term plans in particular. The diary he kept while in prison between the end of the war and his execution in 1948 expresses regret for the 'unfortunate' Sino-Japanese War that had gone on for four years before the outbreak of the Second World War and had been a considerable drain on Japan's resources. He presented that war as a painful and unavoidable necessity, to ensure the stability and economic development of East Asia and peace in the world at large; it was a shame that the Chinese just did not understand Japan's position. This was a grotesque distortion of the reality, and it is possible that he hoped that the statesman-like peace-loving tone of his diary might win him a reprieve from the death sentence that had already been passed on him.

An American negotiator who met Tojo in 1941 wrote that he knew he could expect little from a negotiation with him. 'He was a typical Japanese officer, with a small-bore, straight-laced, one-track mind. He was stubborn and self-willed, rather stupid, hard-working, and possessed a quantity of drive.' Tojo and the rest of his Cabinet were keen to assure the Americans that above all they wanted a negotiated solution. But at the same time Japanese army and navy officers were making inflammatory speeches, and presumably with permission from above. The Director of the naval intelligence section at Imperial Headquarters said in a public speech, 'The Imperial Navy is itching for action, when needed.' The American negotiators realised that Tojo was lying; he was eager for a war with America. Ambassador Grew confirmed in October that the Tojo Cabinet was bent on war, and that it was only pressure from the Japanese Emperor, Hirohito, that made them sue for peace.

By 1938, Tojo was advocating pre-emptive air strikes on both China and the Soviet Union. In 1941, he was (appropriately) made War Minister by Fumimaro Kondoye. He consistently advocated an extremely aggressive foreign policy. He strongly opposed Shigenori Togo's plans to withdraw Japanese troops from China and Korea. Tojo went on to become the Prime Minister of Japan on 16 October 1941.

To begin with he appeared to support his Foreign Office's efforts to reach an agreement with the United States, but war was what he really wanted. Once he believed that a negotiated deal with the US was possible, he ordered the attack on Pearl Harbour on 7 December, 1941. This unprovoked and undeclared act of war was Tojo's single most conspicuous war crime. Tojo later claimed this was a self-defensive action. An American admiral had declared that if war were to break out between Japan and the United States the Japanese navy could be sunk in a matter of weeks. Churchill had also strongly declared Britain's support for America and threatened to join in a war on Japan within 24 hours of its outbreak. Tojo argued, after the war was over, that this amounted to a massive military threat to Japan. In order to protect Japan, 'a decisive appeal to arms was made'. The Japanese decision makers agreed on war on 1 December, 1941, set up the plan to attack Pearl Harbour, though, as Tojo put it in his diary, 'we laid our plans in such a manner that, should there be progress through diplomatic negotiation, we would be well prepared to cancel operations at the latest moment that communication technology would have permitted.' In this way, Tojo tried to justify the unprovoked attack on Pearl Harbour.

Following a series of military disasters in 1944, and in particular the loss of Saipan in July, he came to realise that Japan was bound to lose the war. He resigned on 18 July. When the Second World War ended in 1945, Tojo attempted suicide. He shot himself in the chest just before he was arrested by American troops, but failed to kill himself. He recovered from his injury in hospital.

The American General Douglas MacArthur then had to decide who to try and who not to try as war criminals. The Emperor should have stood trial for the deeds done in his name but, in the end, it was clear that putting Hirohito in the dock would have been too much for the Japanese people to take. In the interests of safety and political stability, it was better not to put him on trial. MacArthur favoured putting on trial field commanders and other military personnel who had committed or permitted atrocities, whether against soldiers or civilians. 'But,' he continued, 'the principle of holding criminally responsible the political leaders of the vanquished in war was repugnant to me. I felt that to do so was to violate the most fundamental rules of criminal justice. I believed that any criminal responsibility attached to Japanese political leaders should be limited to an indictment for the attack on Pearl Harbour, since this act was effected without a prior declaration of war as required by international law and custom.' Beyond that, the matter was handed over to 'distinguished jurists' and MacArthur had only to pass on the final judgements of the tribunal and enforce the sentences. He was, at that point, only carrying out orders, which, ironically, was the defence legitimately offered by several of those tried at Nuremberg, and a defence not accepted by the Nuremberg jurists. There were, in the end, only 28 alleged Japanese war criminals, of which three died or went mad before reaching the courtroom; all the others were found guilty – including Prime Minister Tojo.

Tojo was tried by the International Military Tribunal for the Far East on multiple charges of war crimes, dozens of them. He was found guilty of waging wars of aggression, wars in violation of international law, waging war against the British Commonwealth, waging aggressive war against the Netherlands and France, and ordering, authorizing and permitting inhumane treatment of prisoners of war. On 12 November 1948 he was sentenced to death by hanging. The sentence was carried out on 23 December, 1948.

Before he was hanged, Tojo had time to think and explain himself. His diary from that time argues that Japan had not declared war on civilization. To deflect attention from his own crimes against humanity, he (quite effectively) pointed out that the West had committed crimes in the countries it had colonized. 'In the shadow of the prosperity of Europe and America, the coloured peoples of East Asia and Africa have been sacrificed and forced into a state of semi-colonization. I would point out that the cultural advance of these people has been suppressed in the past and continues to be suppressed in the present by policies designed to keep them in ignorance.' This was all true, and Tojo cunningly tried to take the moral wind out of the Allies' sails by reminding them of their own past crimes in their colonies. It was a good debating point but it was no good as a defence.

Tojo was responsible for taking Japan into a large-scale aggressive war. He was also responsible for committing many crimes against his prisoners, which flouted all the principles of modern warfare. It has been said that Tojo was responsible for the deaths of four million people. It is startling to stumble, in his diary, across comfortable sayings such as 'all nations must hate war.' But he *loved* it.

Ante Pavelic
(1889–1959)

ANTE PAVELIC WAS born on 14 July, 1889 at Bradina, 35km south-west of Sarajevo, the capital of Bosnia-Herzegovina. After completing his secondary education at a Jesuit seminary at Senj in Croatia, Pavelic studied law at the University of Zagreb. After graduating, he set up a small law practice in Zagreb, the capital of Croatia.

As a young man, Ante Pavelic joined the Croat Party of Rights (HSP), which was an extreme right-wing nationalist group that stood for Croatian separatism. The HSP disintegrated in 1908 and Pavelic joined a splinter group led by Josip Frank, becoming its secretary in 1919.

Pavelic believed fervently in a free and independent Croat state 'comprising the entire historical and ethnic territory of the Croat people'. The perceived enemies of the liberation movement were the Freemasons, the Jews, the Communists – and the Serbian government.

In 1918 a Kingdom of the Serbs, Croats and Slovenes was formed and recognized by the Paris Peace Conference a year later. It was to be ruled by the Serbian Prince Regent Aleksandar Karadjordjevicis. The new country was incredibly mixed and multicultural and no single political party would ever gain a majority in elections. The situation was volatile and unstable.

In 1927, Ante Pavelic was elected onto the Zagreb City Council. In 1928, Stjepan Radic, the leader of one of the principal political parties, the Croatian Republican Peasant Party (CRPP), was shot and killed in the Parliament building. The representatives from Croatia and Bosnia-Herzogovina boycotted the parliament, demanded a federal state and refused to acknowledge the King's authority. In a desperate measure to try to save the situation, the King suspended the constitution and declared a temporary 'Royal Dictatorship' and the country's name was officially changed to 'Yugoslavia'. But the King's desperate action simply exaggerated the deep-seated divisions.

Pavelic travelled to Vienna. While there, he took over the leadership of the Croat Youth Movement, a nationalist group that was dedicated to resisting the Royal Dictatorship. Pavelic also met a contact who provided him with an introduction to Mussolini; this was to prove a turning-point in Pavelic's political career.

In 1931 the Yugoslavian Royal Dictatorship came to an end, though the political landscape remained very rocky. Pavelic accepted an invitation from Mussolini to go to Italy, where he started to shape the Croat Youth Movement into a terrorist group. It would later come to be known as the Ustase (or Insurrection). Mussolini was able to provide Pavelic with training camps, protection and financial support. Once the terrorist campaign of bombings began in Yugoslavia, Pavelic started receiving funding from Hungary and Nazi Germany too.

On 14 October, 1934 a Ustase agent assassinated King Aleksandar while he was on a visit to Marseilles in France. Pavelic was behind this shabby act; he had bribed a high-ranking French official to make sure that security surrounding the King was lax. The King was replaced by a three-man regency, and an election was held in Yugoslavia. Now back in Italy, Pavelic found himself arrested along with other leaders of the Ustase, though the Italian authorities refused to extradite them to France, where death sentences had already been passed on them in absentia. Extradition would have meant the guillotine.

In 1939, when the Second World War began, Yugoslavia attempted to remain neutral, but came under pressure from Germany to align with the Axis powers. On 24 March, 1941 the Yugoslav government gave in to the pressure, signing a protocol of adherence to the Axis. Two days later some anti-German air force officers staged a coup, unleashing a wave of anti-German demonstrations in Belgrade. The German response was to bomb Belgrade, killing up to 17,000 Yugoslav civilians; ground troops followed.

Pavelic saw this as his opportunity. He broadcast from Italy a call on Croatian soldiers to mutiny against Serbian officers; 'We are fighting soldier to soldier with our German and Italian allies.' The Yugoslav Army collapsed in the face of the German invasion and the government fled.

On 10 April, German troops occupied Zagreb. On the same day Slavko Kvaternik, the Ustase leader in Croatia, proclaimed an 'Independent State of Croatia' (NDH). Five days later, Pavelic arrived in Zagreb, bringing his 12-year exile to an end. By 18 April, the Yugoslav Army had formally surrendered. The Germans recognized the new Croatia, and occupied most of Serbia and northern Slovenia. The Italians took southern Slovenia, much of Dalmatia and occupied Montenegro.

At Mussolini's request, Hitler agreed to make Pavelic the head of state of the new Croatia, though even Hitler must have wondered whether this was a wise move when he heard of the blood-letting that followed. Pavelic declared that his first aim was the 'purification' of Croatia and the elimination of 'alien elements' – the now-familiar slogans of fascist regimes. This marked the start of an appalling phase of ethnic cleansing, in which two million Serbs, Jews and Gypsies in Croatia were to suffer various kinds of humiliation, injury or death. Ustase storm troopers used forced religious conversion, deportation and murder to achieve Pavelic's aim, to 'kill a third, expel a third, convert a third.'. Identifying armbands were to be worn: Serbs must wear a letter 'P', Jews must wear a letter 'Z'. To add to the horror, the Catholic Church joined in the systematic persecution; the Ustase were supported by the Archbishop of Sarajevo, Ivan Saric, and Franciscan priests enlisted in the Ustase.

The massacres began on 27 April, at the Serbian village of Gudovac, and went on until the end of the war. Tens of thousands of Serbs, Jews and Gypsies died. Orthodox priests were also victimized; 131 were killed. The Ustase killed their victims by knifing and beating to death as well as shooting; some were thrown over cliffs. The brutality of the Ustase shocked the occupying German troops. The German commander in Croatia, General von Horstenau, reported to Berlin, 'The Ustasha have gone raving mad.'. He later commented that the 'Croat revolution was by far the bloodiest and most awful I have seen firsthand or from afar in Europe since 1917.'.

On 6 June Pavelic met Hitler, who agreed that Pavelic could expel the Serb population of Croatia and replace them with Slovenes.

In September 1941, a concentration camp run by the Ustase and Catholic clergy was opened at Jasenovac. There, about 200,000 prisoners were to be killed during the course of the war.

Meanwhile, a Yugoslav resistance movement was beginning to take shape, with Colonel Mihajlovic emerging as its leader. His strategy was to avoid open clashes with the Germans or Italians, but to prepare a general rising to coincide with an Allied invasion of the Balkans. Josip Broz Tito led the Partisan guerillas and favoured overt action instead. He initiated risings in July 1941, but they only led to thousands of civilian deaths in Ustase reprisals. The Germans then joined in with some reprisals of their own, executing 7,000 men and boys at Kragujevac in Serbia after a German squadron was killed in an ambush. The massacres were depressingly like the atrocities of more recent years. Tito continued undeterred.

On 16 April, 1942 Pavelic announced a scorched earth policy; anyone found in an area of Resistance activity may be executed. On 1 October, 1944, the Soviet army crossed the Yugoslav border, joining the Partisans to liberate Belgrade. The Red Army moved on towards Germany, leaving the Western Allies and the Partisans to liberate the rest of Yugoslavia. On 6 April 1945, Sarajevo fell to the Partisans. Ustase leaders fled to Austria, leaving the Partisans in charge in Croatia.

Altogether, the Ustase, Pavelic's monstrous brainchild, murdered 30,000 Jews, 29,000 Gypsies and 600,000 Serbs during his regime. Pavelic himself left Zagreb on 15 April, escaping overland to Austria. From there he went to Rome, where he spent the summer under the protection of the Catholic Church. The Allied occupying forces had information about his whereabouts, but failed to arrest him. By September Pavelic was becoming a problem. He was a very high-profile war criminal. The Allies wanted him brought to trial, but also saw that a formal extradition from the Vatican would deal a body-blow to the Roman Catholic Church. They were reluctant to act against the Pope.

In early 1948, Pavelic was moved to a monastery near Castel Gandolfo outside Rome, where he stayed disguised as a priest. Later in the year he was smuggled to Buenos Aires in Argentina by Vatican agents. There, showing no sign of repentance whatever for his past crimes, Pavelic revived the Ustase movement and became security adviser to Juan Peron, the Argentine dictator.

Back in Croatia, over 200 priests and nuns were charged with participation in Ustase atrocities. They were found guilty and executed. The Archbishop of Sarajevo was sentenced to 16 years in prison for collaboration with the Pavelic government, though he was to serve only five.

In 1957, Yugoslav agents finally caught up with Ante Pavelic in Argentina. On 9 April they tried to assassinate him; he was badly wounded in the attack, but survived. He flew to Madrid, where he died of his injuries more than a year later, on 28 December, 1959.

All the evils of the Pavelic regime have been relived in more recent years, and the way events have unfolded shows how the evil men do lives on long after their death. Pavelic died in 1959, but the Ustase that he created went on. Between 1962 and 1966 three Yugoslav diplomats were murdered by the Ustase. The Ustase claimed responsibility for the bombing of a Yugoslav airliner in 1972. In 1980, the Ustase detonated a bomb in the Statue of Liberty. There are still many in Croatia today who regard Ante Pavelic as a national hero, and long for the day when Pavelic's goal of an ethnically pure homeland is achieved. Pavelic was a self-evidently evil man, yet his portrait is still on show in places of honour in many an office of many a Croatian government and military official.

Ho Chi Minh
(1890–1969)

HO CHI MINH was born in Vietnam in 1890. His father, Nguyen Sinh Huy, was employed by the French colonial authorities as a teacher. He was a highly intelligent and able man, but he was dismissed because as a matter of principle he refused to learn the French language. To make a living, Nguyen was reduced to travelling round offering help in the form of letter writing and medical services to the peasants.

Nguyen was a committed nationalist and he brought up his children to resist French rule – and they did. Ho Chi Minh would contribute greatly to the ejection of the French from Indo-China and go on to achieve something even more remarkable, the ejection of the Americans from Indo-China too. In many respects, then, Ho would turn into a patriotic hero. But it was his refusal to compromise, his refusal to wait, that would cause so much unnecessary loss of life. If he had not involved himself in the affairs of South Vietnam, the Americans would have stayed out.

But all that lay ahead. Ho Chi Minh's sister got herself a job with the French Army, using her position to steal weapons which she hoped could one day be used to drive the French out of

Vietnam. Eventually she was caught and sentenced to life imprisonment.

Nguyen sent the young Ho to a French school, which he thought was the best way to prepare the boy in the struggle against the colonial occupation. Ho himself became a teacher for a short time before becoming a sailor. This enabled him to travel. He saw several other countries that were suffering from exploitation by the French, and this reinforced his view that the French presence in Indo-China must be ended. In 1917, Ho settled in Paris, where he read Marx and other left-wing writers; he became a convert to Communism. In December 1920 the French Communist Party was founded, and Ho was one of its founder members. Like many others in his group, Ho had been inspired by the recent Russian Revolution, and in 1924 he visited Moscow. From there he wrote to a friend that it was the duty of all Communists to go back to their own countries, 'Make contact with the masses to awaken, organize, unite and train them and lead them to fight for freedom and independence'.

Ho also knew that if he returned to Vietnam straight away he would be arrested by the French authorities, so he went instead to China, settling close to the Vietnamese border. While he was there, he organized other nationalists in exile into a Vietnam Revolutionary League. A recurring theme in his political and military strategy is co-ordination

In 1940 the Japanese invaded Indo-China. Paris was occupied by German troops, so the demoralized French troops decided not to resist; they surrendered to the Japanese. Ho Chi Minh saw this as an opportunity to liberate Vietnam, and formed a new organization called the Vietminh, which would run a guerilla war against the Japanese. The Vietminh campaign was supplied with arms by the Soviet Union. After the bombing of Pearl Harbour by the Japanese, the Vietminh got supplies from the USA as well. The events of the Second World War unfolding round them taught the Vietminh a lot about military tactics, and they were able to apply this knowledge in the following years.

When the Japanese surrendered at the end of the Second World War, the Vietminh were in a strong position to take control of Vietnam. In September 1945, Ho Chi Minh declared the foundation of the Democratic Republic of Vietnam. What Ho did not know was that Roosevelt, Stalin and Churchill had already decided at Potsdam what was going to happen in Vietnam. They had decided that Vietnam would be divided in two, the north under Chinese control, the south under British control. It turned out to be even more complicated than that, as the French decided that they wanted their colony back.

In January 1946 the British agreed to withdraw their troops from the south. Later that year the Chinese agreed to leave the north – on condition that France relinquished its claims to territory in the region. But the French did not agree. Fighting soon broke out between French troops and the Vietminh. At first the Vietminh, under General Vo Nguyen Giap, found it hard to match the highly-trained French troops. Their situation improved after 1949, when Mao Zedong and his Communist forces created a safe haven in China where they could train and care for their wounded.

By 1953 the Vietminh controlled large areas in North Vietnam, while the French kept a firm hold in the south, where they had installed Bo Dai, former Emperor of Vietnam, as head of state. The war dragged on, so the French tried to strike a deal with the Vietminh, offering to set up a national government with a view to granting Vietnam eventual independence. Ho Chi Minh did not trust the French, though, and went on fighting. This refusal to negotiate, to prefer armed struggle, was his leading characteristic. In spite of the mild and genial appearance, Ho Chi Minh was a butcher.

In France, there was general loss of confidence in the war in Indo-China. 90,000 French soldiers had been killed by 1952. France was also trying to rebuild its war-damaged economy and the foreign war was costing too much. There were also many in France who, in a post-war world, no longer believed in colonialism.

In Vietnam, the French commander General Navarre saw that time was running out and that he needed to win a quick victory. He was sure that if he could engage the Vietminh in a large-scale battle the French were bound to win it. So General Navarre set up a defensive position at Dien Bien Phu, to block the path of the Vietminh troops attempting to return to their camps in Laos. Navarre thought this would force General Giap to mount a mass attack on the French at Dien Bien

Phu. Giap took up Navarre's challenge, but in an unexpected way. Instead of mounting a huge frontal attack on Dien Bien Phu, he took his time, surrounded it and ordered his men to dig an encircling trench. Then trenches and tunnels were dug radially inwards towards the French, who were now under siege. More Vietnamese troops were brought in. By the time the battle started, General Giap had 70,000 soldiers surrounding Dien Bien Phu, five times the number of French troops bottled up inside.

Navarre realised now that he was fatally trapped and appealed for help. Some US advisers considered the possibility of using nuclear weapons against the Vietminh. Others thought conventional air raids would be enough to overcome Giap. Eisenhower, the US President, in any case refused to intervene without the participation of the other Western Allies. Churchill declined to get Britain involved while the peace negotiations were taking place in Geneva; he perhaps felt that it was through their own folly that the French had made this mess – and they should be left to get themselves out of it. It was on 13 March 1954 that General Giap launched his attack, a relentless and terrifying attack that went on for 56 days. The French were pushed into a smaller and smaller area of Dien Bien Phu. The French artillery commander, Colonel Piroth, blamed himself for the tactics that were obviously failing, told his fellow officers that he was 'completely dishonoured' and committed suicide by blowing himself up with a grenade.

On 7 May the French surrendered; 7,000 French troops had died at Dien Bien Phu, and the remaining 11,000 were taken prisoner. The next day the French announced they were withdrawing from Vietnam. An international conference agreed a division of Vietnam; North Vietnam would be ruled by Ho Chi Minh and South Vietnam would be ruled by Ngo Dinh Diem, who was strongly anti-Communist. The French would withdraw from the South and the North, the Vietminh would withdraw from the south, and the Vietnamese could choose for themselves whether they were going to live in the Communist North or the non-Communist South.

Ho Chi Minh accepted this as a temporary solution, and was sure that in the promised General Election the Vietnamese would elect a Communist government for the whole of Vietnam. Eisenhower shared Ho Chi Minh's view; 'Had elections been held at the time of the fighting, possibly 80 per cent of the population would have voted for the Communist Ho Chi Minh'. But further problems lay ahead. In 1954 the French argued that Ngo Dinh Diem, the proposed new ruler of South Vietnam, was 'not only incapable but mad'. They had a point. It turned out that Diem had no intention of holding elections that might result in a united Vietnam, and cancelled them.

Violence against the Diem regime seemed the only solution. In 1959, an estimated 1,200 of Diem's government officials were murdered by guerillas. At first Ho Chi Minh was against the idea of joining in the violence in South Vietnam and offered non-military support to South Vietnamese opposition forces. He sent a trusted adviser, Le Duan, to South Vietnam to report on the situation. Le Duan returned with the advice that North Vietnam had to encourage armed resistance to Diem; it was the only way to unite the country.

On the strength of Le Duan's advice, Ho Chi Minh sent guerilla units and encouraged the various different armed bands to join together to make a more effective resistance organization. This was agreed and in December 1960 they formed the National Front for the Liberation of South Vietnam (NLF). The Americans were later to call them the Vietcong, and they were made up of many different political and ethnic groups. They were led by Hua Tho, who was a lawyer from Saigon and, as it happened, not a Communist. The tactics of the NLF were very similar to those used by Mao Zedong in China, the tactics of guerilla warfare. Working in small cells with little knowledge of one another, little damage was done to the overall strategy if an individual was captured and tortured; he would know only about his own cell. Ho Chi Minh's speciality was an eye for effective organizational structure. The NLF were under strict instructions to do no damage to the fields and houses of the peasants, but rather to do everything they could to help them. What they actually did, of course, was to implicate the villagers in the campaign of military and political subversion, just by passing through and getting supplies from them, and drew terrible reprisals on them first from the Diem regime and later from the American troops, who notoriously engaged in village massacres.

In 1964, three months after being shot into the Presidency by the Kennedy assassination, Lyndon B. Johnson launched Operation Rolling Thunder. This was a brutal bombing campaign aimed at destroying the North Vietnamese economy and stopping the North Vietnamese from interfering any further in South Vietnam. The plan was for an eight-week campaign; it lasted for three years. In that time, the Americans dropped a million tons of bombs on Vietnam.

Ho Chi Minh himself lived through all this, dying in 1969. He was the visual stereotype of the oriental ascetic, with his emaciated figure, goatee beard, enigmatic smile, mild manner and threadbare bush jacket. He cultivated the image of a humble, benign 'Uncle Ho', perhaps with 'Uncle Joe' Stalin consciously in mind. But behind this mild image was a seasoned revolutionary. He was also totally single-minded. He wanted the French out of his country, he wanted a Communist regime, and he wanted unity. He fought three wars: one to get rid of the French, one to get rid of Diem, one to get rid of the Americans. He was not only single-minded, he was ready to lose a lot in order to win. In 1946, when war with the French was looming, he warned the French, 'You can kill ten of my men for every one I kill of yours, yet even at those odds I will win.'. The French ignored his warning, and suffered badly as a result. In a very similar way, the

Americans were the victims of cultural chauvinism. They were convinced of their own technical superiority and certain that they could win the Vietnam War fairly quickly. They were wrong too. Just like the French, they eventually had to withdraw in total humiliation. Ho Chi Minh and his supporters were too ruthless for even for the Americans to deal with.

Ho Chi Minh was responsible for much of the bloodshed by his refusal to compromise. He could have improved the lot of the North Vietnamese people by holding back from interference in the South, however unsatisfactory it might have seemed to him that unification was being postponed. North Vietnam was a poor country, in need of careful development, and it was not enriched in any way by Ho Chi Minh's doctrinaire policy regarding his neighbour. The orders he gave to the NLF for their behaviour towards the peasants were of an idealistic nature that is reminiscent of eighteenth century France. French revolutionary idealists such as Robespierre spoke in high-flown language (often drawn from Rousseau) of love, nature, peace and patriotism, while all around them, precisely because of their actions, the streets ran with blood. It was the same with Ho Chi Minh. In pursuit of the ideals of anti-colonialism, Communism and nationalism, enormous numbers of innocent Vietnamese people had to die. The sacrifices Ho made to achieve his goals were too great. General Giap spoke in 1990 about the Vietnamese struggle for independence. Asked how long he could have resisted the American onslaught, he said, 'Twenty years – maybe a hundred years – as long as it took to win, regardless of cost.'. But the cost was terrible. Three million Vietnamese people in the North and South died.

Josip Broz Tito
(1892–1980)

JOSIP BROZ WAS born in a village in Croatia, the son of a blacksmith. In the First World war he fought in Russia with the Austro-Hungarian army and was captured by the Russians. He then served with distinction in the Red Army during the Russian civil war of 1918–20. It was only some years later that Broz returned to Croatia, where he became a metal worker and also a prominent union organizer. In 1929 he was imprisoned as a political agitator for five years.

In 1937 the Comintern assigned to Broz the task of reorganizing the Yugoslavian Communist Party, and in 1941 he emerged as the leader of Yugoslavian resistance forces after the occupation of Yugoslavia by the Axis powers. He was the leader of the Partisans, the more active of the two resistance groups. It was at this time that he adopted the name Tito. The core of Tito's Partisan guerilla army was Communist, but the fast-growing force also contained many non-Communists too. Outsiders, Britain included, favoured Mihajlovic and his Chetniks, but within Yugoslavia the Partisans gained the ascendancy. At first Tito and Mihajlovic co-operated with one another, but eventually they clashed. By 1944, it was Tito who was being supported by the British – and the United States.

Tito was Secretary-General of the Yugoslavian Communist Party in the early 1940s. He was also the leader of the Partisans, the guerilla group committed to getting the troops of the fascist powers out of Yugoslavia. The Partisans' slogan was 'Death to Fascism, Freedom to the People.'. In 1941, as resistance to the German and Italian occupation of Yugoslavia was evolving, there were several groups dedicated to ousting the Axis powers. The Yugoslavian Army Colonel Draza Mihajlovic was the best known of the Chetnik commanders, and it was he who was recognized by the British government as the leader of Yugoslavian resistance to the Axis occupation. Mihajlovic's strategy was to avoid direct clashes with German and Italian troops, and instead prepare a co-ordinated general Yugoslav rising to coincide with the anticipated Allied invasion.

Tito's strategy was in conflict with the Chetnik strategy. He preferred direct action, confronting the invading German and Italian troops. In July 1941, he launched risings that were successful in that they gained control of large areas of the Yugoslavian countryside. They were on the other hand very destructive in that they prompted savage reprisals from the Ustase storm troopers; thousands of innocent civilians were killed by the Ustase in revenge.

In September 1941, the German army also hit back at the Partisan action in ambushing and killing a German squadron. A hundred Serb civilians would be killed for every German soldier killed by the Partisans. In October, 7,000 Serbian men and boys were executed. Although it was the Germans who killed these civilians, it is plain that the killings were a direct response to Partisan killings, so Tito was ultimately to blame for all the deaths.

Tito was completely undeterred by the loss of life involved in his strategy, and continued his campaign. He even extended his attacks to include the Chetniks, who were mainly anti-Communist. The Chetniks as a result began to co-operate with the Germans in the hope of preventing a Partisan victory. In 1943, Churchill, Roosevelt and Stalin agreed to give the Partisans their full support, effectively marginalizing the Chetniks. The Partisans gained additional strength in September 1944, when the exiled King called on all Yugoslavs to support them.

In March 1945, Tito became head of the new federal Yugoslav government. In the following month, Sarajevo was captured by Partisans, and soon all Yugoslavia was in the hands of the Partisans. By now, Tito was virtual dictator of Yugoslavia. His position was confirmed in November when he won a major electoral victory, though the opposition abstained, leaving Tito 80 per cent of the vote. The King, Peter II, was deposed and a republic was proclaimed.

From that moment on, Tito ruled as a dictator, suppressing internal opposition by any measures. He had Mihajlovic executed. He had the Archbishop of Zagreb jailed. He set up a highly efficient secret police. He purged dissidents in the Communist party. He nationalized industry and constructed a centrally planned economy. He did not go as far as collectivizing the land of the small farmers, but he did force them to give large portions of their produce to the state.

Tito's Yugoslavia was closely associated with the Soviet Union, but like Ceausescu's Romania often followed independent policies. Tito was not afraid to block the activities of Soviet agents in his country.

Tito was ready to accept loans from the Western powers but at least to begin with he did not let that affect his internal programme. In his later years, though, he did relax many of the stricter aspects of the regime, particularly those affecting small farmers. So it was that in those later years Yugooslavia became the most liberal of the Communist countries in Europe.

Tito's foreign policy was ambitious. He was on good terms with President Nasser of Egypt and Prime Minister Nehru of India, and he tried to develop common policies among the non-aligned nations, in other words those not firmly in the Eastern or Western blocs. In this he was unsuccessful. His relations with the Soviet Union were sometimes friendly, sometimes hostile, as would be likely with Yugoslavia following its own independent line. Tito joined Ceausescu in opposing the Soviet intervention in Czechoslovakia in 1968.

In 1963, Tito's term of office was made unlimited: he was to be dictator for life. He tried in 1971 to set up a succession for the leadership of Yugoslavia after his death. This consisted of a 22-man collective presidency; the members were the presidents of the provincial assemblies.

Attila the Hun on his deathbed. One of the most feared and notorious barbarians of all time, Attila is believed to be of distant Mongol stock. He ravaged much of the European continent during the 5th century AD. According to legend, Attila was as great a menace to the Teutonic tribes people as he was to the Romans.

King Henry VIII, a ruthless dynast who ruled England from 1509-1547. During the course of his reign, he married six times, beheaded two of his wives, broke with the Catholic Church, and dissolved the monasteries in order to gain more land for the crown and gentry.

Mata Hari – an image of her life as a dancer prior to the great war. She was executed in 1917 in front of a firing squad after being found guilty of espionage.

Benito Mussolini delivering a speech to his troops in Italy in 1932. Prior to WWII Mussolini was regarded as a hero by his people, but this soon changed when he became an ally of Hitler, a move that was to ruin Italy and its people.

Adolf Hitler was an architect of evil – he mesmerized a nation and terrorized the world. Here he is seen addressing the crowds through a radio microphone.

Portrait of Pol Pot in his guerrilla base near Thai-Cambodia border.

The bloodthirsty Pol Pot turned the limestone mountain area, about 30 km northwest of Phnom Penh, into a huge prison where many Kampucheans were killed.

A photo of Saddam Hussein after his capture on December 14, 2003. US forces found Saddam, dirty and sporting a greying beard, hiding in a cellar near his hometown of Tikrit. Until then he had been as elusive as al Qaeda chief Osama bin Laden and Taliban leader Mullah Omar.

A wanted poster printed on a full page of a New York newspaper for Saudi-born militant Osama bin Laden. Osama bin Laden was named by US President George W. Bush as the prime suspect in the attacks in New York and Washington on September 11, 2001.

Harold Shipman has the doubtful distinction of being the most prolific serial killer in the history of Britain. Whilst in Shipman's care, 459 of his patients died. Although some of these would have been natural deaths, it is estimated that Harold Shipman killlled between 200 and 400 patients.

Mao Zedong
(1893–1976)

MAO WAS BORN on 26 December, 1893 in the village of Shao Shan in Xiangtan County. He was the son of a moderately prosperous peasant farmer, and the eldest of four children. In his youth, during 1911, he served in the Hunan provincial army, afterwards returning to school, where he became very keen on physical fitness and collective action. In 1918, Mao graduated from Hunan Normal School, travelling to Beijing with his teacher and future father-in-law Professor Yang Changjin. This was during the May Fourth Movement, when Yang was lecturing at Peking University.

On Yang's recommendation, Mao worked under the head of the university library. He also married Yang Kaihui, a Peking University student. When Mao was 14, his father had arranged a marriage for him with a girl in the same village, Lo-Shi, but Mao never accepted this marriage.

Mao spent the early 1920s travelling round China, eventually returning to Hunan, where he took the lead in promoting workers' rights and collective action. In 1921, when he was 27, Mao attended the First Congress of the Communist Party of China in Shanghai, and two years after that he was elected to the Party's Central Committee, and then became director of the Peasant Training Institute. In 1927 he was sent to Hunan province to report on recent peasant risings; his report is regarded as the first important statement of Maoist theory. It was at this time that Mao developed many of his political theories, the most important one being that peasants are the source of revolution. Traditional Marxist-Leninist thinking had it that it was urban workers who led the way to revolution, but Mao argued that in China it would be the rural peasants. He also developed a three-stage theory of guerilla warfare and a concept of a 'people's democratic dictatorship'.

The first attempt at revolution was a failure. Mao led the Autumn Harvest Rising at Changsa in Hunan in 1927, and was lucky to survive. He was being led to execution when he managed to escape from his guards. Together with a band of guerillas, he took refuge in the Jinggang Mountains in south-east China. There, between 1931 and 1934, he helped set up the Chinese Soviet Republic and was elected its chairman.

Mao's first wife was killed by KMT (enemy) forces, and Mao then married He Zizhen. By now Chiang Kai-shek, who had assumed partial control of China, was determined to eradicate the Communists. To avoid being encircled by Chiang Kai-shek's KMT forces, the Communists set off on 'The Long March', which was in effect a retreat from Jiangxi in south-east China to Shaanxi in the north-west. It was during this arduous journey, almost 10,000 km long, that Mao emerged as the natural leader. Mao divorced He Zizhen and misguidedly married the actress Jiang Qing.

After China defeated Japan, the country disintegrated into civil war, in which the Communists defeated the Kuomintang. Mao set up the People's Republic of China in October 1949. It had taken Mao and the Communist Party 20 years to achieve it. Mao became Chairman of the new republic. His main programme now was a phase of fast, forced collectivization, which went on until 1958. Mao also indicated that he was willing to consider different views about the way China should be ruled. Given this opportunity, many Chinese people voiced their doubts about the dogmas of the Communist Party. Mao reversed his policy and rounded up his critics in an Anti-Rightist Movement.

Then came Mao's Great Leap Forward, which was supposed to be a programme of economic growth based on different principles from the Soviet model, which had depended on the development of heavy industry. True to his initial beliefs, Mao based his Great Leap on agricultural growth and the development of small-scale industry. In the midst of this, Khrushchev withdrew the technical support that the Soviet Union had been supplying, because Mao was too aggressive in his demands to precipitate worldwide Communist revolution. Mao was in still greater difficulties because of droughts. The Great Leap came to an end in 1960. Both Chinese and outside observers now see the Great Leap Forward as a fiasco that led to millions of deaths.

A fundamental difference of view led to a distinct cooling of relations between Russia and China in the 1960s.

In the light of all of these economic, social and political failures, other Communist Party members decided that Mao should relinquish power; they included Liu Shaoqi and Deng Xiaoping. Instead of ousting him altogether, they wanted to keep him as a figurehead, but take away his authority. Mao's response to this palace coup was to try to rally the Chinese people in a quite extraordinary way. In his Cultural Revolution, power was given directly to the Red Guards, groups of young people who set up their own tribunals. The Cultural Revolution was an even bigger catastrophe than the Great Leap Forward. It led to the destruction of much of China's heritage, the pointless imprisonment of huge numbers of Chinese academics, and general social chaos.

In 1969, Mao declared that the Cultural Revolution was over. The last years of his life were marked by declining health and the onset of Parkinson's disease, while various factions within the Communist Party squabbled over the succession, jockeying for position in anticipation of Mao's death. Curiously, it was in this final, pathetic decade of disempowerment that Mao created a personality cult in which his image was displayed everywhere and quotations from his writings were included in bold or in red in every conceivable kind of text.

The legacy of Mao is complex. The Great Leap Forward was a terrible economic and social failure. The Cultural Revolution was an even bigger failure. Huge numbers of people died in the aftermath of the Chinese civil war. On the other hand, the numbers of deaths were small compared with those resulting from famine, anarchy and foreign invasion in the period before the Communists took over, and Mao did give China a period free of foreign domination, which it had not enjoyed for a very long time. During Mao's time literacy rates rose from 20 to 93 per cent and life expectancy had risen to over 70 years.

The improvement in life expectancy may not have been due to Communism, though; there were similar improvements in Taiwan, which was ruled by Mao's political enemies. Mao has been denounced for failing to promote birth control; this failure led to a rapid and unmanageable population increase which forced later Chinese leaders to adopt the over-strenuous one-child policy. Another harmful effect of Mao's life has been the imitation of Maoism in communist countries around the world, spawning aggressive revolutionary movements such as the Shining Path in Peru and the Khmer Rouge in Cambodia. While other less economically developed countries have been busily (and often very destructively) imitating Mao and trying to follow his principles, China itself has moved sharply away from Maoism.

In China the official view of Mao Zedong is that he was a great revolutionary leader who made serious mistakes in his later life. The cult of personality in particular is deplored. He is widely regarded as an heroic figure in the first half of his life and an evil egotistical monster once he gained power. He was 'the Four Greats': 'Great Teacher, Great Leader, Great Supreme Commander, Great Helmsman.'. One curious thing about Mao is that, in spite of the apparent radicalism of his political theory, he actually turned into something remarkably close to an ancient Chinese emperor once he was in power – autocratic, self-obsessed, dictatorial, cruel and heedless of the needs of his people. It is as if China has been unable to escape its own past. Even the most radical political thinker and activist imaginable ended up turning into something very like the Qin Emperor.

Kim Il Sung
(1912–1994)

KIM SONG JU was born in Mangyongdae near Pyongyang in North Korea on 15 April, 1912. It is thought his family were middle class. He was the eldest of three sons. The younger brother died young, but the youngest served with Kim until the 1970s. In 1919 Korean intellectuals called for independence from Japan, triggering protests against Japan right across Korea. This brought a harsh response from the Japanese. Kim's family, who were actively opposed to the Japanese, moved away from Korea to Manchuria, where Kim was able to attend a Chinese school. In 1923 Kim returned to Pyongyang for two years' schooling, but was then taken back to Manchuria to continue his education.

Kim's father died aged only 32 in 1926. Three years later, while attending Yuwen Middle School in Manchuria, Kim was sent to prison for being a member of a subversive student group led by the South Manchurian Communist Youth Association. Released the following May, he joined the Anti-Japanese United Army; in 1932, when his mother died, he became the unit leader. At around this time Korean military leaders became involved in the anti-Japanese resistance. More than 200,000 Koreans and Chinese joined guerilla groups, but the

Japanese mounted a bloody counter-insurgency campaign and that number was greatly reduced.

Kim emerged now as an efficient resistance leader, with about 300 men under his command. The Japanese found him sufficiently dangerous to form a special unit to track him down. It was at this time that Kim adopted his new name, Kim Il Sung.

In 1937, when the Second Sino-Japanese War broke out, Japan cracked down hard on dissidents in Korea. Koreans were now required to take Japanese names and to speak Japanese. Kim's wife, Kim Hye Sun, was captured by the Japanese on 6 April 1940 and later killed. By 1941, Kim himself was the only surviving leader of the Anti-Japanese United Army still operating in Manchuria. He decided to flee with 120 of his men across the border into Siberia, where they were forced to join a Soviet guerilla group and assigned to intelligence-gathering in Manchuria. To this end, Kim was given training in espionage, radio communication and sabotage. He had no choice but to stay with the Soviets until the end of the war.

In 1942, Kim's son Kim Jong Il was born to his second wife, Kim Chong Suk, at Khabarovsk. The personality cult that was later elaborately built up around Kim and his son would have it that Kim Jong Il was born in a log cabin on North Korea's highest and most sacred mountain, Paektu-san, on the border of North Korea and Manchuria. To add to the mythic nature of this birth, it would later be said that it was accompanied by a double rainbow, and a bright star in the sky, and a swallow descending from Heaven. None of this is true. Kim Jong Il was born in an army camp in the Siberian town of Khabarovsk.

On 14 August 1945 Japan surrendered, bringing both the Second World War and the Second Sino-Japanese War to a dramatic end. Korea was suddenly a power vacuum. The country was divided into two, with the USA administering the south, and the Soviet Union administering the north. This division was intended to be temporary, to make handling the surrender of Japanese troops easier, but it became permanent as the Cold War set in. Kim and 40 of his guerillas returned to Pyongyang in September, aboard the Soviet warship Pukachev. Kim was selected by the Soviet secret police to take control of the creation of a provisional government for North Korea.

In 1946 the Korean Workers' Party was set up under the joint leadership of Kim Tubong and Kim Il Sung. The KWP introduced a series of reforms that included an eight-hour working day, equality of the sexes, and the suppression of religion. Soviet-style economic planning was introduced. The following year, the People's Committee of North Korea was formally set up, with Kim Il Sung as its leader. North Korea refused to abide by a United Nations resolution demanding a general election to determine the government of a unified Korea. Elections meanwhile went ahead in South Korea, where a democratically elected republic was established in August 1948. Already Kim Il Sung was acting undemocratically; it was a hint of the out-and-out dictatorship that was shortly to come.

In 1948, any opponents to Kim within the KWP were purged in order to ensure his absolute power. In 1949, the USA started withdrawing its troops from South Korea. Kim indicated that he saw this withdrawal of the peace-keeping force as a prelude to an invasion of North Korea by the South; he was bullish about it – he would both fight and win a war of reunification. This entirely unnecessary aggressive war was vetoed by Stalin, even though it was at the time assumed in the West that the invasion was Stalin's idea. What Stalin did, unwisely, was to offer military support to enable Kim to build up a strong 'defensive' force along the frontier with South Korea. The border was fortified. The Chinese leader, Mao Zedong, also told Kim that the time was not right for a pre-emptive invasion, asking him at least to wait until the Communists were in full control in China itself.

But in 1950, Kim went to Moscow to try again to persuade Stalin that he could win a war with South Korea. Then he went to Beijing to try to persuade Mao. Both Stalin and Mao said he could go ahead, though they were reluctant and it seems extraordinary that Kim should have thought he knew better than either of them. Kim's invasion of South Korea was totally unprovoked and illegal. The UN condemned it as 'initiated without warning and without provocation, in execution of a carefully prepared plan.'. The UN demanded that the North Korean troops withdraw. Kim refused, so the UN authorised military action against North Korea. It was the third time Kim Il Sung had gone against United Nations rulings, a sure sign that he was an extremely dangerous dictator.

The initial invasion of South Korea was almost totally successful, but then the American-led UN Command force arrived, launching a surprise counter-offensive behind the North Korean lines and driving Kim's army almost back to the Chinese border. Then Mao intervened, sending a massive army numbering three million to push the UN army back. The Korean War ended in July 1953, after which a 2 km wide demilitarized zone was set up along the border.

The Korean War was short and localized, but incredibly intense and bloody, with huge losses of life. North Korean casualties included 419,000 dead and 304,000 wounded. Chinese casualties included 445,000 dead and 487,000 wounded. South Korean casualties included 58,000 dead and 175,000 wounded. US casualties included 54,000 dead and 103,000 wounded. The loss in human life had been horrific. In addition, through much of Korea, and especially the North, a lot of the basic services had been destroyed. A poor country had been made even poorer, by the stupid aggressive policy of the man the North Koreans would be brainwashed into idolizing – Kim Il Sung.

In September 1953, senior people within the KWP attempted to overthrow Kim Il Sung. Eleven of the conspirators were put on trial, found guilty and later executed. A purge of KWP members followed, to remove anyone from South Korea. Later purges were to remove pro-Chinese and pro-Russian members. Like all dictators who feel threatened by dissidents, Kim set up a harsh deterrent regime. He set up seven huge penal labour colonies, similar to the Soviet camps, where 'political' prisoners could be sent. Up to 200,000 were held in these colonies. Most of the people incarcerated there were found guilty of trivial offences which nowhere else in the world would be regarded as offences at all, such as reading a foreign newspaper or singing a South Korean pop song. But these minor infringements were enough to get people sent to the labour camps, and it was often for life.

Maddest of all was Kim's decree about sentencing. 'Factionalists or enemies of class, whoever they are, their seed must be eliminated through three generations.' What this meant in real terms was that not only was a political criminal (of the newspaper-reading type just described) sentenced to life imprisonment – so were his children and their children. It was one of the cruellest and wickedest decrees of all time.

In 1955, just as Kim began to preach self-reliance to his people, he with unconscious irony went on a tour of China, the Soviet Union and Eastern Europe to raise loans for the rebuilding of his country's damaged infrastructure. Kim also began to set up a personality cult around himself, similar to those surrounding Mao in China and (until relatively recently) Stalin in the Soviet Union. Kim had become 'iron-willed, ever-victorious commander', 'the great father', 'the sun of the nation', 'the supreme brain of the nation', 'the matchless patriot' and many other marvellous things besides. The North Korean media, state-controlled, inevitably, promotes a substantially laundered and mythicized version of Kim's biography.

By the late 1980s, Kim had raised over 34,000 monuments to himself. His portrait was everywhere, in private houses, in offices, even on items of clothing. The calendar had been rewound to start in the year of the Great Father's birth, so that 1912 became Year 1. Questioning and dissent became illegal. All religion was illegal except the worship of Kim Il Sung. Here we see symptoms of the endlessly repeating pattern of power-mania, the leader spiralling out of control like a Messerschmidt in flames.

The personality cult was extended to include Kim's son, as you will remember – the one who wasn't born on the sacred mountain. He became 'Dear Leader' and 'Genius of Ten Thousand Talents'.

The Soviet-style development programme was initially quite successful, but flagged in the 1980s. The main problem was the dependence on aid, and North Korea had to bear the shame of becoming the first Communist country to fail to repay its loans from free-market countries. By 1986, Kim had got his country a spectacular six billion dollars into debt.

In 1967 Kim became a target of Mao's Cultural Revolution. Red Guards denounced him as a counter-revolutionary revisionist and as – what could be worse? – a millionaire. The following year, North Korean commandoes tried to assassinate the South Korean President Park Chung Hee. Kim claimed to know nothing about it. Several further incidents happened during the next few years, as Kim tried to infiltrate South Korea. In 1972 Kim stepped down as head of government though not head of state. Kim's 60th birthday celebrations triggered new heights in the deification of the leader and a bronze statue of Kim 21 metres high was unveiled. Further attempts on the life of the South Korean President Hee resulted in the killing of President Hee's wife in 1974.

In 1982, Kim Il Sung celebrated his 70th birthday, though the old man showed no sign of receding into the background; he had been enjoying the limelight too much for too long. Kim Il Sung's 70th birthday was celebrated with the opening of an Arch of Triumph and the Juche Tower, a larger version of the Washingon Monument, featuring one block of granite for each day of Kim's life. In 1983, North Korean agents tried to kill the South Korean President again, while on a visit to Burma; the bomb killed 17 people, but not the President. The South Korean President, now President Chun, made a formal complaint. Kim Il Sung replied that the South Korean President's statement was 'a preposterous slander' and that President Chun masterminded the bombing himself for a 'hideous purpose' – presumably to frame Kim. But further plots by North Korean agents to kill Chun were to be uncovered.

In 1986, North Korea acquired a nuclear

reactor. It was widely feared that this announced an intention of developing nuclear weapons, that would be used against South Korea, and this was confirmed by Kim three years later. In 1987 a South Korean passenger plane was blown up and destroyed off the coast of Burma; two North Korean agents were tried and convicted of the crime. The following year US Secretary of State James Baker declared North Korea 'a country which has repeatedly provided support for acts of international terrorism'.

By the 1990s, the huge loans, the mounting interest debts they trailed behind them and the over-spending on soldiers and weapons had all put the North Korean economy into serious decline. Industrial output fell. Kim was wasting up to a quarter of the country's income on the military.

In 1992, Kim Il Sung began handing over some of his roles to his son and appointed successor. But he still had not let go of the idea of unifying Korea, calling for an 'end to the national division'. Kim had a third wife, Kim Song Ae, whom he married in 1962, and he had four children with her. One of these, a son called Kim Pyong Il was becoming prominent in Korean politics, so Kim Il Sung had him banished; he was made Ambassador to Hungary to avoid a power struggle with the favourite son. In response to repeated UN queries, Kim Il Sung denied that North Korea had, or had been developing, nuclear weapons; UN weapons inspectors were nevertheless denied access. North Korea confirmed that a ballistic missile capable of delivering a nuclear warhead to

Japan was being developed; a provocative test of this missile was conducted over the Sea of Japan in May 1994.

Kim Il Sung died suddenly in Pyongyang on 8 July 1994 of a heart attack. It later emerged that the heart attack was brought on by a row with his son, Kim Jong Il. The state funeral on 18 July was the occasion of a great and heartfelt outpouring of grief among the thoroughly indoctrinated population of North Korea. The funeral marked the start of a three-year period of national mourning. Kim Il Sung, like all dictators, made the people in his country see everything through a kind of kaleidoscope of his own design. The whole population was conditioned to see him, his past, his policies, themselves and the place of North Korea within the world through a distorting lens of Kim Il Sung's making. No doubt many North Koreans still think Kim was the best possible leader. But he was a great transgressor of human rights. He was running an international terrorist operation. He did try to assassinate two successive Presidents of the neighbouring state. He did set up concentration camps for alleged dissidents, many of whom had committed very minor offences. Worst of all, he was guilty of causing hundreds of thousands of deaths by causing the Korean War. As an enemy of the human race, Kim Il Sung knocks Saddam Hussein into a cocked hat. Presumably the Americans decided to turn a blind eye on North Korea because of their memories of Korea in the '50s – and Vietnam in the '60s.

Ferdinand Marcos
(1917–1989)

FERDINAND MARCOS WAS born at Sarrat in Ilocos Norte at the north-west tip of Luzon on 11 September, 1917 and became the tenth President of the Republic of the Philippines. His parents were teachers. He studied law at the University of the Philippines, where he came first in the bar exams.

He was, in spite of his profession, engaged in criminal activity from an early age. In April 1939, at the age of only 21, he was arrested for the murder of a political rival of his father, which meant, among other things, that he had to complete his law studies in prison. In September 1939 Marcos stood trial for murder and he was found guilty. Given Marcos's record in later life, and in particular his evident complicity in the assassination of Benigno Aquino, his own political rival, in later years, it seems all too likely that the young Marcos was guilty. The following year, Marcos staked everything on his recent law training by representing himself in his appeal against the murder conviction. The conviction was overturned and Marcos became a trial lawyer in Manila.

In the Second World War, Marcos served as an

officer in the Philippine armed forces. After the war he claimed to have led a band of guerillas, the Maharlikas, against the Japanese, but it was later discovered that he played no part in anti-Japanese activity. Dictators have a habit of revamping their CVs in this sort of way. In 1946 he returned to his law practice, becoming an aide to Manuel Roxas, the first President of the Philippines, in the following year. In 1949 Marcos was elected as Liberal party representative for his home province in the Philippine Parliament, becoming the youngest ever Philippine MP. From the beginning, he used his political position dishonestly, for personal enrichment, and he quickly became a millionaire.

In 1957 Marcos married Imelda Romualdez. In 1959, he moved from the lower house to the Senate, becoming the opposition leader in parliament. In 1961, Marcos stood down from his candidacy as Liberal Party candidate for the Presidency, on the understanding that he would be supported for the nomination next time round, in 1965. In 1963 he was elected President of the Senate. The following year the Liberal Party refused to honour the agreement made in 1961, having decided in the meantime, for some reason, that they did not after all want Marcos for President, so Marcos promptly changed his allegiance to the Nationalista Party. In November 1964 he was nominated as the Nationalista candidate for the following year's presidential election, which he won, defeating Diosdado Macapagal. The land reforms he promised would never be carried out, but the promise to improve living conditions for average Filipinos was achieved through a big programme of public works; he helped to form the Assocation of Southeast Asia Nations in 1967. In 1969, Marcos became the first president in the short history of democracy in the Philippines to win a second term, but from then on the situation deteriorated. Whether he was the worst President of the Philippines is for history to decide, but he was without doubt the least democratic.

Economic growth slowed down, the quality of life declined, crime and violence increased. General dissatisfaction with the state of affairs led to increasing social unrest. Students tried to storm the president's mansion on 30 January 1970 and there were random protest bombings in the city of Manila. Marcos blamed left-wing agitators for the disturbances and suspended habeas corpus in August 1971. Marcos's opponents tried to introduce a blocking provision to prevent Marcos remaining head of state at the end of his second term, but Marcos got this overturned in 1972.

Marcos alleged that there had been an assassination attempt against his Defence Minister and declared martial law on 21 September. Later it was revealed that the assassination attempt was a piece of play-acting staged by the military. Leading opposition figures, including Benigno Aquino, as well as journalists and labour activists, were arrested and detained in army compounds. Newspapers were shut down. Strikes were outlawed.

In 1973 a new constitution was introduced; this allowed Marcos to stay in power indefinitely – for life – and rule by decree. This measure was approved by a rigged referendum. Imelda Marcos was made Governor of Manila and Minister of Human Settlements and Ecology. Industries were nationalized or handed over to Marcos's relatives or friends in an orgy of nepotism. In the time-honoured way, absolute power led on to ever-madder and ever-more corrupt decision-making. The wealth of the Philippines, once a prospering country, was siphoned off and mismanagement escalated.

Worse still was the increasing overriding of human rights. The army had unrestricted powers to search, arrest and detain civilians. The civilian courts were stripped of their autonomy and authority. Over 60,000 people were arrested in the five years after 1972. Political prisoners were routinely subjected to torture. Suspected political activists often 'disappeared'. The increasing brutality of the Marcos regime caused a great many Filipinos to turn to the Communists for support.

The patterns repeat in one dictatorship after another. Like most dictators, Ferdinand Marcos wanted grand monuments to himself, and the bigger the better. Marcos ordered a Mount Rushmore type of monument, a gigantic portrait of himself sculpted into a hillside. It was subsequently destroyed by Communist rebels.

The turning-point in Marcos's career was the way he dealt with one of his major political rivals and critics, Benigno Aquino. Marcos was by this stage so used to getting his own way, so used to 'disappearing' dissidents and opponents, that he took an absurd risk – assassinating a much-respected rival in public in front of the world's press. It was the biggest mistake of his life.

In 1977, Benigno Aquino, the opposition leader, was tried by a military court, convicted of subversion and sentenced to death. The sentence was not carried out. In 1980, Aquino, who was ill, was released to get medical treatment in the USA, where he remained as leader of the opposition in exile. In 1983, in full knowledge of the risk that he was taking, Aquino decided to make the heroic decision to return to the Philippines to help bring the Marcos regime to an end. As the plane landed he gave a filmed interview to journalists in which it was clear that he understood the danger that he was in. Just moments after stepping onto the runway while disembarking from his plane at Manila, Aquino was shot in the head. The lone assassin was shot dead on the spot by soldiers who happened to be close by. Marcos claimed that the assassin was a Communist, but an enquiry found that Marcos's own military conspired to assassinate Aquino. Marcos rejected the enquiry's finding and the suspects were released.

It was the last straw. Aquino's funeral attracted hundreds of thousands of mourners, who assumed that Marcos was behind the murder. It became the largest popular demonstration in the history of the Philippines and it marked the beginning of the People's Power movement; this was led by Aquino's widow, Corazon Aquino.

The economy of the Philippines had virtually

ground to a halt under the weight of mismanagement by Marcos's friends and relations, and the business community began to denounce the Marcos regime. What had once been South East Asia's strongest economy was now one of its poorest. Communist support gradually grew. The results of the 1986 election gave Marcos as the winner, but there was a widespread conviction that the election had been rigged. The Defence Minister, the Police Chief and the Vice Chief of Staff of the Armed Forces rebelled against the flagrant injustice; it was very clear during the run-up to the election that Mrs Aquino had a huge popular following and therefore should have won the election. With the backing of the Church and the people, the rebels called on Marcos to resign. Mrs Aquino assumed, rightly, that she had won the election, and she went on to become President in Marcos's place.

On 25 February, 1986 the Marcoses abandoned their presidential palace and flew to Hawaii. Ferdinand Marcos's 25-year regime had come to a sudden end. Corazon Aquino was sworn in as president. Marcos arrived at Hawaii airport with suitcases loaded with jewels, 24 gold bars and certificates for billions of dollars' worth of gold bullion. His Swiss bank accounts were estimated to contain up to five billion dollars stolen from the Philippines. It would be appropriate for all of this loot to be returned to the Filipinos, but the exact whereabouts of the stolen Marcos billions remain a mystery, in spite of extensive investigation by US officials.

In 1987 Marcos was conspiring to launch an invasion from Hawaii to re-establish his position, but it was no use. Moves were afoot in the USA to put him on trial for a variety of offences including mail fraud, misappropriation of property and obstruction of justice. But the game was up in more ways than one. His life was running out. On 28 September 1989 he died of kidney failure in Honolulu, Hawaii. Imelda Marcos eventually managed to get permission for her husband's body to be returned to the Philippines. It is currently contained in a glass box at his birthplace in Ilocos Norte, Luzon.

The Federal Grand Jury attempted to pin some of the blame on Mrs Marcos, but when she was brought to trial in July 1990 she was acquitted. In a trial in the Philippines, Imelda Marcos was successfully convicted of embezzlement. In the popular press, Imelda Marcos became something of a figure of ridicule, because of the pseudo-royal lifestyle she adopted, as witnessed by the thousands of pairs of shoes she left behind when she left the presidential palace in such a hurry.

The problem of compensating people, indeed whole peoples, for the injustices they experience at the hands of people like the Marcos family has never been resolved. How do you make up for a ten-year reign of terror? Obviously lives that have been lost cannot be brought back, but money and property that have been stolen can be returned, though even that has proved very difficult to do. In 1994 the District Court of Hawaii awarded close to 2 billion dollars in damages to the victims of the Marcos regime but, extraordinarily, a court in the Philippines blocked payment in 1999. In 2003, the Philippine Supreme Court ruled that 700 million dollars of the Marcos fortune must be handed over to the Philippine government to pay for the distribution of land to poor farmers, but the Marcos family blocked this with an appeal. The situation became more complicated still in September 2003, when the District Court of Hawaii slapped a global freeze on Marcos assets. In November, the Philippine Supreme Court criticized the Hawaiian court for overreaching its jurisdiction.

Ferdinand Marcos's legacy to the Philippines is all too obvious. Not only did he leave thousands of people dead, he also left the country's democracy in ruins after years of rule-bending and ballot-rigging, with corrupt practices and procedures firmly entrenched, and institutionalized nepotism on a grand scale. He left the economy in ruins, and the country struggling just to pay the interest on the huge foreign debts that he took on. One of the big prestige projects for which he borrowed a huge sum of foreign capital was a nuclear power station. This was built at the junction of three plate margins, deep faults in the earth's crust where big earthquakes are likely to happen. It is an extremely dangerous place to build a nuclear power station and it can never be operational. It was a complete waste of money. It was a typical dictator's white elephant.

It took Ferdinand Marcos 20 years to loot and wreck the Philippines. Unfortunately it may take a lot longer for that damage to be repaired.

Nicolae Ceausescu
(1918–1989)

NICOLAE CEAUSESCU WAS born of Romanian peasant stock and educated at the Academy of Economic Studies at Bucharest. He joined the Communist Party when he was 15 and during his youth he was imprisoned twice for anti-fascist activities. In 1945, Ceausescu became Secretary of the Bucharest branch of the party and climbed gradually to power through a succession of promoted positions within the party.

He became Secretary-General of Romania's Communist Party in 1965 after the death of Gheorghe Gheorgiu-Dej. In 1967 Ceausescu also became President of the State Council, which meant that he now occupied the leading posts in both party and state. He was elected President of Romania in 1974. His nationalist stance won him initial popularity among Romanians; he showed a certain degree of courageous independence from Moscow, refusing to break diplomatic ties with Israel in 1967 and even daring to condemn the invasion of Czechoslovakia by Warsaw Pact troops in 1968.

His independent line similarly won him friends abroad, and US President Nixon visited him in 1969. Ceausescu was invited on state visits to

France, the USA and UK. He stayed as a guest of the Queen at Buckingham Palace in 1979. Romania was given 'Most Favoured Nation' status by the USA and the first formal pact (on textiles) to be made between the EU (then the EEC) and an Iron Curtain country. As the leader of the only East European country to recognize both Israel and Egypt, Ceausescu was able to help to arrange Anwar Sadat's historic peace-making visit to Israel in 1977.

That, as far as the West was concerned, was the positive face of Nicolae Ceausescu: a friendly face behind the Iron Curtain. But behind this mask of friendship was a fearful Stalinist regime with a terrible record of human rights infringement, including persecution of ethnic Hungarians. Ceausescu went on visits to China and North Korea and came back with a programme of large-scale industrialization and social engineering that would blend town and country into an ugly, soulless industrial society. Again, copying what he saw in the East, and copying earlier fascist leaders, Ceausescu worked on a personality cult centring on himself and his wife Elena, the 'doctor, engineer and academician'. He also saw to the accelerated promotion of other family members. The state-controlled media included a daily party newspaper called Scinteia. This made the glorification of Ceausescu and praise of his wife a great focus.

Ceausescu's 'Era of Light' began to grow dim in the 1970s. The Romanian economy first grew, but then began to fail. By 1979 the massive un-economic oil refineries were functioning at only

10 per cent of their capacity; unrealistic targets were being set for agricultural and industrial workers; the standard of living for ordinary people dived. Ceausescu's Stalinist programme of collectivization and quota-setting on the farms created a stultifyingly rigid environment within which food yields dropped and dropped. Bread rationing had to be introduced in 1981. There were food shortages leading to food queues in many shops.

Ceausescu's response to the crisis that he had created was to comment that Romanians ate too much. In 1985 he announced a scientific diet for all Romanians, a euphemism for rationing, but food supplies could not reach even these low-level rations. Austerity measures bit harder and harder. Food and all goods of any quality were exported in order to repay international debts.

Ceausescu's socio-economic reform of the rural areas hinged on a mad scheme called 'systematization'. This involved destroying half the villages in Romania and moving the people to agro-industrial centres where they could be controlled more easily. The arguments given for doing this were that it would free up land for more efficient food production and provide better services. The plans for systematization were drawn up in 1972, but not activated until 1988. This was understandably intensely unpopular in Romania itself. There were vigorous protests from many European states, including Germany, Belgium and even Hungary (a Warsaw Pact country). In the end it seems that instead of the threatened

8,000 only two villages were completely destroyed, though the experience for the people living in those two villages must have been intensely traumatic. They had only 24 hours' notice before their houses were flattened and the land was ploughed up. For the most part the systematization was restricted to demolishing old houses in small towns and the rehousing of the displaced people in new apartment blocks.

Like most dictators, Ceausescu wanted to build great monuments to himself. The most outrageous building project was the Palace of Parliament, designed by Anca Petrescu in 1982. To create space for this gigantic building, the Uranus district of Old Bucharest had to be completely cleared. In spite of its name, the new building was really a palace for Nicolae and Elena Ceausescu, surrounded by apartments for the party faithful. This extravagant project was built at a time when standards of living for ordinary Romanians had sunk very low. As a piece of architecture, this monstrous mountain of white marble is a recognizable descendant of inter-war fascist design. It has 3,700 rooms and is seven times the size (in volume) of the Palace of Versailles. The appalling, top-heavy proportions of the facade are due to the fact that Ceausescu was initially shown a scale model of the design - beautifully made and fully detailed by Petrescu. Yet the dictator lacked imagination. Looking down at the model on the table, he thought the building should be higher and insisted on adding what was in effect an extra building on top.

Another big project was the Danube-Black Sea Canal. The idea of this short-cut for shipping had been around since 1856, when the region was under Ottoman rule. It was re-launched in 1949 when the Communist Party revived it. Work began, and it was soon known as the 'Canal of Death'. Between 1949 and 1954, when the project was abandoned, 60,000 people died while working on it. Those who died were basically slaves – people who had had all their human rights withdrawn because they had resisted collectivization, or tried to leave the country, or opposed the regime in some way. They were regarded as traitors and housed in concentration camps under appalling conditions. Many died because of extremes of heat and cold, others of malnutrition, still others of dysentery or tuberculosis. Ceausescu ordered work to begin again in 1973, but following a more practicable route across lowland rather than through hills. It took 30,000 workers and represents a huge investment by a very poor country. Though the completed canal is useful, it does not justify the investment and is widely regarded as a Ceausescu white elephant.

The Securitate, the secret police, were greatly feared. They ensured that any criticism of the regime was instantly suppressed. The Securitate were everywhere. It was said that a third of the population were either members of the Securitate or informers for Securitate, so it was not safe to criticize the regime even in private; even your close friends or relatives might be informers.

Phones in the workplace were routinely tapped. The threat of arrest and imprisonment was very effective in silencing opposition. It was only when Gorbachev came to power in Russia and things became rather more relaxed there, with greater freedom of speech, that conditions in Romania became a major focus of interest in the West. Suddenly the abuses of human rights in Romania stood out as startlingly more extreme than in the rest of Eastern Europe. The West's diplomatic and press attack on Romania was cynical. The human rights abuses had been overlooked while the West feared Russia, and Romania was a thorn in Russia's side; now that the Cold War was ending and Russia looked friendlier to the West, Romania had served its purpose.

Ceausescu's invasion of human rights reached its worst excesses in his strategy to increase Romania's population. Abortion and contraception were banned. Women workers in factories were given monthly gynaecological examinations to ensure the law was being obeyed. After 1983 it was the duty of every woman to produce at least five children. Unmarried women and childless married women had to pay higher taxes as a penalty for being unproductive. Women who did their patriotic duty by having over five children were called 'Heroine Mothers'. The result was indeed an increase in the birth rate as Ceausescu wanted, but also a huge increase in unwanted children who ended up in orphanages; many women died as a result of trying to get illegal 'back street' abortions.

The Romania that Ceausescu created was a total disaster, socially, economically, demographically, ethically, culturally. Even the television programmes were terrible. TV was restricted to a two-hour programme each day, and most of that was devoted to showing Ceausescu on various visits, and receiving praise and applause. The academic world also suffered. The history of Romania was rewritten, in order to give Ceausescu a higher profile. Ceausescu's part in the rise of Communism was highlighted. The arrest of Antonescu and King Michael's switch of alliance from Axis to Allies in 1944 was transformed into a glorious Communist rising against imperialism and fascism.

Most Romanians knew something of the truth and distrusted the barrage of propaganda the Ceausescu regime bombarded them with, but fear made them silently acquiescent. When the 1989 revolution came, it was like the eruption of a long-dormant volcano; it was by far the most violent and bloody of all the Warsaw Pact countries. Once people saw that Ceausescu could be brought down and that they could regain their freedom, the overthrow of the tyrant who had degraded and abused them for so many years became inevitable.

When there were anti-government demonstrations in Timisoara in 1989, Ceausescu ordered the army to suppress them with great brutality. It was a tactical mistake, as it alienated the army; he now had the army against him. Ceausescu fled from Bucharest with his wife on 22 December,

1989, but they were soon captured. They were charged with murder and embezzlement of government funds and tried in secret. On 25 December, both were found guilty, given a quick medical to make sure they were well enough to be executed - a final pointless formality, then unceremoniously taken outside and brought down in a hail of machine-gun fire.

Jean-Bedel Bokassa
(1892–1980)

Jean-Bedel Bokassa was born at Bobangui in the Central African Republic on 22 February, 1921, and became one of the most infamous African tyrants. He started off as a career soldier, enlisting in the Free French Army in 1939, and ending the Second World War as a Sergeant Major with the Légion d'Honneur and the Croix de Guerre.

By 1961 he had risen, rather slowly, to the rank of captain. He left the French Army for the army of the Central African Republic. Here he advanced more quickly, possibly because he was the cousin of the President, David Dacko, and the nephew of the previous President, Barthelemy Boganda. Bokassa was duly promoted to colonel and then commander in chief of the armed forces.

On 1 January, 1966, Bokassa successfully overthrew his cousin, David Dacko, in a quick and efficient coup; he assumed power for himself as President of the Republic and leader of the country's only party, the Movement for the Social Evolution of Black Africa (MESAN). By 4 January Bokassa was abolishing the 1959 constitution and ruling by decree. He was a dictator.

In April 1969 there was an attempt to topple

him, which simply gave Bokassa the excuse he wanted to strengthen his personal power. In 1972, he made himself President for Life. He survived another attempted coup in December 1974 and an attempt on his life in February 1976.

After meeting Colonel Gaddafi of Libya, President for Life Bokassa decided he would convert to Islam. This involved changing his name to Salah Eddine Ahmed Bokassa.

In September 1976, Bokassa dissolved his government and put in its place a Council of the Central African Revolution. Megalomania was now taking over in a big way. On 4 December 1976, Bokassa told the MESAN congress that the country was no longer a republic but a monarchy, called the Central African Empire. He issued an imperial constitution, converted back from Islam to Catholicism, and had himself crowned Emperor Bokassa I on 4 December 1977. He had coronation robes specially designed in ivory, black white and gold, with a fur-trimmed, red-lined cape, and naturally an ermine-trimmed gold crown. The throne was a spectacle in itself: a red plush seat embedded in the breast of a colossal golden eagle with wings outstretched. His idea seems to have been to outshine the Emperor Napoleon. The spectacular lavishness of the coronation brought down global ridicule and disapproval upon Bokassa. The errors of judgement and taste were strikingly similar to those of General Amin.

The new imperial regime was even more stringent than the old. Dissent was punished severely. France remained a supporter of Bokassa, in spite of Bokassa's high-profile descent into megalomania. The French President Valery Giscard d'Estaing was a friend of Bokassa's and a loyal supporter; he made sure the Bokassa regime had adequate financial and military support. If this support seems strange, Bokassa in return invited Giscard d'Estaing on frequent hunting trips to Africa and supplied France with uranium, which was vital for its nuclear power programme. The French press nevertheless became increasingly critical of Giscard d'Estaing's excessively friendly relationship with Bokassa, and all the more so after it emerged that Bokassa had given the French President presents of diamonds. The reason for Giscard's support now seemed clear.

There were many infringements of human rights in Bokassa's empire. One high-profile incident received international coverage. Riots in Bangui led to a massacre of civilians. On 17-19 April some schoolchildren were arrested over a protest about school uniforms. Almost incredibly, about a hundred of them were killed. It was alleged that Bokassa himself had taken part in these killings and that he had eaten some of the bodies.

French support for the dictator Bokassa instantly evaporated. David Dacko, the previous president, enlisted French support for a coup. While Bokassa was out of the country visiting Libya on 20 September, 1979, Dacko led a coup using French troops and replaced him. Dacko remained President until he too was overthrown, for a second time, in 1981.

Bokassa had by then been sentenced to death

in absentia. Remarkably, and very exceptionally in such cases, Bokassa returned from exile in France to answer his accusers. He arrived back in his empire on 24 October, 1986, when he was arrested and put on trial. The charges were treason, murder, cannibalism and embezzlement. The trial was an emotional affair and dragged on for some months. Bokassa was eventually cleared of the charges of cannibalism, but found guilty of the other charges, and sentenced to death on 12 June 1987. Some months later the death sentence was commuted to life imprisonment, then commuted to 20 years. With the return of democracy in 1993, the outgoing President Andre Kolingba announced a general amnesty for all prisoners. Bokassa, who was incredibly lucky not to have been executed back in 1986, now found himself released from prison, a free man, in August 1993.

Bokassa's lucky break was short-lived. He died of a heart attack three years later, on 3 November, 1996. Whether he ate the children or not we shall probably never know, but the killings certainly happened – lots of them. Bokassa ruled with the same capricious cruelty that Amin displayed in Uganda, and in a similar way he spread untold misery among his unfortunate subjects. His country was a poor one, and it was entirely inappropriate for him to siphon off such a high proportion of his country's wealth to pay for his own lavish lifestyle. Like many such political leaders, he kept his people poor, instead of enriching them; he took away their rights instead of empowering them.

Pol Pot
(1925–1998)

SALOTH SAR, WHO is better known as Pol Pot, was born in Prek Sbauv in French Indo-China (now the province of Kompong Thom in Cambodia). In 1949 he won a scholarship to study radio engineering in Paris. There he became a Communist and joined a Khmer Communist group.

He returned to Cambodia in 1953, when a Communist-led revolt against French occupation was under way. The rising was centred on Vietnam, but spread into neighbouring Laos and Cambodia. Saloth Sar joined the Vietminh, but was disappointed to find that they were interested only in Vietnam; they had no interest in freeing Laos or Cambodia. In 1954, when the French left, King Sihanouk called an election. The king abdicated and formed a political party so that he could take part in the election. Using his name, popularity and certain amount of intimidation, Sihanouk won and swept away the Communist opposition.

Sihanouk's secret police were after Pol Pot, so he fled. He spent twelve years in hiding, during which he trained recruits. By the late 1960s, Lon Nol, the head of Sihanouk's security organization, was taking brutal action against the revolutionaries who called themselves the Communist

Party of Kampuchea. Pol Pot then started an armed rising against the Sihanouk government. He was supported by China. In 1970, General Lon Nol, now backed by the Americans, deposed Sihanouk; the Americans saw Sihanouk as supporting the Vietcong in Vietnam. Sihanouk now allied himself with Pol Pot.

President Nixon ordered an invasion of Cambodia to destroy Vietcong refuges close to the Vietnam border. The US bombings drove many Cambodians to support Pol Pot and it was not long before Lon Nol only held control over the cities. Pol Pot owed his rise to the war in Vietnam and the bonus of the misguided American invasion of Cambodia.

When the American troops left Vietnam in 1973 the Vietcong left Cambodia, but the Communist Party of Kampuchea carried on fighting. General Lon Nol's government collapsed and Lon Nol fled to the USA. Sihanouk returned to power in 1975, but few people were interested in his scheme to restore the monarchy. The following year, the Communist Party put Sihanouk under house arrest and in May Pol Pot was appointed Prime Minister of Cambodia.

Pol Pot introduced sweeping and devastating socialist reforms. The countryside had been emptied by guerilla fighting and American bombings; the cities had become overpopulated refuges for those in flight from the fighting. He evacuated the overcrowded cities – Phnom Penh had grown by a million people immediately before 1976 – in order to repopulate the empty rural areas. Property was communalized. Many politicians, officials and intellectuals who refused to participate in the revolution were killed. The city of Phnom Penh became a ghost town. The result of these wrenching and catastrophic changes was that many people died. Some died of starvation, some of illness, some by execution. The overall death toll may have been as high as 2 million.

In 1978, Vietnam invaded Cambodia, easily defeating the Cambodian army. Pol Pot hurried to safety near the Thai border. Many in the east defected to the Vietnamese, fearing that they would be charged with collaboration if they did not. Pol Pot managed to keep fighting in the west. China even intervened for a short time, in a brief Sino-Vietnamese War.

The USA also supported Pol Pot, partly because he was seen as anti-Soviet. The US connived to create an anti-Vietnam alliance among Pol Pot, Sihanouk and the nationalist Son San. To help achieve this, Pol Pot formally resigned in 1985, while remaining the leader of the Communist Party in Cambodia. In 1989 Vietnam retreated from Cambodia. Pol Pot would not co-operate with the peace process, and fought against the new coalition government. But his demoralized troops, who must have started wondering what on earth they were fighting for now, started deserting.

In 1997, Pol Pot executed his life-long deputy Son Sen when Son Sen proposed making a settlement with the government. Then Pol Pot was arrested by Ta Mok, the Khmer Rouge military chief, and sentenced to lifelong house arrest. In April 1998, Ta Mok fled into the forest after a renewed attack by government forces. He took Pol Pot with him. A few days later, on 15 April, Pol Pot died at the age of 72. It was said that he died of a heart attack, which is possible but it seems more likely that he was killed by his captors.

Pol Pot caused the people of Cambodia untold misery by keeping the fighting going for so long. His socialist revolutionary changes to both town and country during his time in power caused massive economic and social disruption. Too many people died. Even Pol Pot's own, conservative, estimate of the number of deaths that he caused was nearly one million, and it is more likely that over two million died.

Idi Amin
(1928–2003)

GENERAL IDI AMIN Dada Oumee was born near Koboko in Uganda on 17 May, 1928, as a member of the Kakwa tribe. He was brought up by his mother, who was thought to be a witch doctor, and had very little in the way of education. In 1946, Amin joined the King's African Rifles as a private in the British colonial army. He saw action in the Mau Mau revolt in Kenya and was promoted to the rank of lieutenant. He was a keen, over-eager soldier with a reputation for cruelty, rising gradually through the ranks to sergeant-major before being made an effendi, which was the highest rank an African could reach in the British army.

The young Amin was a great sportsman. He was a champion swimmer and also Uganda's light heavyweight champion from 1951 to 1960.

After Uganda became independent in 1962, the first Prime Minister of Uganda, Milton Obote, promoted him to Deputy Commander of the army in 1964. The following year, Amin and Obote were involved in a scandalous gold and ivory smuggling deal. An investigation demanded by President Frederick Mutesa II, who was also the Kabaka (King) of Buganda, and known as King Freddie, put Obote on the defensive; he made Amin General and Chief-of-Staff, had five ministers arrested, suspended the constitution and declared himself president. King Freddie was forced into exile in 1969; he went to London, where he died the same year under mysterious circumstances.

Amin started recruiting members of his own tribe into the army and relations with Obote began to deteriorate. Obote tried putting Amin under house-arrest. When Amin heard Obote planned to arrest him for misappropriating army funds, he seized power. The day he chose, 25 January, 1971, was when Obote was out of the country, attending a Commonwealth meeting in Singapore. Amin was a dictator from the start. He began to accumulate titles and self-awarded decorations, and called himself 'His Excellency President for Life, Field Marshal Al Hadji Doctor Idi Amin, VC, DSO, MC, Lord of All the Beasts of the Earth and Fishes of the Sea, and Conqueror of the British Empire in Africa in General and Uganda in Particular'.

Amin was initially welcomed by the international community, and within Uganda. No-one knew then what horrors were in store. He gave King Freddie a state funeral and disbanded the Secret Police. But he also set up killer squads who hunted down Obote supporters. Military leaders who had not supported his coup were executed. By 1974, Amin was murdering hundreds of thousands of his own people, feeding the heads of his enemies to crocodiles, boasting of eating human flesh and keeping human heads in his freezer.

Obote meanwhile had taken refuge in Tanzania, and from there he tried to regain control of Uganda in 1972; it was a failure. In retaliation, Amin did not flinch from bombing Tanzanian towns. After that, Amin became more paranoid and more bloodthirsty than ever. The Nile Mansions Hotel in Kampala became notorious. Far from being a hotel, it was Amin's interrogation and torture centre. The killer squads rampaged across Uganda, abducting, raping, murdering. Amin even ordered the execution of the Anglican Archbishop of Uganda, Janani Luwum, the Chief Justice, the Chancellor of Makerere University, the Governor of the Bank of Uganda and many others.

A different kind of atrocity followed. On 9 August, 1972, Amin gave the 70,000 Asians in Uganda 90 days to leave the country. He claimed he had had a dream in which God told him to expel them. The same year, he severed diplomatic relations with Israel. In 1976, he severed relations with Britain. He turned instead to Libya and the Soviet Union for support. Amin developed links with the PLO, and he offered the PLO the former Israeli Embassy as an HQ. The Air France Airbus hi-jacked from Athens in 1976 was invited to stop at Entebbe. The hi-jackers demanded the release of 53 PLO prisoners in return for the 256 hostages. Amin himself visited the hostages on more than one occasion. In an extraordinarily daring raid, Israeli paratroopers attacked Entebbe airport on 3 July, 1976, freeing nearly all of the hostages. The attack badly damaged Uganda's air force, as its fighters were destroyed by the Israelis.

There is no doubt that Idi Amin was dangerous and evil, but was he also mad? One expert view is that he was suffering from neurosyphilis. As the years passed, even his harmless child-like eccentricities turned into manias. He began wearing so many medals that his shirts tore under their weight. He thought up ever-grander titles for himself, including King of Scotland. Curiously, in 1975, he was elected President of the Organization of African Unity. Perhaps by flattering Amin the heads of neighbouring states hoped to calm him down. As the Tanzanians found, Amin was not just dangerous to the people of Uganda.

By 1978, he and his killer squads had killed up to 500,000 people. In a final piece of madness, with the help of Libyan troops, Amin ordered the invasion of Tanzania and tried to annex its northernmost province, Kagera. By April 1979 President Nyerere of Tanzania had driven the Ugandan and Libyan troops out of his country; he also succeeded in driving Amin out and taking Kampala, the Ugandan capital. Subsequently, Obote was reinstated.

Amin went into exile, bringing to an end one of the worst regimes since Stalin's. First he travelled to Libya. It is not clear how long he stayed there – maybe as little as one year or as much as ten years – before finding asylum in Jeddah in Saudi Arabia. On 20 July, 2003, one of his four wives reported that he was in a coma and close to death in hospital in Jeddah. She pleaded with President Museveni of Uganda to let her husband return to die in Uganda. The reply was that if he returned he would have to answer for his sins. He did not return. Amin died in Jeddah on 16 August 2003 and was buried there. David Owen was British Foreign Secretary in 1977–79. While in office, he proposed that General Amin should be assassinated in order to bring the bloodshed to an end, but his proposal was turned down. It is certainly remarkable that the same international community that intervened with such alacrity in Kuwait, Afghanistan and Iraq should have stood back from Uganda and watched – while a madman killed half a million innocent people. That is evil by doing nothing.

Haile Mengistu
(1937–)

HAILE MARIAM MENGISTU was educated at Hoeltu military academy. He joined the Ethiopian army and rose to the rank of colonel. As an officer in the Ethiopian army, Mengistu played a prominent part in the overthrow of Emperor Haile Selassie in 1974. Several groups were involved in toppling Haile Selassie, but it was Mengistu's group, known as the Derg, which came out on top. It is thought that it was Mengistu who ordered the strangling of the deposed emperor in 1975.

In a second coup, which he led in 1977, he himself seized power as head of state and chairman of Derg. He achieved this by having his two predecessors killed. He became, through a programme of violence alone, head of state in Ethiopia. He set up a totalitarian-style government and launched a reign of terror to eliminate any opposition. From 1974 until 1991, Mengistu's regime was responsible for human rights violations on a huge scale. Tens of thousands of Ethiopians suspected of being enemies of the Derg were tortured, murdered or 'disappeared' in a purge known as 'the red terror'. Tens of thousands more Ethiopians were killed as a result of the breakdown of law and order during the many internal armed conflicts. Many more, and perhaps over 100,000 people in all, died as a result of forced relocations ordered by Mengistu. He had major problems with drought and secessionist risings, especially in the north, and only survived with aid from the Soviet Union, Cuba and the West.

The collapse of the Derg was hastened by natural phenomena, droughts and famine in particular, especially the Ethiopian famine of 1984–5. There were also rebellions in the northern regions of Tigray and Eritrea.

In 1987 he reintroduced civilian rule, but it was a socialist one-party state, a people's republic on the Soviet model. The party in question was the Marxist-Leninist Workers' Party of Ethiopia. He fought off Somali incursions and Eritrean rebel forces. Regional rebellions gained in strength as Soviet aid receded and the Ethiopian economy broke down. In 1989, the Tigrayan People's Liberation Front (TPLF) merged with other ethnically based opposition groups to form the Ethiopian Peoples' Revolutionary Democratic Front. In 1991, EPRDF forces converged on the Ethiopian capital, Addis Ababa, and it was clear to Mengistu that his reign was over. He fled the country with about 3,000 Derg officials.

Mengistu blamed the collapse of the Derg on the policies of Mikhail Gorbachev, who had let the Soviet Union collapse and hence cut off the funding for the Mengistu government. It was a poor explanation. Mengistu was eventually given asylum in Zimbabwe. In 1995, he was tried in absentia on charges of mass murder, relating to the murder of Emperor Haile Selassie and the deaths of thousands of his political opponents during the period known as the Red Terror in 1977–79. There was an assassination attempt in November 1995, which he survived.

He was finally overthrown with some violence by rebel forces. Mengistu was a combination of cruel military dictator and total incompetent. The colossal numbers of violations of human rights committed during his time as leader are documented in the Human Rights Watch's book-length report, *Evil Days: 30 Years of War and Famine in Ethiopia*. Mengistu goes unpunished for his crimes, living on a private ranch in Zimbabwe. The Ethiopian authorities have repeatedly tried to have Mengistu extradited to face trial. Several former Derg members have already been tried in absentia – and sentenced to death.

Saddam Hussein
(1937–)

SADDAM HUSSEIN WAS born in the village of Al-Awja in the Tikrit district of Iraq to a family of shepherds. His father, Hussein Abd al-Majid, either died or disappeared before Saddam was born. When pregnant with Saddam Hussein, his mother, Subha Tulfah al-Mussallat, tried to abort, but failed. She later remarried and Saddam gained three half-brothers. The new step-father, Ibrahim al-Hassan, treated him harshly, forcing him to steal.

His bond with his home town was strong and his relatives from Tikrit, 'the Tikrit mafia', as they were later called, would be among his most influential advisors and supporters. One of the half-brothers, Barzan Ibrahim Hasan was chief of the Iraqi secret police and ambassador to the UN in Geneva. Another, Sabawi Ibrahim Hasan, became head of Iraqi intelligence. The third half-brother, Watban Ibrahim Hasan, became Iraqi interior minister. Barzan and Watban were both eventually arrested by coalition forces.

When he was 10 years old, Saddam Hussein moved to Baghdad to live with an uncle, Khairallah Tulfah, who was a devout Sunni. From him, Saddam learnt never to back down, no matter how superior the enemy numbers may be. In 1955, he went to secondary school in Baghdad.

The rise of Gamal Nasser in Egypt in 1952 was a highly significant event in the Near East, foreshadowing a series of revolutions that would topple monarchies in Iraq, Egypt and Libya. The collapse of the Iraqi monarchy in 1958 was another landmark for the rising new urban classes; it was not just the monarchies that were going, it was the imperialist collaborator elites that went with them. Nasser's populist pan-Arab nationalism in Egypt made a strong impact on Saddam Hussein. Nasser challenged and faced down the British and the French, nationalized the Suez Canal, and went several steps towards modernizing Egypt.

Saddam joined the Ba'ath Party in 1957, and became known for his brutality. He was 19 when he committed his first murder. It was in 1958 that a non-Ba'athist group led by General Abdul Karim Qassim overthrew the king in a massacre. The following year, Saddam Hussein was involved in a plot sponsored by the CIA to assassinate Prime Minister Qassim. Saddam was shot in the leg, managed to get away and remove the bullet from his own leg as he escaped; he fled to Syria and then to Egypt. He was sentenced to death in absentia.

Saddam resumed his education at the University of Cairo. He gained a Law degree from Baghdad University in 1968.

Saddam came to power as a result of the Ba'athist revolution of 1963. He was imprisoned in 1964 following a change in the ruling faction, but he escaped from prison in 1967. In 1968 he played a part in leading the successful – and peaceful – Ba'athist coup. He was then appointed Vice-Chairman of the Revolution Command Council and Vice President of Iraq. In 1973 he was appointed a General in the Iraqi armed forces.

Iraqi society is deeply divided among Arab Sunni, Kurdish Sunni, Assyrian, Turkoman and Arab Shiite camps. A major problem for Saddam Hussein since 1968 has been to consolidate his power in Iraq in the face of such deep divisions. There have also been tribal conflicts, class conflicts, rural-urban conflicts. Saddam's power base was Arab Sunnis of the middle and working classes, which make up perhaps a fifth of the population. The new Ba'athist regime, of which Saddam was a part, was therefore characterized by a very strong – oppressively strong – security regime, in order to prevent coups. The new regime also reduced poverty through the nationalization of oil; oil revenues were used to build schools, hospitals, acquire imported technology. But they were also used to strengthen the security services. In 1972, Saddam led the process of nationalizing the Western-based oil companies who had a monopoly on Iraq's oil. He led a programme of modernization out in the countryside as well as in industry. He worked to raise literacy levels. At the same time he was purging members of the Ba'ath Party who might oppose him. It was a curious mixture of good and evil.

The improvements under Saddam were palpable. There was universal free education up to and including university, support for families of soldiers killed in war, free hospital treatment, subsidies for farmers, land reforms so that peasant farmers could have more land. This was the general pattern up to the point where Saddam began his destructive military adventures. The programme of modernization was looking good, until the invasions of Iran and Kuwait and the twelve years of UN-imposed economic sanctions that were Saddam's – and Iraq's – punishment for lawless behaviour.

As Vice President Saddam consolidated his power over the Iraqi government and the Ba'ath party, the elderly President, Ahmed Hassan al-Bakr became increasingly unable to do his job. Saddam began to take a more and more prominent role as the public face of the Iraqi government. It was not long before he was shaping foreign policy, and representing Iraq on visits to foreign countries. By the late 1970s, he was still Vice President, but the de facto leader of the country.

In 1979, the President began to make treaties with Syria that would lead to a unification of the two countries. The President of Syria Hafez al-Assad was to become Deputy Leader in this union, and Saddam would be nowhere. Saddam was forced to act. He compelled Bakr to resign on 16 July, 1979 in a bloodless coup, and took over the Presidency. Then the horrors began.

One of Saddam's first acts was to call a meeting of Ba'ath leaders on 22 July and have one of them read out a list of the names of members that

Saddam thought might oppose him. These members were labelled 'disloyal'. They were taken out of the room one at a time and immediately shot by firing squad. Then Saddam congratulated those still sitting in front of him. The room erupted in applause and praise of Saddam.

To the consternation of Islamic fundamentalists, Saddam gave women additional freedoms, opening high-level government and industry posts to them. He abolished the old Sharia laws except for personal injuries and small claims. He also introduced Western-style banking and legal systems. So, there were some enlightened and liberal developments. The strong, oppressive style of government had the effect of keeping the lid on tribal, ethnic, class and religious divisions that could easily have erupted at any time. But the systematic use of torture for political ends was a very negative development, and it is claimed by human rights groups that there are documented cases of state-sponsored rape.

The end result was the creation of the most oppressive and suffocating of the Middle East's autocratic regimes. Few sectional interests were satisfied. The traditional Sunni and Shiite aristocracies disliked the populist, modernizing nature of Saddam's policies, even though they had dramatically raised living standards overall. Saddam's later attempts to use some of his giant portraits to show himself off as a devout Muslim were an effort to win round the more religious elements in Iraqi society. However horrible the Saddam Hussein regime was, at least there was no bloody fundamentalist insurgency of the sort seen in Egypt, Algeria and Tunisia.

Instead, Saddam espoused the concept of Iraqi patriotism, emphasizing the role that Iraq has played through history, especially the Abbasid period, when Muslim Baghdad was the political, cultural and economic capital of the Arab world. He also referred in his speeches to Iraq's glorious pre-Islamic past when the land between the Tigris and the Euphrates was a cradle of civilization. Saddam's sincerity in this regard seems to have been genuine; he devoted enormous resources to archaeology.

Whether Saddam was ever actually popular is hard to say. In the time-honoured way, there were elections, but with only one presidential candidate and voting was mandatory. In 2002, there was a referendum to find out whether Saddam should continue to lead Iraq. One hundred per cent of voters thought he should. The 'show referendum' was one aspect of the Saddam Hussein personality cult. During his time as President, Saddam used propaganda on a big scale, and like other dictators he used his own image to project an identification of leader with state. Gigantic portraits, huge statues and colossal murals appeared all over Iraq. They were all different, some showing him in traditional Arab costume, some in a Western suit. One of the oddest is an image of him in a three-piece 'City' suit, tie and trilby, brandishing a rifle in his right hand. Other dictators, notably Hitler, Stalin and Mao, have used their own portraits to project a personality cult, but nothing on the scale of Saddam. One western commentator said that Saddam's publicity campaign made Stalin look as if he suffered from low self-esteem.

The Islamic Revolution in Iran in 1979 threatened to destabilize Saddam's programme of modernization, not least because the majority of Iraqis were Shiites, and Shiites were on the whole sympathetic to the Ayatollahs who were coming to power in Iran. Saddam found a pretext – a territorial dispute – and declared war on Iran. With hindsight it seems extraordinarily misguided, but Saddam was supported in this war by both the USA and the Soviet Union. Neither of the great powers wanted radical Islamic fundamentalist revolution to spread and destabilize the Middle East; if Saddam was willing to contain it, they would help him. During this terrible war, Saddam ordered the use of chemical weapons on Iranian soldiers. There was no overall victory, just a stalemate with 1.7 million people dead. The economies of both Iran and Iraq were left wrecked.

For a long time, Iraq has been troubled by the desire of the people in the north of the country, the Kurds, to have their independence. During the Iraq-Iran War, a side-swipe against the separatist Kurds was almost inevitable, and Saddam did not shrink from using chemical weapons against both Kurdish troops and settlements. The worst atrocity took place on 16 March, 1988, when Iraqi troops attacked the Kurdish town of Halabjah with poison gas and nerve agents. They killed 5,000 people, mostly women and children. It is also the case that many Kurds have been driven out, in some cases over the mountains into Turkey, where they are no more welcome. According to one estimate 100,000 Kurds have been driven into exile since 1991.

The Iran-Iraq War left Iraq bankrupt. To rebuild, Iraq needed money. The only country ready to lend money was the USA, but borrowing from the USA would have made Saddam an American 'client-king' rather like the old Shah of Iran. It may be that these considerations drove Saddam into his next military disaster, the attempted conquest of Kuwait.

In 1990, Saddam Hussein complained to the USA about slant drilling in Kuwait. It is possible to drill boreholes vertically or at a slight angle to the vertical. In a deep borehole, this slanting may mean that oil is being siphoned from behind a territorial boundary, and that is what Saddam accused the Western oil companies of doing. Having had no satisfactory response, Saddam drew troops up to the Iraq-Kuwait border. A further problem was that the desert border had been inappropriately defined in relation to some palm trees. Obviously, palm trees come and go, and new ones can be planted in different places. It seems likely that Saddam had additional palms planted further south, in order to make it appear that the correct line of the frontier should be further south. He had exploited a loophole in order to create an international dispute. Saddam had a meeting with a high-ranking US official, who indicated that the USA would not interfere in border disputes. Saddam interpreted that to mean that the USA would not intervene if he invaded Kuwait. He invaded Kuwait.

The Iraqis had long held the view that Kuwait was really part of Iraq and Saddam lacked the seaport that Kuwait occupied, a grievance that pre-dates and cannot be blamed on Saddam. In 1961, the British narrowly prevented a similar Iraqi invasion. A reluctant UN Security Council declared war on Iraq. By the end of the Gulf War, Iraq had lost at least 20,000 troops and perhaps as many as 100,000, and been ejected from Kuwait.

Following the Gulf War, there were popular risings against Saddam in both the north and the south. They were brutally suppressed. In the south, in addition to a purge, Saddam began a programme of drainage, to destroy the age-old swamps where the Marsh Arabs live. A UN trade embargo was clamped on Iraq and living conditions in the country deteriorated further.

Relations between Iraq and the US were strained. Bush was criticized for not pursuing the retreating Iraqi troops all the way to Baghdad and 'finishing the job'. An opportunity to seize, depose, possibly kill the now-hated Saddam Hussein had been missed. In 1991, Bush visited Kuwait to meet the restored Emir. Iraqi soldiers tried to assassinate the American president and failed. During the Clinton administration, the Americans complained that Saddam was violating the terms of the Gulf War cease-fire, and accused Saddam of manufacturing weapons of mass destruction (WMD). The Americans tried to intimidate Saddam by making isolated strikes inside Iraqi territory, such as Operation Desert Fox in 1998.

When Gorge Bush's son, George W. Bush, became US President in 2000, he appeared to have a mission to complete the job his father had begun. Bush alleged that Saddam had WMD, that he was a threat to the West and that the overthrow of Saddam by force was the only solution. In March 2003, American troops together with troops from a few other countries (Britain, Poland and Australia) invaded Iraq. The Iraqi government, and the Saddam Hussein regime, fell in about three weeks. The removal of Saddam Hussein from power had been accomplished.

Since that time the major problem has been that no amount of searching has produced the weapons of mass destruction that were the United States pretext for invading. It begins to look as if the invasion of Iraq was just as unethical as Iraq's invasions of Iran and Kuwait.

A problem in fighting extreme evil is that sometimes 'clean' methods don't work. The British Prime Minister, Tony Blair, said that Saddam Hussein was an evil man and needed to be got rid of – but that is another argument entirely, and actually transgresses one of the accepted codes of international conduct of the last three centuries. One country may only invade another country if it is itself threatened with invasion; invasion may only be defensive. And how virtuous is it to lie about your reason for going to war? Is there anyone left standing on the moral high ground?

In the weeks following the fall of Baghdad on 9 April, 2003, there was much uncertainty about the whereabouts of Saddam Hussein. Saddam was placed at the top of the US list of most wanted Iraqis. Many of the other leaders were arrested. After a tip-off from an informant, his sons and likely successors, Uday and Qusay, were killed in a shoot-out with American troops in July 2003. It was assumed that Saddam Hussein would choose to go down fighting in a similar way, and the manner of his capture surprised everyone. It was on 14 December, 2003 that Saddam was found cowering in a small concrete-lined underground pit. He was bearded, dirty and dishevelled, and surrendered without a struggle. The problem then was deciding what to do with him. Alive and in captivity, he continues to be a major problem to the 'Coalition'. With his record for waging un-provoked war, indiscriminate use of torture, political murders, war crimes, and attempted genocide of both Kurds and Marsh Arabs, it is difficult to see how, if he was brought to trial in the Middle East, anything but a death sentence could be the outcome. Would the Coalition powers want to make a martyr out of this enigmatic monster?

PART SEVEN

REIGNS OF TERROR

Tomas de Torquemada
(1420–1498)

TOMAS DE TORQUEMADA was born at Valladolid in 1420, a nephew of the celebrated cardinal and theologian Juan de Torquemada. As a boy Tomas entered the Dominican monastery at Valladolid and later became prior of the Monastery of Santa Cruz at Segovia, where he stayed for 22 years.

His name has become notorious as the personification of the Spanish Inquisition.

While at Segovia, the Infanta Isabella chose Tomas de Torquemada as her confessor. When in 1474 she succeeded to the throne of Castile he became one of her most influential councillors. He refused all the ecclesiastical promotions he was offered, preferring to remain a humble friar, though in his behaviour he was far from humble. It was a difficult time for Catholicism in Spain. There were many Jews and Muslims in Spain, and a high proportion of them pretended to convert to Christianity in order to make life easier for themselves. The Inquisition was set up by Catholic monarchs acting under instructions by Pope Sixtus IV in 1478, but it failed to achieve much in spite of inflicting a good deal of cruelty, mainly because it was not centrally organized. Torquemada was to change all that. Torquemada was assistant inquisitor from February 1482 and the following year the Pope appointed him Grand Inquisitor of Castile. A few months later, the Pope extended Torquemada's jurisdiction to include Aragon as well.

As the Pope's representative and the highest official of the court of the Inquisition, Torquemada was able to control the entire business of the Inquisition in Spain. He was able to delegate his power to other inquisitors of his own choosing. Torquemada immediately set up tribunals at seven cities including Seville and Saragossa. He also set up a high Council, whose job it was to help him in the hearing of appeals, and called a General Assembly of Spanish Inquisitors in Seville in 1484, and presented a set of guidelines.

Torquemada's self-appointed task was to cleanse Spain of heresy and dissent. The Jews were a great barrier to this. There were, to begin with, a lot of them; Spain had more converted Jews than any other country in Europe, some converted by choice, some by force. They were all regarded with distrust by the Christians, because some, called Marranos, were only nominally converts, and they continued to practise their Jewish customs in secret. Because many of them were rich and therefore politically powerful they were able to evade the tribunals.

The result was a kind of crusade to cleanse Spain of impure blood and establish sangre limpia, the pure blood of Christianity. It was a fantastic, unrealistic and foolish enterprise, not only because there were so many Jews in the country but because although everybody claimed it almost nobody actually had sangre limpia. Most people had some Jewish or Moorish blood flowing in their veins, Torquemada included. Even so, it became Torquemada's mad mission to achieve sangre limpia in Spain. He wanted to root out heresy and destroy the Marranos. It was one of the most barbaric and cruel enterprises ever undertaken in the name of Christ.

The Inquisition published guidelines for identifying Marranos.

> *If your neighbours wear clean and fancy clothes on a Saturday, they are Jews.*
> *If they clean their houses on Fridays and light candles earlier on that night, they are Jews.*
> *If they eat unleavened bread and start a meal with celery and lettuce in Holy Week, they are Jews.*
> *If they say prayers facing a wall, bowing back and forth, they are Jews.*

If people saw their neighbours doing any of these things, they were to report them and the Inquisition would do the rest. The mildest penalty imposed was the confiscation of property, which was a handy fund-raising method for the war against the Moors. This was followed by public humiliation; the Marranos were paraded through the streets wearing only the sambenito, a yellow shirt covered with crosses. Then they were flogged at the church door. The grandfather of Teresa de Avila was one of many who were treated in this barbaric way.

But there was far worse. The scale of punishment escalated up to burning at the stake, which was turned into a public spectacle called an *auto-da-fe*. Public executions were of course quite routine in the middle ages. If the condemned recanted and kissed the cross, they were spared the pain of the burning by being garrotted (strangled) first. If they recanted only, they were burned with quick-burning wood; if they refused to recant, the agony was protracted by using slow-burning wood.

In 1490, Torquemada staged a show trial involving eight Jews and Jewish converts whom he accused of crucifying a Christian child. It was an absurd lie, but people were ready to believe it. There was no body and no victim was identified. Even so, all eight were found guilty on the strength of their confessions extracted under torture. They were burned at the stake. Folk tales about Jews sacrificing Christian children had been circulating across Europe for hundreds of years. There was no truth in them whatsoever, yet Jewish communities were repeatedly persecuted in one country after another on the strength of this malicious 'blood libel'. There is no evidence that any Christians were sacrificed by Jews. There is, unfortunately, a huge amount of evidence that Christians murdered enormous numbers of Jews. Torquemada himself was responsible for many of these ritual murders of Jews in Spain.

Torquemada used the crucifixion trial as a lever. He urged the sovereigns, Ferdinand and Isabella, to force the Jews to choose: they had to convert to Christianity or leave Spain. The wealthy Jews cunningly subverted this by offering the sovereigns large sums of money to be left alone. Ferdinand was sorely tempted by the huge amount of money offered. As Ferdinand wavered, Torquemada is said to have appeared before him brandishing a crucifix and accusing him of being a Judas, of being prepared to sell his Saviour for 30,000 ducats. Torquemada put the crucifix down on the table in front of Ferdinand and left him to contemplate both it and his impending betrayal of Christ. In this way, Ferdinand was brow-beaten by his Grand Inquisitor into expelling the Jews from Spain.

In March 1492, Ferdinand and Isabella issued their Edict of Expulsion. '[We] have decided to command all of the aforesaid Jews, men and women, to leave our kingdoms and never to return.' The Jews were given until 1 July to get out. Any found in Spain after that date would be killed. Some went to North Africa, where they faced more persecution. A few took ship with Columbus. Some risked remaining in Spain as 'secret Jews'.

After spectacularly achieving his main goal, the expulsion of the Jews, which we would now regard as the grossest abuse of human rights, Torquemada retired to the monastery of St Thomas in Avila, which he had designed himself. He feared that he would be poisoned there by his enemies and he kept what he thought was the horn of a unicorn beside his plate as an antidote. He was not in the end poisoned, but died a natural death in 1498.

Torquemada was responsible for an enormous amount of mental cruelty, in questioning his victims under threat of torture and death. The forms of torture he favoured were many: foot-roasting, the use of the garrucha and suffocation. He was also responsible for the confiscation of property, and ordering the humiliation and burning of heretics. It is impossible to be sure how many suffered these miseries during Torquemada's period in office, between 1483 and 1498. A high estimate is that 8,800 suffered death by fire and 9,654 were punished by other methods including hanging. Other estimates put the number of burnings much lower, at about 2,000. It is difficult for most people today to understand how questioning people under torture can ever have been regarded as a sane, let alone civilized, method of arriving at a true account of events, but it is important to remember that torture was regularly and officially used in one European state after another in the medieval period and on into the Renaissance. It was a 'normal' practice. As for Torquemada's commitment to the Inquisition, it has to be remembered that he thought Spain was in danger, that Christianity could be toppled, and that extreme methods were justified to prevent that catastrophe from happening. He may have had a personal agenda in that his own grandmother was a converso, a converted Jew; he had something to prove. He was seen as something of a hero by contemporary Christians. A contemporary Spanish chronicler called him 'the hammer of heretics, the light of Spain, the saviour of his country, the honour of his order.'.

Cardinal Richelieu
(1585–1642)

ARMAND JEAN DU Plessis de Richelieu was born in Paris in September 1585, into an ancient family of the lesser nobility of Poitou. Armand's father Francois, Seigneur de Richelieu fought through the wars of religion, first as a favourite of Henry III and then under Henry IV. Armand's mother Susanne came from a family of a lawyers. Armand was the third son and, as was often the fate of younger sons, he was destined for the Church.

At the age of only 21 he was nominated Bishop of Lucon by Henry IV. As he was so young, he went to Rome to receive a special dispensation and was consecrated bishop there in April 1607. Armand returned to his poor bishopric and devoted himself conscientiously to his episcopal duties there for six years. In 1614, he was elected by the clergy of Poitou to the last States-general to meet before the Revolution. It was there that he attracted the attention of Marie de' Medici, the Queen Mother, and was chosen at its close to present a plenary statement on behalf of the clergy, embodying its petitions and resolutions.

After the assassination of Henry IV of France in 1610, there was a power vacuum. The dead King was succeeded by his nine-year-old son, Louis

XIII. The young King's mother Marie de' Medici, acted as regent. Four years later, Armand, became the Queen's adviser, during her exile at Blois. One of the duties involved in this complex role was to spy on the Queen Mother and report back to the young King on his mother's activities. The situation was made more complicated still, it was said at the time, by the Queen Mother's un-requited love for the young man. Armand's own patron, Concini, had been assassinated, so he was very vulnerable, and he did his best to ingratiate himself with the King. Two years later in 1616 he was promoted to secretary at war and for foreign affairs. It is hard to understand his meteoric rise, though he certainly had tremendous ability and cunning as a diplomat.

But Richelieu's tight-rope walk between the King and his mother brought no instant gratitude. He was of course a priest as well as a politician and he was able to retreat to his diocese (Lucon) for a while. He was even so exiled to Avignon with his brother and brother-in-law in 1618. But his august personality saved him. Even the King quailed before his stern, severe, ascetic face. He was thin-faced, sickly, wasted by disease, but still an awe-inspiring presence – and even more so after 1622, when he was created a cardinal, and could wear the red robes. He also tried his hand at writing drama.

When Louis XIII came of age in 1624 he appointed Richelieu as his minister of state. Richelieu was now a great churchman, at least in title and appearance, with his scarlet robes, but his true ambition was to make France greater than she was. He used his new position at the young King's right hand to set about destroying his rivals in France. He was a harsh ruler as far as his fellow countrymen were concerned. He also pursued a very aggressive foreign policy.

It was in 1628 that Cardinal Richelieu personally supervised the suppression of the Huguenots, the French Protestants who had for a long time been a thorn in the King's side, resisting his overlordship. Richelieu organized a military strike. He destroyed the Huguenot stronghold at La Rochelle after starving the occupants out in a siege that lasted a year. Richelieu went on to destroy the last Huguenot refuge at Montauban. After that, the Protestants in France were too weak to cause Richelieu any further trouble.

Richelieu appointed intendants, officers who toured France, supervising taxation, policing and law courts. The intendants were in effect spying for Richelieu, reporting back to him any subversive activity. Anybody who plotted against Richelieu was taking a terrible risk; ahead lay prison and possibly death.

In 1630, the two Queens, Louis XIII's wife Anne of Austria and his mother Marie de' Medici, made friends at last and made a pact that they would get rid of Richelieu. Together they might do it. They persuaded the King to promise to get rid of him. He agreed to do so when the war with Spain was over. When news of the truce of Regensburg came through, the King went to his mother's apartments at the Luxembourg Palace to discuss the situation, ordering that nobody was to disturb them. Richelieu entered by way of the unguarded chapel door. Marie was flabbergasted at Richelieu's audacity in entering her chamber uninvited, then rebuked him in the strongest terms, declaring that the King must choose between them. Richelieu withdrew, certain that all was lost. Later, though, the King sent for Richelieu and assured him of his support. The King hated Richelieu personally, hated him deeply, but knew also that he needed his abilities to run France. He could not overthrow him, even though he detested him just as much as everyone else in France did.

When the Austrians had overrun Germany and threatened the whole of Europe in 1631, Richelieu paid Sweden, Denmark and the Netherlands to fight the Habsburgs. In 1635, Richelieu initiated a war with Spain, a war that dragged on after his death, which came in 1642. By that stage the French army had proved itself to be one of the best fighting forces in Europe. Richelieu certainly succeeded in setting France up as a great European power, but it was at a very great cost. By the end, when he was both a cardinal and a duke, Armand Jean Du Plessis, duc de Richelieu was deeply hated by the French, and by all levels in French society, for his harsh and tyrannical style of government. He was hated for being over-bearing, for being a dictator, for creating a universally oppressive climate of fear and distrust. The bad plays could just be ignored, and he did at least offer patronage to some better writers, such as Corneille. He was the most arrogant of courtiers, claiming precedence even over princes of the blood. He was proud, ambitious and behaved as if he were the king. He was gratified to find that he had created a dynasty of sorts. His nieces and nephews were people of great consequence and status, because of their kinship with him, and their hands were sought in marriage by the noblest aristocrats in France.

When Richelieu died in December 1642, he was buried in the chapel at the Sorbonne, which still stands as he built it. His tomb, built in 1694, was desecrated and looted during the French Revolution.

Murat Rais
(1590–1650)

THE WHITE SLAVE trade sounds like a colourful theme from eighteenth or nineteenth century romantic fiction. It sounds like a sensational yet wholly imaginary peril that an imaginative lady novelist might throw in the path of her heroine. But the white slave trade was not a fiction. It really did exist, and it was big business from 1530 right through to 1780. Ship-loads of pirates from the Barbary Coast of North Africa made repeated raids on the Mediterranean coast of Europe at that time, successfully capturing, abducting and enslaving huge numbers of white European Christians.

The Muslim slavers captured as many as 1,250,000 Europeans in the two-and-a-half centuries ending in 1780. This is more than the number of black African slaves that were transported to America in the same period. The horrors of the black African slave trade have been given a very high profile by historians and human rights campaigners in recent decades. A substantial burden of guilt has been attached, retrospectively, to the white American and white European societies that were responsible for organizing the mainly transatlantic black slave trade, and these colonial powers have been shunted further into the moral low ground because of it. But the very similar horrors of the white European slave trade have until recently been overlooked, partly because the Barbary Coast slave traders did not keep detailed records, so that the evidence is harder to find, but mainly because it has not been fashionable – or politically correct – to condemn the behaviour of Muslim countries. It is clear from the evidence that the Muslim countries of North Africa have a past for which they too are answerable.

The main organizational centres for the white slave trade were Tripoli, Algiers, Tunis and Morocco. The slaves came mainly from ships at sea and coastal villages and towns on the opposite side of the Mediterranean, but the Barbary pirates also sailed along the Atlantic coast, reaching Britain, Ireland and even Iceland. The pirates were skilled navigators, latter-day Vikings, who sailed lateen-rigged xebecs (ships with distinctive triangular sails) and oared galleys. Mostly they captured ships on the open sea, because there the crews and passengers were out of reach of help. They nevertheless also regularly raided coastal villages, preferably isolated villages. They would land on a secluded, unguarded beach at night and creep through the streets, literally taking people from their beds.

Because they were the closest targets, the coasts of Spain, France, Italy and Portugal were particularly hard hit by the white slave trade. Many coastal settlements were just abandoned; the inhabitants fled inland and founded new villages in safer places. It is why there are so many picturesque hilltop villages in southern Italy, and probably why early medieval monasteries in south Wales were often hidden a little way inland. Slaving has a long and dishonourable history.

The length of the voyage did not put the pirates off raids on Britain. Villages on the coasts of Devon and Cornwall were particularly vulnerable, not just because they were nearer but because the low population density meant that it was safer for the pirate captains to risk landing. A raid on London, Chatham or Portsmouth would have been reckless. In the 20 years after 1622 7,000 English men, women and children were abducted by pirates. Towards the end of the seventeenth century, Samuel Pepys met two slaves who had escaped from North Africa. 'To the Fleece tavern to drink and there we spent till four-a-clock telling stories of Algier and the manner of life of Slaves there; and truly, Captain Mootham and Mr Dawes (who have both been slaves there) did make me full acquainted with their condition there. As, how they eat nothing but bread and water, how they are beat upon the soles of the feet and bellies at the Liberty of their Padron.'

Some slaves were well treated and regarded as companions by their masters, but the majority of white slaves were subjected to terrible living conditions. The local rulers in North Africa, the pashas, were entitled to keep one-eighth of the captured Christians, who were often kept in crowded bath-houses and fed on scraps. They were used mainly as a cheap labour force, doing jobs such as cutting down trees, quarrying, building or, notoriously, rowing the pirate galleys when they went off in search of more slaves. Some of the female slaves were selected for the pasha's harem. Boys were forced to convert to Islam, and some were castrated to turn them into eunuchs (harem minders).

The regime was severe. If a slave did not work hard enough, he might be beaten on the soles of the feet hundreds of times. If a slave tried to escape, he was executed by crucifixion, burning or impalement on huge iron hooks.

The Muslim pashas and sultans often used European captains who knew their way round the European coastline. The most infamous of these pirate leaders was Murat Rais, a Dutch sailor who turned to piracy and became a favourite of the Sultan of Morocco. Murat Rais was responsible for carrying out one of the few well-documented Barbary pirate raids on the British Isles, in 1631.

On 20 June, 1631, Murat Rais sailed two shiploads of pirates into Baltimore harbour in West Cork, and they were pirates straight out of nineteenth century novels, ruthless and cruel, with beards, turbans and cutlasses. Murat and his pirates set fire to many of the houses, cutting the heads off anyone who got in their way. With the skull-and-crossbones flying from the mast, they set sail again for Africa with 20 men and 89 women and children on board. Ironically, virtually none of the captives were Irish; they were the offspring of English pirates who had fled to Ireland from the English West Country to escape from justice a couple of decades earlier.

The Baltimore captives spent nearly two distressing months at sea, living under appalling conditions, 'crammed like capons fattened for sale'.

Only one of the Baltimore villagers ever made it back to the village. Her name was Joan Broadbrook. She was taken to Algiers and only set free 14 years later, when the English government paid a huge ransom for her. A pub in Baltimore is called the Algiers Inn, commemorating the pirate atrocity. Ransoming slaves like Joan Broadbrook was another motive for taking them, and Christian communities, Catholic ones in particular, soon organized slave ransom funds. Raising money to buy back white slaves became the major European charity. The English authorities were very lax about the matter, raising an 'Algerian Duty' out of customs tax ostensibly to pay ransoms, but actually the money was used elsewhere – rather like today's Petrol Tax.

The Barbary pirates who took white slaves were organized and employed by the rulers of Barbary Coast states. Those same rulers and other Arab chiefs were equally deeply implicated in the black slave trade. From the moment when the Arabs swept into Africa under the banner of Islam way back in the seventh century, the enslavement of native Africans was under way. Over the next 1,200 years, an estimated 12 to 14 million black Africans were enslaved by Arab Muslims. This is roughly the same number that the European Christians took across the Atlantic to work in their colonies in the Americas. The slave trade was abolished in the British Empire in 1807. Slavery itself was made illegal throughout the British Empire in 1834 and in America in 1863. It was not abolished in Saudi Arabia until the 1960s, and slavery still goes on in the Sudan and Mauretania. It seems odd that certain governments, so keen to justify their military interventions overseas on ethical grounds, have turned a blind eye to this blatant transgression of human rights. Thousands of Africans are still slaves.

Jean Paul Marat
(1743–1793)

JEAN PAUL MARAT, one of the leading figures of
the French Revolution, was born at Boudry in
Neuchatel on 24 May, 1743. He was the son of
Jean Paul Marat, a designer of Cagliari in Sardinia,
and Louise Cabrol who came from Geneva. When
his mother died in 1759, Marat set off on his
travels, studying medicine for a couple of years at
Bordeaux before going to Paris. There he applied
his already considerable medical knowledge to
find a cure for an eye disease. After that he
travelled to the Netherlands and London, where
he practised medicine.

In 1773, Marat published a *Philosophical Essay
on Man*, in which he argued that physiology
alone was enough to account for the connection
between soul and body. In 1774 he published *The
Chains of Slavery*, his first 'revolutionary' piece, in
which he advocated that constituencies should
vote for members who were likely to serve the
people's interests, and reject the king's friends. In
1775, he went to Edinburgh and was made an MD
at St Andrew's. On his return to London he published a paper on the eye disease he had been
researching, dedicating it, with unconscious
irony, to the Royal Society. In the same year,

Marat published a third volume of the *Philosophical Essay on Man*. This book exasperated Voltaire, who attacked the young author in print and so drew far more attention to him and his writings than he would otherwise have received.

Marat was by now famous as a doctor. He presented papers on heat, light and electricity to the Academy of Sciences in Paris, but the academicians were horrified that he had the temerity to disagree with Newton and would not admit him to the Academy. In 1787, he produced a new translation of Newton's *Optics* and his own *Academic Memoirs*. It is easy to forget that Marat was a significant scholar and a great doctor – because of the spectacular second career that he was about to begin.

In 1788, there was a flood of pamphlets relating to the elections for the States General. Marat wrote *Offering to the Country*, followed the next year by *The Constitution and Picture of the Vices of the English Constitution*, which he presented to the Assembly. This was an extraordinary thing to do, when the Assembly was full of Anglophiles – Anglomaniacs, even – who thought the English constitution was the only one, and certainly the best available one, to follow. Marat had spent time in England, and saw the realities behind the declared forms of English liberty; he saw that England was ruled by a land-owning class which pretended to represent the country and the interests of ordinary people, but was really being mastered by royal power. It was a penetratingly honest observation of pre-Reform Act England.

By now, Marat was deep in politics, heart and soul. He decided to found a newspaper. A single number of the *Moniteur Patriote* appeared, then another number, then a continuous run of the newspaper, now entitled *L'Ami du Peuple (The Friend of the People)*, which he went on editing from September 1789 more or less continuously for the next three years.

From this point on, Marat became one of the legendary figures of the French Revolution. From first to last, he stood alone, never joining any political group or faction. His attitude was to suspect whoever was in power, and to speak out against anything he believed wrong. No wrong, no poverty, no misery, no persecution could silence him. He was endlessly shouting, 'We are betrayed!'. If anyone suspected anyone else of anything, they had only to denounce them to Marat, and the newspaper did not let up until the accused was found innocent or guilty. He made lots of enemies, and it is astonishing that he lasted so long.

Marat started by denouncing the most powerful institutions in Paris, the ministers, the constituent assembly, the court of the Chatelet. He was himself denounced and arrested on 8 October, 1789 and held in prison for a month. On a second occasion he narrowly avoided arrest after a very aggressive campaign against Lafayette, and he managed to escape to London. There he wrote a *Denunciation against Necker*, and in May 1790 he made a daring return to Paris, where he resumed his editorship of *L'Ami du Peuple*. He launched one attack after another. Finally, he attacked the King himself. To avoid being attacked or arrested, he spent all his time hiding in cellars and sewers. It was by living like this that he picked up a horrible skin disease. He was tended by only one trusted friend, Simonne Evrard, who remained true to him.

By December 1791, almost in despair, he fled again to London. He returned in the spring of 1792, when summoned by the Cordeliers' Club. The war was now the big question, and Marat saw that the point of the war was to serve the interests of the Royalists and the Girondins – not the people. He denounced it. Himself denounced, Marat had to hide in the sewers again until August. Then he took his seat at the Commune and demanded a tribunal to try the Royalists who were in prison. No tribunal was formed and instead, as both Marat and Danton had foreseen, there were massacres in the prisons in September. Marat then took his seat as one of the 24 deputies for Paris. When the Republic was declared, Marat closed his newspaper, *L'Ami du Peuple* but opened a new paper, *Journal of the French Republic*, which adopted exactly the same tone as the previous one. It was still very audibly the voice of Jean Paul Marat.

In spite of his position in the Assembly, Marat went on denouncing people in his newspaper just as before, making himself well hated by everybody. His position in relation to the King was peculiar. He was implacably hostile to the King, and saw him as the one man who must die for the people's good, but he would not hear of the King being tried for anything that pre-dated the acceptance of the new constitution. He also went out of his way to be fair to the King's counsel, Chrétien de Malesherbes, referring to him in his newspaper as a 'wise and respectable old man'.

After the King's execution, in which Marat played his part, there were five months in which the struggle between Marat and the Girondins went on. Marat despised the Girondins because he thought that they had suffered nothing for the republic, and because they talked too much of their high-flown feelings. They were too patrician, too self-consciously re-creating the Roman Republic of a bygone age. Marat had no time for that. The Girondins hated Marat because he represented a raw red republicanism of the people, one that would not bow the knee to themselves in their fantasy roles as Roman tribunes, orators and generals. The Girondins sought to silence Marat by having him tried before the Revolutionary Tribunal, but this backfired on them very badly. Marat was acquitted by the Tribunal on 24 April, 1793 and returned in triumph to the Convention with the people of Paris behind him. The fall of the Girondins on 31 May was now almost inevitable. It was Marat's final triumph.

The skin disease that he had picked up in the cellars and sewers of Paris had dogged him for years. It was worsening now – and killing him. He could only ease the pain by sitting in a bath. He used often to sit in the bath, writing on a wooden board resting across the sides. On 13 July, he heard a young woman, Charlotte Corday, begging to be let in, saying that she had news from Caen, where the escaped Girondins were trying to raise troops in Normandy. He asked for her to be let in. He asked her for the names of the deputies at Caen, and wrote down their names on a piece of paper. Then he said, 'They shall soon be guillotined'. At this, the young woman stabbed him through the heart. The painter Louis David painted an unforgettable picture of the scene immediately afterwards, the pale body of Marat slumped in the tin bath, still holding his quill. Only the murderess is missing, dragged off to prison and shortly to be guillotined.

The Convention attended his funeral and put his bust in the hall where its sessions were held. Marat had become a hero of the Revolution, and was certainly much safer dead than alive. A year later, his ashes were transferred to the Pantheon with great pomp on 21 September, 1794. But celebrity of the kind Marat achieved is fragile. His is a type of fame that can switch like the batting of an eye to infamy. A decree of February 1795 saw to it that Marat's ashes were removed from the Pantheon. Quite rightly too. Marat proceeded by way of a particularly nasty kind of power play. His was the politics of the tabloid press – the naming and shaming of alleged criminals, regardless of the process of law – his was the ethical standard of the lynch mob. He was ready to send countless numbers of people to prison and death on somebody else's say so. The final conversation is in a way the most revealing. A total stranger, who may be sane or insane, well-informed or ignorant, well-meaning or malicious, turns up at his house with news that may or may not be true. All Marat wants to know are the names of the people involved. He writes them down. Charlotte Corday may be telling him the right names, she may be telling him the wrong names, the names of people she happens to hate. It was always that way with proscription – one of the most evil practices not only used, but condoned and encouraged by the French Revolutionaries. 'They shall soon be guillotined,' he says, with a flourish of his quill, and no doubt gives Charlotte Corday a thin smile of reassurance.

Maximilien Robespierre
(1758–1794)

MAXIMILIEN MARIE ISIDOR de Robespierre was born on 6 May, 1758 in the French town of Arras. He was the eldest child of François de Robespierre, a lawyer, and Jacqueline Marguerite Carraut, the daughter of a brewer. Robespierre's childhood was unhappy, especially after the death of his mother in 1767, and he was left, along with three orphaned siblings in the care of relatives when his father abandoned them. The father left Arras immediately after his wife's death, wandering disconsolately round Europe until he too died, in Munich, two years later.

Maximilien was sent to the college of Arras and the college of Louis-le-Grand in Paris. It was in Paris that he met and befriended Camille Desmoulins. As a boy and as a man Maximilien was nervous and hesitant when speaking, disliked crowds, and might have been thought timid and lacking in self-confidence, but his reserve concealed a steely certainty and an underlying arrogance.

In spite of the hesitancy of his ordinary speech, and his solitary nature, he turned out to have the gift of oratory and he became the greatest public speaker of his time.

In 1780, Robespierre became a Bachelor of Law, receiving his licence the following year and opening a law practice in his home town of Arras. As a young man he had a reputation for honesty and compassion. He was not a good lawyer, and lost many of his cases, though he began to think of ways in which society might be reformed through the law. He wanted to see the death penalty abolished and, when he became a criminal judge in the diocese of Arras in 1782, refused to give a death sentence when the law required it. He resigned his post rather than pronounce the death sentence.

He turned now to literature and society. He came to be admired as one of the best writers and most popular dandies of Arras. He was a member of a musical and literary society known as 'The Rosati'. It was the beauty of his speaking voice when he recited at meetings that won him great applause rather than the quality of his verses, which were not very good.

In 1788 Robespierre took part in the discussion on the way in which the Estates General should be elected. He argued lucidly that if the old mode of election were used, the next Estates General would not represent the people of France.

In this way the following year he found himself elected, at the age of only 30, to the Estates General, to represent Artois. He gravitated to the extreme left wing and soon commanded attention because everything he said was aflame with fanatical fervour. His charisma ensured that his influence grew daily. Initially he had no intention of overthrowing the monarchy or setting up a revolutionary government. Mirabeau referred to the left wing contemptuously as 'the thirty voices', because they were so few, but they were fanatically determined. Mirabeau's death brought Robespierre into higher profile. The radical Jacobin Club to which Robespierre belonged was soon advocating exile or death for the aristocracy.

In 1791 Robespierre proposed the motion that no member of the present Assembly should be eligible for the next, and revealed for the first time in public the streak of jealous suspicion that would come to the fore during the Terror to come. Robespierre's first great triumph as a demagogue came on 30 September, when the Constituent Assembly was dissolved and the people of Paris crowned Pétion and Robespierre as 'the two incorruptible patriots'.

In August 1792, Robespierre presented to the Legislative Assembly a petition for a Revolutionary Tribunal and a new Convention, where some bitter attacks launched against him by the Girondins threw him into a closer alliance with Georges Danton. Interestingly, and somewhat inconsistently, during that summer Robespierre took no part at all in the movement to end the Bourbon dynasty. At this stage, almost incredibly, it seems that Robespierre was still shocked at the idea of shedding blood. Robespierre opposed the Girondins' idea of a special appeal to the people of France on the King's death. By December 1792 his position had changed to the extent that it looks as if his personality had changed. He said, 'This is no trial; Louis is not a prisoner at the bar; you are not judges; you are – you cannot be – statesmen, and the representatives of the nation. You have not to pass sentence for or against a single man, but you have to take a resolution on a question of the public safety, and to decide a question of national foresight. It is with regret that I pronounce the fatal truth: Louis ought to perish rather than a hundred thousand virtuous citizens. Louis must die, that the country may live.'.

The execution of the King without appeal to the people on 21 January, 1793 represented a personal triumph for Robespierre and inaugurated the final life-and-death struggle between the Girondins and the Jacobins.

Robespierre's personality changed, or rather different traits emerged, after he gained power. There was now a strong streak of paranoia. He became extremely intolerant. He treated people who disagreed with him and criticized his ideas as 'enemies of the nation', and suspected conspiracy everywhere. In his position as leader of the Committee of Public Safety, he was easily able to send those enemies of the nation to the guillotine. People became terrified of him. Robespierre now developed a great love of power and acquired a reputation for self-righteousness and cruelty. He used his great skill as an orator to win the death sentence for both the King and the Queen.

It was largely due to Robespierre's efforts that Louis XVI went to the guillotine in January 1793 and Marie Antoinette followed ten months later. The first Committee of Public Safety was decreed in April 1793. It assumed the governance of France and now Robespierre, elected in July, formally became one of the rulers of France along with the rest of the Twelve. In his capacity as ruler, Robespierre supervised a three-year Reign of Terror. During this terrible episode, Robespierre and his associates committed the wholesale murder of entire families of aristocrats, and sent thousands of ordinary people to their death without proper trials.

In addition to launching this bloodbath, Robespierre was capricious and inconsistent. His paranoia led him to suspect everyone about him. His friends Danton and Desmoulins were sent to the guillotine. He placed his own men in all positions of influence in the Commune of Paris and assumed complete control of the Revolutionary Tribunal. Jacques-René Hébert, an atheist, closed the Catholic churches and started the pagan-style worship of a Goddess of Reason. Robespierre condemned this Cult of Reason and sent him and his friends to the guillotine in March 1794, and then in May recommended the Convention to acknowledge the existence of God. On 8 June he introduced his own alternative faith, the Reign of Virtue, at the inaugural Festival of the Supreme Being. It says a lot about Robespierre's vanity and megalomania that he thought he could make up a whole new religion and force France to adopt it. He gave an extraordinary speech 'On the Festival of the Supreme Being', the text of which has survived. It is full of ringing generalities and eloquence.

'The day forever fortunate has arrived, which the French people have consecrated to the Supreme Being. Never has the world which He created offered to Him a spectacle so worthy of his notice. He has seen reigning on the earth tyranny, crime and imposture. He sees at this moment a whole nation, grappling with all the oppression of the human race, suspend the course of its heroic labours to elevate its thoughts and vows toward the great Being who has given it the mission it has undertaken and the strength to accomplish it.

'Is it not He whose immortal hand, engraving on the heart of man the code of justice and equality, has written there the death sentence of tyrants? Is it not He who, from the beginning of time, decreed for all the ages and for all the peoples liberty, good faith and justice?

'He did not create kings to devour the human race. He did not create priests to harness us, like vile animals, to the chariots of kings and to give to the world examples of baseness, pride, perfidy, avarice, debauchery and falsehood. He created the universe to proclaim His power. He created men to help each other, to love each other mutually and to attain happiness by way of virtue.'

After reading a page or so of this a kind of ethical weightlessness takes over, and then one can begin to sense what it must have been like to be there, listening to Citizen Robespierre persuasively rhapsodizing as the death sentence becomes more and more certain for some unlucky victim.

'O hapless People, would you triumph over all your enemies? Practise justice, and render the Divinity the only worship worthy of Him. O People, let us deliver ourselves today, under His auspices, to the just transports of a pure festivity. Tomorrow we shall return to the combat with vice and tyrants. We shall give to the world the example of republican virtues. And that will be to honour Him still.

'The monster which the genius of kings vomited over France has gone back into nothingness.' And so on.

Robespierre's friend St Just demanded the creation of a dictatorship in the person of Robespierre. On 8 July, the dictator delivered another long and neurotic tirade, this time complaining that his enemies were out to get him. Many felt threatened and menaced by his tone.

Robespierre's grasp of France was mercifully short-lived and imperfect, so at least his Reign of Terror was quite brief. He succeeded in the course of a few months in executing many of his enemies, but the groups opposed to him quickly recognized that they must act against him or they too in their turn would be executed. The only way to save themselves was to bring Robespierre down.

In 1794, the Committee of Public Safety impeached Robespierre. Most of his co-members of the Jacobin Club betrayed him during this trial. St Just was a rare exception. When Robespierre hesitated in his own defence, someone shouted, 'It's the blood of Danton that chokes him!' He had sent one too many of his comrades to the guillotine. He was rescued from prison and taken to the hôtel de ville, but Barras followed him there with the national guards to re-arrest him. They found Robespierre signing an appeal to one of the sections of Paris to take up arms for him. A young gendarme fired his pistol at him and hit him in the jaw. After a night of agony, Robespierre was taken before the tribunal where he was identified as an outlaw and taken away to be executed. On 28 July, 1794, Robespierre was taken to the Place de la Concorde along with nineteen of his comrades and executed with the same guillotine, on the same spot, as Louis XVI.

After Robespierre's death the Reign of Terror came to an end. At the time, Robespierre was blamed for instigating many of the horrors, probably rightly. Robespierre did not single-handedly invent the Terror, but he served it with his oratory. He persuaded his hearers of his honesty and virtue and made it seem that everything that happened was laudable and necessary, rather than monstrously evil. Robespierre liked to lay 'all the crimes and misfortunes of the world' at the door of the poor, dead, feckless King Louis, but the Reign of Terror was much more of Robespierre's making than the King's. He spoke of 'all mortals bound by a boundless chain of love and happiness' and willed 'the tyrants who have dared to break it' to perish. Robespierre was himself the tyrant and deserved to be consumed by the machinery of the Terror.

In himself, Robespierre was a respectable, hard-working, well-dressed, well-mannered, honest, truthful, charitable man. But for the Revolution, he would probably have made a comfortable and happy life for himself as a provincial judge and a writer – a traditional pillar of eighteenth century bourgeois society. But reading Rousseau when young gave him disturbing, subversive, revolutionary ideas. Even those might not have led to trouble, but for his election to the Estates General, where he met a score of other fanatical young Rousseau addicts – and there among them the Revolution was kindled. It was a personal tragedy that the honest and incorruptible idealist who detested the idea of sentencing someone to death should have ended up successfully arguing for the death of his King and his Queen and thousands of other innocent people besides.

François 'Papa Doc' Duvalier
(1907–1971)

FRANÇOIS DUVALIER WAS born and brought up in Port-au-Prince, trained as a doctor and worked mainly in the rural areas. There he won praise for his battle against typhus and other diseases among the poor, and earned himself the affectionate nickname 'Papa Doc'. He married Simone Ovide in 1939 and became Director General of the Haitian health service in 1946. In 1949 he became Minister of Health and Labour. When he opposed the coup of Paul Magloire, he was obliged to go into hiding; he was only able to re-emerge after an amnesty in 1956.

Then, with the army behind him, and campaigning as a populist leader, Duvalier won the 1957 elections. Duvalier brought back the old traditions of Vodun, and used them to consolidate his power. He worked hard to consolidate his position, and there were attempts to unseat him. There was an attempted coup in 1958, and he purged the army and wrote a new constitution. He won the 1961 election a little too easily. The official votes cast were 1,320,000 votes in favour of Duvalier, none against. It is very rare for an election to be unanimous.

Now a dictator, Duvalier made himself president for life in 1964 and his regime became more repressive and cruel. He did not entirely trust the army, so he created a separate militia, called the VSN (Volontaires de la Securité Nationale), who were responsible for maintaining his power outside the capital. The VSN became known as the Tonton Macoute. They had no salaries and were forced to make their living by criminal extortion. Duvalier created a second militia, the Garde Présidentielle, to act as a personal bodyguard.

When Kennedy came to power in the USA, he put pressure on Duvalier to clean up Haiti, which was clearly corrupt; aid money was being diverted. In 1962, the USA suspended aid to Haiti, but after Kennedy's assassination, the hard line was relaxed. Duvalier was after all adopting the persona of a virtuously anti-Communist presence in the Caribbean, a counter-balance to the evil presence of Castro's Cuba.

By the mid-1960s, it was clear that Duvalier had no intention of standing down. He set about building a personality cult around himself, or rather around the image of himself as the embodiment of Haiti. There were rumours that Duvalier, like some of his predecessors, was dreaming of making himself Emperor of Haiti and establishing a monarchical system.

Duvalier used evil methods to maintain his grip over the island. He used political murder and expulsion to get rid of enemies. He may have killed as many as 30,000. Many of the killings were counter-attacks against people who would have liked to see him dead. Attempted coups by the military were treated as particularly serious offences. In 1967, when some bombs were detonated close to the presidential palace, he had 20 Garde Présidentielle officers executed.

Papa Doc Duvalier maintained his reign of terror until his death in 1971, when he nominated his 19-year-old son Jean-Claude Duvalier to take his place.

Osama bin Laden
(1957–)

OSAMA BIN LADEN was born in Saudi Arabia in 1957. For some years past now, he has figured in the FBI's list of Ten Most Wanted Fugitives, and it is revealing to see bin Laden through the eyes of the FBI for a moment. He is wanted for 'murder of US nationals outside the United States; conspiracy to murder US nationals outside the United States; attack on a federal facility resulting in death'.

The FBI give his details as follows. 'Height: 6ft 4in to 6ft 6in; Weight: approximately 160 pounds; Build: Thin; Occupation: Unknown; Hair: Brown; Eyes: Brown; Complexion: Olive; Sex: Male; Nationality: Saudi Arabian; remarks: Bin Laden is the leader of a terrorist organization known as Al-Qaeda, 'The Base'. He is left-handed and walks with a cane. Osama bin Laden is wanted in connection with the August 7, 1998 bombings of the United States embassies in Dar es Salaam, Tanzania and Nairobi, Kenya. These attacks killed over 200 people. In addition, bin Laden is a suspect in other terrorist attacks throughout the world. Considered armed and extremely dangerous. The US Department of State is offering a reward of up to 25 million dollars for information leading directly to the apprehension or conviction of Osama bin Laden.'

This sum of 25 million dollars would not be easy money, though.

Osama bin Laden is a remarkable, ascetic-looking Islamic fundamentalist. He was a Saudi millionaire, and is now an Islamic terrorist leader. He has been known to the US authorities ever since the days when he was fighting with the CIA against the Soviet army in Afghanistan. Now he is US public enemy number one. He was born on 30 July 1957, the seventeenth of 20 sons of a Saudi construction magnate of Yemeni origin. He took a degree in public administration in 1981 in Jeddah. Bin Laden came to prominence in the Afghan war of independence against the Soviet Union. In 1989, when the war was over, he returned to Saudi Arabia to work in the family firm, the Bin Laden Construction Group.

As a result of his radical Islamic contacts and opposition to the ruling Al Saud family, the Saudi government revoked his citizenship in 1994 and his family disowned him. In 1996, in response to US and Egyptian pressure, Sudan expelled him too and he returned to Afghanistan, where he has lived ever since under the protection of the Taliban. He has put himself in the unusual position of being an incredibly wealthy outcast, rich but dispossessed. His already distorted vision of the world has become yet more distorted. America has become the evil empire, the corrupter of Islamic cultures, the supporter of a Zionist Israel against the Muslim Palestinians, and the source of all the evils of the Near and Middle East; America is the enemy.

In February 1998, bin Laden issued a fatwa against all American citizens – military and civilian. 'The ruling to kill the Americans and their allies - civilian and military – is an individual duty for every Muslim who can do it in any country in which it is possible to do it, in order to liberate the al-Asqua Mosque (Jerusalem) and the holy mosque (Mecca) from their grip, and in order for their armies to move out of all lands of Islam, defeated and unable to threaten any Muslim.'. In June 1999 bin Laden was added to the FBI's Ten Most Wanted List and a 5 million dollar reward was offered.

Bin Laden has an extraordinary ability to move effortlessly from place to place. During his time in Afghanistan, bin Laden was able to disguise his movements from the 50 US special officers who worked full-time on tracing his movements by regularly varying his style of movement. He varied the number of vehicles in his convoy, and varied the type of vehicle. Sometimes he gave his entourage hours of notice, sometimes only minutes. Since September 11, when US officials are more determined to find him, far less has been known. It is thought that only 20 dedicated guards know exactly where he is and that they are pledged to die rather than reveal this.

During the war in Afghanistan it seemed impossible that he could survive the systematic ambush in the Tora Bora hills, yet he escaped. Today, no-one knows for sure where he is. The last time he was heard for sure was close to the Pakistan border. In late 2001, the US military searched the mountains of western Pakistan, where a pattern of phone communication between bin Laden and his friends was picked up. Most analysts think he is still holed up in that area. It is possible that he has changed his appearance. Some people have argued that without a beard and in western clothes he might pass unnoticed, but his tall, gaunt appearance and distinctive facial features make that extremely unlikely.

Bin Laden used to communicate with his organization and the outside world generally by satellite phone. Unfortunately, the US leaked that they were not only listening in but using the calls to locate him. Since then, he has naturally taken to using other methods – e-mail or couriers. The couriers carry computer discs with encrypted messages, which are carried from country to country and only de-encrypted in the destination country. Bin Laden is often referred to by aliases, such as the Sheikh, Hajj, Abu Abdullah, the Director. Multiple aliases are the hallmark of Al-Qaeda chiefs. Ramzi Yousef, who masterminded the World Trade Centre attack, used 15 different identities and 11 passports.

Bin Laden is the undisputed leader of Al Qaeda, its undoubted evil genius. He is called 'emir' or 'prince' by his followers, who have to swear an oath of personal allegiance to him, and violation of that oath is punishable by death. Under bin Laden is a consultative council. His two aides are Egyptian, Ayman al-Zawahiri, a doctor and leader of al-Jihad, and Muhammed Atef, his military commander who also served in al-Jihad. It was al-Jihad that was responsible for the massacre of tourists at Luxor in 1995. Then there is a fatwah committee of the council which makes the decisions to carry out terrorist attacks. Al-Qaeda is a transnational organization with operations in 60 countries and active cells in 20 of those. It is believed to operate training centres in Sudan and Afghanistan. There are active cells in Pakistan, Afghanistan, Kosovo, Chechnya, Philippines, Egypt, Tunisia and USA.

Bin Laden's organization is meticulous in its organizational methods. Operations are planned months and even years ahead. Sites are often carefully researched using fieldwork. The 1995 assassination attempt against the President of Egypt, Hosni Mubarak, in Addis Ababa was based on surveillance of Mubarak's security arrangements in Ethiopia two years earlier. The East African embassy bombers phoned in credible but hoax threats to the embassies and then observed the embassy response; this was an operation that was planned over the course of five years.

Responsibilities for each operation are clearly divided, with a planning cell that mulls over and researches every aspect of the attack for months or years beforehand, and an execution cell that is brought in at the last moment, in some cases only a few weeks before the attack. The greatest weakness in Al-Qaeda's style of operation is the slow and monolithic construction of the plans; any change to the plan has to be approved by superiors. An observer commented that 'They have one idea. Alter it for them, and they have to go back to the drawing board. They are not agile.

They have to re-load, and that takes months, about four to six months.'. The success of each operation depends absolutely on operational security.

Bin Laden and his team plan several different attacks at once, and a series of co-ordinated attacks is well within his operational ability.

A peculiarity of the cells is that both the planners and the operators are very young. The masterminds are often 25. Another surprising feature of the terrorist attacks is that they are relatively cheap. It has been estimated that the 1993 World Trade Centre attack cost Al-Qaeda 18,000 dollars altogether, excluding 6,000 dollars in unpaid phone bills. It was once assumed that bin Laden's huge personal fortune enabled him to finance these lavish projects, but it is not so. His personal fortune is not as great as was once thought, though still tens of millions of dollars, and his operations are relatively inexpensive.

The US are naturally disappointed not to have apprehended or killed bin Laden, but several senior Al-Qaeda officials have been eliminatcd, imprisoned or detained. There were also some successes in foiling several planned attacks, but pride in those successes diminished considerably after the September 11th catastrophe in 2001. The more recent train bombings in Madrid in March, 2004, when 199 people were killed are a reminder that bin Laden is still a great force for evil in the world.

The thing that will never be forgotten about this evil and misguided man is that he bears the ultimate responsibility for the attacks on the

World Trade Centre and the Pentagon on 11 September, 2001, attacks in which over 3,000 people died unnecessarily.

Osama bin Laden's health is not good. He has an enlarged heart, chronically low blood pressure and has lost toes on one foot from a battle wound sustained in Afghanistan. He is regularly attended by a doctor. It has also emerged that he is dependent on kidney dialysis, which is why President Musharraf of Pakistan assumed bin Laden had died in the mountains of Afghanistan – from lack of treatment. That appears to have been incorrect. Inevitably all sorts of stories and rumours circulate round such a figure. The only certainty is that the world is a much more dangerous place – for all of us – for having Osama bin Laden living in it.

PART EIGHT

MASS MURDERERS

Sawney Bean
(about 1350–1400)

GALLOWAY IN SOUTHWEST Scotland was always a
bleak, windswept, empty landscape. In the late
fourteenth century very few people lived there
and most of those who did lived round the edges.
Travellers in those days sometimes went missing,
as victims of falls, bandits, or simply losing their
way at night and dying of the cold. But around
1400 so many travellers were disappearing in
Galloway that the locals began to wonder if packs
of wolves were on the loose in the hills. But there
were no signs of attacks by wolves: no remnants
of bloodstained clothes or other belongings.

James I of Scotland sent officers into Galloway
to investigate. A few suspicious-looking vagrants
and inn-keepers were rounded up and hanged,
but the disappearances went on just as before.

One day, a man and his wife were riding home
from a fair, both on the same horse, when they
were set upon by a wild man who jumped out of
some bushes by the roadside. The rider was
armed and fired a pistol at the wild man. There
was a shout, and more wild men appeared.
Surrounded, the rider slashed at the attackers with
a sword. His wife was pulled off the horse from
behind and her throat was cut by one of the

attackers; then the rider too was pulled down. Another moment and he too would have died.

By chance, a crowd of two dozen or more people, also returning from the fair, came into view. They were stunned by what they saw. The poor woman's clothes had been ripped off her and she had been disembowelled. Her attackers were tearing at her flesh – and apparently eating it. The advancing crowd shouted and the attackers ran off. The poor woman was dead, but her husband and the horse were still alive. They were the only creatures to have survived an attack from the pack of cannibals in 25 years. The woman's body had been dragged off the road for butchery. Any bloodstains there, among the heather, would not have been noticeable from the road. Within hours of the attack, no-one would have known anything had happened there at all.

The news was conveyed to the King in Edinburgh. In four days, he was in Galloway with 400 men. They visited the scene of the ambush, where there were plenty of rocks and bushes, and then set off in the direction seen to be taken by the fleeing marauders. They soon arrived at the coast, which was dominated thereabouts by tall cliffs. There they waited for low tide and then rode along the beach until they found some caves, none of them big enough to make a human dwelling. They were about to turn back when the dogs they had brought with them started barking at a crack in the cliff. It seemed hardly big enough to let a person in, but the dogs went in and started barking excitedly.

The King sent for torches while a few of his men went into the crack. When the torches arrived, the King sent more of his men in. They followed the dark tunnel beyond the crack until eventually it opened into an evil-smelling cave. There were people crouching in the corners and everywhere there were piles of money and jewels. Human body parts dangled from the cave ceiling. The wild people were cornered and ready to fight, but they were quickly overpowered by the armed soldiers.

The cave-dwellers were cannibals, almost unbelievably eating human flesh raw. The soldiers buried the human remains in the beach sand and took the cannibals to the Tolbooth in Edinburgh.

It emerged that the head of this appalling family was Sawney Bean, who had been born in East Lothian, near Edinburgh. As a young man he had run off with a woman and they had ever since then lived in this cave where she had produced six daughters and eight sons; they in their turn had produced 14 granddaughters and 18 grandsons. They were transferred from the Tolbooth to Leith.

There was no trial. The chronicler of these events, John Nicholson, said that it was decided there was no point in bringing them to trial, 'It being thought needless to try creatures who were even professed enemies to mankind.'. The Bean clan had lived in a barbaric way. They died too in a barbaric way. The men's hands and feet were chopped off and they were left to bleed to death. The women were made to watch this grisly spectacle, which was not so different from the scenes they saw in their everyday lives, before being burnt to death on three fires. Nicholson noted that they died 'without the least sign of repentance, but continued cursing. . . to the very last gasp of life.'

In executing the Bean family without a trial, King James was in effect declaring that they were not in his view human beings but animals. But it was an evil response to evil. As so often, evil breeds evil.

Gilles de Rais
(1404–1440)

GILLES DE RAIS was born at Machecoul, in the area of France that lies on the border of Brittany and Poitou, in 1404. His was a quite extraordinary double career, as a great land-owning aristocrat and soldier, and as a black magician and serial child-killer.

It is almost as if we are looking at the distinct and separate lives of two distinct and separate people. Gilles was born into a noble French family, and became one of the paragons of the French aristocracy. As a boy he showed intelligence and was a good pupil; he learned to speak fluent Latin.

At the age of 16, in 1420, he found himself at the court of the Dauphin, the then-uncrowned King of France. He was present at the Dauphin's court nine years later, when Joan of Arc arrived and proposed a plan for the Dauphin to retrieve his throne from England. From 1427 to 1431, Gilles de Rais served as a commander of some note in the Hundred Years' War between France and England. His exploits in battle against the English made him almost as famous as Joan herself. After achieving a notable victory at the Battle of Patay, Gilles was rewarded with the post of Marshal of France.

He acquired five huge estates and ran a chapel that required the attendance of 30 canons. He had a proud, muscular bearing; he was cultured, sophisticated, rich, pious, and brave in battle. He fought with his personal retinue of 200 knights alongside Joan of Arc and was so highly esteemed that in his post as Marshal of France he was able to crown Charles VII King of France. He reached a pinnacle of glory in France just as his contemporary, and apparent antithesis, Vlad the Impaler, was reaching a nadir of infamy. Yet Gilles de Rais was not what he seemed, not what he seemed at all.

Behind the public image there was another Gilles de Rais that was almost a mirror image of all that nobility. He had the darkest of dark sides. He had become fascinated with alchemy and became convinced that to succeed in alchemy he would have to sell his soul to the Devil. A magician offered to introduce him to the Devil and, according to Gilles's story, persuaded him to sacrifice a child. It was by this route, he claimed, that he became a serial child-murderer. It is believed that he sadistically tortured and murdered somewhere between 150 and 800 children. He was so obsessed with the letting of blood that he would order his servants to stab his victims in the neck so that the blood would spurt over him.

Local children started to disappear, and their disappearance was noticed. The remains of many of these children were found in his castles of Machecoul and Champtogne. They were discovered in 1440, after Gilles quarrelled with someone to whom he had sold another of his properties.

Ten years after Joan of Arc was charged and tried for heresy, Gilles de Rais was charged with heresy too after attacking a priest. He was taken into custody on 13 September, 1440, on a charge brought against him by the Bishop of Nantes. He loftily denied the charge, but was then charged with a number of other offences including murder. His ecclesiastical accusers charged him with being a 'heretic, sorcerer, sodomite, invoker of evil spirits, diviner, killer of innocents, apostate from the faith, idolator.' It is an astonishing list of crimes, and it reads like a series of preposterous trumped-up charges. In fact the Church had good reason to want de Rais out of the way. He had become far too powerful in France and was a major threat to the power of the Church, and in particular to the Church's influence over the new King. Moreover, if de Rais was found guilty, the Church was in a good position to acquire some of his lands. The evidence against de Rais was acquired by force. His servants were tortured until they produced enough evidence to convict their master.

On the face of it, it would seem like any other medieval or Renaissance show trial, where the accused has committed no offence at all, but the perjured evidence has been wrung from witnesses by torture in order to achieve a conviction – and execution. But what is extraordinary about this case is that de Rais, who was evidently not tortured, freely admitted his crimes. He made a full confession not only to the murder of the 140 children with which he was charged, but to the murder of at least 800. It is not at all clear why he made this confession, but then he was not a normal personality.

De Rais killed some girls, but most of his victims were young boys, whom he sodomized both before and after decapitating them. He enjoyed watching his servants butchering the children's bodies after the killings.

Gilles de Rais gave two reasons for committing all these murders. One was the impact of a book. It was an illustrated copy of *Lives of the Caesars* by Suetonius, which included graphic descriptions of the mad sexual excesses of emperors such as Tiberius and Caligula, which included sadism – a word not yet invented, of course. The second reason was the approach of an alchemist, Prelati, who promised to reveal the secret of turning base metal into gold by way of black magic rites and human sacrifices.

Probably these were mere attempts at rationalization. De Rais may not have fully understood what he was doing. Today his behaviour would be described using words such as paedophililia and sadism, though it has to be said that naming the impulses does not bring us much closer to understanding them. We have an illusion of analysis and understanding of sexual deviation which is really a self-deception. In the middle ages, concepts like sorcery, black masses and sacrifice came more readily to mind.

Gilles de Rais was, inevitably, found guilty of all these crimes. In a public display of repentance he begged the forgiveness of the parents of the children he had killed. Like Joan of Arc, he was sentenced to burn, but he was shown some mercy because of the full confession, and so garrotted before being burned. He was executed on 26 October, 1440.

Jack the Ripper
(possibly 1857–1888)

THE INFAMOUS JACK the Ripper murders were really just one manifestation of a low-life nineteenth century East End of London. The awful slum conditions bred disease, poverty and violence. There were huge numbers of prostitutes, there was high child mortality, high incidence of sexual abuse of every kind - and lots of murders. Prostitutes were particularly vulnerable, then as now, and prostitute murders were two-a-penny.

Jack the Ripper was responsible for only five of these murders – a drop in the ocean – and his reign of terror in the East End was a surprisingly short one, yet his name became notorious unlike any other murderer's before or since, a by-word for gratuitous, sadistic violence. The Ripper murders made a huge impact on late Victorian England.

One minor mystery is exactly when the Ripper murders began. It is generally agreed that the period over which they happened was fairly short – but how short? Two early victims have been suggested: Emma Smith and Martha Turner. Emma Smith was described as 'a drunken Whitechapel prostitute' which might make her look like a classic Ripper victim, but there the similarities end. She was staggering home drunk to her lodgings in Spitalfields on 3 April, 1888 when she was attacked. Before she died, 24 hours later she was able to tell the police that she had been attacked by four men, the youngest about 19 years old. She had been stabbed with something like a spike and robbed. It has never been suggested that any of the authentic Ripper murders was carried out by a gang.

The second possible early victim was Martha Turner, another prostitute. She was seen drinking with a soldier late one night before being murdered – with 39 stab wounds, nine in the throat, 17 in the chest, 13 in the stomach. It was a frenzied attack and looked as if it might have been done with two hands at once. Martha Turner was murdered on 6–7 August, 1888. Rather surprisingly, soldiers at the Tower of London took their bayonets with them when off duty. After the Turner murder that practice was stopped. All the soldiers at The Tower were lined up for an identity parade, but Martha Turner's friend, who had seen her with the soldier earlier in the evening of the murder, either could not or would not identify the murderer. Sir Melville Macnaghten, who was in charge of the CID after the last Ripper murder and had the job of wrapping the case up, discounted these two murders; he did not believe they were the work of the maniac who committed the Jack the Ripper murders.

The murders began on 31 August, 1888. Mary Ann Nichols, a Whitechapel prostitute, was found murdered in an alley. The police thought from witness accounts that she had approached a tall stranger with the line, 'Want a good time, mister?'. She took him into the dark alley for sex and had her throat savagely cut. The police surgeon who examined her body said, 'I have never seen so horrible a case. She was ripped about in a manner that only a person skilled in the use of a knife could have achieved.' This idea that skill had been used was to return again and again, as people wondered whether the killer was perhaps a butcher or a surgeon.

It was a horrible murder, but 'one-off' prostitute murders were relatively common, and the police assumed it was one of these. But a week later another prostitute, Annie Chapman, was found dead in Hanbury Street close to Spitalfields Market. She had not only had her throat cut, she had been disembowelled, and her possessions as well as her entrails laid out beside her body. The thorough dissection of Annie Chapman suggested that the murderer had an interest, however warped, in anatomy.

Then, on 25 September, came the first letter from the Whitechapel murderer. It was sent to a Fleet Street news agency. 'Dear Boss,' it read, 'I keep on hearing that the police have caught me. But they won't fix me yet. I am down on certain types of women and I won't stop ripping them until I do get buckled. Grand job, that last job was, I gave the lady no time to squeal. I love my work and want to start again. You will soon hear from me with my funny little game. I saved some of the proper stuff in a little ginger beer bottle after my last job to write with, but it went thick like glue and I can't use it. Red ink is fit enough I hope. Ha! Ha! Next time I shall clip the ears off and send them to the police, just for the jolly. Jack the Ripper.'

Shortly afterwards, on 30 September, he murdered Liz Stride, another prostitute, in Berner's Street. Like the others, she had her throat cut, almost certainly from behind, but was not mutilated in any other way. The police, probably rightly, assumed that Jack had been disturbed during this murder and had run off before finishing the job. To compensate, he killed again a few streets away, in Mitre Square. This fourth victim was Catherine Eddowes. She was disembowelled.

Panic gripped Whitechapel. Women began to equip themselves with whistles to raise the alarm and knives to defend themselves.

The Eddowes murder introduced a new dimension. Not only was it much bloodier than all the others – so far – but a trail of blood led to a wall where a message was inscribed in chalk: 'The Juwes are the men who will be blamed for nothing'. Fearing reprisal attacks on Jewish men, the head of the Metropolitan Police Force, Sir Charles Warren, had the message scrubbed off. In doing so, he may have destroyed some vital evidence. It would be useful to know, for instance, whether the handwriting was the same as that in the 'Dear Boss' letter.

Warren's fears about reprisals were well-founded. All sorts of rumours were going round the East End about the identity of the murderer. One suspect was Michael Ostrog, a Russian-born doctor; it was rumoured he had been sent from Russia to incriminate expatriate Russian Jews. Nevertheless, the spelling of 'Juwes' may suggest something else – the involvement of freemasonry. The disembowelling too may be connected with Freemasons' lore. The police were flooded with suspects nominated by the public, and the general atmosphere in the East End approached hysteria.

The Ripper's final victim was Mary Kelly, a 25-year-old prostitute, who was murdered on 9 November in her rented room in Miller's Court. The following morning her landlord, Henry Bowers, called to collect her rent. He looked in through the window and saw the horrific sight of Mary's dismembered body lying on the bed. 'I shall be haunted by this for the rest of my life,' he told the police. The previous evening Mary had been desperately trying to earn her rent. She was seen approaching strangers for business. The last one she was seen approaching was tall, dark and wore a deerstalker hat.

After Mary Kelly's death there were no more Ripper murders, and that is in itself one of the great unsolved mysteries about them. Compulsive psychopathic killers tend to go on killing until they are stopped, yet the police had not apprehended anyone. There was no arrest, yet there were no more killings. One possible explanation is that the Ripper was prevented from continuing by his own death, that he committed suicide. This has led to the identification of Montagu John Druitt as the Ripper. He was last seen alive on 3

December, 1888, four weeks after the Kelly murder. His body was found floating in the Thames a few days later. Druitt was a failed barrister who had fallen on such hard times that he had to resort to teaching to make a living. In favour of Druitt as the murderer are the history of mental illness within the family and Druitt's acquisition of basic medical skills as a young man.

Druitt was born on 15 August, 1857 at Wimborne in Dorset. His father William was a distinguished surgeon, a Justice of the Peace, a pillar of the community. Montagu Druitt was sent to Winchester in 1870 at the age of 12. At school he was successful, except as an actor. Even the school magazine slated his performance as Sir Toby Belch. His great passion was for cricket. He went on to New College Oxford to read Classics, graduating in 1880. His decision to become a barrister seems to have been the beginning of a decline. He fell back on teaching at a private 'cramming shop' in Blackheath. He went on playing cricket. Interestingly, he is known to have been playing in matches the day before or the day after several of the murders – whatever that proves.

In 1888, Montagu Druitt was going to pieces, and finally killed himself in December. It may be that he even gave the police his address too. On 29 September, 1888, the Ripper wrote from Liverpool, 'Beware, I shall be at work on the 1st and 2nd inst., in Minories at twelve midnight, and I give the authorities a good chance, but there is never a policeman near when I am at work.' After the Catherine Eddowes killing he sent another letter from Liverpool: 'What fools the police are. I even give them the name of the street where I am living.' Was Jack the Ripper really living in the Minories, a street near the Tower of London? Druitt had a relative called Lionel Druitt, who qualified as a doctor in Edinburgh in 1877, and he had lodgings near The Tower. It was at 140 Minories. Lionel seems to have moved in as a junior partner of Dr Gillard in Clapham Road in 1886, but it may be that the Minories rooms were passed on to his cousin Montagu, who was four years younger than him. It was quite common for upper and middle class young men to go 'slumming' in the East End. Charles Dickens and Wilkie Collins had done it when looking for material for their fiction; others did it when looking for sex. A room in a lodging house in the area would have been useful for the purpose. The connection between Montagu Druitt and the Minories is tenuous, but it is the address he mentions in his letter. It is also intriguing that Lionel Druitt left for New South Wales in Australia in 1886, yet he was able to produce, in 1890, a tantalizingly elusive document entitled *The East End Murderer – I knew him*. Since he was out of the country at the time of the murders, he can only have picked up the key information from other family members. Unfortunately, though the title and author of this document are known, no copy has so far been traced. In spite of having a promising career in both medicine and cricket in England, Montagu's brother Edward suddenly decided in 1889 to emigrate to Australia. Maybe, after his brother's murder spree and suicide, England was no longer so attractive. In 1889, he doubtless met Lionel and told hem everything, giving him the material for the 1890 monograph.

Dr Neill Cream is a known murderer who may have the Ripper murders added to his CV. Cream's career as an arsonist, abortionist and murderer was brought to an end in 1892, when he was convicted of the murders of four London prostitutes. He had picked them up in the boroughs of Walworth and Lambeth and poisoned them with strychnine. It is said that on the scaffold he exclaimed at the last moment, 'I am Jack the – ' just as he dropped. Unfortunately, as well as the hangman, who swore that this happened, there were others present, including Sir Henry Smith, who later boasted that nobody knew more about Jack the Ripper than he did, and he did not mention this key information. Actually, even if Cream had claimed at that crucial moment that he was the Ripper, it could have been a ruse to gain a stay of execution. If he had owned up to being Jack the Ripper, surely those with him on the scaffold would have wanted to hear more?

In fact, regardless of what Neill Cream shouted, or whether he shouted, Cream could not have committed the Ripper murders. From November 1881 until July 1891 he was serving a life sentence for murder in Illinois.

Another convicted murderer often brought forward as a suspect for the Ripper murders is

George Chapman. He was born in Poland in 1865 as Severin Klososwski. He was hanged in 1903 for the murder by arsenic poisoning of Maud Marsh, Mary Spink and Bessie Taylor. He is linked to the Ripper cases by being, according to one source, in Whitechapel at the right time. He is said to have run a hairdresser's business at George Yard, which is where Martha Turner was murdered. Inspector Abberline, who led the Ripper enquiries, came to believe in his retirement that George Chapman was the Ripper. Abberline presumably suspected Chapman because he was living in the area (but so were a lot of other people) and he fitted the description of the man seen with Mary Kelly on the night of her murder. But the nature of the Ripper killings is totally different from that of the Chapman killings. One murderer used a knife; the other used poison. They could not have been more different.

Some writers have proposed that the Duke of Clarence was the murderer, on the grounds that the Duke was mentally unstable and keen on London low-life, and was confined after the Ripper murders. The Duke's sexual proclivities seem to have lain elsewhere, though, and it is difficult to see how he could have been involved in slaying female prostitutes. Many other people have been named as Ripper suspects, including the painter Walter Sickert, though none carry real conviction. The Jack the Ripper murders seem destined to remain the great unsolved murder mystery of modern times.

Who was he? At least we know what he looked

like, because of one or two sightings of him immediately after the murders. The best description is the one given by a detective, Steve White, who saw a lone figure moving away from the scene of the Mitre Square murder. This is his memorable description of Jack the Ripper;

'I saw a man coming out of the alley [where the body was found two minutes later]. He was walking quickly but noiselessly, apparently wearing rubber shoes, which were rather rare in those days.

'He was about five feet ten inches in height, and was dressed rather shabbily, though it was obvious that the material of his clothes was good. Evidently a man who had seen better days, I thought. His face was long and thin, nostrils rather delicate and his hair was jet black. His complexion was inclined to be sallow and altogether the man was foreign in appearance. The most striking thing about him was the extraordinary brilliance of his eyes. The man was slightly bent at the shoulders, though he was obviously quite young – about 33 at the most – and gave one the idea of having been a student or professional man. His hands were snow white, and the fingers long and tapering. As the man passed me at the lamp, I had an uneasy feeling that there was something more than usually sinister about him, and I was strongly moved to find some pretext for detaining him; but it was not in keeping with British police methods that I should do so . . . I had a sort of intuition that the man was not quite right. The man stumbled a few feet away from me, and I made that an excuse for engaging him in conversation. He turned sharply at the sound of my voice, and scowled at me in surly fashion, but he said "Good-night" and agreed with me that it was cold.

'His voice was a surprise to me. It was soft and musical, with a touch of melancholy in it, and it was the voice of a man of culture – a voice altogether out of keeping with the squalid surroundings of the East End.'

When Steve White's vivid description is compared with Montagu Druitt's photograph, there is not much doubt that the two are strikingly similar. White got Druitt's socio-economic class right. He even got Druitt's age right. The rubber-soled plimsolls were consistent with Druitt's sporting activity. Immediately after the detective's encounter with Jack the Ripper, he was called urgently by one of the other officers to 'come along' and look at the body of a woman he had just found in the alley. Steve White went and looked, remembered the man he had just seen and ran after him as fast as he could.

But of course he didn't catch him.

Peter Kürten, the Vampire of Düsseldorf
(1883–1932)

PETER KÜRTEN STARTED his career as a sadist when still a child. When he was nine years old he worked for the local dog-catcher near his home town of Cologne-Mulheim. At this tender age, he started torturing the unfortunate animals he caught. Later he went on to torture pigs, sheep and goats. He was fascinated by the sight of blood and loved chopping the heads off geese and drinking the blood that came spurting out. It was not long before he graduated to killing people.

While still a boy, he was swimming in the Rhine with friends and succeeded in drowning two of them.

As an adult, he looked for new thrills, and tried fraud, theft and arson. He also tried beating prostitutes. But murder seems to be what he was destined for. It is rather strange, given the trail of death he had already laid, that the first premeditated murder he planned went wrong. He attacked a girl in a park and left her for dead, but she recovered and staggered away from the scene, too ashamed to report what had happened. The next attack was more successful, if that word can be used appropriately in this situation. He strangled and raped an eight-year-old girl he found asleep in a room over an inn at Cologne-Mulheim, then cut her throat. After committing this awful deed, Kürten locked the door, and returned to his home in Düsseldorf. He returned to the scene of the crime the next day and sat at a café opposite the inn. He felt elated and important when he heard people round him talking about the murder. This murder had an inevitable second victim – the man who was wrongly accused of the little girl's murder. He was the girl's uncle. He was arrested, tried and eventually acquitted, but the trauma and the 'no smoke without fire' suspicion that continued to hang over him wore him down; the poor man died prematurely two or three years later. This landmark in Peter Kürten's career of murder took place in 1913.

In 1914, Kürten was called up. If he had stayed in the army, he would have had more than his fill of killing, but he deserted straight away and consequently spent most of the First World War in prison. When freed, he turned to fraud again and was sent back to prison. Then, in 1921, he was freed again and he made a decision to go straight. He married an ex-prostitute, started dressing smartly, and took a job in a factory. He was courteous and well-liked. But it did not last. In 1925 he started attacking prostitutes, then complete strangers in the street, still mesmerized by the sight of blood.

In 1929, Kürten attacked two sisters aged five and 14 as they walked home from a fair, strangled them and cut their throats. The next day he stabbed a housemaid with such ferocity that the knife-blade broke off in the young woman's back. She was lucky to survive; her screams attracted the attention of passers-by who came and saved her life, but unfortunately they did not arrive in time to catch Peter Kürten.

By this stage, the city of Düsseldorf was in a panic. Police had records of over 50 attacks which they thought must have been committed by the same psychopath. This unknown madman was known as The Vampire, but no-one knew who he was.

The breakthrough happened in 1929, as Kürten was trying to set up another atrocity. A girl arrived at the main railway station in Düsseldorf on 14 May and was intercepted by a stranger who offered to direct her to a cheap hotel. He took her along a main street, but then tried to get her to walk through the park. At this point she became nervous, remembering the stories about the Düsseldorf monster. Just as the man was becoming frighteningly persistent, another man arrived to rescue her, and he introduced himself as Peter Kürten. The first man disappeared. Kürten invited the girl to his house in the Mettmannerstrasse to recover and have a meal. She was concerned when she saw how poorly furnished his attic rooms were. Then he walked her through the Grafenburg Woods, where he assaulted her. Suddenly, mid-assault, Kürten released her, courteously escorting her back to the public highway. He asked her if she remembered where he lived. She said no, a lie that saved her life. Remarkably, the girl did not report the incident to the police. Kürten might still have been in the clear, but for a strange coincidence. The girl wrote about the incident to a friend, but addressed the enveloped wrongly. A post office clerk opened the letter to find out the sender's address and his eyes fell on the account of the attack, which he reported to the police.

Policemen visited the girl and made her retrace her steps back to Kürten's house. She had not remembered the number, but picked out the likeliest. When she saw Kürten's room she was sure. At that moment Kürten came up the stairs, saw what was happening and ran off. The landlady gave the police his name. They spotted Peter Kürten, but he ran off through the city streets. As a last resort he turned to his wife. He told her everything. She was appalled, arranged another secret meeting with him and went straight to the police, who ambushed and arrested Kürten at the appointed meeting place.

Kürten was charged with nine murders and seven attempted murders. Kürten, confined in a hastily improvised wooden cage, startled the judge and jury with the clinical way in which he described his appalling crimes. His defence counsel was reduced to describing his client as 'the king of sexual delinquents, uniting nearly all perversions in one person, killing men, women, children and animals, killing anything he found.'.

The counsel's intention was to portray Kürten as a madman. It did not work. Kürten was sentenced to death. For a time it seemed the death sentence might not be carried out. There was lot of controversy about the use of the death penalty, which had not been used since 1928, and Kürten appealed. On 30 June, the Prussian Ministry of Justice turned down the appeal. He was guillotined at 6 a.m. on 2 July, 1931 in the courtyard of the Klingelputz prison in Cologne. He went happily to his death, eating two breakfasts of Wienerschnitzel, fried potatoes and white wine and telling the prison doctor how he looked forward to 'the pleasure to end all pleasures, that after my head has been chopped off I will still be able to hear, at least for a moment, the sound of my own blood gushing from the stump of my neck.'.

Fritz Haarman, the Vampire of Hanover
(1879–1925)

WHILE PETER KÜRTEN, the Düsseldorf Vampire, was gaining notoriety for his murders, another brutal serial killer was coming to the end of his criminal career in another German city. He was Fritz Haarman, and he was known as the Vampire of Hanover.

Fritz Haarman was born in 1879 and spent the First World War safely in prison, serving a five-year sentence for theft. As the war ended, he came out of prison and returned to Hanover to try to make a living. He became a purveyor of meats, pies and second-hand clothes in a poor district of Hanover. His business was based on murder: the raw materials of his trade came from young men and boys.

Haarman went out at night, picking up homeless and jobless boys at the railway stations and offering them food and a bed for the night. When they reached Haarman's home they were fed and sexually abused, which they probably expected. Some of them, though not all, were murdered, which they did not expect. Their bodies were butchered and their flesh cooked and put into Haarman's pies; their clothes too were sold.

It was the way Haarman killed his victims that gave rise to his nickname. He bit their throats.

Remarkably, Haarman was in regular contact with the police, who must have suspected at least the lesser of his crimes. He was a police informer, passing on information about suspicious new-comers to the town, the whereabouts of stolen goods and plans for criminal activities. The police were so used to working with Haarman that when a 17-year-old boy went missing and his parents raised the alarm, the police made only a cursory visit to Haarman's room, even though a witness had seen the boy with Haarman. Haarman later boasted at his trial that when the police visited his room the boy's head was there, wrapped in newspaper behind the oven.

In 1919, Fritz Haarman acquired an accomplice, a 20-year-old called Hans Gans. It became Hans's job to go out and select the victims. Together, they stepped up the murder rate – and the production of meat.

It became evident that Hanover was a very dangerous place. People were literally vanishing from the streets. The police found Haarman's information so useful that they turned a deaf ear to the stream of complaints coming in about Haarman. People were reporting the one-way traffic of boys into Haarman's home, buckets of blood being carried out, the bloodstained clothes he was selling – yet the police took no action against him.

The discovery of two human skulls, one of a boy, beside the River Leine, pushed the police into action. More human remains were found along the river bank. Some boys found a sack packed with human organs. Hundreds of human bones were found on the river bed. Eventually the police raided Haarman's blood-stained rooms.

Haarman and Gans went on trial in December 1924. When asked how many he killed, Haarman said, 'It might be 30, it might be 40.'. He freely admitted killing them by biting through their throats. In the circumstances, Gans was treated fairly lightly. He was given a life sentence, of which he served 12 years. Haarman was found to be sane, in the sense that he was entirely responsible for his actions, and therefore sentenced to death by beheading. He said he looked forward to it.

Herman Mudgett
(H. H. Holmes)
(1861–1896)

HERMAN WEBSTER MUDGETT is one of those rare mass murderers whose activities defy belief even decades after they have happened. The events, the circumstances are so bizarre and extraordinary that they read like a work of cheap sensational fiction – so absurd, as well as so appalling, that they cannot be true.

Herman Mudgett was born in Philadelphia, Pennsylvania, the son of Levi Horton Mudgett and his wife, Theodate Page Price. In 1878 he married Clara Lovering. In 1887 he bigamously married Myrta Belknap in Minneapolis; they had a daughter called Lucy. He married a third time, to Georgiana Yorke, in 1894.

His early career was based mainly on fraud and forgery, including a patent cure for alcoholism and a gadget for making natural gas from water. But Mudgett would also become a sadistic killer who enjoyed dismembering his victims. He researched his methods at the incredibly named Ann Abhor medical school, becoming an expert in acid burns. He found that he could supplement his student allowance by body snatching. He stole corpses, made them unrecognizable by burning them with acid, and claimed on life insurance policies he had taken out under made-up names. He managed to pull off this trick several times before he was stopped. A nightwatchman caught him removing a woman's body from a cemetery, and Mudgett ran off empty-handed.

Mudgett then went to Chicago, where he ran a pharmacy, ominously adopting an alias, Dr H. H. Holmes. By defrauding the pharmacist, Mudgett acquired not only the pharmacy but the land next to it; in 1890 he was able to build himself a house on the vacant plot. It was to be no ordinary house. The ground floor was shops, the top floor was his personal office, and the floor in between con-sisted of a maze of over a hundred windowless rooms. Mudgett called it The Castle, and like a medieval castle it contained a remarkable range of special features such as secret passages, trap doors, chutes, shafts and dungeons. He managed to avert any suspicion about what he was up to by commissioning a different builder for each part of the house.

Mudgett's Torture Castle was completed in time for the great Columbian Exposition of 1893. This attracted huge numbers of visitors to the city. He offered rooms to let in his house, and killed several of his guests. He lured young women to his castle where he drugged them, shot them down one of the shafts or chutes into an airtight chamber, which he pumped full of lethal gas. The bodies were sent down chutes into the cellar where he had installed vats of acid and lime – and a dissecting table. Here Mudgett cut his victims up, saved the organs that interested him and put the rest into the vats for disposal. Some victims were cremated, some sold to medical schools.

Mudgett later admitted to killing 28 young women during the period of the Exposition, but he may have killed as many as 200. He might have gone on committing more and more murders, but for his avarice. Two of his victims were sisters from Texas. Instead of disposing of their bodies in his usual way, he set fire to the house in order to get the insurance money and moved away from Chicago. The insurance company was suspicious and called in the police. Unfortunately, and surprisingly, the initial police investigation revealed no direct or circumstantial evidence of any of the terrible crimes Mudgett had committed in the house.

Mudgett did not know this, and was by now in Texas, where he traced the relatives of the two Texan sisters. He tried to defraud them of $60,000 and they became suspicious. Before any action had been taken, Mudgett took to the road again, stealing a horse to make his getaway. The police stopped him in Missouri, where he was charged with another attempt at fraud. He managed to get a grant of bail, and promptly absconded.

The mass murderer next turned up in Philadelphia, in 1894, where one of his criminal associates had been running an insurance fraud racket for him. Mudgett took the extraordinary risk of murdering him and moving to Toronto with his victim's wife and three children. The children too were to be murdered; their bodies were later found in the cellars of rented houses.

There is so often an ironic twist in these cases that is tempting to think that there is a resistance in the human heart to believing in evil on the grand scale. Right up to this point, no-one had any suspicion that Mudgett had killed anyone at all, let alone that he was a serial killer. The police were on his trail, but for the theft of the horse and for bail-jumping. The police went to Mudgett's mother, who was proud of her successful son and happy to tell them where they could find him. Mudgett was arrested in Boston and charged with horse-stealing, bail-jumping and fraud. Only then did the police return to the burnt-out remains of the Chicago Torture Castle. There they found the remains of many human bodies.

Mudgett confessed to 28 murders and was hanged on 7 May, 1896. He was one of the most spectacular serial killers, indeed serial criminals, in American history.

Henri Landru
(1869–1922)

HENRI DÉSIRÉ LANDRU was born of fairly poor
Parisian stock. His father worked as a fireman at
the furnaces of the Vulcain Ironworks in Paris.
Henri attended a Catholic school and was
admitted as a sub-deacon in the religious order of
St Louis en l'Ile. He left school at 16 after taking
an engineering course, and shortly afterwards did
his four years' military service, by the end of
which he had reached the rank of sergeant.

Henri Landru had been considered a bright
boy, and as a young man he realised that his
glibness was useful in seducing young women. In
1891 he seduced his cousin. She became pregnant
and gave birth to a daughter. Two years later, he
married her. He had been quartermaster of the
regiment at St Quentin, but he left the military life
behind when he got married and went into
business, in a small way, as a clerk. He was
unlucky in his choice of employer; the man in
question absconded with the money Landru had
given him as a bond. It may be that this incident
gave Landru a motive to get back at society in
some way, or just confirmation that the world is a
jungle.

In addition to being a furniture dealer and

garage owner, Landru turned into a swindler. His victims were mainly middle-aged widows whom he met through his furniture business. Often they came to him with their possessions to sell, as a desperate means of making some money. Landru preyed on their weakness and vulnerability, and persuaded them to let him invest their pensions, which he then stole. This trick worked for a time, but by 1900 he found himself in court being sentenced to two years in prison for fraud; he had tried to withdraw funds from the Comptoir d'Escompte using a false identity.

Over the next ten years, Landru was in and out of prison no less than seven times, serving sentences as long as three years. In 1908, quite undeterred by the law's opinion of his activities, he struck on a new scam. He put an advertisement in the newspaper, posing as a well-to-do widower looking for the companionship of a widow in a similar situation. It looked harmless and respectable enough. What he was looking for was more vulnerable widows, but this time he was going to get hold of all of their money, and all at once. Landru was becoming more ambitious. Mme Izore, a 40-year-old widow, was persuaded to hand over a 15,000 franc dowry with some fake deeds as surety. Mme Izore was left destitute. She was naturally unhappy about it, and went to court to get compensation and justice. Unfortunately the dowry had gone by the time the police caught up with Landru, so all she had was the satisfaction of seeing Landru going to prison for another three years.

Landru was released just before the outbreak of the First World War, probably on the understanding that he would re-enlist in the army. Landru's mother had died in 1910. His father had committed suicide, in despair over his son's lawless behaviour, which had left the family penniless and degraded. He drifted around the countryside, knowing that he had been convicted in absentia for various new offences and sentenced to deportation, for life, to New Caledonia.

It is not clear what happened to Landru psychologically during the communal trauma of the First World War, but something happened to escalate his criminal behaviour. Perhaps it was estrangement from his wife. Perhaps it was the death of both of his parents; he may have felt released from such slight moral controls as they had exerted over him. Perhaps it was the cumulative coarsening effect of too many years in prison. Perhaps it was the daily reports of terrible slaughter at the Front that made human life seem even cheaper to him.

The series of murders that followed do not fall into any 'normal' pattern of female serial killings. The motive does not seem to have been in any way sexual. Lust did not enter into it at all. Bloodlust does not seem to have been the motive either. In this case, killing was a means to an end. The murders are probably best understood in relation to the pattern of the earlier swindles. Landru started by buying furniture from vulnerable women, then went on to conning them out of part of their pensions, then went on to conning a wealthier woman out of her dowry. That was where he encountered a major problem; Mme Izore had afterwards brought a charge against him. If she had not been alive to bring the charge, there would have been no problem. So the logical next step was to take the money and kill the victims. The murders were therefore entirely cold-blooded. As Colin Wilson has said, he was 'a callous ruffian'.

He was evidently a good talker. He was not good-looking. He was rather small, with a bald head and a thick, reddish-brown beard, bushy eyebrows and sunken cheeks. He looked sinister or comical, and swept people along with his amusing patter. He even made jokes at his trial. It was not just women he charmed, but men. All the while he was robbing widows, he was defrauding discharged soldiers of their pensions too. What they all had in common was their position in society; they were all vulnerable people, and that tells us that Landru had no conscience. He was a psychopath.

He had a sense of right and wrong, but did not apply it to himself. He was able to justify swindling one soldier out of his pension on the grounds that he had a mistress, yet Landru himself had a mistress and was cheating on both the mistress and the wife. He expressed no remorse over the murders at his trial, only embarrassment that his estranged wife would now find out that he had been unfaithful to her. By that stage the unfortunate Remy must instead have been feeling very relieved that she had got away from Landru alive; the infidelity was a negligible detail.

Landru planned his killings with some care, making sure first that the victims were separated from their families. After he had killed them, he went to the trouble of assuring the families that they were alive and well. Two of Mme Guillin's friends had postcards from Landru to say that she was unable to write herself, which was true. He forged a letter from Mme Buisson to her dressmaker and another to the caretaker at her apartment in Paris. Landru posed as the solicitor of Mme Jaume, who had been in the process of divorcing her husband, and closed her bank accounts.

Two years after Mme Buisson had the misfortune to meet Landru, her son died. Obviously the family wanted to inform Mme Buisson, but could not contact her. Her sister remembered that she had said something about running away with a M Guillet, so she wrote to the mayor of Gambais to see if he could locate either of them for her. The mayor knew nothing of either party but suggested that she should contact the family of Mme Collomb, who had also mysteriously disappeared in Gambais under rather similar circumstances. At that stage nobody knew where Mme Collomb had gone – except Henri Landru.

The mayor directed the Buisson family and the police to a villa. The tenant there was a M Dupont, but when the police called at the Villa Ermitage they did not find any of the people they were looking for. There was no Mme Buisson, no Mme Collomb, no M Dupont – and no Henri Landru either. The villa was Landru's. Mme Buisson's sister, Mlle Lacoste, went on hunting the streets of Paris. There she had a remarkable piece of luck. She spotted the distinctive Henri Landru coming out of a shop and recognized him as someone she had seen accompanying her sister and who had been called 'Fremiet'. She lost him in the crowd but had the presence of mind to go into the shop to ask the man's name. She was told he was not M Fremiet but M Guillet, and that he lived in the Rue de Rochechouart. She called the police and Landru was arrested.

Landru was immediately suspected of murdering both Mme Collomb and Mme Buisson, but Landru was unhelpful and the police had no evidence on which to hold him. Where were the bodies? The police returned to Gambais, dug up the gardens, but found only the bones of two dogs. They searched another villa Landru had occupied at Vernouillet, but found nothing there either. All the police did find was a notebook, in which Landru had usefully recorded all his financial dealings. On one page was an intriguing list of names that told an alarming story: 'A. Cuchet, G. Cuchet, Bresil, Crozatier, Buisson, A. Collomb, Andrée Babelay, M. Louis Jaume, A. Pascal, M. Thr. Mercadier'. In the middle were the names of the two missing women, but who were these other people? Were they perhaps missing too? The police suspected that this was a list of murder victims.

Landru maintained his silence, confident that with no bodies there was no case against him. The police went on investigating the case for two years, with Landru consistently and frustratingly refusing to admit to anything. Gradually the story emerged. Each of the women had answered Landru's marriage advertisements and subsequently disappeared. Landru had recorded the purchase of tickets from Paris to Gambais – in each case return tickets for himself but one-way tickets for his victims. It was clear now that Landru had taken all the women to Gambais with the deliberate intention of killing them and disposing of their bodies there.

The grounds of the Villa Ermitage and Vernouillet were dug up again, with no result. Then the neighbours at Gambais mentioned the terrible evil-smelling fumes that had come from Landru's kitchen stove. The stove was examined and it gave the investigators the evidence they were looking for. Amongst the ashes they found the remains of fasteners characteristic of women's clothing. *The Times* added that they also found small human bones, though this seems not to have been the case. The police could not tell how the 11 women had been killed, but it was now obvious how their bodies had been disposed of. Landru had cremated them. Landru could now be charged on 11 counts of murder and sent to trial.

The trial of Henri Landru caused a sensation. In a depressing post-war world, the lurid details of Landru's shenanigans were a welcome distraction. The court case had all the ingredients of a high-camp melodrama; Landru's extraordinary villainous appearance, racy lifestyle and long criminal record made him a fascinating figure; his current mistress, Francoise Segret, was a 27-year-old he had picked up on a Paris bus; there was the sensational string of mysterious disappearances; there was the total mystery surrounding the deaths of the 11 women; finally, there was Landru's cavalier, rascally, impudent personality. There were queues to get places in the court-room. On one occasion, there was such a scrum between some women fighting over seats that Landru called out to them that one of the ladies would be welcome to have his place.

The trial opened in November 1921 and went on for a month. Landru was still convinced that he could not be convicted without the evidence of a body, so he carried on refusing to give away anything at all. His stock replies were that it was no-one else's business what he knew about the disappearance of the women, and that to say what happened would be to betray a woman's confidence. He also believed that because he had been judged sane enough to stand trial he would have to be found innocent, and said as much to the newspaper reporters, who enthusiastically covered his trial in great detail. Landru was bombarded with questions, day after day, but he stood firm. 'I have nothing to say.'

During the trial, Landru's health began to deteriorate and he became less circumspect in his answers. Although he never admitted killing any of the women, he said enough to show the court that he was deviously concealing a detailed knowledge of what had happened. This was an error of judgement. He needed to create a favourable impression if he was withholding information, and he was creating a very unfavourable impression with his impudence and heavy sarcasm. Increasingly he came across as just the sort of devious, heartless, callous villain who would lure women out to his place in the country and kill them for their money. He came across as guilty.

It did not take the jury long to decide that he had indeed killed the 11 women, and he was duly sentenced to death. When the time came for Landru to say goodbye to his lawyers, he presented them with a picture. If they had looked behind the picture, they would have found Landru's written confession admitting to the murders, but they did not; the confession remained hidden for 50 years. Landru was guillotined in February 1922.

Ted Bundy
(1946–1989)

THEODORE ROBERT COWELL was born on 24 November, 1946 in a home for unmarried mothers in Burlington, Vermont. To cover the illegitimacy, his mother, Eleanor Cowell, told the boy he was her brother, leading him to believe that his grandparents were his parents. It has been suggested that the grandfather may have been the father, and that the trauma of discovering that he was the product of incest may have tipped the boy towards psychopathic behaviour; but none of that is certain. There is in fact nothing known that can satisfactorily explain the series of brutal killings that began in 1973.

In 1950 Eleanor Cowell moved to the West Coast, settling in Tacoma, Washington, where she changed the boy's name from Cowell to Nelson. It is not clear why she did this. Then a year later she married John Bundy, and the boy took his step-father's surname. There seem to have been no abnormal childhood problems except that Ted referred to Eleanor alternately as his sister and his mother, and changed his name twice in quick succession, which suggests a level of confusion. In his teens, Ted Bundy started stealing on a regular basis and, on his own admission, was socially retarded.

Bundy attended the University of Puget Sound for two semesters, then transferred to the University of Washington. There he met and fell in love with Stephanie Brooks. She was a good-looking young woman with long dark hair parted in the middle, in fact strikingly similar in appearance to the young women Bundy was later to select as murder victims. It could be that a few years later Bundy was killing Stephanie, over and over again. Back in 1966, the relationship with Stephanie seems to have been developing smoothly, but by 1968–9 difficulties were emerging and Stephanie broke it off. Bundy was devastated. It was at about this time that he revisited Burlington, the place where he was born, and looked up the records to check whether Eleanor was his sister or his mother. She was his mother. A man called Lloyd Marshall was listed as his father. No-one had ever mentioned him at all. It is not clear what effect these revelations had on Bundy, but he returned to Washington to try, unsuccessfully, to restart the affair with Stephanie.

Two more relationships began at this time, with Liz Kendall and Ann Rule, and Bundy seemed outwardly calm and normal. In 1973 he entered law school. Then he abruptly dropped out – and the killing started.

Kathy Devine, a 15-year-old, took a lift in a green pick-up on 25 November, 1973. Her body was found a couple of weeks later; her throat had been cut. In January 1974 Bundy brutally attacked 18-year-old Jonu Lenz in the basement bedroom of a house she shared with some other girls in

Seattle. She was sexually assaulted and savagely beaten over the head; she was lucky to survive. The third victim, on 1 February, was Lynda Ann Healy. She was abducted, again from a basement bedroom. The fourth was Donna Manson, who was abducted from Evergreen College; her body was never found. The list of abductions and murders goes on, seemingly endlessly: Susan Rancourt, Kathy Parks, Brenda Ball, Georgia Hawkins, Brenda Baker, Janice Ott, Denise Naslund.

The police had little to go on, except the report of a green pick-up and the description of a man with a plaster cast on his arm who was seen by several people approaching women and heard introducing himself as 'Ted'. The composite sketch was published in the press. The likeness was good enough for Ted Bundy's workmates to tease him about being the serial killer.

The remains of one of his victims were discovered near Lake Sammamish, but by then Bundy had moved on to the University of Utah, where he started killing more young women: Nancy Wilcox, Melissa Smith and Laurie Aimee. Then one of the abductions went wrong for Bundy. On 8 November, 1974 he approached Carol DeRonch at a shopping centre in Murray. He pretended to be a policeman and told her that her car had been broken into. He got her into his car, pulled out a gun and snapped a handcuff onto one of her wrists. Before he could secure the other cuff, Carol had the presence of mind to get away and flag down a passing motorist who took her straight to the police. Unfortunately there were no fingerprints left on the handcuffs that were clear enough to be used for identification. Bundy was still free to go on killing, and another long list of victims followed: Debbie Kent, Caryn Campbell, Julie Cunningham, Denise Oliverson, Melanie Cooley, Lynette Culver, Susan Curtis, Shelley Robertson, Nancy Baird and Debbie Smith.

By now the authorities in Washington knew they had a serial killer on their hands, and the Utah authorities knew that they did too, but because of Bundy's travelling it was difficult to be sure whether the killings were linked. One murderer? Or two, three or four? The scale of the mystery escalated when an investigator found the crushed skulls of several of the missing girls, one of them transported 260 miles from the scene of the abduction.

The task force in Washington made gradual progress, compiling a list of suspects. Using a computer, the list was reduced to 25. They were interviewed one by one. As it happened, Bundy was to be next, when a Highway Patrol officer, Bob Haywood, noticed an unfamiliar light-coloured Volkswagen in his neighbourhood. He turned his car lights on the vehicle, it sped away, and Haywood gave chase. Eventually Haywood caught up with the VW and made it pull over to the roadside. He asked for identification. It was Ted Bundy. Haywood noticed that the vehicle had been customized in an unusual way. The passenger seat had been removed. Haywood decided to search the vehicle. He found a bag containing a stocking mask, an ice-pick and some handcuffs. Haywood arrested Bundy for evading a police officer and released him.

Soon after that, the investigators began to make a link between Bundy and the DeRonch attack. They searched his apartment but found nothing significant. Bundy's photograph was circulated, but unfortunately Carol DeRonch could not positively identify him. A witness at one of the other abductions did recognize him, though. Bundy's girlfriend was interviewed and she told police about his odd collection of possessions, such as a false moustache, crutches and plaster of Paris. It was one of Bundy's favourite tricks to pretend to be disabled by an arm or leg injury, and use this disability to persuade a girl to load something into his car for him. Once the girl was halfway into the car, the plaster cast and crutches would be thrown aside and the girl bundled into the vehicle. It became increasingly obvious that Bundy was the serial abductor and killer.

Almost incredibly, Bundy was granted bail and he moved in with Liz Kendall until his trial. He was convicted of aggravated kidnapping and sentenced to up to 15 years in prison. The main purpose of this conviction was to hold Bundy until he could be tried for one or more of the murders. The first murder charge would be for the death of Caryn Campbell, one of whose hairs had been found in Bundy's VW. The preliminary hearing was nearly a fiasco when one of the witnesses, asked to identify Bundy, pointed to someone else. The case was still supposed to go to a full trial, though. During a visit to the courthouse on 7 June, 1977, Bundy leapt to freedom from a second storey window. He spent several days in the woods near Aspen, but was then caught while driving yet another stolen vehicle through the streets of Aspen.

Once again he was in captivity. Once again he escaped. On 30 December, 1977, he broke out of his cell in Colorado Springs by dismantling an old light fixture in the ceiling. He took a bus to Denver, and then a plane to Chicago. By the time the Colorado Springs authorities knew he had gone he was hundreds of miles away. Once in Chicago, Bundy stole another car, drove to Atlanta in Georgia and took a bus to Tallahassee in Florida, where he assumed two new identities – Chris Hagen and Ken Misner.

By travelling these long distances and repeatedly crossing state boundaries, Bundy was cleverly exploiting the disunity of the United States. He just might have got away with his appalling list of past crimes, but for the fact that he just couldn't stop committing new ones. He launched into another series of killings, while he lived off the proceeds of shoplifting, purse-snatching and stolen credit cards. On one night, 14 January 1978, Bundy attacked five girls: Lisa Levy, Margaret Bowman, Karen Chandler, Kathy Kleiner and Cheryl Thomas. They were all house-mates at the Chi Omega sorority in Tallahassee. Four of them had been sexually assaulted and strangled, bitten and beaten to death; Cheryl survived, but in a terrible state; she suffered permanent hearing loss. The savagery of the Chi Omega killings implied that Bundy was falling apart psychologically.

On 8 February, 1978, Bundy tried to abduct a 14-year-old girl in Jacksonville, using a stolen van. Luckily the girl's brother turned up just in time and frightened Bundy off. The next day would prove to be the last in Bundy's career as a serial killer. On 9 February he abducted a 12-year-old girl, Kimberly Leach, from her school campus in Lake City, Florida. It was the first period of the day. She had left one school building to go to another to collect her purse. She got her purse, but was intercepted by Bundy before she made it back to her classroom. She was last seen by a passer-by, who saw Kimberly being led towards a white van by an angry-looking man. The witness did not interfere, assuming that the pair were father and daughter. The girl's body was found a month later 30 miles away underneath an old pig shed.

After this final murder, Bundy dumped the stolen van in a high-crime area, presumably guessing that it would be stolen; it was in fact never found. Bundy stole another vehicle, was stopped by the police, but managed to escape while the officer was checking the registration number. He returned to his Tallahassee apartment, wiped it clean of fingerprints, stole yet another car, and left Tallahassee. Yet again Bundy was stopped by police, when an officer recognized the stolen number plates. He tried to make a run for it, pretended to be shot when fired at, then leapt up ready to fight off the policeman, but was eventually overpowered.

Bundy attempted to pass himself off as Ken Misner, but by now his photograph was to be seen everywhere – he was on the FBI's Ten Most Wanted list – and he was identified as Ted Bundy. He was taken to Tallahassee and charged with the Chi Omega killings. In court, Bundy was confident, controlling and aggressive, unsuccessfully demanding that the judge and defence lawyers should be replaced. The Chi Omega trial was held in Miami, and he was found guilty on 23 July 1978. There was overwhelming forensic evidence tying him to the atrocity; the bite marks on one of the victims matched his teeth. There were character witnesses at the trial, including Bundy's mother. Bundy wept as she gave her evidence of his good character. On 31 July, he was sentenced to death. Then he was tried and convicted for the Leach murder. During this trial, Bundy exploited an odd law that allowed marriage in a courthouse, and he married his current girlfriend, Carol Boone, while she took the witness stand.

Twice condemned to death, Bundy did not give up and made full use of the lengthy appeal procedures to prolong his life. The final death warrant was issued on 17 January 1989. He and his lawyers tried to get an extra three years to enable Bundy to have time to confess properly to all the killings. They even tried to press the families of missing girls to plead for a stay of execution on this basis, but no-one supported it. Bundy gave a torrent of interviews during his last few days, confessing to some murders but not others. He was unwilling to own up to the killing of the younger girls, perhaps because in a corner of his warped mind even he recognized that that was evil, perhaps because he knew they were too young to have been Stephanie. Refusing a last meal, Ted Bundy was electrocuted early in the morning on 24 January, 1989.

Albert De Salvo
(1930–1973)

ALBERT DE SALVO, better known as the Boston
Strangler, was born on 3 September, 1930. The
reign of terror of the Boston Strangler was as brief
as that of his notorious London counterpart, Jack
the Ripper.

All the murders happened within an 18-month
period between June 1962 and January 1964.
Between those two dates, 13 women of various
ages, all single and living quiet, self-contained
lives on their own, were murdered in the city of
Boston, Massachusetts. The youngest victim was
19 years old, the oldest was 85. All of them were
murdered in their own apartments, first sexually
assaulted and then strangled with items of their
own clothing. A peculiarity of all the cases was
that there was no sign of forced entry into the
apartment, implying that either the murderer was
in each case known to the victim or he was
extremely plausible and persuasive, able to talk
his way in. Somehow and for some reason that
we still don't know, in each case the women
invited the murderer into their homes.

The attacks were not necessarily all the work of
the same person. The police working on the
murder cases at the time were not convinced that

a single serial killer was to blame. There is always the possibility, when details of a crime are well-publicized, that attention seekers will copy the crime. Nevertheless, the people of Boston believed that the murders were all committed by one man, and he became known as the Boston Strangler.

De Salvo might have got away with the string of 13 murders, but in the end he gave himself away. It is often the way with psychopaths that they have a psychological need to be caught or stopped; often after a run of 'successful' killings, they will unconsciously give themselves away, and make it easier for the police to apprehend them. Sometimes they advance deeper into insanity. Sometimes they simply get careless.

The breakthrough in identifying Albert De Salvo as the Boston Strangler came in the autumn of 1964. On 27 October, De Salvo got into a young woman's apartment posing as a detective. He tied the victim to her bed, sexually assaulted her and then suddenly changed his mind, apologizing to her and leaving. The woman was lucky to have survived this visit, and she was able to give the police a detailed description of her visitor. This led to the identification of the attacker as Albert De Salvo. Even at this point, the police were not thinking of this attacker as the Boston Strangler, but when he was charged with rape and interviewed, De Salvo confessed in detail to all the crimes of the Boston Strangler.

The case against De Salvo might therefore seem to be open and shut. But there was no physical or witness evidence, no evidence of any kind, to support his confession, and it is relatively common for people with personality disorders to confess to crimes they have not committed. There is in addition something profoundly disorientating about being questioned by professional interrogators, and history is littered with the corpses of unfortunate people who have agreed to all manner of crimes they have not committed, confessed to almost anything, in these stressful situations. There were some significant discrepancies between De Salvo's account of the killings and the autopsy reports. Both investigators and psychiatrists were ready to discount his implausible and apparently rehearsed or coached confession.

After careful consideration, the law enforcement officers decided that De Salvo was not to be charged with the serial stranglings at all, but for some earlier crimes, robbery and sexual assault. He was found guilty of these and sentenced to life imprisonment in 1967. There was a general assumption that the Boston Strangler had been de-activated, and that he was now safely behind bars, though some people thought there was more to the series of killings than had been satisfactorily explained. The case is not closed.

De Salvo himself was unable to throw further light on the matter, as he was murdered in prison six years later, in 1973. One reason for believing De Salvo was not responsible for the crimes was that people who knew him personally were convinced that he was not capable of committing such crimes. But we know from the lives of many other evil people that this is a common pattern. A great many quiet, kind, well-mannered people have turned out to be mass killers.

In De Salvo's case there is some forensic evidence in favour of his innocence. The 19-year-old Mary Sullivan, who was the eleventh of the Strangler's victims, and died on 4 January, 1964, may not have been killed by De Salvo. She was found dead by her room-mates, strangled with a stocking. Her nephew Casey Sherman later explored the crime scenes, the initial police investigations, the primes suspects, and also De Salvo's confession tapes, which have never been made public. Sherman alleges that the Boston Strangler Task Force was driven by political motives, and that the defence attorney manipulated De Salvo's confession. Casey Sherman also gathered forensic evidence, including DNA evidence, that suggests that Mary was not killed by De Salvo but by somebody else. Sherman's campaign led to his forming an alliance with De Salvo's family; together they attempted to get the law enforcement officers in Massachusetts to declare De Salvo innocent and re-open the Mary Sullivan murder enquiry. Sherman believes he knows who the real killer of Mary Sullivan was. If De Salvo did not kill Mary Sullivan, then quite possibly he did not kill any of the other victims either.

In 1971, Albert De Salvo was awarded an extraordinary commendation by the Texas House of Representatives, who in their citation said that he was 'officially recognized by the state of Massachusetts for his noted activities and unconventional techniques involving population control and applied psychology.' The commendation was made at the instigation of Texas legislator Tim Moore, with the idea of highlighting the lack of legislative scrutiny in Massachusetts.

Behind all these complex wrangles rests a truth that is uncomfortable to live with. Albert De Salvo may have been the Boston Strangler. If so, he was sent to prison, even if for another crime, and because he was stabbed to death while in custody he was unable to re-offend. Society was saved from further attacks. But if De Salvo was not the Boston Strangler, then somebody else was – and that somebody else was never caught.

Peter Sutcliffe, the Yorkshire Ripper
(1946–)

THE YORKSHIRE RIPPER murders started in October 1975, with the killing of a 28-year-old prostitute named Wilma McCann. Her body was found on a playing field in Leeds. It had some distinctive wounds – hammer blows to the head and some stab-wounds made with a screwdriver. Three more murders, all of prostitutes in the Leeds-Bradford area, followed a similar pattern.

The pattern changed in June 1977 when a 16-year-old girl, not a prostitute this time, fell victim to a Ripper attack. Other non-prostitute victims were to follow, creating widespread fear and panic among women in West Yorkshire.

It was almost by chance that the Ripper was caught in January 1981. He was discovered by Sheffield police in his Rover with a prostitute named Ava Rivers. The car had false number plates and carried the Ripper's sinister armoury: a garotte, a hammer and a sharpened screwdriver. Ava Rivers was very lucky that the police intervened when they did, as she would almost certainly have become the Ripper's next victim.

When the suspect was taken into custody for

questioning, it emerged that he was Peter William Sutcliffe, a married man living in a respectable middle-class district of Bingley. He had had a variety of jobs, including digging graves in Bingley cemetery. It also emerged, worryingly, that the police had interviewed him no less than nine times before and not realised that he was their man.

Sutcliffe was described by a friend as a quiet, unaggressive man. One of a family of six, he had left school at 15 and gone through a series of different jobs including labouring and two spells as a grave-digger. A workmate recalled that his behaviour even then was irregular. He usually opened the coffins to rob the corpses of rings or other jewellery. Even more macabre, he would sometimes play with the corpse like a ventriloquist's dummy. He was eventually sacked from this job for poor time-keeping. Sutcliffe had married a schoolteacher with a history of mental instability called Sonia Szurma in 1974 and he started murdering women just a year later. It is possible that Sutcliffe was in reality releasing the aggression he felt towards his wife. Although outwardly demure, Sonia was giving him a difficult time at home, frequently shouting at him. In response, the slightly-built Sutcliffe did no more than ask her to keep her voice down. There was a great deal of tension in the relationship, and it found its outlet in the series of terrible killings.

The Yorkshire Ripper attracted a great deal of press interest, not merely because of the series of horrible murders, but because of the suspicion that the mishandling of the case by the police had delayed the arrest and therefore allowed Sutcliffe to kill more women. The manhunt, costing 4 million pounds, had been seriously misled and substantially delayed by three letters and a tape that had apparently come from the Ripper in 1978. The police accepted the tape as authentic. The voice on the tape had a Geordie accent, which meant that police for a time ruled out non-Geordies from their enquiries; meanwhile the murders continued. The tape turned out to be a hoax.

Another cause for interest was the application of the 1957 Homicide Act. Under this Act, Sutcliffe asked for a reduced charge of manslaughter on grounds of diminished responsibility. He was in effect pleading insanity. The Attorney General and the judge were uneasy about shrugging off a whole series of murder charges, and it was with murder that Sutcliffe was charged. The Attorney General said what the jury had to decide was whether Sutcliffe as 'a clever, callous murderer, deliberately set out to create a cock and bull story to avoid a conviction for murder.' He added that there was a marked difference between the stories Sutcliffe had told the police and the doctors. It is still uncertain whether Peter Sutcliffe was technically insane or not. Sutcliffe's defence went in the direction of establishing his unfitness to be tried for murder, and he claimed that he heard 'voices' telling him to kill prostitutes. He had a divine mission from God to kill prostitutes. He was examined by psychiatrists in prison, and they reported that he was a paranoid schizophrenic, but it is possible that Sutcliffe was fooling them.

There are good reasons for supposing that he was faking insanity. For instance, in prison he was overheard telling his wife Sonia that he expected to get 30 years for what he had done but if he could convince people he was mad he might only get ten years in a 'loony bin'. He did not mention the heavenly voices in the initial interviews at all. In court, he was careful to give no clue as to the state of his mental health. More damning still was the fact that not all the victims were prostitutes. Jayne Macdonald, Josephine Whitaker, Barbara Leach, Jacqueline Hill and Margo Walls were numbered among Sutcliffe's victims, and none of them were prostitutes.

It turned out that Sutcliffe normally went out murdering on a Friday or a Saturday night, the two nights when Sonia worked as an auxiliary nurse. For the Crown, Mr Ognall asked one of the consultant psychiatrists, 'Why did God only direct him on Friday and Saturday Nights?' Mr Milne, the psychiatrist, answered, 'Paranoid schizophrenics are extraordinarily cunning, extremely involved in premeditation and determined not to be found.'. Mr Ognall replied, 'That isn't the hallmark of a schizophrenic. It is the hallmark of the normal criminal.'.

Much of the case hinged on Sutcliffe's motive for killing. It was fairly clear that there was a sexual motive; he had actually had sex or attempted to have sex with several of the victims while he was murdering them. But Sutcliffe was intelligent enough to know that he had to deny, if possible disprove, a sexual motive if his insanity plea was going to work. The voices, the divine mission, had to be the reason for the attacks, not sexual gratification.

In May 1981, it took the jury at the Old Bailey just six hours to find Peter Sutcliffe guilty, by a majority of ten to two, of 13 charges of murder and seven charges of attempted murder. He was given life imprisonment with the recommendation that he should serve not less than 30 years. The judge added that the psychiatrists were of the opinion that he should never be released. Meanwhile, Sutcliffe spends his time at Broadmoor, diagnosed with paranoid schizophrenia, his state of mind having deteriorated markedly since going into prison. It is a chilling thought that this man will, according to the judgement passed on him, possibly be at liberty again in 2011. Whether mad or faking, there can be no doubt that Peter Sutcliffe is an extremely dangerous man.

Harold Shipman
(1946–2004)

DR HAROLD SHIPMAN was born on 14 January, 1946. He has the doubtful distinction of being, as far as we know, the most prolific serial killer in the history of Britain.

A report on Shipman's activities published in July 2002 revealed that he had killed at least 215 of his patients between the years 1975 and 1998, when he was practising as a general practitioner at Todmorden in West Yorkshire (1974–75) and Hyde in Greater Manchester (1977–98). The judge who compiled the report, Dame Janet Smith, said that there were many more suspicious deaths that he may have been responsible for but which could not definitely be ascribed to him. Altogether, 459 of Shipman's patients died. A proportion of those will have died naturally, of the conditions he was treating them for, so it is fair to assume that Shipman killed over 200 people, but significantly under 400.

At the time of writing, a new investigation is opening into Shipman's time as an assistant doctor in a practice at Pontefract. If Shipman was killing at Hyde, and killing at his earlier practice in Todmorden, it is not beyond the bounds of possibility that he was killing even before that.

The level of human misery Harold Shipman caused is hard to imagine. The murder victims themselves had their lives needlessly and undeservedly cut short, but at least they died very quickly and had no knowledge of what was happening to them. The families of the victims have the ongoing torture of living with the knowledge that the doctor they trusted and respected, and in some cases recommended, betrayed them and robbed them of their loved ones. Then there are the families of the possible though not certain victims, who are left with the uncertainty; did their mothers or grandmothers die natural deaths or were they murdered? The people of Hyde will take a very long time to recover from the trauma of the Shipman murders.

The reason why there is still much uncertainty is that Shipman was often the only person in attendance at the time of death, he signed the death certificate, and the death was often followed by cremation, so there was no possibility of a later exhumation and post mortem to establish forensically the true cause of death.

Shipman's technique was usually to visit his victims, who were often elderly but in good health, and persuade them to let him give them an injection. He injected diamorphine in lethal doses, from which they died almost instantly. It seems that Shipman enjoyed watching people die and enjoyed having the power of life and death over them. His bedside manner was good, and most of his patients thought he was a wonderful doctor. Just occasionally the mask slipped. He could for instance be inexplicably callous when dealing with bereaved relatives. He nevertheless went unchallenged for a very long time because of his professional status as a doctor.

He might have got away with this incredibly long series of murders, but for greed. He tried to forge a will for one of his victims. It was a transparently poor forgery, pointing to foul play, and the police had the woman's body exhumed. Traces of diamorphine (heroin) were found. It turned out that Shipman had hoarded diamorphine, which is legally used in small quantities for pain control in Britain. One of the local undertakers became suspicious too; rather a lot of Dr Shipman's patients seemed to be dying. This too was reported. Other suspicious deaths were investigated. There were more exhumations, and Shipman was finally arrested.

In January 2000 Harold Shipman was convicted of murdering 15 patients with lethal injections of diamorphine. He was sentenced to life imprisonment and given no hope of release; life would mean life. In prison, Shipman continued to behave as though he had professional status and expected to be treated accordingly. The prison staff finally withdrew some of his privileges because of his high-handed behaviour and he became depressed. At 6.20 on the morning of 13 January, 2004, Shipman was found dead in his cell at Wakefield Prison in West Yorkshire. He had used bed sheets to hang himself from the bars of his cell. He was pronounced dead at 8.10 a.m.

We can only guess at Shipman's motives for

murder. He consistently denied the murders and never explained his actions. He was, as a youth, profoundly disturbed by seeing his mother die, and it may be that in the series of murders of elderly women he was in some way re-enacting and coming to terms with that episode. It may also be that the 'will to power' was at work, that it gave Shipman satisfaction to make decisions about whether other people should live or die. Maybe it was a way of asserting his importance as an individual. It may have been these same motives that led to his suicide. He gave no clues to the prison staff that he was planning to kill himself, so he was as deceitful about his suicide as he was about the other killings. It must also be significant that he killed himself on the eve of his birthday; the prison authorities had refused to let him have a visit from his wife on his birthday. Harold Shipman was not getting enough of his own way, so by killing himself he took total control of the situation.

PART NINE

SINGLE ACTS
OF EVIL

John Wilkes Booth
(1838–1865)

JOHN WILKES BOOTH, who was for a hundred years America's most infamous assassin, led a double life. He was not only the conspirator who succeeded in murdering perhaps the greatest president of the United States, he was also a much-admired actor; it is often forgotten that, unlike Lee Harvey Oswald, he was a well-known figure before the presidential assassination.

Booth came from a theatrical family. His father, Junius Brutus Booth, left England for the United States in 1821 and made a great name for himself on the American stage. His mother was Mary Ann Holmes. John Wilkes Booth was born on 10 May 1838 on a farm (worked by slaves) near Bel Air, Maryland. He was the ninth of ten children, and his siblings were later to write of his waywardness and eccentricity. John went to several private schools including a Quaker school before attending St Timothy's Hall, an Episcopalian military academy at Catonsville. During the 1850s, he became a Know-Nothing. The Know-Nothing Party was formed by 'nativists', people who wanted to preserve the country for native-born white citizens. This white supremacist theme was to prove a crucial element in Booth's decision to kill Lincoln.

Booth worked on the farm for a time after his father died in 1852, but it was too dull for him and he fantasized about doing something remarkable. According to his sister Asia, he cried 'I must have fame! Fame!' and decided he would become a famous actor like his father.

Booth followed his father and two elder brothers onto the stage, making his stage debut at the age of 17 in 1855 in Baltimore, as the Earl of Richmond in *Richard III*. He started acting in earnest two years later, but early notices were not favourable and he disliked being compared with his much-respected father. Junius Booth had been one of the most famous actors of his day, though he had an eccentric personality, problems with alcohol and (significantly) bouts of insanity. In spite of later achieving a great deal as an actor, John Wilkes Booth may have felt that he could never outshine his dazzling father and this may have driven him to make a mark in some other way.

Theatre companies often used big-name touring actors to pull in larger audiences, and Booth was eventually to achieve this 'star' status, though it led him into a very punishing lifestyle. Often a different play was performed each night, so after a performance Booth might have to stay up the rest of the night learning his new part, then go to the theatre for a morning rehearsal. This irregular lifestyle involved keeping unusual hours, and may have helped to make him less visible as a conspirator, even though he was recognized wherever he went. Booth began his stock (repertory) theatre appearances in 1857 in

Philadelphia, which was then the drama capital of America. His early acting lacked confidence, and he frequently needed prompting; he forgot his lines and missed his cues. The acting and stage manager at the Arch Street Theatre, William Fredericks, commented that the new actor did not show promise as a great actor. Other actors in the company were more forthright, saying that he had no future as an actor at all. But he was only 19 and he was determined to make his mark.

In 1858, he moved to Richmond, Virginia for a season of repertory at the Marshall Theatre. Here he became more confident and was liked by audiences. He also became more positively committed to the southern way of life and more entrenched in southern political views.

In 1859, Booth appeared to make a fresh start altogether, joining the Richmond Grays. But he enlisted, on 20 November 1959, with the sole purpose of witnessing a political assassination, the hanging of the fiery abolitionist John Brown in Charles Town, Virginia. He was part of the armed guard standing near the scaffold to prevent anyone from rescuing John Brown. Shortly after the historic hanging, Booth was discharged. The episode shows Booth's fanatical support of the southern cause, his desire to be involved in historic events, his interest in political assassination, and his unstable, maverick behaviour.

During the Civil War, Booth promised his mother he would not join the Confederate Army, but he was involved in some covert operations and may have been a southern agent. Some have suggested he was involved in smuggling medical supplies to Confederate troops.

John Wilkes Booth was a charismatic figure, good-looking, with a slim athletic build and magnetic eyes. Charles Wyndham, another actor, commented that 'when his emotions were aroused, his eyes were like living jewels. Flames shot from them.'. He was attractive to women. Booth was often seen 'lounging' in the arms of Ellen Starr. In 1861, an actress called Henrietta Irving slashed his face with a knife when she realised Booth had no intention of marrying her. After Booth was killed, the photographs of no less than five women were found in his pockets. One of them was a picture of his fiancée, Lucy Hale, the daughter of Senator John P. Hale who, ironically, was a prominent abolitionist. Here we see more signs of Booth's inconsistency and waywardness. He wanted to see Brown hanged, but was also happy to accept Hale as a father-in-law: both were abolitionists.

Booth's acting career took off in 1860, and he played leading roles in many plays. In Shakespeare's *Julius Caesar*, he played Mark Antony with his brothers Edwin and Junius as Brutus and Cassius. In November 1863, the Lincolns saw John Wilkes Booth acting in *The Marble Heart* at Ford's Theatre. With them in the box was a guest, Mary Clay. She reminisced that Wilkes Booth twice, when uttering disagreeable threats, came up close to Lincoln and pointed at him. When he came close a third time, Mary Clay said, 'Mr Lincoln, he looks as if he meant that for you.' Lincoln replied, 'Well, he does look pretty sharp at me, doesn't he?'

By now Booth was earning 20,000 dollars a year. He was able to invest in oil. In May 1864, he left the stage and went to Pennsylvania to concentrate on his oil investments. He formed a company, the Dramatic Oil Company, with three actor friends. But Booth was too impatient; when success was not immediate, he dropped out, handing most of his investment over to a friend and his brother Junius.

In October 1864, Booth made a mysterious journey to Montreal, where he held secret meetings with Confederate sympathisers. In November, he returned, carrying a letter of introduction which eventually led him to meet Dr Samuel Mudd. Booth was assembling a conspiracy to capture the President, take him to Richmond as a hostage and compel the Federal government to return the Confederate prisoners of war who were held in Union prisons. The intention was to re-invigorate the Confederate army and enable it to win. It was a plot to kidnap, not to kill.

He must later have wished that he had taken his chance on 4 March, 1865, when he attended Lincoln's second inauguration as the invited guest of his fiancée. Booth later said to another actor, 'What an excellent chance I had to kill the President, if I had wished to!'

All through these years, Booth behaved in a secretive, erratic way, but his brothers and sisters seem to have thought little of it. Asia later recalled how when he stayed with her in Philadelphia 'strange men called late at night for whispered consultations'. She knew her brother was a spy, a blockade-runner, a rebel.

The capture of the President was due to take place on 17 March, 1865. But after five months of detailed planning on the part of the conspirators, Lincoln changed his plans at the last minute. Instead of visiting the Campbell Hospital outside Washington to see a play, *Still Waters Run Deep*, he decided to attend a luncheon at the National Hotel, where he would speak to officers of the 140th Indiana Regiment and present a captured flag to the Governor of Indiana. Booth was thwarted.

Two weeks later, the Union siege of Richmond ended in Confederate defeat. One week after that, on 9 April, 1865, General Lee was obliged to surrender. Booth was doubly frustrated; his own conspiracy to kidnap Lincoln had failed and the Confederates had lost the war. On 11 April, Lincoln gave his last speech at the White House. Booth and two of his co-conspirators, Powell and Herold, were in the audience. Lincoln proposed conferring rights on certain black people, 'on the very intelligent and on those who serve our cause as soldiers'. Booth was now beside himself. 'That is the last speech he will ever make.' Booth's fury made him think up a wild, last-throw attempt to get the better of Lincoln. Just four days later, he would murder him.

Booth made a big mistake in thinking that the conspirators who had been ready to kidnap were just as ready to kill.

At 9 a.m. on 14 April, 1865, Booth went to a barbershop to have his hair trimmed, then returned to the National Hotel, where many of the guests recognized him. Later in the morning he went to Ford's Theatre to pick up his mail. There he learned from Henry Ford that Lincoln would be attending that evening's performance of *Our American Cousin*. He decided that this was his opportunity to kill Lincoln. He spent some time walking round the theatre. He knew the play well, and knew that the biggest laugh would come at 10.15 p.m.; that would be the moment to shoot. At noon he went to a stable and hired a fast mare before returning to the hotel.

At 2 p.m. Booth visited Lewis Paine and told him he was going to kill Lincoln. He also told Paine that he, Paine, was going to kill Secretary of State William Seward. Booth then went to Mary Surratt's boarding house and left her a package containing field glasses; she was to take them to her tavern at Surrattsville, where he could collect them that night. At 3 p.m., Booth visited George Atzerodt to tell him to assassinate Vice-President Andrew Johnson, who lived in the same building, but Atzerodt was out. Inexplicably, Booth left a note for Johnson, who was then at the White House. After picking up the mare, Booth went to a tavern for a drink and wrote a letter to the press, which was to be delivered the next day; he signed the letter with his own name and three others: Paine, Atzerodt and Herold. At that stage poor Atzerodt didn't know what was in store for him. It was only by chance that Booth met him in the street at 5 p.m. and told him to kill Johnson at 10.15 p.m. Atzerodt did not want to do it.

At 6 p.m. Booth rode to the theatre to rehearse the route he would use in the assassination, everything except the leap onto the stage. Then he returned to the hotel to rest, dine and change. He put on calf-length boots, new spurs and black clothes and picked up a compass, a bowie knife and a derringer, a single-shot pistol. At 8 p.m., Booth held a final meeting with the other conspirators. Paine would assassinate Seward, Atzerodt would assassinate Johnson, Booth would assassinate Lincoln; all the attacks would take place at 10.15 p.m. They would meet at the Navy Yard Bridge and ride to Surrattsville. After that, Booth rode to Ford's Theatre, left his horse round the back and went to a tavern to get a bottle of whiskey. Another customer, assuming he was acting that night, quipped, 'You'll never be the actor your father was.' Booth answered cryptically, 'When I leave the stage, I'll be the most famous man in America.'.

At 10 p.m., Booth climbed the stairs to the dress circle, saw the white door of Lincoln's State Box. Forbes, the President's footman, sat next to it. Booth gave him his card and opened the door into the dark area at the back of the box, wedging it shut with the leg of a music stand he had left there earlier. Then Booth opened the inner door, approached the President from behind and shot him in the head at close range. In the confusion that followed, Booth may have shouted 'Sic semper tyrannis!' (Thus always to tyrants), though some in the audience thought he shouted this after he leapt down onto the stage. Major

Rathbone, who was sitting in the box, thought he shouted 'Freedom!' immediately after the shot. Rathbone grappled briefly with Booth, but was stabbed in the arm. Booth jumped over the front of the box and onto the stage. One of his spurs caught in one of the decorative flags draped over the balustrade, and he landed awkwardly, breaking his left leg just above the ankle. He managed to run across the stage, out of the theatre and rode away.

At 11 p.m., Herold caught up with Booth and they made for Mary Surratt's tavern. Booth was preoccupied with the pain in his leg and as yet did not know that the rest of the conspiracy had failed. Paine had not killed Seward and Azerodt had made no attempt to kill Johnson. Booth had some whiskey and reached Dr Mudd's house at 4 a.m. Mudd attended to his broken leg.

It was several days before the army caught up with Booth and Herold. They were rumoured to be in the area between the Potomac and Rappahannock Rivers. Lieutenant Edward Doherty of the Sixteenth New York Cavalry followed their trail, picking up sightings from fishermen and ferrymen on 24 April. It was clear that Booth was assisted along his escape route by a rebel, Captain Willie Jett. Jett was tracked down to the house of his girlfriend's parents, the Goldmans, where he was found in bed with the Goldmans' son. Jett was compelled to tell the soldiers where Booth was, and he undertook to lead them to the barn where Booth and Herold were hiding. Booth was defiant. He refused to surrender. When Doherty threatened to set fire to the barn, Booth admitted that Herold was keen to surrender, which he was allowed to do. As soon as Herold was out, a fire was started at the back of the barn. Sergeant Boston Corbett shot Booth in the neck for reasons that were not explained in Doherty's otherwise very detailed report, and Booth died two hours later. Ironically, Corbett was commended by Doherty for his action in 'bringing the murderers to justice'.

Booth had always wanted fame. In the end he achieved not fame, but infamy. But to an alarming number of people, it seems to make little difference whether they are famous or notorious. Perhaps what matters most to them is to be noticed, to be remembered – even if it is for an evil act, the destruction of something good.

George McMahon
(about 1900–1960)

FOR SOME REASON the British have never seen their royal family as targets for assassination. This is odd, because several attempts have been made on them. A madwoman attacked George III with a knife, but it was too blunt to do any harm. There were no less than five unsuccessful attempts on the life of Queen Victoria, all, apparently, representing the evil dreams of would-be lone assassins.

More recently there was an attempt to abduct Princess Anne; a young man fired blanks to frighten the Queen when she was on her way to the Trooping the Colour ceremony; and Lord Mountbatten was murdered by the IRA.

In 1936, in spite of what is almost a tradition of gaining notoriety by attempting a royal assassination, there was no apprehension that anyone might make such an attempt on the new King, Edward VIII. It was 16 July, 1936 and the crowds lining Constitution Hill were three or four deep, waiting to catch a glimpse of Edward VIII as he returned to Buckingham Palace from a Colours ceremony in Hyde Park. Standing in the front row was an agitated, thick-set middle-aged man in a brown three-piece suit. He was holding a newspaper. At 12.30 p.m. the military band that led the procession came into sight under the Wellington Arch, and close behind the band was the King himself, in his scarlet tunic and perched on his horse – a perfect target. As the King rode by, the thick-set man dropped his newspaper revealing a gun. He aimed the revolver at the King.

Alice Lawrence, who was standing next to the gunman, shouted and instinctively made a grab for the man's arm. Her action was very timely and it was a matter of seconds before policemen had piled on top of the gunman and pushed him onto the ground.

They took him to Hyde Park police station, where the gunman identified himself as Gorge Andrew McMahon. Within hours, the police were proudly telling the King that they had unravelled the mystery. Based on their cursory enquiries, they described McMahon as 'a frustrated Irish journalist who had convinced himself that the Secretary of State for Home Affairs had conspired to prevent him from publishing a journal called the *Human Gazette*'. The incident was thus no more than an attempt to bring his perceived injustice to everyone's attention; he had not meant any harm to the King.

But had Scotland Yard really 'unravelled the mystery', as they believed? Special Branch were later able to establish that the man's name was not really McMahon at all, but Jerome Bannigan. He had been born in Dublin and moved at the age of eight with his family to Glasgow. He had been unable to settle in Glasgow and found it hard to stay in work, so he drifted to London. There, his extreme right-wing political views and preoccupation with guns had brought him to the attention of the police. He was known to be a Nazi sympathizer. In fact, once photographs of his spectacular arrest had been seen in the national newspapers, a number of people came forward to say that they had seen the man, McMahon-Bannigan, selling the *Blackshirt*, a fascist newspaper, on the streets in the Paddington area of London.

When McMahon appeared at the Old Bailey in September 1936, he gave another account of what had happened, which may or may not have been true. In October the previous year he was approached by an English agent of 'a foreign power' outside the relevant embassy. There had been a second meeting at which the two men discussed the unjust way Britain had treated Ireland; it emerged that there might be a way in which McMahon could help the Irish cause. McMahon then, rather oddly, claimed that he had reported this to MI5 and had kept in touch with them subsequently. Then, after the death of George V and the accession of Edward VIII, it was suggested by the agent of the foreign power that McMahon should attempt the assassination of the new King. McMahon seemed to be protecting his own position during his trial by maintaining that he never had any intention of doing the King any harm. He was just going along with the outline of the plot and passing the information on to MI5.

At the time of the trial all this was dismissed as hokum, but when McMahon's files were released to the National Archives in 2003, it was clear that McMahon really had been in contact with MI5, just as he had said at his trial.

The public perception of the McMahon incident

was, and still is, that it was the work of one, lone, mad, would-be assassin. But the reality is that there was a conspiracy of some kind. The foreign power may or may not have been Germany, but the meetings with the agent of that power evidently had taken place. McMahon had passed on information about the conspiracy to kill the King to MI5. It may be that the very prompt and efficient action by the police on that occasion can be explained very simply; they knew that an assassination attempt, or something that was supposed to look like an assassination attempt, was going to happen, and they knew who was going to carry it out. They were able to pounce and wrestle the gunman to the ground because they knew exactly who and where he was – and when he would act.

But several questions remain. Why did MI5 go along with the conspiracy to this final and rather risky moment? Was there some diplomatic or political gain in having the King's life threatened in this melodramatic way? Perhaps there was something more sinister behind it. Perhaps elements in the English establishment would have been quite relieved to see Edward VIII assassinated. He was evidently going to be an embarrassingly incompetent King, and the Mrs Simpson scandal gave the establishment the lever it needed, in the summer and autumn, to force his abdication in December 1936. However this mystery unravels, it is very hard to make out what George McMahon or Jerome Bannigan was doing. A final irony is that, like McMahon, Edward VIII too was a Nazi sympathizer.

Lee Harvey Oswald
(1939–1963)

LEE OSWALD WAS a very different character from John Wilkes Booth. Until the fateful moment when he killed President John F. Kennedy, Oswald had achieved nothing and his life had meant nothing. It was as if that was the only thing that could make people remember him, his only way into history.

Oswald was born on 18 October, 1939 in New Orleans. He never knew his father, who died two months before he was born. For a time he was left in an orphanage, and after that he moved with his mother Marguerite from place to place, mainly because she could not hold down a job. By the age of 18, Oswald had lived at 22 different addresses and attended 12 different schools. He was a persistent truant, missing 80% of his high school classes. He grew up rootless, insecure, unsocialized, always the odd one out. By the age of 14 he was already showing signs of having a disturbed personality and was remanded in youth custody. He was referred to a psychologist, Dr Renatus Hartog, for an evaluation; Dr Hartog found that he had 'personality pattern disturbance with schizoid features and passive-aggressive tendencies'. Dr Hartog believed that Oswald had 'definite traits of dangerousness', and advised that he should be kept on probation and given psychiatric help. Not long after that, Oswald was ordered to be put into a home for disturbed boys and subject to mandatory psychiatric care.

The mother's response to this was unhelpful. She fled New York, taking her son to Texas. After the assassination, the New York authorities were asked what action they had taken about the boy at the time. The New York Probation Service told the Warren Commission, 'There is very little one can really do. We don't have the extra-state jurisdiction, and we didn't even know where she [Marguerite Oswald] had gone'.

Lee Harvey Oswald joined the US Marine Corps, evidently as much as anything to escape from the suffocating clutches of his mother. During his military career he became an expert marksman with a rifle. In December 1956 he, on two occasions, achieved 48 and 49 out of 50 during rapid fire at a target 200 yards away. After the assassination, there were sceptics who doubted Oswald's ability to fire three shots in rapid succession and score hits with two of them, and this led them on to the idea that there must have been other marksmen in the plaza. But the evidence still exists that Oswald was certainly capable of firing all the shots.

During his military career, Oswald learned Russian, then travelled to Russia in 1959; he seems to have thought of it as defection. The Russians were not interested in acquiring Oswald's services as a spy, possibly because they sensed that he was a weak and defective personality, possibly because they thought he would play games and attempt to become a double agent. The Soviet authorities wanted to return him to America, but he attempted suicide by cutting one of his wrists and they allowed him to live in Minsk, where he got a job in a television factory. He married a Russian woman, Marina Prusakova. Oswald maintained that he was a Marxist and tried to renounce his American citizenship. The Soviet authorities recognized that he was unstable after the suicide attempt and handed him over for psychiatric evaluation. Two psychiatrists concluded that he was 'mentally unstable' and warned that he was capable of further irrational acts.

Then, in 1962 he changed his mind, as no doubt the Soviet authorities thought he would, and returned to America, taking Marina and his infant daughter with him. He had got tired of Soviet authoritarianism. Oswald hung on to the fantasy that he was a high-powered spy, telling one of his friends that he had been responsible for giving the Soviets the information that enabled them to shoot down the U-2 spy plane. He desperately wanted to be important, to influence historic events.

Oswald next took a job at a graphic arts firm in Dallas. This company produced some classified government work, including detailed maps of Cuba. Oswald boasted to friends that not only was he working on the Cuba maps, but the CIA arranged the job for him. Although this may have been true, his CV up to that point does not make it very likely, and his indiscretion made him a poor security risk. In the spring of 1963 the Oswald family moved to New Orleans, where he befriended Judyth Vary. According to Judyth, Oswald interviewed the female Cuban refugees who came to work at the Reily Coffee Company, where both Oswald and Judyth now had jobs. Oswald was on some kind of mission, finding out the names of safe contacts in Cuba. Oswald's employers seem to have known that he was doing some kind of secret work and nodded at it.

In late March 1963, Oswald bought himself a rifle and a handgun. Rather peculiarly, Oswald got Marina to take a photograph of him wearing the handgun at his right hip and holding the rifle and a copy of a Yugoslav newspaper, *Politika*. Why was he creating a trail of evidence against himself in this way? Or was it all juvenile play-acting that eventually got out of hand? And what did Marina think he was doing?

In the summer of 1963, Oswald became secretary of the Fair Play for Cuba Committee (New Orleans chapter). When Oswald gave out *Hands Off Cuba* leaflets on the streets of New Orleans, he was heckled by anti-Castro Cuban exiles and arrested by the police for disturbing the peace. A local reporter hosting a radio show interviewed Oswald on air. But what Oswald was up to is not at all clear. Although the leaflets supported Castro, the address printed on them, 544 Camp Street, was that of a racist ex-FBI agent called Guy Banister who was running a training camp for anti-Castro exiles preparing to take over

Cuba. Oswald spent a lot of time in Banister's office. According to Judyth, Oswald often went through a garage next door to Reily's to reach Banister's office; so as not to arouse suspicion, he befriended the garage owner, Adrian Alba, and took to whiling away time at the garage reading gun magazines. The garage was frequently used by CIA and FBI agents. Alba later testified that he saw the driver of one of these cars pass an envelope to Oswald. It is far from clear what Oswald was doing or where his loyalties lay.

Before the Kennedy assassination, Oswald had already aimed his rifle at a prominent local politician, trying to shoot him from the street through a window in his home. His target moved, and he missed. At the time the police were unable to identify the would-be assassin but, after the death of the President, when Oswald's life was carefully sifted over, it became obvious that this shooting was his work too. It is a sobering thought that if the earlier assassination had been 'successful', Oswald would probably not have been free to commit the later one, and the course of American history would have been changed.

The chance visit of President Kennedy to Dallas that autumn provided Oswald with a much higher-profile target. By chance he was looking for someone to assassinate. By chance he had a job in a building that overlooked the route of the President's motorcade. The opportunity must have seemed like a gift from destiny.

At 12.30 p.m. on 22 November, 1963, Oswald shot President Kennedy from a window on the sixth floor of the Texas School Book Depository in Elm Street, where he was temporarily employed during the Christmas rush. The window had a view across Dealey Plaza. Oswald fired perhaps three shots at the President's motorcade as it moved slowly across the plaza away from him, hitting the President twice, fatally, and wounding Governor Connally. Their wives, who were also in the car, were unhurt.

Whether there were more snipers behind a wooden fence at the top of a grassy bank in front and to the right of the President's car is still not known. Those who favour a conspiracy put one or more snipers in that location, to account for the dramatic way Kennedy's head jerked back at the impact of the second shot, implying a shot from in front. The large wound in the back of the head would also be more consistent with an exit than an entry wound. So, there is some circumstantial evidence for a second gunman. One of the bullets appeared to have followed a zig-zag path through the bodies of both Kennedy and Connally, and this so-called 'magic bullet' has often been used as evidence that at least one additional shot must have been fired. But recent virtual reality reconstructions have shown that the path followed by the magic bullet was a dead straight line. The earlier misinterpretations did not allow for the fact that Connally's seat was positioned significantly lower than the President's, in order to make the President more visible. Nor did they allow for the fact that Governor Connally's body was twisted because he had turned round at that moment to speak to Kennedy.

After the shooting, the dying President was raced to a nearby hospital where the surgeons found that his brain was so badly damaged that they could do nothing for him. Oswald left the Book Depository, took a bus and a taxi back to his room, changed his clothes and (according to the Warren Commission) picked up a pistol. A little later, the official report states that Oswald killed police officer Tippit in Tenth Street, though witnesses who saw the shooting describe a different man, not at all resembling Oswald.

Oswald was arrested at the Texas Theatre in the Oak Cliff neighbourhood at 1.50 p.m., initially for the murder of Tippit. He was only later charged with murdering Kennedy. Police Officer McDonald, who arrested Oswald in the theatre auditorium, told him to stand up so that he could handcuff him; Oswald shouted, 'Well, it's all over now', punched McDonald and pulled his revolver from his belt. He was going to kill McDonald as he had earlier killed Tippit. This time the gun did not respond when he pulled the trigger and Oswald was overpowered.

Oswald's behaviour while in custody was unnaturally calm. When challenged about the two ID cards he was carrying, one in the name of Lee Harvey Oswald and one in the name of Alek Hidell, Oswald smirked at the officer and said, 'You figure it out'. He smiled complacently and appeared to be enjoying all the attention; he spoke to the press in a measured, almost pompous way. It was if this was the moment he had been waiting for. This was his inauguration. He still denied shooting anyone, but he was only teasing his audience. While he was being transferred to the county jail, two days after the assassination, a nightclub owner called Jack Ruby rushed forward and shot Oswald in the stomach. Oswald died shortly afterwards.

Because of the doubts and uncertainties surrounding the assassination, one week after the assassination the new President, Lyndon B. Johnson, ordered an investigation by a specially appointed commission, the Warren Commission. The report the Warren Commission eventually released concluded that Oswald had fired all three shots – the initial shot that missed altogether and the two that hit Kennedy – and that he had acted alone, without accomplices. The conspiracy theories were fuelled by a desire to see this momentous event resulting from a complicated and deep-laid plot involving some powerful underground organization, perhaps the Mafia or the CIA. But the truth seems to be that the catastrophic end to Jack Kennedy's presidency was down to the caprice of one lone, mad gunman desperate for his place in history. And he got it.

PART TEN

EVIL FOR THE FUN OF IT

Marquis de Sade
(1740–1814)

ONE OF THE classic arguments against pornography, or against the legalization of pornography, has always been that it feeds the appetites of evil people and provokes them into going out and committing sexual crimes. When the police searched the house of the Moors murderer Ian Brady, they found the works of the Marquis de Sade, as well as Hitler's *Mein Kampf.* Hitler was dangerous politically. De Sade was dangerous sexually. Those, like Longford, who wanted pornography to be outlawed, argued that here was proof that pornography turns weak men into predatory monsters.

Donatien Alphonse François de Sade was born in June 1740, in Paris. De Sade's father was a courtier, a diplomat, and related to the royal family. His mother was a lady-in-waiting to the Princess de Conde. The young de Sade, who was handsome, rich and very spoilt, was brought up by his uncle, the Abbé de Sade of Breuil. By the age of 18 he had experimented in every imaginable sexual activity, and from all of this experience he had deduced that, for him at least, the acutest sexual pleasure was to be had from pain and cruelty.

He served in the army during the Seven Years' War. He left the army in 1763, to marry a judge's daughter, but within a few weeks he was having an affair with an actress and inviting prostitutes to his (and his wife's) house at Arceuil. It was then that he started putting into practice his sexual cruelty theories, and the principle that was subsequently named after him – sadism. It seems odd that many of his victims were ready to put up with his cruel treatment, but prostitutes of every period have had to endure maltreatment of one sort or another. Even so, some complained about the abuse, and de Sade was arrested and held in prison for a short time in Vincennes.

After his release, he re-offended. In 1768 a Parisian prostitute called Rose Keller made a formal complaint to the authorities after being locked up and tortured by de Sade. This time de Sade was imprisoned at Lyons. But he was socially well connected and therefore released relatively soon afterwards. In 1772 he moved to Marseilles. Here, in the back streets of the busy port, de Sade's pock-marked manservant Latour was able to procure a steady supply of prostitutes for his master to torture. De Sade fed the girls sweets laced with aphrodisiacs. They were sick, and understandably complained to the police that de Sade had tried to poison them. De Sade and his manservant left Marseilles.

Both of them were sentenced to death in their absence at Aix, and were executed in effigy. Eventually the pair were caught and imprisoned in the castle of Miolans. Remarkably, de Sade still seemed to be able to extricate himself. He escaped from Miolans and hid, with his wife, at their chateau. He was in debt, the debauchery continued, and further brushes with the authorities were inevitable. A new scandal broke, this time involving young boys, and both de Sade and his wife, who was by now also implicated, fled. The Marquise hid in a convent, while de Sade went to Italy with his wife's sister, the Canoness de Launey, who had become his mistress.

In 1777, de Sade recklessly returned to France and was arrested in Paris. He languished in dungeons at both Vincennes and the Bastille, where he was roughly treated by both warders and other prisoners. He was still unrepentant, though, and used his time in prison to develop his ideas on sexual cruelty in writing. There was no god but Nature, he wrote, reflecting the revolutionary ideas of Jean-Jacques Rousseau, and Nature was part creative, part destructive. Since man's destiny ran parallel with Nature, man too had destructive impulses, which should not be ignored. The true natural man had to fulfil himself by being cruel. This theorizing formed the backdrop for his stories of sexual deviation. *120 Days of Sodom* was written in the Bastille on a single roll of paper 12 metres long.

Then, on 14 July, 1789, almost as if in apocalyptic fulfilment of his own wild and elemental theories, the people of Paris stormed the Bastille and demolished it, freeing all the prisoners, including the mad Marquis. De Sade was free once more. Astonishingly, in spite of his aristocratic background, de Sade now became Citizen Sade and headed of one Paris's revolutionary committees. From this position he was able to do one good deed, which was to save his father-in-law from execution. Then, more astonishingly still, de Sade began to voice disapproval of the leaders of the new France. They were too brutal for him, too cruel; it was a final irony. Labelled a moderate by the other revolutionaries, he was himself in great danger now. He was sentenced to be guillotined and only escaped being taken off to be executed because of a mistake. He was somehow overlooked on the day of execution. The very next day, Robespierre was overthrown and de Sade was safe. Once again, this most undeserving of men had escaped punishment.

He was now free, but desperately poor. He set up home with a widowed actress and wrote *Justine* and *Juliette*. These books were a big mistake. In 1801, they were judged to be the ravings of a madman, he was pronounced insane and locked up in the Charenton lunatic asylum. It was Napoleon himself who ordered that he must never be released.

He was able to receive visitors, and his young mistress used to visit him. he also went on writing and his plays were performed by the other inmates of the asylum. He died at Charenton in 1814. His son visited the asylum after his death, gathered up all the writings he could find – and burnt them all. It became clear from his will that de Sade wanted to be buried in a thicket on his old estate and the ground sown with acorns so that 'the traces of my grave must disappear from the face of the earth, as I flatter myself that my memory will be effaced from the minds of men.'. Unfortunately his wishes were overridden in both respects. He was given a Christian burial and a stone cross memorial. Shortly afterwards his grave was robbed. The skull eventually found its way into the hands of a phrenologist, who inferred from its shape that he was man of 'tender character' – which he clearly was not.

De Sade remains an extremely controversial figure. He had a distorted view of life, outlining his 'philosophy' in books such as *Juliette, Justine, Philosophy in the Bedroom* and *120 Days of Sodom* so that others could, if they wished, copy him. His books are full of anecdotes of sexual perversion, told with positive approval and relish. His writings have been read by many, the sane, the insane, the innocent, the corrupt and the downright bemused, and it is by no means certain that he had any influence on anyone at all. Ian Brady would have been an evil man without any help from the Marquis de Sade. De Sade represents and typifies a particular type of sexuality, but it cannot be conclusively demonstrated that he or the story of his life made anyone else behave sadistically. Whatever his precise influence, he has certainly not been forgotten.

Aleister Crowley
(1875–1945)

EDWARD ALEXANDER CROWLEY was born in Leamington in Warwickshire on 12 October, 1875, the son of Edward Crowley, a brewer and Plymouth Brother. He was initially sent to a school for the sons of Plymouth Brethren, where the Bible and the birch were the main teaching aids. He was accused at the age of 12 of trying to corrupt another boy. Then he was sent to Malvern and Tonbridge, which he hated. He also had a tutor at one point, who introduced him to cards, racing, billiards, betting and women; this was the sort of education the boy really wanted, though he then caught a sexually transmitted disease from a Glasgow prostitute.

A lot of the stories he told about his childhood are unexceptional, but there is one about torturing a cat that is profoundly disturbing. It shows him as being both unimaginative and pitiless.

From the age of 20 he decided to call himself 'Aleister', just as the broadcaster Alfred Cooke decided to adopt 'Alistair', though there the similarities end. For some reason Crowley liked to think of himself as descended from Louise de Keroualle, the Duchess of Portsmouth, though he wasn't. Crowley's father travelled about the countryside, preaching that true Christianity could be found only among the Plymouth Brethren. Alcister liked to think he had nothing in common with his father, but his own life was similar; he too joined a small sect of the elect, tried to convert the world to his point of view, and immersed himself in an esoteric religious world. He even started off emulating his father by becoming a Plymouth Brother, thinking of himself as a Christian knight. But in adulthood, he was drawn to the dark world of black magic.

He found that descriptions of torture or bloodshed aroused and inspired him. He liked to imagine himself in agony, especially suffering at the hands of a wicked and independent-minded woman.

When he was 21 he had a kind of awakening. He was suddenly aware that he could explore whole areas of his personality, so far inaccessible, by resort to magic. He had the idea that he could control reality by magical thinking. Two years later he produced a long poem called *Aceldama*. He had a hundred copies privately printed in Cambridge, where he was an undergraduate. It was an attempt to transplant Baudelaire's satanism into England, following Swinburne's example.

Poetry and magic were two threads in Crowley's twisted life; mountaineering was an unlikely third. It was while he was climbing at Zermatt that he met Julian Baker, a chemist, who pointed out some of the scientific flaws in the alchemical ideas Crowley was propounding. Crowley wondered if Baker was perhaps the Master he was looking for. If not, perhaps Baker could introduce him to the man who was. Baker tried to oblige by introducing Crowley to a member of a flourishing and fashionable magical dining society called the Golden Dawn. Crowley was now in his element. The Golden Dawn arranged its members in an ascending hierarchy of office. There were four grades in the First or Outer Order, who took part in esoteric ceremonies but did not actually practise any magic. Magic was only learnt and practised by members who reached the Second or Inner Order. The highest of these, grade seven was called Adeptus Exemptus.

Crowley's initiation into the Golden Dawn led on to a series of weird relationships involving various kinds of psychological, sexual and magical dependence. Crowley was very active sexually, and had been since his first encounter, with a girl in Torquay, at the age of 15. He was determined to try every possible kind of sexual experience before he reached the age of 20, which he apparently succeeded in doing. Side by side with this huge appetite for sex was a very low opinion of women. He thought they should be delivered to the back doorstep, like bottles of milk. The Golden Dawn relationships also involved drugs; opium, morphine and cocaine were relatively easy to get hold of, and many members were taking them.

In 1900, Crowley left London for Scotland. Adopting the magical pseudonym Perdurabo, Crowley went off to look for a suitable place to 'build an oratory'. He settled on a single-storeyed house called Boleskine near the village of Foyers beside Loch Ness. Crowley promptly adopted the style 'Laird of Boleskine'. By this title, Crowley understood more than the normal Scottish concept of 'landlord', but something closer to the English concept of the peerage. Consequently he had a coronet embossed on his notepaper.

Shortly after this, Crowley returned to London demanding advancement in the Golden Dawn. He was refused, and he set about breaking it up by espousing the cause of the paranoid – mad, even – MacGregor Mathers, who lived in a kind of exile in Paris, and quarrelling with the poet W. B. Yeats. Crowley expected Yeats to acknowledge him as fellow genius, but was disappointed. 'It would have been a very dull person indeed who failed to recognize the black, bilious rage that shook him to the soul. I instance this as proof that Yeats was a genuine poet at heart, for a mere charlatan would have known that he had no cause to fear an authentic poet. What hurt him was the knowledge of his own incomparable inferiority.'.

By now Crowley was showing all the personality traits that would mark the rest of his career; vanity, arrogance, self-deception, the desire to acquire grandiose titles, the desire to control other people, the under-valuing of fellow human beings, the absurd belief in his own genius, the destructiveness. He lacked any inhibition. When it came to a new adventure, there was no still small voice inside telling him that it was unreasonable, or inconsistent with what he had been doing hitherto; he just went ahead and did it. And – worst of all – he did not fear madness, which was always just round the corner. Another peculiar trait was that he had no respect for his own or anyone else's body, which helps to explain the headlong plunge into sexual activity with almost anybody.

In middle age he set up his Abbey of Thelema and while there he described himself in remarkable terms. 'I have made my flesh rotten, my blood venomous, my nerves hell-tortured, my brain hag-ridden, I have infested the round world with corruption.' It is not hard to catch the boastful tone here, but how could anyone think it was a good or worthwhile thing to do – to infest the round world with corruption? It is probably easiest to understand it in simple terms of the will to power. Crowley wanted to have an effect on the world. If the only effect he could have was destructive, then so be it.

He was, of course, mad. He was always accusing those he quarrelled with of stealing his possessions. As he aged, this came to be a mania. The absurd *grand guignol* descriptions he wrote of his own depravities are obviously designed to shock, and they read more like the scandalous talk of small boys when they want to shock one another or their elders and betters. Or the flasher in the park. He took to elaborating his signature so that the initial A turned into a phallus. He was an *enfant terrible* on a very big scale. But why did Crowley want to shock his elders and betters? It does not take a great leap of imagination to see that it was the deceased Plymouth Brother father he was really seeking to scandalize.

A lot of Crowley's magic writings are derivative. The first poem was drawn from Baudelaire by way of Swinburne. Later, he drew on the erotic writings of Sir Richard Burton, whom he greatly admired, and on eastern writers when he was travelling in India, Nepal and China. He also drew quite a lot from the esoteric writings of Dr John Dee, Elizabeth I's magician.

In Victor Neuburg, Crowley found the perfect acolyte. Neuburg had a psychological need to be mastered, to be Crowley's slave, and Crowley was only too keen to enslave him. Crowley enoyed humiliating Neuburg and even carried out a ritual that persuaded Neuburg he had been turned into a camel. Neuburg was useful to Crowley in other ways too. He had money and Crowley needed money. More expensively-produced editions of Crowley's books started to appear. In one of these, Crowley was intending to reveal the secrets of the Golden Dawn, and MacGregor Mathers succeeded in getting an injunction to block publication on the grounds that he had proprietory rights to the material. Mr Justice Bucknill granted the Golden Dawn the protection Mathers wanted. Crowley was surprised, appealed against the decision, and won the appeal. Crowley had by 1909 broken with the paranoid Mathers and started to hanker for an order of his own. Mathers died in the 1918 influenza epidemic, but it was said that Crowley had killed him.

Crowley founded his order, contrived elaborate ceremonies for his followers in which sex was usually on offer. His taste for notoriety was unquenchable. He was absolutely delighted when Somerset Maugham featured him in *The Magician*, as Oliver Haddo, 'a big stout fellow with a taste for wild-looking clothes'. 'I was not in the least offended by the attempts of the book to represent me as, in many ways, the most atrocious scoundrel, for he had done more than justice to the qualities of which I was proud . . . *The Magician* was, in fact, an appreciation of my genius such as I had never dreamed of inspiring.' And so on for about a page.

Oddly, Crowley relentlessly pursued a public reputation as the wickedest man in the world, and came to be called just that in the popular press, while at the same time being very quick with litigation. He loved to sue for libel. He was friendless, partly because of his relentless need to control people. It was followers, disciples, he needed, not friends. There was one who came close to being a friend and that was Herbert Pollitt. Crowley met Pollitt when he was 23 and in his final year at Cambridge. Pollitt was ten years older than Crowley and, according to Crowley, he had appeared at Cambridge solely to dance for the Footlights Club. Pollitt was a female impersonator. Crowley described the beauty of Pollitt's hair, which does seem much of a recommendation, and Pollitt was not interested in any of Crowley's preoccupations. The mutual interest seems to have been purely sexual. Crowley says, 'The relation between us was that ideal intimacy which the Greeks considered the greatest glory of manhood and the most precious prize of life.'.

One night in 1912, there was a knock at Crowley's door. It was a mysterious stranger with a huge moustache. It was Theodor Reuss, the head of the Ordo Templi Orientis; he was also, incidentally, a member of the German Secret Service. He straight away accused Crowley of publishing the innermost secret of his organization, the Ninth Secret. Crowley denied it. Reuss went to Crowley's bookshelf and picked up *The Book of Lies* and opened it at a page reading 'Let the Adept be armed with his Magick Rood.'. Crowley was very taken with Reuss's earnestness and eloquence and the two men talked into the night. They pooled secrets. Shortly after this, Crowley was elevated once more in the hierarchy of magicians; he became Patriarch Grand Administrator General.

At the outbreak of the First World War, Crowley rushed back to England from Switzerland to be of service to his country, but the British government did not want his services. They knew enough about him and his antics to want nothing to do with him. They may, besides, have known about his association with Reuss. So, in October he sailed for America on the *Lusitania*, which was unfortunately not torpedoed until a couple of years later. In America he got lots of media attention, which he enjoyed. Crowley's appearance fascinated many. A reporter for *The World Magazine* said, 'At times I have seen him look 70, and at times barely 25. His looks seemingly change at will. Now he is a priest-like old man; now apparently a somewhat effeminate youth with soft plump hands and heavy womanish face.'.

Crowley took up painting, but characteristically took it up in a bizarre, attention-demanding way. He posted an ad in the newspaper for models; 'WANTED: DWARFS, Hunchbacks, Tattooed Women, Harrison Fisher Girls, Freaks of All Sorts, Coloured

Women, only if exceptionally ugly or deformed, to pose for artist. Apply by letter with a photograph.'.

In the 1920s, Crowley worked on setting up his new religion at the so-called Abbey of Thelema, and publicizing it. It is odd to think of Crowley performing grotesque and obscene acts of black magic, trying very hard for notoriety, then sitting down in the Mediterranean sunshine, tut-tutting over the *Sunday Express*'s lurid account of his lurid lifestyle. 'COMPLETE EXPOSURE OF DRUG FIEND AUTHOR. Black Record of Aleister Crowley. Preying on the Debased. His Abbey. Profligacy and Vice in Sicily'. All on the front page. Was he scandalized? Was he delighted? His reaction was as remarkable and unpredictable as everything else he did. He found some sheets of writing paper and wrote Lord Beaverbrook, the newspaper's proprietor, a letter urging fair play and a spirit of independent inquiry. But it was true that people were having their minds played with, their lives wrecked, by Crowley's psychological games. One young man, Raoul, even died. It was not clear why he died, but his wife suspected some kind of poisoning; Crowley sometimes asked his followers to drink blood – a sure way of passing on infections.

Crowley, now proudly adding the title 'The Great Beast' to his long list of self-awarded titles, was invited to give a lecture to the Oxford University Poetry Society. He proposed reading a paper on Gilles de Rais, an earlier black magician and therefore, in Crowley's mind, one of his predecessors. Father Knox, the Catholic Chaplain of the University got to hear of the projected lecture and had it stopped. Hugh Speaight, the Poetry Society's secretary, was forced by Knox to write to Crowley to tell him the booking was cancelled. Crowley was happy to be interviewed about the matter by the *Oxford Mail*; 'Perhaps the refusal to let me lecture has come because Gilles de Rais is said to have killed 800 children in ritual murder and,' he said airily, 'in some way this was connected with myself, since the accusation that I have not only killed but eaten children is one of the many false statements that have been circulated about me.'. As with the *Sunday Express*, Crowley manages to adopt a tone of wronged innocence that is either shocking or funny, depending on your point of view.

But overall Aleister Crowley's career was not a laughing matter. Like a magnet, he drew to him an endless stream of emotionally damaged or psychologically flawed people; he manipulated and played with them, physically, sexually, emotionally and psychologically, invariably leaving them more damaged than they were before.

On one occasion, when he was suing someone for libel, Crowley was asked, 'Are you asking for damages because your reputation has suffered?'.

'Yes,' Crowley replied.

'Have you, from the time of your adolescence, openly defied all moral convention?'

'No.'

'And proclaimed your contempt for all the doctrines of Christianity?'

'Not all. . .'

'Did you take to yourself the designation "The Beast 666"?'

'Yes.'

'Do you call yourself "The Master Therion"?'

'Yes.'

'"Great Wild Beast".'

'Do these titles convey a fair expression of your practice and outlook on life?'

'"The Beast 666" only means "sunlight". You can call me "Little Sunshine".'

Laughter in court. But when the judge heard later the nature of the paintings on the walls of Crowley's Chamber of Nightmares, he could not contain himself; 'I thought that everything which was vicious and bad had been produced at one time or another before me. I have learnt in this case that we can learn always something more if we live long enough. I have never heard such dreadful, horrible, blasphemous and abominable stuff as that which has been produced by [Aleister Crowley]'. Crowley lost his case.

He became a retired magician, dosing himself with huge quantities of drugs. Crowley died at the age of 72 on 1 December, 1947 of myocardial degeneration and chronic bronchitis. As he lay dead, someone stole his watch. He was cremated in the Brighton Crematorium. The coffin was borne in and then one of Crowley's followers recited the Hymn to Pan. There was a ruffling of municipal feathers at this last scandal. It was said that the crematorium was afterwards re-consecrated.

PART ELEVEN

FAKERS AND FRAUDS

Horatio Bottomley
(1860–1933)

HORATIO WILLIAM BOTTOMLEY was born at Bethnal Green in London in 1860 and after his parents died he was brought up in an orphanage. He eventually ran away from the orphanage to become an errand boy, then a solicitor's clerk, then a shorthand writer in the law courts. It was there that he learned about the workings of the law.

For many years Bottomley pretended to be the illegitimate son of Charles Bradlaugh, the celebrated atheist MP, probably because he looked very much like Bradlaugh. But this was just the first of many lies that Horatio Bottomley would tell – or at least the first lie that we know about. In fact Bottomley's father had been a tailor's foreman – and he had ended up in a lunatic asylum.

In 1884 Bottomley started his first business venture, a local paper, *The Hackney Hansard*. In spite of his lack of formal education, he turned out to be a gifted journalist with a persuasive turn of phrase – and a brilliant public speaker. He had a good ear for ringing phrases. The newspaper business ended in bankruptcy and the first of several prosecutions for fraud. He was acquitted and the judge was so impressed by Bottomley's conduct of his defence that he recommended he should become a barrister. Unfortunately, as an undischarged bankrupt he was ineligible for the Inns of Court, so he was to stay on the wrong side of the law.

By 1900 he had promoted getting on for 50 companies with a total capital of 20 million pounds. But his companies failed as regularly as he launched them. He was tried for conspiracy and fraud in 1891 and again in 1909 in spectacular trials, but acquitted on each occasion. In another trial, the judge refused to convict him of starting an illegal lottery in spite of the evidence against him. Between 1901 and 1905 he had as many as 67 bankruptcy petitions and writs filed against him. His businesses failed almost as soon as they were set up. One major problem was his fondness for the good life; he had to milk his companies' assets in order to maintain his champagne lifestyle.

He started a racing stable. This was successful in that one of his horses won the Cesarewitch, but he squandered the profits on a luxury flat in London, a large country house in Sussex and a villa in the south of France.

In 1906 he founded a weekly paper, *John Bull*, and also became MP for South Hackney. One of Bottomley's most nauseating characteristics was his pose as a philanthropist. He was a grabber, not a giver, yet he managed through his oratory to persuade people that he was a great philanthropist, and it was through this massive hypocrisy that he won his seat in Parliament.

In 1911 he presented a petition in bankruptcy

and resigned his seat in Parliament.

During the First World War he raked in sub-
scriptions amounting to nearly 900,000 pounds for
various enterprises. He exploited the outbreak of
war to foist another great confidence trick on the
British public. Not Bottomley as philanthropist this
time, but Bottomley as patriot – another piece of
hypocrisy. He became a recruiting officer, touring
the country to give barnstorming speeches that
would goad young men into enlisting in the
armed forces. He charged 50 pounds a time for
these speeches, a lot of money in those days. This
activity made him a national celebrity, which in
turn helped him to discharge his bankruptcy.

In 1918 he was discharged from his bankruptcy
and became an MP again. The government floated
a Victory Loan, in which the smallest bonds had
a nominal value of five pounds. Bottomley had
the brilliant idea of forming a club, so that the
'little man' and the 'little woman' could share in
the loan by subscribing smaller sums. With these
small sums, Bottomley would buy Victory Bonds
or National War Bonds in the club's name.
Bottomley's scheme was hugely popular. By the
end of 1919, he had collected getting on for half
a million pounds. Some of it was used properly,
to buy bonds, but some was not; instead it was
used to shore up various ailing companies. Some,
inevitably, just went straight into his pocket.

In 1921, Chancery appointed a receiver to look
into Bottomley's enterprises. At this critical
moment, Bottomley quarrelled with an associate,
Reuben Bigland. This was an unwise move, as

Bigland knew enough about Bottomley to do him a lot of harm. Reuben Bigland published a defamatory pamphlet, describing the Victory Bond Club as Bottomley's 'latest and greatest swindle' and accused him of duping 'poor subscribers to invest one pound notes'. Like Oscar Wilde not long before, Bottomley made a second big mistake in suing for libel. Bigland put in a detailed written plea of justification explaining the exact nature of the swindle, and in the face of this Bottomley withdrew the prosecution; Bigland was formally acquitted. Now Bottomley's prosecution became inevitable.

In 1922 he faced his final trial, the one that was his undoing. He was charged with 24 counts of fraudulently converting over 150,000 pounds to his own use. This money had been entrusted to him by members of the public for investment in his Victory Bond Club and three other enterprises. Mr Travers Humphreys, the greatest criminal lawyer of his time, led the prosecution. Bottomley, as usual, conducted his own defence. By this stage, Bottomley was 62 and bloated with food and drink. Humphreys said afterwards, 'In truth it was not I who floored Bottomley. It was drink.'. Bottomley's brain could by then 'only work on repeated doses of champagne'. Before the trial began, Bottomley sought an interview with Humphreys. He wanted a special deal. He wanted a mid-morning break each day so that he could have a pint of champagne, and he wanted the name of a certain lady kept out of the trial. Disarmed, Humphreys readily agreed to both requests. Bottomley had evidently lost the plot.

It was clear from the facts and figures that Humphreys produced that a lot of 'little men' and 'little women' had been robbed by Bottomley. Eighty-five thousand people had written in wanting their money back. Bottomley had not paid up. Obviously they could not all be called as witnesses, but a sample was summoned. There was even a colonel who had lost 10,000 pounds ; most had lost very small sums, but sums they could not afford to lose. Many of Bottomley's victims had been deceived by the propaganda published in Bottomley's own newspaper, *John Bull*. He had posted ads that read, 'A New Road to Fortune – £1 gives you an opportunity of winning £20,000'.

Bottomley put up a showy and spirited defence, cross-questioning all the witnesses in a thorough and professional way. He then made a great speech to the jury, which began, 'You may have entertained a great opinion of me, and thought that, whatever my faults in days gone by, I have endeavoured to do my duty to my King and country. Now you are asked to change your opinion, and to say that all the time I was an arrant humbug and scoundrel.' It was outrageous stuff. Of course he had been an arrant humbug and scoundrel all the time. 'You have got to find,' he went on, 'that I had the intention to steal the money off poor devils such as ex-soldiers who subscribed to the Club. You have got to find that Horatio Bottomley, editor of *John Bull*, Member of Parliament, the man who wrote and spoke throughout the war with the sole object of inspiring the troops and keeping up the morale of the country, who went out to the front to do his best to cheer the lads – you have got to find that that man intended to steal their money. God forbid!'.

Travers Humphreys managed to prove that even the patriotism was for money. 'Were you not paid for your patriotic speeches during the war?' he asked.

'Never a farthing for my recruiting meetings,' Bottomley answered, untruthfully. 'But later on, as lecturer on the war, I got certain remuneration.' Pressed for details, Bottomley admitted what the sums of money were. They added up to 27,000 pounds.

'So the war did you pretty well?' Humphreys commented drily.

In a final, rather wild, speech to the jury, Bottomley cried, 'You will not convict me. The jury is not yet born who would convict me on these charges, It is unthinkable. The sword of justice will drop from its scabbard if you give a verdict of Guilty against me. I know my country and my country's people, and knowing you, and knowing myself, and knowing the truth about this matter, I know by the mercy of God and the spirit of justice you will liberate me from this ordeal.' He was so moved by his own oratory that he ended in a series of choking sobs.

Within half an hour, the jury found Bottomley guilty of fraud. The sword of justice remained firmly in its scabbard. The judge said he had been rightly convicted of a series of heartless frauds.

'These poor people trusted you, and you robbed them of 150,000 pounds. The sentence of the Court upon you is that you be kept in penal servitude for seven years.' Bottomley then audaciously asked the judge whether it was not usual to ask the prisoner if he had anything to say. 'It is not customary in cases of misdemeanour,' said Mr Justice Salter.

'Had it been so, my lord,' said Bottomley, 'I should have had something rather offensive to say about your summing up.' He was taken off to Wormwood Scrubs.

Bottomley was expelled from the House of Commons a few days later, as he began his sentence. He served five of the seven years. When he came out, he earned 12,500 pounds for a series of articles about his experiences in prison and even started another magazine, this time called *John Blunt*. This too was a financial failure. He was bankrupt again and had to part with The Dicker, his big house in Sussex. He was so hard up now that he was reduced to applying for a state pension, which was granted and then summarily withdrawn without explanation.

In his last days, after his wife died, he was looked after by a retired musical comedy actress called Peggy Primrose. He had backed her shows long before. He made a pathetic series of appearances at the Windmill Theatre – he would do anything for a bit of money – but collapsed and died in May 1933. When Travers Humphreys, his old adversary, heard the news he said, 'What a wasted life. What a pity.'. It was indeed a waste.

Horatio Bottomley had enormous intelligence and talent as a speaker and journalist and could have used those talents for good ends. Instead he used them for evil, pretending to be someone he was not, pretending his motives were other than they were, raising and dashing the hopes of 'little people' who had few prospects, pilfering small sums of money from people who couldn't afford to lose any money at all, and spending the proceeds on his own extravagant life style. Bottomley was the sort of parasite every society can do without.

Charles Dawson
(1864–1916)

IN 1912 CHARLES Dawson discovered the first of two skulls found in the Piltdown quarry in Sussex. The second was discovered, by Dawson and an unnamed 'friend', in 1914 or 1915. They were apparently the skulls of a very primitive human being, a hominid, or early man. The discovery was a sensation and the new sub-species was named *Eoanthropus dawsoni* in the full expectation that it would prove to be the long-awaited missing link between the human species and the apes. British palaeontologists were especially excited at the prospect that Dawson's early man was a Briton.

During the nineteenth century and the early years of the twentieth century a partial picture of the evolution of the human race was gradually emerging. Neanderthal Man was discovered in 1856, Cro-Magnon Man in 1869, Java Man in 1890, Peking Man in 1903 and Heidelberg Man in 1907. A find in Australia, Talgai man in 1914, seemed to support the Piltdown discovery.

But some scientists were sceptical from the start and as the years passed other discoveries of hominids were made, for example in Africa, and it became increasingly clear that Piltdown Man didn't fit any emerging sequence in the evolution of the human race. Ramapithecus was discovered in 1934, Swanscombe Man in 1935. In 1931, though, Sir Arthur Keith, a stout defender of Piltdown Man, was still saying, 'It is therefore possible that Piltdown Man does represent the early Pleistocene ancestor of the modern type of man. He may well be the ancestor we have been in search of during all these past years. I am therefore inclined to make the Piltdown type spring from the main ancestral stem of modern humanity.'. But the remains looked increasingly like an anomaly, not part of the mainstream of human development at all. Sherwood Washburn said, 'I remember writing a paper on human evolution in 1944, and I simply left Piltdown out. You could make sense of human evolution if you didn't try to put Piltdown into it.'. In 1949 the Piltdown bones were subjected to fluorine tests, showing that they were relatively recent.

Then in 1953 it finally emerged, just as spectacularly as the original discovery, that Piltdown Man was a hoax. Careful investigation of the bones and the site itself showed that there were never any significant fossil bones in the Piltdown quarry. They had all been planted. Oakley carried out various tests to find out what the bones were and where they had come from. His conclusions:

Piltdown I skull: medieval, human, dating from about AD 1330.

Piltdown II skull: the same.

Piltdown I jawbone: jaw of orangutan, about AD 1450, from Sarawak.

Elephant tooth: genuine fossil, from Tunisia.
Hippopotamus tooth: genuine fossil, probably
   from Malta or Sicily.
Canine tooth: genuine fossil chimpanzee
   tooth.

The hoaxer had treated the whole set of remains carefully to give an impression of great age. The bones were iron stained, and several of them were treated with chromic acid to make them more receptive to the staining process. The canine tooth was painted with Van Dyke brown. The teeth were filed to make them fit and patched with chewing gum. There was no doubt that this was a very deliberate hoax, though it must have taken a considerable amount of time and effort to prepare.

Piltdown had collapsed. Now it was no longer a question of finding out how the bones fitted into the human family tree. A whole new set of questions had erupted overnight. First, how was it that the scientific community had not spotted before that it was a hoax? Second, who perpetrated the hoax?

The palaeontologists who first examined the Piltdown remains were not really experts in this particular field. The British Museum people, Pycraft and Arthur Smith Woodward, made several errors of reconstruction and interpretation. The only expert in the expanded team, Grafton Eliot Smith, was curiously silent about some of these mistakes. We also have to bear in mind that some of the key forensic techniques available today were simply not available in 1915–20, so scientists were rather easier to fool. The forger appears to have known exactly what tests would be used and adapted the remains accordingly, which carries implications. Was the forger perhaps well known to the team? The 'experts' should, even so, have spotted the use of stain, paint and chewing gum. They could also have taken better quality x-ray photographs of the specimens than they did; sharper images would have exposed several problems, such as the peculiar wear patterns on the teeth, which had been produced by filing.

Naturally, from the exposure of the hoax onwards, the men who found the remains were the chief suspects: Charles Dawson, Teilhard de Chardin and Woodward. Of these, Dawson was the leading suspect, not least because he had played other practical jokes and he was the common link connecting each stage in the discovery to the next. Obviously he planted the bones. Even so, over the last half century, other candidates have been identified, and candidates with plausible motives for carrying out the hoax. Grafton Smith and Sir Arthur Keith were prominent scientists playing key roles in the discovery, and it has been argued that Dawson and Keith together could have organized the hoax between them. Probably the labourer, Hargreaves, who did most of the digging, was in on the hoax; there would have been no point in preparing the remains if the digger dug in the wrong place. Sir Arthur Conan Doyle, the geologist W. J. Sollas, the amateur geologist and Hastings shop-owner Lewis Abbot and the palaeontologist Martin Hinton have also been accused.

What is so evil about carrying through a harmless practical joke about a prehistoric man who never existed? No-one died. No-one was injured. No-one was robbed. No crime was committed.

It was an evil act because it misled not only the general public, who had no way of knowing whether the Piltdown man claims were true or not, but it misled the scientific community. In science, the accumulation of knowledge proceeds slowly and gradually, each piece of research taking several years to complete and building on the results of earlier research. The knowledge is hard-won. If people are sent down intellectual blind alleys, they may waste years of their lives in pointless research. 'Wrong' knowledge can clutter up the information systems across the globe, as scholars try to invent new evolutionary models that will cater for the anomalous data. The Piltdown hoax sent many earnest researchers down a blind alley for 40 years – a whole lifetime of wasted research effort.

Charles Dawson remains the prime suspect. He made the initial finds of both Piltdown I and II skull fragments and he was the one who decided to make the Piltdown quarry a special focus for research. He was also the chief suspect in a number of other hoaxes. There was the Beauport statuette, the Blackmore flint weapon, the Bexhill boat, the Uckfield horseshoe, the Pevensey Brick and the Hastings clock-face hoaxes – all of which are laid at Dawson's door. He was a dabbler, a man of many interests, both palaeontological and antiquarian. It doubtless amused him and gave him an inflated sense of self-worth, as an amateur and an outsider, to fool the professionals from time to time.

Dawson just conceivably could have carried out the hoax single-handed, and some have argued that he did have sufficient knowledge to do it. It nevertheless seems more likely that at Piltdown he had a co-conspirator – among the experts. The reason for thinking this is that Dawson was so obviously suspect. But if he had a friend or friends at the museum who would verify the finds for him he could expect that others would be ready to accept the finds as genuine, at least for a while. He could hardly have expected that his hoax would be so successful. Most practical jokes are uncovered fairly quickly, and Dawson would probably have been quite happy with his hoax if it had lasted five years. Why would anyone at the museum have been interested in helping Dawson? In any academic institution there are people with academic aspirations that remain unrealised, people who are frustrated because their work has not been justly rewarded and who feel bitter resentment towards 'superiors' who do not merit their promoted positions. It would be quite possible for a group of malcontents within a department to get together with the intention of making a fool of their head of department. We have only to think of a more recent example of a high-profile historian who was made to look very foolish when the 'Hitler Diaries' which he had publicly endorsed were shortly afterwards shown to have been written on recently made paper. It may well be that one or more of the academics involved on the Piltdown work wanted to make a fool of someone in exactly this way.

In the 1970s, Ian Langham, an Australian science historian, started to re-evaluate the events surrounding the forgery. Initially he favoured Ronald Millar's suspect, Grafton Eliot Smith, but later settled on Sir Arthur Keith. Langham died suddenly in 1984 before revealing his conclusions and Frank Spencer, an Australian anthropologist, completed Langham's project, publishing the results in a book, *Piltdown: a scientific forgery*. The central pillar of the Langham-Spencer theory is an anonymous article that appeared in the British Medical Journal on 21 December, 1912, just three days after the discovery of Piltdown Man was announced at a Geological Society meeting. A superficial reading suggests that the article is just a report on the meeting, but it contains additional information about the location and the story of the discovery, known only to those directly involved with the digging.

Arthur Smith Woodward thought this odd, wondered who the author was, and how he knew these extra details – but he was never able to find out. Ian Langham found that the author was Arthur Keith. What is more, Keith's diary shows that the piece was written three days before the Geological Society announcement. As Keith was not part of Woodward's inner circle, it is hard to understand how he knew these things. There are other documents that imply a covert connection between Keith and Dawson. One shows Keith claiming that he met Dawson for the first time in January 1913; others show that Keith had met Dawson at least three times before that. Langham also noticed that Keith had destroyed all of his correspondence with Dawson. The thrust of the Langham-Spencer theory is that Dawson initiated the hoax and began to prepare it in 1905. Keith was brought into the plot in 1911, and during 1911–12 Keith prepared the various specimens, which Dawson then planted.

A more likely collaborator for Dawson would seem to be Martin Hinton, a curator of zoology at the British Museum at the time of the fraud. Various items found among Hinton's possessions after his death in 1961 strongly imply that he was involved in the staining of the bones. Hinton was a rodent specialist, and a canvas travelling trunk bearing Hinton's initials was found in the loft space at the museum. As well as a lot of rodent specimens, it contained a collection of carved and stained pieces of hippopotamus and elephant teeth and assorted bones that look as if they belong with the Piltdown collection. Here, at last, is the smoking gun.

What would Hinton's motive have been? Hinton was famed for his wild sense of humour and elaborate practical jokes, so the Piltdown fraud would certainly have been in character. The shaping of an elephant bone into a tool that looked suspiciously like a cricket bat was obviously a joke about 'the earliest Englishman'. It was also the case that his head of department, Woodward, was irritatingly pompous and self-important and it may have amused Hinton to watch Woodward taking the limelight with something that could easily blow up in his face at any moment. As time passed, and the hoax went undetected, Hinton may have derived a sadistic pleasure in watching his 'superior' spending years of his professional life supporting Piltdown Man and simultaneously digging himself a deeper and deeper pit as far as posterity was concerned.

Hinton had plenty of contacts in the Sussex Weald and was an expert on Wealden geology. In 1954, Hinton wrote a revealing letter to Gavin de Beer, the Director of the British Museum, 'the temptation to invent such a "discovery" of an ape-like man associated with late Pliocene Mammals in a Wealden gravel might well have proved irresistible to some unbalanced member of old Ben Harrison's circle at Ightham. He and his friends (of whom I was one) were always talking of the possibility of finding a late Pliocene deposit in the Weald.'.

There are some loose ends. The Piltdown specimens contain gypsum; the Hinton specimens do not. The Hinton specimens contain manganese; the Piltdown specimens do not. But there is no reason to suppose that the BM trunk contains all the dummy-run specimens that Hinton worked on; some were probably thrown away. Whatever the detail, Hinton clearly knew far more about the

Piltdown affair than is likely if he was not involved. It seems unlikely that Hinton could have worked alone, because he would not have had access to the Piltdown site in 1912-14, but in partnership with Charles Dawson. Dawson's responsibility for the hoax is clearly signalled by the fact that no further finds were made at Piltdown after 1916, the year when Dawson died.

L. Harrison Matthews, who respected Hinton, described informal dinner conversations with Hinton in 1945-50. Hinton was keen to get across the fact that 'Piltdown was not a subject to be taken seriously.'. Matthews surmised from this that Hinton knew more than he was saying.

There is another possibility, which is that Woodward was in on the hoax as well. At first this seems unlikely, as the man seemed stuffily conventional, a 'straight arrow', but he stood to benefit greatly in terms of enhanced academic status from his part in the discovery. The finds also neatly fitted the particular evolutionary theories he believed in. But then, Martin Hinton would have known that too.

The Piltdown hoax had, and still has, endless ramifications. It is even used by fundamentalists as a club to beat evolutionists. If we cannot trust scientists to tell us the truth, who *can* we trust?

Han van Meegeren
(1889-1946)

OVER FIVE HUNDRED years ago, Vermeer said, 'As long as there is art there will be forgeries.'. This is a nice piece of irony, as one of the most celebrated forgers of the twentieth century, Han van Meegeren, specialized in forging Vermeer's paintings. Why are forgeries evil?

It is not just that a fake Old Master is worth far less than a real one and therefore a financial fraud is involved when the picture is auctioned – though that certainly does happen – it is more that the past itself is being falsified. Lying in a courtroom may get someone wrongly convicted or wrongly acquitted; that is lying about the present. Painting a picture in the style of Vermeer is equivalent to fabricating a view of the sixteenth century Europe and therefore bearing false witness to the past – it is a kind of perjury.

Some art forgeries teeter on the brink between art forgery and archaeological hoax. The famous Turin Shroud, for instance, may be the cloth which wrapped up the body of Christ or a medieval art work made as a devotional aid. Until we know for sure what it is, we don't really know how to respond to it.

Art dealers say that 15 per cent of all art sold at

auctions is fake. Thomas Hoving, the former curator of the Metropolitan Museum of Art, says that 40 per cent of the art and artefacts offered to him for the Museum were forgeries. For some artists, the percentage of fakes in circulation is alarmingly high. Some experts believe that 60 per cent of the Giacometti sculptures in existence are fakes.

Modern forensic techniques make it easier to identify forgeries; fabric and wood can be radiocarbon dated, and x-rays make it possible to see older paintings under the surface layer. There was a painting alleged to be a Picasso, dating from his early blue period. An x-ray revealed an abstract painting underneath it, which must have been painted at a later period. Another painting called *St Antony the Hermit* was alleged to be by Bernhard Strigel and painted around 1460. An x-ray showed a painting underneath it that had been painted by an artist who lived 250 years after Strigel's death.

Perhaps the best known forger of all time was Han van Meegeren, who was born on 10 October, 1889 at Deventer in the Netherlands. He did not copy existing Vermeers, but created new compositions in Vermeer's style. One, *Christ and his Disciples at Emmaus* was based on the composition of Caravaggio's *Supper at Emmaus*, but in Vermeer's style. It seems van Meegeren forged six in all. He took care to use pigments that were available in the seventeenth century. The canvases came from the seventeenth century. The ageing process he subjected his pictures to took four years of research. Van Meegeren famously sold one of his fake Vermeers to Hermann Goering in exchange, it is said, for 200Dutch paintings that Goering had looted.

After the fall of Nazi Germany at the end of the Second World War, Hermann Goering's collection of priceless old masters was discovered at his house at Berchtesgaden. Most of this haul had been looted from churches, galleries and private houses during the German invasion of one European country after another. A few of them had been honestly purchased, which is ironic, as they had not been honestly sold. One of these purchased paintings was *Woman Taken in Adultery*, and it was signed by Jan Vermeer. The investigators discovered that the painting had been acquired by Goering's agents from a dealer in Amsterdam, though for too low a price.

Suspicions were aroused when as many as six hitherto unknown Vermeers turned up during the short period of the Second World War. An x-ray revealed a face on the underpainting left on the canvas that van Meegeren had been unable to remove. One picture had too many layers of paint to be a Vermeer.

Van Meegeren was a prosperous night club owner. He had made a small fortune by selling previously unknown old masters to major art galleries. Quite apart from the painting he sold to Goering, he sold six other 'Vermeers' to galleries in the Netherlands. Van Meegeren was arrested and imprisoned on suspicion of being a collaborator; this was a much more serious charge than the art forgery – it carried the death sentence. This gave Van Meegeren his reason for telling the truth. When he was brought to court he came out with the most astonishing story. Far from collaborating with the Nazis, he had actually fooled them, deceived them, duped them. He had after all not sold the Nazis a Vermeer: he had not sold them a Dutch national art treasure, but a van Meegeren.

At first the judge did not believe him, but decided to give him a chance to prove that what he was saying at least *could* be true. He was put under guard in his cell in Amsterdam and told to paint another 'Vermeer' that was good enough to fool the experts. Under these unusual conditions, he painted *Jesus Among the Doctors*. The painting was impressive, and so difficult to tell from a real Vermeer that the judge acquitted him on the collaboration charge. He was free. But not for very long.

As more and more van Meegerens came to light, the scale of the forger's deception became more obvious. He was brought to trial again, this time charged with deception. After a two-year forensic investigation, van Meegeren was sentenced to a year in prison, but he died of a heart attack in Deventer on 30 December, 1947, just six weeks later before he could serve his sentence. He was 57.

What made van Meegeren a forger? His fakes made huge sums of money, yet it was not the money that motivated him. He had been a very successful young painter. He had had a major exhibition of his own, unfaked, work at The Hague when he was 33. His work was very popular. It was the critics who hated it, among them a pompous academic called Bredius, who treated van Meegeren's work with contempt. The fakes were a way of getting back at critics like Bredius. The painter Bredius most admired was, of course, Vermeer.

In 1936, van Meegeren shut himself away in a rented French villa to work on his masterpiece, which he called *Christ and his Disciples at Emmaus*. It was not a direct copy of a Vermeer, and would be seen by Bredius as a previously unknown painting. In 1937, van Meegeren put the painting on the market through a Paris lawyer, with a fake provenance: a Dutch family living in France had owned it. Naturally, the Paris lawyer first approached Dr Bredius, who was best qualified to verify the painting's authenticity. Bredius had no hesitation in confirming that it was a Vermeer. Van Meegeren was delighted, and all the more so when Bredius claimed to have discovered the art treasure and urged the Boymans Museum in Rotterdam to buy it for 50,000 pounds. Bredius visited the painting there to study it. Van Meegeren went too, though for different reasons.

Tom Keating

TOM KEATING CAME to notice in 1976, when it emerged that he had created 13 drawings attributed to Samuel Palmer. He went on trial in 1979, charged with fraud. During his trial it emerged that he had painted over 2,000 paintings in the style of 150 artists.

Keating was a big, bearded ex-naval man, a stoker, and a Cockney. He seems now, and seemed at the time, an unlikely figure to take on and challenge the art world. He became disillusioned and angry when he was leading a very poor existence, living in a prefab, and being paid five pounds to produce copies of pictures by other artists, especially when he shortly afterwards saw his paintings, the same paintings, on sale in galleries for 500 pounds. He denounced the art dealers as crooks. 'Those dealers are just East End blokes in West End suits. They don't give a damn about the paintings. All they are after is the profit.' He decided to get even with them.

When his marriage ended in 1950, Keating went to Scotland to restore murals. While he was there he started imitating the works of other painters and sending them for sale at auction. He was later to claim that at auction the pictures were selling themselves at their own value, that he was not defrauding anyone at all.

His biggest commission was restoring the paintings in Marlborough House in 1960; the house had been empty since Queen Mary had died in 1953. While he was restoring a huge mural painting of the Duke of Marlborough on the stairs, the present Queen went to watch him at work. She was astonished. She had run up and down the stairs hundreds of times as a little girl and been unaware that these pictures lay hidden on the walls. Tom Keating said, 'Well, they are, madam, and there's a lot more under the black varnish on the other walls'.

But restoration work like this was not enough to make a continuous income. He went on producing his fakes by the score. He referred to them using Cockney rhyming slang – 'Sexton Blakes'. He became obsessed with Samuel Palmer, a painter he greatly admired, and scoured galleries looking for Palmers to copy. He took care to use the right paper. He also prepared himself mentally, thinking himself into Palmer's view of things before drawing 'automatically' in Palmer's style. Unfortunately, Keating signed some of them with Palmer's name, which opened him squarely to the charge of fraud. He was later contemptuous of his own 'Palmers', saying they were far inferior to the real thing; the point he was making was that he knew the difference between the real Palmers and the fakes, and the dealers knew too. They were tacitly conspiring with the forger in order to make money. A pencil sketch he made of a barn at Shoreham, Palmer's favourite haunt, was sold initially at a country auction for 35 pounds. Later a London gallery sold it to Bedford Museum for 2,550 pounds – after it had been restored by the National Gallery. Somebody should surely have spotted that it was not really by Palmer, or did no-one really care?

The scandal broke after an art expert wrote to the press suggesting that a sepia ink-wash of Sepham Barn, sold for 9,400 pounds as a Palmer, was not genuine. This led to the investigation that in turn led to Keating's trial. Keating could no longer remember which pictures he had painted, but he reckoned that at least 2,500 paintings hanging on gallery walls or in the homes of private collectors were – and still are – fakes.

During the trial, Keating became ill and the trial was stopped. Because of the media coverage of his case, Tom Keating was suddenly very famous. Everyone wanted to buy Keatings now. It was evident that some of his fakes were very clever. Van Meegeren had tried producing Caravaggio's composition in the style of Vermeer, with great success, but Keating went several steps further. When faking a Constable, instead of simply reproducing *The Leaping Horse*, *The Cornfield* or *The Hay Wain*, which would have been spotted by everyone as fakes because the originals and even their rough drafts were so familiar, he visited the scene of *The Hay Wain* and painted the view across the water in the opposite direction, just as the original artist might have done if visiting the spot on another occasion. It was part of the exercise of thinking himself into the artist's place, but it produced something very close to an original piece of work.

The art dealers were flocking round him now. The general public too were very intrigued by the talent of this man who seemed able to paint convincingly in the styles of so many very different painters. He was on TV, talking about art. He was offered some very big commissions and a 250,000-pound contract with a London gallery, but he turned them down. He said, 'I have enough work to make me rich beyond my wildest dreams. All I have ever wanted to do is paint. I would give the damn things away if I could afford to.'.

PART TWELVE

ORGANIZED CRIME

Henry Morgan
(1635–1696)

HENRY MORGAN WAS a seventeenth century priva-
teer or buccaneer, but an unusual one in acquiring
a knighthood. This rare distinction was bestowed
on the buccaneer in 1674 after pulling off a daring
and spectacular raid on Panama City. Whether he
deserved the title has long been debated, but
these days that debate seems rather pointless; now
that 'celebrity' (semi-officially indistinguishable
from 'notoriety') is the only criterion that counts,
and even pop singers seem to be able to command knighthoods, it is no longer clear at what
depth the threshold achievement lies.

The notorious buccaneer Henry Morgan was
born in 1635, possibly at Penkarne in Monmouth-
shire or at Llanrhymny in Glamorgan. Not much
is known about his early days, but it is assumed
that he spent his childhood in south Wales. Two
of his uncles, Edward Morgan and Thomas
Morgan, were officers in the English Civil War,
Thomas (a Colonel) for the Royalists and Edward
(a Major-General) for the Parliamentarians.
Conflict was very much in the family, even before
Henry went to the Caribbean.

Henry Morgan seems to have sailed against
Spain in the mid-seventeenth century, but it is not

clear how he reached the Caribbean. One story has it that he was 'Barbadosed', in other words beaten over the head while going about his business in South Wales and abducted, only waking up on a ship on the way to be sold as an indentured labourer in Jamaica or Barbados. Later, in 1655, Cromwell sent an army to the Caribbean under General Venables to attack the Spaniards, and this gave Henry an opportunity to escape his indenture by joining Venables's army. Another version of Morgan's life has it that Morgan joined General Venables's army as a volunteer in Plymouth in 1654. Venables's attack on the city of Santo Domingo was defeated. The bruised and beaten British force dragged itself back to its ships and limped, with a following wind, to the then-worthless island of Jamaica. There, the 7,000 troops stormed and took the weakly-defended only town, Santiago de la Vega, which was defended by only 200 Spanish soldiers.

This apparent success was in fact a disaster, as Venables had been sent to achieve a significant victory by capturing a major Spanish stronghold, like Santo Domingo, Havana, Vera Cruz or Cartagena. Venables had taken an insignificant Spanish outpost, wasting the huge army he had been entrusted with. When Venables and Admiral Penn, the fleet's commander, returned to London they were both thrown into the Tower. Meanwhile in Jamaica the British troops were dropping like flies from tropical diseases they did not understand: yellow fever, malaria and dysentery killed hundreds. A Spanish resistance group and bands of runaway slaves called Maroons also accounted for British deaths. Somehow, Henry Morgan was lucky enough to survive all this.

During the succeeding years, there were expeditions led by Vice-Admiral Goodson and Commodore Mings. During Commodore Mings's raid on Santiago de Cuba in 1662, Henry Morgan at last emerged from obscurity, when he was documented as being the captain of one of the ships. This attack was a resounding success; the infamous Castillo del Morro guarding the entrance to Santiago Bay was completely destroyed.

In 1663, Morgan was again a captain of one of the ships under Commodore Mings's command, during a daring attack on San Francisco de Campeche. The English naval vessels once again returned home groaning with plunder. Later in 1663, Morgan was involved in attacks on Villa Hermosa, Trujillo and Grenada, all of which fell to the buccaneers. By the time the buccaneers reached Port Royal, Jamaica's main harbour, Henry Morgan was a rich man.

By 1665, the Morgan family had arrived in Jamaica in significant numbers, and it may have been at this time that Morgan married his cousin Mary Elizabeth, though the exact date is not known. Colonel Edward Morgan had also arrived, though he died shortly afterwards during an attack on the Dutch island of Statia.

Morgan's name only became widely known in 1665, when he was made second-in-command of a group of buccaneers, or licensed pirates, who had fought the Dutch in the Anglo-Dutch War. He was not a pirate, which would have put him outside the law, but a buccaneer. The difference is that he had a document from the representative of the British government, the Governor of Jamaica, to fight and steal from Spaniards. The actions of a buccaneer were to all intents and purposes the same as the actions of a pirate, but with official sanction. His first major achievement was the capture of Puerto Principe in Cuba. He was not content with the booty that raid yielded, and he sailed for Panama, sacking the city of Portobello. This made him both rich and famous.

In 1666, Morgan was made Colonel of the Port Royal Militia, a defence force in which he had long served as a captain; now he commanded it. The Dutch leader of the *Brethren of the Coast*, Edward Mansvelt, died and the buccaneers asked Henry Morgan to take his place as their 'Admiral'. Morgan was now the official leader of the buccaneer force in the Caribbean. He went on to attack Puerto del Principe on Cuba, which yielded him another 50,000 pieces of eight. His men were disappointed with this, which induced him to lead a new attack on the harbour of Portobello on the north coast of the Isthmus of Panama. In this daring attack, Morgan took the town, held its citizens to ransom and beat back an army of 3,000 Spanish troops coming to help Portobello from Panama City. Morgan and his men returned to Port Royal with a haul of 250,000 pieces of eight in the holds of their ships.

In October 1668, Morgan sailed again. He and Governor Modyford thought the Spaniards were preparing to attack Jamaica, and decided on a pre-emptive strike on Cartagena, the main Spanish harbour. Morgan set up his base for this attack on Cow Island but his flagship, the *Oxford*, exploded and he lost 300 of his 900 men. He knew he now had too few men to take Cartagena and, taking the advice of one of his French captains, decided to take the port of Maracaibo instead. This raid was a failure, because everyone in Maracaibo had fled before Morgan arrived. He sent search parties to look for people hiding in the forest; they found a few, but little in the way of money. Morgan moved on to another harbour town, but had the same problem. After spending eight unproductive weeks in the Maracaibo Lagoon, Morgan sailed back to Maracaibo itself. Then he encountered a Spanish Vice-Admiral, Alonso del Campo y Espinosa, with three great men o' war.

On 1 May 1669 there was a battle between this Spanish squadron and Morgan's fleet. Morgan sent a fireship towards one of the Spanish ships, the *Magdalen*, which caught fire and sank. The second Spanish ship, the *Santa Louisa*, sailed away to safety, leaving the third, the *Marquesa*, to be captured by the buccaneers. Don Alonso managed to escape to the fort of San Carlos Island. Its guns ranged across the narrow entrance to the Maracaibo Lagoon. The result was a stalemate. Morgan had control of Maracaibo and all the ships. Don Alonso was marooned in the fort, but controlled Morgan's only escape route.

The citizens of Maracaibo now agreed to pay a ransom of 20,000 pieces of eight to prevent Morgan's men from torching their city. Morgan also retrieved more treasure from the sunken Spanish warship.

Morgan then pretended to prepare an attack on the fort. He deceived Don Alonso by setting up a fake landing on the landward side, and causing Don Alonso to move all his guns to point in that direction. Then he set sail on the ebb tide and quickly escaped to the open sea through the unguarded channel. Don Alonso was completely outflanked. The Spanish authorities arrested him and deported him to Spain for questioning; he was exonerated and commended for his bravery. Meanwhile, Henry Morgan sailed back to Port Royal, arriving there in triumph on 17 May 1669.

During the following year, Morgan consolidated his land investments, expanding his sugar planta-tions rather than harrying the Spanish. He was turning himself into a man of status and property.

Undoubtedly the greatest exploit in Morgan's career was the attack on Panama City. For this he knew he needed a large force, so he united the two buccaneer forces in the Caribbean, those based at Port Royal and those at Tortuga. On 19 January 1670, Henry Morgan led a fleet of 36 pirate ships against the city, which was believed to be the richest city in the world. It was a collecting-point for the Spanish gold that was on its way to Europe. Morgan met the Viceroy of Panama, Don Juan Perez de Guzman, in battle just outside the city. De Guzman's forces outnumbered Morgan's by about 500. Morgan massacred de Guzman's forces, mainly because Morgan's reputation as a cunning and ruthless fighter had preceded him; many of the Spanish soldiers took fright and made a run for it as soon as the first shots were fired. He burned the city to the ground and seized 400,000 pieces of eight. This was a great fortune, but because Panama was believed to be the Spaniards' principal centre it was assumed by many of the buccaneers that it would be even wealthier. Morgan's men were disappointed with the treasure. It seems that the silver taken from the Peruvian mines and the merchants' fortunes had all been removed to places of safety before Morgan's fleet arrived.

The Panama attack was poorly timed as far as diplomacy was concerned, though. When Morgan got back to Port Royal in April 1671, he received some very bad news. It turned out that, a few days earlier, Britain had signed a treaty with Spain, so Morgan had technically attacked an ally during a time of peace between the two kingdoms. Morgan had not known about it, because the message arrived from England shortly after his departure for Panama. The scale of Morgan's attack on Panama gradually became known in both England and Spain. The Spanish court made formal protests to London. Towards the end of 1671 orders for the arrest of both Morgan and Governor Modyford arrived in Jamaica. The new Governor, the unfortunately named Sir Thomas Lynch, was reluctant to carry out the order for Morgan's arrest because of Morgan's huge popularity in Jamaica; he feared an outbreak of public disorder if he arrested a public hero. Eventually, Lynch obeyed and sent Morgan back to England. Modyford was by now already in the Tower of London, but because of Morgan's continuing special status – a kind of immunity that sometimes goes with success – Morgan was not sent to join him.

In 1673, England started a new war with the Dutch, and in July Charles II sought Morgan's (written) advice on Caribbean matters. He was so impressed by Morgan's memorandum and the pirate's grasp of the region that he released him and made him Deputy Governor of Jamaica, working under Lord Vaughan, who had succeeded Lynch. Morgan's advice was to strengthen the defence of England's most lucrative colony, because of the huge tax income it produced for the Crown. Just before Christmas 1675, Henry Morgan was knighted.

On 6 March, Morgan was back in Port Royal, but as a changed man. He had left the Caribbean under arrest, a buccaneer charged with serious offences. He had returned a respectable establishment figure, a man of wealth and status, the second most important figure in the colony. He gave up piracy, and concentrated on affairs of defence and the business of running his sugar plantations. In his new roles he showed great skill and diplomacy, well able to deal with the countless intrigues and quarrels that went with the new territories. He even played a part in re-writing his own history. A book of ripping yarns about his exploits as a buccaneer appeared, and he sued the publishers for libel; the book represented him as a sadistic, drunken lout – which he was. Like many other people who have committed terrible crimes, he 'rewrote' his past in his own mind and tried to impose his own revisionist view of himself on those around him.

Morgan died on 7 June, 1696. As if in divine judgement on the city Morgan had done so much to build on the back of his criminal activities, a massive earthquake destroyed Port Royal shortly afterwards. What was Sir Henry Morgan? Slaver, pirate, ruthless buccaneer, brutal murderer, sadist? Plantation owner, administrator, statesman, empire-builder, diplomat? Henry Morgan was probably all of these. The legalistic distinction between pirate and buccaneer is a fine one. Morgan's attacks on the harbour towns of the Caribbean may have been sanctioned by his licence, but there was no difference between their effect and the effect of freelance piracy. People died in large numbers, homes and businesses were burned to the ground, people were robbed at knife-point. Morgan made his money – and his name – out of slavery, robbery, violence and murder. It was what we now call organized crime, and on a grand scale.

Salvatore 'Lucky' Luciano
(1895–1962)

SALVATORE LUCIANO WAS a thug from early on; he was in and out of trouble from the age of ten onwards. At the age of 21, together with Benjamin 'Bugsy' Siegel, he was assaulting a girl in a New York street doorway when the pair of them were set upon by Meyer Lansky, a respectable 16-year-old Polish immigrant who happened to be passing; he saw it as an opportunity to rescue a young woman in distress. He did not know that by attempting this good deed he was stepping into a life of crime.

The fight that broke out in the doorway brought the police out and the three youths were put in the cells for two days for brawling. During those 48 hours Luciano and Siegel took Lansky under their wings and bonded with him.

Salvatore Luciano was a Sicilian immigrant, arrested within hours of disembarking for stealing fruit from a handcart in the street. In 1915 he was jailed for drug dealing, and it was immediately after that that he met Meyer Lansky. Luciano at first tutored Lansky, then they worked together, controlling several New York gangs engaged in robbing shops, warehouses and apartments. Luciano specialized in prostitution and Lansky would have nothing to do with that. Lansky had had a bad experience. He had fallen in love with a prostitute as a teenager, then found her in an alley one night with her throat cut, presumably by her pimp.

The young Salvatore Luciano and Meyer Lansky became members of Jacob Orgen's gang. Orgen, 'Little Augie' as he was known, was making a lot of money out of union rackets. Luciano became the most feared hit-man in New York. His favoured weapon was an ice-pick. His reward was a string of brothels which by 1925 were earning him a million dollars or more a year. He was already rich, when Prohibition brought yet more opportunities to make even bigger money.

In 1927, Lansky and Luciano were joined by a third ruthless killer, Vito Genovese. Genovese had been a friend and neighbour of Luciano's since he arrived in New York at the age of 16. He joined Orgen's gang. Lansky, Luciano and Genovese were by now acquiring formidable reputations as mobsters, but they were still not the biggest gangsters in town. There were two older-style Mafia leaders, Salvatore Maranzano and Giuseppe Masseria, two rival gang bosses whose savage territorial warring had left 60 of their gang members dead. Both Maranzano and Masseria wanted Lansky, Luciano and Genovese in their gangs, but they refused to join. Luciano was lured to an empty garage, where several armed men lay in wait for him. Maranzano had him strung up by the thumbs and punched and kicked until he lapsed into unconsciousness; Maranzano had him revived and punched again. In the end, Maranzano cut him savagely across the face with a knife. It was at this point that Luciano told Maranzano he had changed his mind. He would join the Maranzano mob after all.

Maranzano gave him as his first assignment the assassination of his hated rival, Masseria. Luciano invited Masseria for a meal under the pretext that he was ready to join forces with him. They agreed, drank to the deal, and Luciano went off to the lavatory. At this signal, four gunmen appeared – Vito Genovese, Bugsy Siegel, Albert Anastasia and Joe Adonis – and Masseria knew what they were there for. He tried to escape, but he fell to the floor in a hail of bullets.

Now there was only Maranzano between the Orgen gang and total control of the New York underworld. Maranzano rightly saw himself as top man, and he drew up a constitution for what he termed La Cosa Nostra, and declared himself its Godfather. But Luciano had been maltreated by Maranzano and was not going to forget it. Lansky and the others agreed to help Luciano to settle his score with Maranzano. In September 1931, four gang members posing as Internal Revenue Service investigators called at Maranzano's real estate agency in Park Avenue. They were ushered into Maranzano's private office, where it emerged that they were not tax investigators at all, but Bugsy Siegel, Albert Anastasia, Red Lavine and 'Three Fingers' Lucchese. They drew their knives and stabbed Maranzano several times, and then shot him as well. He had lasted as the New York Godfather for just five months.

For safety's sake, as much as anything, Luciano had 40 more of Maranzano's associates killed – the whole Maranzano mob had gone. The new mob was now firmly in power. The older generation of Mafia leaders, nicknamed 'Moustache Petes' had gone. In their place were accountants and company executives, with the hired guns much more in the background. The operation was divided into two operations, the National Crime Syndicate and Murder Incorporated. Murder Incorporated, the death squad, was headed by Albert Anastasia, who had been involved in killing both Masseria and Maranzano. He was nicknamed the Lord High Executioner of New York and carried out contract killings for over two decades; he also became the head of one of the five big Mafia families in New York, the Mangano family. But his power grew too great for his rivals, including Genovese. Two of Genovese's men followed Albert Anastasia to his barber's shop one morning in 1957. As a warm towel was placed over his face, Anastasia did not see the two gunmen take position behind him. They shot him in the back of the head.

The shoot-outs and revenge assassinations were weakening the organized crime, though. Lansky seems to have disapproved of the dynastic killings. His aim was to weld together the hot-tempered Mafia families into a more 'federal' operation. One associate said of Lansky and

Luciano, 'They were unbeatable. If they had become President and Vice-President of the United States, they would have run the place far better than the idiot politicians.'.

Lansky made millions for the Mafia and it is estimated that he made 300 million dollars for himself. Somehow he had evaded any criminal charges. His main concern as he grew older was to evade the Internal Revenue investigators. At one point he left the USA to live in a hotel in Israel, but the Israeli government was not at all pleased with this arrangement. He eventually returned to spend his last years in the USA.

Genovese was to become Godfather for about a year before being sent to prison in 1959 for drug smuggling. He died of a heart attack after spending ten years in prison.

The third of the trio, Lucky Luciano, was not always lucky. He was tried, convicted and sent to prison for between 30 to 50 years for 90 offences relating to prostitution. That looked like the end of him. Then, in 1942, he got a prison visit from Lansky, who had managed to do a deal with the US naval intelligence. Information about Allied convoys was being leaked by pro-Mussolini Italian migrants working on the waterfront. The spectacular loss of the French liner *Normandie*, set on fire while at anchor in New York harbour, suggested that intelligence was being leaked out and that there were Axis saboteurs in New York. Lansky struck a deal to the effect that the Mafia, under Luciano's direction from prison, would work with a special intelligence unit to flush out

Italian spies and saboteurs. In return, Luciano would be released at the end of the war. Luciano agreed to the deal and must indeed have been very grateful to Lansky for setting it up for him.

Apart from keeping peace and preventing further acts of sabotage on the New York waterfront, the odd alliance of naval intelligence and Mafia co-ordinated by Luciano was responsible for pinpointing an enemy submarine off Long Island. Four German spies were caught as they came ashore from the submarine; under interrogation they revealed a whole North American network of Nazi agents. Before the Allies invaded Sicily, Luciano sent word to the Sicilian Mafia leaders that they must give the Americans every assistance. This collaboration in Italy proved invaluable. In Rome, the Mafia was able to give advance warning of an assassination attempt against General Sir Harold Alexander.

The American authorities kept their part of the bargain. In 1945, when the war in Europe ended, Luciano was released, but he was not to be a free man in America: he was to be deported to Italy. The ever-loyal Lansky was there to see him off, giving him 500,000 dollars to help him start a new life in Rome. But the new life was not stimulating enough, not dangerous enough for Luciano. He pined for the complexity of the New York underworld, and yearned for the bright lights and the power. In Italy he was nobody. He suddenly turned up in Cuba, issuing invitations to the leaders of organized crime in Amercia to meet him in Havana. He was pushing his luck if he thought he could make a come-back. The US government put pressure on President Batista of Cuba to send Luciano back to Italy, and back he went.

Then there were plans to make a film about Salvatore Luciano's life. On 26 January, 1962 he went to Naples airport to meet the American producer, and died of a heart attack in the airport lounge. The three loyal friends – Lansky, Genovese and Lucky Luciano – all died natural deaths, in spite of the lives of incredible violence they had led.

Robert Maxwell
(1923—1991)

ROBERT MAXWELL COMES from a long line of migrant serial criminals who change their identity as they move from one field of operation to another and pose as respectable and trustworthy high-powered businessmen; they go on to commit large-scale white-collar crimes such as embezzlement.

It is a fascinating and dangerous personality type, one that was explored brilliantly by Anthony Trollope in his 1875 novel *The Way We Live Now*, in the semi-fictional character Sebastian Melmot. Though they may not kill, they steal, they cheat and defraud, they bully and disempower the people round them, they ruin countless lives in countless ways in their self-seeking greed. With Maxwell the chief crime, but only one of many, was robbing people of their pensions.

Robert Maxwell was not what he seemed in any way. Even his name was false. He was born on 10 June, 1923, with the name Jan Ludwig (or Ludvic) Hoch, one of seven siblings, in a village called Slatinske Doly in the province of Ruthenia; at the time of Hoch's birth the village was in Czechoslovakia, but after 1945 it was in the Ukraine. His parents, Mechel and Hannah, were

Orthodox Jews. Mechel made a poor living as a cattle dealer, woodcutter and farm labourer.

During the Second World War, Hoch allegedly joined the Czech Resistance, and he certainly made his way to France to escape from the Nazis. His parents were Nazi victims. Exactly which parts of Maxwell's life story are true and which he invented it is still difficult to tell. He later claimed the classic self-made man's 'rags to riches' story, going so far as to say that he did not have a pair of shoes until he was seven.

In May 1940 Hoch arrived in England. Here he assumed the name Leslie Du Maurier and joined the North Staffordshire Regiment. Later he transferred to the Fifth Battalion of the West Surrey Regiment, stationed in Belgium, and changed his name again, to Ian Robert Maxwell.

On 29 January, 1945 he was leading a platoon of soldiers towards Paarlo when he captured a machine-gun post. For this he was awarded the Military Cross and was promoted to Captain. After this he married a French girl, Elisabeth Meynard, in Paris. They had four sons and five daughters; one son and one daughter died in childhood.

It was at the end of the war that Hoch/Du Maurier/Maxwell went into business, publishing academic textbooks and scientific journals and in 1949 founded Pergamon Press. He was keen to be accepted as English but also wanted to become part of the English establishment. He was eventually to set himself up in a manor house. In 1959, as a next step in this direction, he stood for Parliament as Labour candidate for Buckingham.

He was defeated, but won the seat in 1964 and kept it in 1966, losing it again in the 1970 election; he failed to regain it in both the elections in 1974. Being an MP no longer looked like an option.

Meanwhile, in 1971, an American entrepreneur called Saul Steinberg showed interest in buying a subsidiary of Pergamon Press dealing in encyclopaedias. Maxwell inflated the share price to make it appear more profitable by using transactions between Pergamon and his family companies. When Steinberg discovered that he was being tricked in this way he understandably withdrew from the deal. A Department of Trade investigation into the matter resulted in the following damning verdict; 'Notwithstanding Mr Maxwell's acknowledged abilities and energy, he is not in our opinion a person who can be relied upon to exercise proper stewardship of a publicly quoted company.'.

Maxwell was very lucky that the Director of Public Prosecutions decided not to press charges, so he was allowed to recover from this particular scandal. Even so, it is incredible that any businessman could recover a career in business after such comments had been publicly made, yet he did.

Though heavily in debt he was able to buy back Pergamon in 1974. In this way he earned the press nickname 'the Bouncing Czech'. By the time he came to take over the troubled British Printing Corporation in 1980, renaming it Maxwell Communications Corporation, most people had had time to forget the DTI's warning about him. Maxwell had long hoped to be able to take over one of the national newspapers in Britain, but twice lost out to Rupert Murdoch, who successfully took over *The Sun* and *News of the World*. He then got a chance to gain control of the Mirror Group. He borrowed heavily in order to buy Mirror Group Newspapers from Reed International for 113 million pounds in 1984 and later in the 1980s he bought the American publishing house Macmillan. These business ventures were extravagantly over-ambitious, and Maxwell pushed himself deep into debt. As a result in 1991 he floated Mirror Group Newspapers as a public company as a desperate measure to raise cash; the idea was to save the rest of his business empire, which was drifting towards bankruptcy. Maxwell's debts had reached over two billion pounds.

Maxwell's business practices were often questionable, though rarely questioned openly in the press. He was very quick to sue for libel. When the whole story, or what we now think of as the whole story, eventually came out after his death, it became very obvious why he had to silence investigative journalists who wanted to expose his goings-on. Anyone who implied that he was dishonest was sued. A high-profile victim of this aggression was the public-spirited satirical magazine *Private Eye*, whose writers seemed to know far more about Maxwell than they were allowed to print.

On 5 November, 1991, just as his empire was on the point of collapse, Maxwell went missing under very mysterious circumstances from his yacht off the Canary Islands. The boat, the *Lady*

Ghislaine, was named after one of his daughters. His body was found floating in the North Atlantic shortly afterwards and taken for burial on the Mount of Olives in Jerusalem. It has never been established whether Robert Maxwell accidentally fell off his yacht or deliberately committed suicide or was murdered. There was much speculation about what might have happened.

Immediately following Maxwell's death there were eulogies for his business achievements. But just a few days after the funeral, it emerged that in order to keep his companies solvent and to subsidize his own extravagant lifestyle he had stolen hundreds of millions of pounds from his employees' pension funds. Obviously Maxwell himself was unaccountable for this crime, and it is probable that this is why he took his life. His sons Kevin Maxwell and Ian Maxwell were tried for the misuse of Maxwell Group pension fund stocks to assist a faltering Maxwell company and risking pension fund shares to secure a loan for another Maxwell company. This was one of the largest fraud cases in Britain; Maxwell's two sons were both acquitted in 1996.

Once the true state of Maxwell's business empire became known, his long-silent critics gained courage, and his memory was damned by press and public alike for the unscrupulous way in which he had run his businesses. Commentators speculated that his extraordinary behaviour might be partly explained by the extreme deprivation of his childhood.

For a long time before his death at the age of

68, British intelligence officers had suspected that Maxwell was both a rogue and possibly a traitor. One theory was that he was a Soviet agent. One report submitted to the Information Research Department, a covert Foreign Office unit, described Maxwell as 'a thoroughly bad character and almost certainly financed by Russia.'. The report remained secret until its release in 2003. Another theory is that Maxwell was a secret Israeli agent. The generally shady dealings in the east suggest a figure not unlike Harry Lime, the shadowy anti-hero in the novel and film *The Third Man*, who traded across the Cold War iron curtain. But, ultimately, it is as the destroyer of people's pensions that he will be remembered, and hated for, most.

Ronnie Kray
(1933—1995)
and Reggie Kray
(1933—2000)

IN 1969, THE Kray twins were sentenced to serve long prison sentences. The judge, when passing these sentences after listening to the catalogue of their villainies, said wearily, 'In my view society has earned a rest from your activities'. The judge, Mr Justice Melford Stevenson, could not have put it better. The Krays' activities included theft, intimidation, extortion and murder during a Mafia-like reign of terror in the London underworld.

For some reason, they were regarded by many as loveable Cockney 'cheeky chappies', and it was fashionable for well-known singers, comedians, actors and actresses to be seen partying with Ronnie and Reggie Kray. The Krays enjoyed their partying too, and loved being photographed with the rich and famous. They even gave money generously to charities, which allowed the indulgent celebrities to portray them as 'Robin Hood' characters. But loveable they were certainly not. They held the underworld in a vice-like grip and they were feared like few other criminals. They were in many ways like the American gangsters of the '30s, and they had in fact consciously modelled themselves on the American Mafia.

The Kray twins were born on 17 October, 1933 at Hoxton in the East End of London. Ronnie was the elder, Reggie was 45 minutes younger. They had an older brother called Charles. The Krays were of mixed ancestry – Jewish, Irish and Romany. Their father Charles Kray was dealing in old clothes, silver and gold; their mother Violet was just 21. As boys, the Kray twins became known as the Terrible Twins because they loved to fight, first with bare hands, then later with bicycle chains and flick-knives. By the age of 16 they were carrying guns and at 17 they were in court. So far, it is a story of appalling parenting; in a well-run society Charles Kray Sr and Violet Kray would have been brought to book for their children's behaviour. As it is, no blame has ever been directed at the Krays' parents.

At 17, the Kray twins became professional boxers. Shortly after that they were called up for National Service. The Army would seem like the most natural place for the naturally violent, yet the Krays absconded and were briefly imprisoned. They have the distinction of being among the last, if not the very last, criminals to be imprisoned in the Tower of London. Regrettably, their stay there did not end at the executioner's block; they were released on an unsuspecting London to wreak havoc.

Following their dishonourable discharge in 1954, they went straight into the protection racket. If a shopkeeper or club owner wanted no trouble, he had to pay the Krays a weekly retainer. As this easy money came in, the Krays were able to recruit more collectors. They were able to extend their operation to cover much of East and North London. With the money they made, they were able to start their own clubs, one in Knightsbridge, where the shallow rich found the 'rough trade' pair attractive and charming. The Krays were capable of putting on charm and were even known to be loyal.

Ronnie Kray was known as 'the Colonel' and Reggie as 'the Quiet One'. Their home at Vallance Road was called 'Fort Vallance'.

In 1965, Ronnie Kray shot a man in the leg. He was identified in a formal identity parade at a police station, but was able to wriggle out of a charge by claiming he was Reggie. But it did not always work. Later the same year, Ronnie was convicted of stabbing someone with a bayonet during a raid on a rival gang. It was at this time that Ronnie's dangerous instability became evident. In prison he went berserk. He developed fears that someone was trying to have him killed. In the end he was sent to a mental hospital where he was certified insane. It seems likely that of the two, it was Ronnie who was the one with the entrenched criminal personality. Reggie, the slightly weaker and quieter younger brother, was always having to prove himself; he was constantly copying and being pulled along by the more aggressive Ronnie.

Even the detention in mental hospital became a

jape for the twins. Reggie paid his brother a visit
and swapped clothes with him. When Ronnie was
safely out and away, Reggie owned up to the
trick. Ronnie had a few weeks of freedom, during
which he made surprise calls on East End pubs
just to tease the police, who were of course
looking for him. But he was still mentally ill and
the family, who were sheltering him, became
alarmed when he tried to commit suicide and
they thought it best to let the police recapture
him. He was diagnosed as fit for release in 1958.

But Ronnie was still mad. Reggie knew this.
Reggie Kray was developing a good head for
business and while Ronnie was in prison or
hospital the Kray business ventures were thriving.
There was the founding venture, the Double-R
Club in Bow, another club in Stratford and an
illegal gambling club right next to Bow Street
police station. Ronnie's return from prison meant
a return to the bullying and violence that put
businesses like these in danger. Reggie could
really have done without Ronnie's release just
then. In fact separation from Ronnie could have
meant that Reggie would be able to go straight, or
at any rate straighter.

In 1960, it was Reggie's turn to be jailed, for
demanding money with menaces. This gave
Ronnie a free hand at running the businesses.
Ronnie fell in with the notorious slum landlord
Peter Rachman. The deal was that, for a
commission, the Kray gang would act as guards
for Rachman's rent collectors. This brought in
more cash, and another new club was opened,

Esmeralda's Barn; this became a favourite with the entertainers who liked slumming with the new London Mafia. It also became a magnet for young men on the make; it became known that Ronnie was gay.

When Reggie came out of prison in 1961, he fell in love with a 16-year-old girl. Now the lifestyles of the two brothers became markedly different. Ronnie spent more and more time with his new swinging friends up in the West End, while Reggie returned to their home area in the East End. Reggie married, but unfortunately his new young wife could not adjust to the insane gangster world Reggie inhabited and in 1967 she committed suicide.

It may have been the widening gap between the twins' lifestyles, or it may have been the problematic private lives that both were experiencing – whatever the reason, the Krays' regime took a more violent turn in the later '60s, with sadistic knifings, beatings and brandings. A former friend who drunkenly insulted Ronnie was so violently assaulted that his face needed 70 stitches. They were making plenty of enemies now. There were three attempts on their lives.

One cause of the escalating violence was competition from a rival gang, the Richardson gang. Charles Richardson was operating mainly in South London, but trying to extend into the West End. One of Richardson's heavies was a man called George Cornell. He rashly tried to talk down the Krays. In the East End he said, 'Ronnie Kray is a big fat poof and don't take any notice of him. He can't protect you from anything.'. Ronnie was given a tip-off that Cornell would be in a pub called the Blind Beggar in Whitechapel. Ronnie walked into the pub and put a gun to Cornell's head, looked him in the eyes and pulled the trigger. He put the gun in his pocket. The body fell off the stool. Ronnie walked out of the pub. In Ronnie's view, Cornell was vermin. 'He was simply nothing. I done the Earth a favour ridding it of him.'

The Krays were now becoming a liability to the East End. Ronnie's openly homosexual activities and the expansion of the business into pornography and drugs did not really fit in with the East Enders' view of their area. Ronnie had been unstable from way back, but now Reggie was behaving psychotically too, shooting at the legs of people who offended him. Even their rich and famous friends in the West End began to avoid them. Feeling threatened by the contraction of their world, the Krays decided to test their gang's loyalty by carrying out a meaningless and entirely unnecessary murder.

Jack 'The Hat' McVitie owed the Krays 500 pounds and was said to have insulted them in their absence. They were by any normal standards not sufficient reasons to kill anybody, but the Krays were just looking for an excuse to kill. Four members of the Kray gang lured McVitie to a party in a house in Stoke Newington. Ronnie, Reggie and two more heavies lay in wait there. When he arrived, McVitie realised what was in store and tried to escape. Ronnie held him against a wall a said, 'Come on, Jack, be a man.' At the back of much of the Krays' antisocial behaviour lay this Achilles's heel. Deep down, they were insecure about their masculinity. All the fighting, bullying and facing down was to do with proving that they were 'real men'. Given the standards of the day, Ronnie in particular may have felt insecure. 'Come on, Jack, be a man.' Terrible, school playground stuff, but all the more terrible that this was being acted out by middle-aged men on a daily basis – with weapons. McVitie was required to 'die like a man', like a character in an old black-and-white Western. But poor Jack McVitie didn't want to die.

Ronnie led McVitie into a basement room. Reggie pointed a gun at his head and pulled the trigger, but the gun jammed. Ronnie stuck a carving knife into McVitie's back but it did not penetrate the thick coat. McVitie made a valiant attempt to get out of the window, but he was caught by the feet and dragged back. Ronnie held him, screaming at his brother to do the killing. Reggie ineptly stabbed McVitie several times in the throat.

So out of touch with reality were they by this stage, that the twins thought this horrible sadistic fiasco had been a success. The only thing that was successful about it was that they managed to conceal or destroy the body; it has never been found. They were so elated by the crime that they decided to form a 'Murder Incorporated' outfit, along American lines. By now they were being monitored by Detective Superintendent Read ('Nipper' Read) of Scotland Yard. He collected evidence against the Krays as they plotted more absurd and meaningless killings. One of them involved murdering a Maltese club owner by blowing his car up with dynamite. 'Nipper' Read's problem was that he knew witnesses would disappear or have amnesia unless both of the Krays were safely behind bars. Unless he had witnesses, a court case would crumple and the Krays would go free.

A member of the Kray gang was stopped in Glasgow while boarding a plane bound for London. He was found to be carrying four sticks of dynamite, which Read assumed were to be used to kill the Maltese club owner. Further evidence was found at the gang member's home. On the night of 8 May, 1968 the Kray twins went drinking at the Old Horn in Bethnall Green, then to the Astor Club in Berkeley Square, before going on to their mother's flat in Shoreditch at four in the morning. Reggie went to bed with a girlfriend, Ronnie with a boyfriend. Shortly afterwards, Superintendent Read's men swooped and arrested them.

The Kray twins were charged with murdering George Cornwell and Jack McVitie. Eight other gang members, including the older brother Charles Kray were charged with a range of other crimes. They tried a Not Guilty plea, but were found guilty after a trial lasting over a month. They were jailed for life, with the recommendation that they should serve not less than 30 years. They were 35 years old when sentenced. Ronnie and Reggie were sent to two different high-security prisons. For a short time in 1972 they were reunited in Parkhurst Prison on the Isle of Wight. In 1979, Ronnie was once again sectioned and sent to Broadmoor.

In 1987 there was an abortive campaign to have them released.

Reggie Kray found prison hard to cope with. He was graded a Category A prisoner, which means that he was (rightly) regarded as dangerous and likely to try to escape. He was followed all the time by prison officers and he had restricted visits. He was unable to appeal. In desperation, in 1982, he tried cutting his wrists but, characteristically, bungled it. Ronnie, as a Broadmoor inmate, had more privileges. He was able to have visits from gang members and from the following of shallow showbiz celebrities; they brought him hampers from Harrods and classical records. He also had a colour TV. He was free to regale journalists with highly coloured and slanted versions of his criminal career. 'We never hurt ordinary members of the public. We only took money off other villains and gave a bundle of that away to decent people who were on hard times. . . Then people could take ladies into pubs with them without the risk of their being insulted. Old people didn't get mugged either. It couldn't have happened when we were looking after the East End.'

All this nonsense was larded up with sentimentality about their 'dear old Mum'. Violet Kray had been a loyal visitor throughout their time in prison. When she died at 72, the Krays were allowed one day out of prison for Violet's funeral, which turned into a big media event with all the showbiz friends flocking back again. It was said that Violet was the only person who had any control over the Kray twins. It could be said that she and her husband never exerted enough parental control or guidance when they were bringing the boys up.

PART THIRTEEN

EVIL BY DOING NOTHING

Captain Stanley Lord
(1877–1962)

AT 2.20 IN the morning on 15 April, 1912, the greatest ship in the world went to the bottom of the Atlantic Ocean. With her died 1,522 people, some by drowning, many by hypothermia in the freezing water. Seven hundred and five people were saved in the lifeboats, and they were picked up later by the Cunard liner Carpathia after spending four lonely and terrifying hours freezing in the open boats, drifting among ice floes, not knowing whether rescue was on its way. It was a second terrible ordeal. A third ordeal was waiting those four hours or longer to find out whether the rest of the family had been rescued or not. Ever since the official enquiries into the loss of the Titanic, and there were two – one on each side of the Atlantic, it has been accepted that the management of the White Star Line, the ship's owners, were at fault in several ways. There were not enough lifeboats for all the passengers and crew; Captain Smith was taking the ship at 22 knots – far too fast – through seas that were known to be strewn with icebergs; the watertight bulkheads did not rise high enough inside the ship's hull; the crew were not given enough time to familiarize themselves with the layout of the ship; and so on.

But even after the disaster had happened, even after the ship had collided with the iceberg and been fatally damaged, there was one man who could have saved everyone on board – at least everyone except the handful of men in the boiler room who had been killed on impact. One man with the power to save them all.

He was Captain Stanley Lord.

Stanley Lord was born in Bolton in 1877. He went to sea in 1891, serving first in sailing ships. At the age of 23 he gained an extra master's certificate, the highest voluntary qualification that can be had by an officer in the British Mercantile Marine. At the young age of 29 he was taken on by the Leyland Line to be a captain on their passenger cargo liners.

That fateful spring, he was captain of the Leyland Line *Californian*, a 6,000-ton cargo vessel with a licence to carry passengers, bound from London to Boston. On 14 April 1912, the *Californian* was on a similar westward course to the *Titanic* but a little to the north. On encountering sea-ice, Captain Lord wisely stopped his ship until the morning brought a clear view of the hazard. It was at 10.20 p.m. that Lord stopped his ship and told the wireless operator to send out a general ice report. The ship remained stationary in the water until 5.15 the next morning. In the meantime, not very far away, the *Titanic* steamed catastrophically into an iceberg weighing an estimated 500,000 tons, ten times as much as the *Titanic*, and sank with the loss of 1,500 lives. The *Titanic* hit the iceberg at 11.40 p.m. Some time after that, perhaps at midnight, the *Titanic*'s Fourth Officer Boxhall went to the bridge to look at a light ahead; through glasses he saw the two masthead lights of a steamer. Boxhall told Captain Smith about the steamer in the distance and told him that he had sent for some distress rockets to attract her attention. Smith told him to carry on. Obviously transferring the passengers to another ship was their best chance of saving lives. As he sent off the rockets – 'between half a dozen and a dozen' – Boxhall thought the steamer was getting closer. The distress rockets were very distinctive: they were bigger than ordinary firework rockets, white, with a luminous tail, they exploded quite loudly and they produced a shower of white stars. They could not be mistaken for anything other than distress rockets. Boxhall thought the steamer was close enough to read the *Titanic*'s electric Morse signalling lamp, so he signalled, 'Come at once. We are sinking'. Captain Smith also saw the distant steamer. There was no doubt at all that it was there.

Boxhall left the *Titanic* at about 1.45 a.m. in one of the lifeboats and, although he was now right down at sea level instead of perched up on the ship's sinking bridge, he could still see the lights of the steamer, which he estimated must have been only about five miles away. Second Officer Lightoller also saw the lights of the steamer. He also estimated that it was around five or six miles away. Frustratingly, the distant steamer did not respond in any way. No reply by Morse lamp, no rockets, no attempt to come to the *Titanic*'s aid.

At 11 p.m., the officer of the watch on the *Californian* was Third Officer Groves. He saw the lights of an unknown steamer approaching from the east. Captain Lord told him to call her with the Morse lamp, but the steamer did not respond. Lord went into the wireless cabin and asked the wireless operator, Evans, who was very inexperienced, if he had had any communication with any other ships. Evans said he had had the *Titanic*, but from the strength of her signal she was 100 miles away (he thought). Lord told Evans to call the *Titanic* to let her know that the *Californian* was surrounded by ice and stopped. Evans started an inappropriately informal message – 'Say old man we are surrounded by ice and stopped' – but the *Titanic*'s chief operator, Phillips, told him to shut up as he was busy. At 11.30 p.m. Evans listened in to the *Titanic* sending passengers' telegrams to New York. Unfortunately, at 11.35 p.m., which was just five minutes before the collision, Evans stopped eavesdropping and turned in. If he had stayed listening for another ten or 15 minutes he would have picked up the *Titanic*'s first call for help.

At 11.40 p.m. Groves saw that the unknown vessel had stopped and thought he saw the steamer's lights go out. In fact the *Titanic*'s lights stayed on for a surprisingly long time during the sinking, so it may be that once the *Titanic* had stopped powering across the Atlantic her sinking bow section was gradually turned by the current so that at a certain point the crew of the *Californian* were looking at her end on and were no longer able to see the huge array of lights along her side. Lord for some reason decided she was not a passenger steamer. Grove disagreed and said she was. At midnight, Second Officer Stone came on duty as officer of the watch, relieving Groves, and met Lord at the wheelhouse. Lord pointed at the steamer and said she had stopped; he would have thought nothing of this, as he himself had stopped his ship for the night and probably thought the other ship had done the same. Stone observed one mast-head light, a red side-light (which suggests that the *Titanic* was after all not being viewed end-on) and one or two indistinct lights round the deck that looked like portholes. Stone thought she was about five miles away.

At 12.15 a.m., James Gibson, another inexperienced crew member on the *Californian*, arrived on the bridge with coffee. He tried the telegraph, but with no response. Was he actually using the equipment correctly? At 12.45a.m. Stone saw a flash of white in the sky above the mystery steamer and thought it was a shooting star. Then soon afterwards he saw another and realised it was a rocket. In the next half hour he watched three more of these rockets, all of them white. He had the impression they were coming from beyond the steamer.

At 1.15 a.m. Stone whistled down the speaking tube to Captain Lord. Stone told Lord about the rockets. Lord told Stone to call the steamer on the Morse lamp and try to find out more: 'When you get an answer let me know by Gibson'. Gibson and Stone watched as the *Titanic* in desperation sent up three more rockets. They also noticed that the steamer was apparently steaming away to the southwest. In fact she wasn't: she was sinking. By 2 a.m. Stone thought the steamer was moving away from them rapidly. She was now showing only her stern light and one masthead light. In fact what was happening was that the *Titanic* had sunk to the point where the front half of the ship was under the water and the stern was coming up out of the water.

Gibson was sent down to tell Captain Lord that he and Stone had seen eight rockets and that the steamer was moving out of sight. Lord said, 'All right. Are you sure there were no colours in them?'. Gibson confirmed that they were all white. In other words there was no doubt that they were distress rockets. At 2.45 a.m. Stone again whistled down the tube to tell Lord that they couldn't see the lights any more and the ship had gone. It had in fact sunk 25 minutes earlier. Captain Lord's sleep would be disturbed no more by the *Titanic* – not that night, anyway.

At 4 a.m. Chief Officer Stewart arrived on the *Californian*'s bridge to relieve Stone. Stone told him of the events of his watch. Stewart first woke up Captain Lord, then Evans the wireless operator, to find out what was going on. Stewart seems to have been the first officer on the *Californian* to realise the gravity of the situation and to have the courage to wake and challenge the captain. Evans picked up a telegraph message from a Canadian Pacific liner, saying that the *Titanic* had struck an iceberg and was sinking. Meanwhile, the Cunard passenger liner *Carpathia* had picked up the *Titanic*'s distress calls and had been steaming at full speed for a couple of hours through the icefield towards the *Titanic*'s last position.

Captain Rostron of the *Carpathia* had acted exactly as we would all expect a ship's captain to act; he dropped everything, changed course and without regard for anything else at all he raced to the scene of the disaster to offer help. He was the opposite of Captain Lord, who had ample evidence that a ship nearby was in deep trouble and did nothing whatever to help – and he was close enough to have saved everyone. Several witnesses on the *Titanic* and the *Californian* put the distance between the two ships as five miles. The icy night air was unusually clear and it may be that they were deceived. Maybe the distance was greater, but still between five and ten miles. The *Californian* could have been on the scene of the disaster within half an hour, well before the *Titanic* sank, and taken all the crew and passengers safely on board. Captain Rostron would have done his bit, but Captain Lord would have been the hero of the hour.

As it was, the *Carpathia* arrived at the scene of the sinking far too late to save any of those in the water, but rescued those in the lifeboats. The *Californian* spent between 8 a.m. and 9 a.m. in the area looking for bodies, having (significantly) been asked to do so directly by Captain Rostron. But even Lord's search for bodies was desultory. After 9 a.m., the *Californian* resumed her voyage to Boston.

News of the sinking of the *Titanic* dominated the newspapers in England and America for the next few days. On 18 April, the *Carpathia* arrived in New York harbour with the survivors, to be greeted by chaotic, grief-stricken crowds. On the same day the *Californian* docked in Boston met by nobody. One or two newspapers began latching onto the *Californian*'s proximity to the scene of the disaster. The figure of five miles was quoted. Lord appears to have tried to protect himself by giving a figure nearer 20 miles. Then a *Californian* crew member gave an interview in which he confirmed that the *Titanic*'s distress rockets had been seen from the deck of the *Californian*. Ernest Gill said that he had seen, about ten miles away, 'a big vessel going along at full speed. She looked as if she might be a big German'. This describes the *Titanic* very well. She was similar in size to the big prestige German liners of the day, and Captain Smith was, as notoriously emerged during the official enquiries, taking her at full speed – probably around 22 knots – through the dangerous icefield. Gill was adamant that the *Titanic* must have been closer than the 20 miles claimed by some of his officers, since he could not have seen her at 20 miles and he saw her plainly.

Gill's statement to the press seemed watertight. As he himself said, he was losing a good berth by making the statement, putting himself out of a job, but 'no captain who refuses or neglects to give aid to a vessel in distress should be able to hush up the men.'. Unfortunately it then emerged that Gill had been paid 500 dollars for his story, more than a year's wages, and certainly a large enough sum to tempt him to bend the truth. It was also worrying that he claimed to have seen the *Titanic* steaming along at full speed at 11.56 p.m., which was 16 minutes after she hit the iceberg, and that couldn't be right. Even so, Gill stuck to his story at both the American and the British enquiries, whereas Captain Lord changed his story and was far from direct in his answers to questions.

Lord's defence – it became just that – was that the vessel seen from the *Californian* was not the *Titanic* and the vessel seen from the *Titanic* was not the *Californian*. But in spite of extensive enquiries in 1912 and in subsequent years, no evidence emerged of any third ship in the area at the right time. Neither the US Senate enquiry nor the British Board of Trade enquiry could find a third vessel. The conclusion is inescapable. The big ship that Lord and his officers watched, perhaps seven miles away, setting off eight distress rockets and then disappearing can only have been the *Titanic*. The stationary or gradually moving small steamer seen by the officers of the *Titanic* and failing to respond to their desperate pleas for help by rocket and Morse lamp can only have been the *Californian*.

At the enquiries, attempts were made to pinpoint the two ships' positions. Captain Lord gave the *Californian*'s position at the crucial moment as 42 degrees 5 minutes N, 50 degrees 7 minutes W. The *Titanic*'s final position was 41 degrees 46 minutes N, 50 degrees 14 minutes W. But the French attempt to find the wreck at this location failed, and Robert Ballard's discovery of the wreck at a different location implies that the 1912 calculations of position were not accurate. If the *Titanic*'s officers gave their ship's position incorrectly when their lives depended on being found quickly, how dependable would Lord's calculation of the *Californian*'s position have been? There were enough witnesses, though, from both ships for it to be fairly certain that the two ships were more than 5 miles apart, but less than 10 miles.

At the British Board of Trade enquiry, Lord Mersey summed the situation up. 'The truth of the matter is plain. The *Titanic* collided with the berg at 11.40. The vessel seen by the *Californian* stopped at this time. The rockets sent up from the *Titanic* were distress signals. The number sent up by the *Titanic* was about eight. The *Californian* saw eight. The time over which the rockets from the *Titanic* were sent up was from about 12.45 to 1.45. It was about this time that the *Californian* saw the rockets. At 2.40 Mr Stone called to the Master that the ship from which he had seen the rockets had disappeared. At 2.20 the *Titanic* had foundered. It was suggested that the rockets seen by the *Californian* were from some other ship not the *Titanic*. But no other ship to fit this theory has ever been heard of.'

These circumstances convinced Lord Mersey that the ship seen by the *Californian* was indeed the *Titanic* and that the two vessels were only five miles apart; he was assuming that the coordinates given by Lord were correct. 'The ice by which the *Californian* was surrounded was loose ice extending for a distance of not more than two or three miles in the direction of the *Titanic*. The night was clear and the sea was smooth. When she first saw the rockets the *Californian* could have pushed through the ice to the open water without any serious risk and so have come to the assistance of the *Titanic*.'

There were other, suspicious circumstances surrounding Lord's evidence. Captain Lord's 'scrap' log, the rough copy from which the fair log was later made, had been destroyed. Why was that? Why did the fair log make no mention of the rockets? After abandoning the search for bodies and turning to head for Boston, Captain Lord told Stone and Gibson to make written statements about what they had seen and done between midnight and 4 a.m. Both of these statements make it clear that they were written under some duress, in that they both open with covering remarks to indicate that the statements were Lord's idea. There are no discrepancies whatever between the two statements, even though they were made three days after the disaster; they were evidently harmonized, if not actually dictated, by the captain. The preparation of the documents and the 'loss' of the scrap log strongly suggest that Captain Lord knew he was going to be called to account for his inaction. Lord claimed under cross-examination that he had no recollection of Gibson's visit to his cabin, no recollection of asking about the colours of the rockets. Why would he have asked about the colour of the rockets? 'I really do not know what was the object of my question,' he said under cross-examination. It was obvious why he asked. It was not a random question asked by someone not fully awake. The significance of the colour was that a white rocket was a distress rocket. He was told that the rockets were white and he was unwilling to admit that he knew all the information he needed to know to justify starting the *Californian*'s engines and steaming cautiously towards the rockets.

Captain Lord was by contemporary agreement one of the worst witnesses to give evidence, uninformative, evasive, unconvincing. His career as a ship's master should have ended there and then. Given the damning verdicts of both American and British enquiries, Lord was forced to resign from the Leyland Line. Yet somehow he managed to continue his career at sea. Surprisingly, he was soon employed by Lowther, Latta and Co to skipper nitrates cargo ships. He retired from the sea in 1927, without any further incident. Captain Stanley Lord did not behave like a man who felt any guilt through negligence. He instead behaved like a man who had been hard done by. In August 1912 he was writing to the Board of Trade to put them right on some facts. He emphasized that he had given his position that fateful night before he had any knowledge of the *Titanic*'s final position and that that was 17 miles away from the *Titanic*. He also pointed out that Boxhall observed the unidentified ship approaching the *Titanic* between one and two in the morning, whereas the *Californian* was stationary. He added that when the *Carpathia* arrived at the scene of the sinking at dawn (4.30 a.m.) Captain Rostron saw two steamers in the area, neither of which was the *Californian*. The *Californian* was still stationary at that time and had therefore not been in the vicinity of the sinking.

These were good points, but not entirely convincing. As we have already seen, the calculated positions are not 100 per cent reliable. It is also the case that the area was the meeting place of two powerful currents, the Labrador Current (which had been responsible for delivering the iceberg and the rest of the sea-ice) and the Gulf Stream. Even if the *Californian* was stationary in the water, the water itself was gradually moving along – and the ship with it. From the moment when the *Titanic* stopped, at 11.40, she too would have been moved around by the currents. This is probably why the wreck lies a long way from the last calculated position. Boxhall's observation that the *Californian* was getting closer was probably nothing more than wishful thinking. They had signalled to the *Californian* that they needed help, therefore she must be coming to help. Ignoring their call for help was unthinkable. She must be coming.

In his letter, which is very revealing in being a compilation of answers to questions Lord wished he had been asked at the enquiry, he makes some misguided points about the *Titanic*'s bearing from the *Californian*. 'At 2.00 a.m. the steamer we had in sight at 11.30 p.m. had altered her bearing from

SSE to SW (to do this she must have steamed at least 8 miles, the *Titanic* did not move after midnight) and had fired 8 rockets and was then out of sight.'

This argument is pure folly and can be disproved by simple trigonometry. We can assume for the moment that the *Californian* and the *Titanic* were seven miles apart at the time of the sinking; that seems the likeliest distance. When the *Titanic* was observed in the SSE at 11.30, she was still steaming westwards at about 20 m.p.h. She did not hit the iceberg for another ten minutes, giving her another three miles of westward travel. Although immediately after the collision the engines were shut down, the *Titanic* would have continued under momentum – she weighed 60,000 tons (her displacement weight) – for at least a further mile before stopping. That would have put her to the southwest of the *Californian* and only two miles from the position Captain Lord gives, which is just over six miles from the 11.30 position rather than the eight miles he states. The two-mile discrepancy can easily be accounted for by the 'stationary' *Californian* drifting two miles eastward with the Gulf Stream. At 2 a.m., according to the evidence of his own officers, the *Titanic* was not out of sight at all. She was still visible from the *Californian* but 'steaming away'. It was not until 2.45 that the *Titanic* was reported as having finally disappeared. Ironically, Captain Lord's additional evidence and argument, including poor mapwork, poor calculation and misrepresentation of his own officers' evidence, only ensnare and incriminate him more deeply.

Boxhall, when pressed under cross-examination, thought the *Californian*, or whatever ship it was that came within five miles of the *Titanic*, had eventually moved away to the west ('I should say it was westerly'). But in the darkness, Boxhall's obvious frame of reference was the *Titanic* herself, and it seems from the orientation of the wreck that the ship very slowly rotated in the water, which may have temporarily disorientated the officers until the ship finally sank. If Boxhall's 'westerly' only means that the *Californian* seemed to move in the direction the *Titanic*'s bows were pointing, it could mean that Boxhall was actually seeing the *Californian* moving eastwards – or indeed not really moving at all.

Both the British Board of Trade enquiry and the US Senate enquiry condemned Captain Lord's behaviour. Both concluded that, 'She [the *Californian*] might have saved many if not all of the lives lost'. The *Californian*'s stand-off was highlighted in Walter Lord's book *A Night to Remember* and also in the film of the same name. The film's scenes on the bridge of the *Californian*, as the *Titanic*'s distress rockets go up one after another, are persuasively re-created and agonizing to watch: the apathy, the officers' curious refusal to believe the evidence of their own eyes, Captain Lord's determination to turn in and get some undisturbed sleep. Stanley Lord was still alive in the 1950s when the film was released and he thought he was being libelled. He wanted the Mercantile Marine Service Association to take legal action on his behalf, but the organization decided to issue statements in Lord's support instead, not least (they said) because of Lord's age and infirmity.

Lord died in the 1960s, still with many supporters. They have done much with discrepancies in times of various events, such as the firing of rockets. But it is all to no avail. The officers and crew of the *Californian* admitted that they did watch a series of eight distress rockets fired by a big unidentified steamer. How many big steamers were there in that area of the North Atlantic letting off eight distress rockets at around midnight on 14 April 1912? Only the *Titanic*. Captain Lord knew full well what a white rocket meant and he knew full well that a ship letting off eight white rockets meant a ship in serious trouble. He decided to do nothing because that was easier. Perhaps he assumed someone else would help instead. Perhaps he assumed his presence on or near the scene would remain undetected. How could he have known that the greatest marine disaster of all time was taking place in full view of his ship, and that every factual detail about what everybody did that night would be gone over again and again for decades? The fact is that he failed in his duty as a human being in not troubling to find out. He went to bed. He stayed in his cabin from 12.40 until 4.30 in the morning - not wanting to know. He was the Bad Samaritan. His mid-watch officers seem to have been similarly apathetic.

His defenders have argued that he was looking

after the safety of his ship by remaining stationary, but he got his ship moving first thing in the morning. Nor did he behave like a man with an entirely clear conscience during the two or three days after the sinking. It can only have been from motives of self-protection that he obliged Gibson and Stone to write down their (identical) accounts of what had happened - and they sensed that too. When he was questioned he prevaricated, which was not only dishonourable but foolish as the rest of his crew, including Gill, knew what had happened, or more to the point what had not happened that night. Captain Lord had not taken his ship to the aid of the passengers and crew of the *Titanic*.

There are many different kinds of evil in the world. In some ways this kind of evil – evil by doing nothing — is the most insidious and widespread. People do it all the time. Seeing something happening and doing nothing about it. Seeing a crime being committed and not reporting it. Seeing someone being bullied and not intervening. Seeing people in desperate need of help and not helping. Often the incident is blotted out: we make an excuse for ourselves – we were too busy, perhaps, or too tired – and maintain a comfortable feeling of balanced self-righteousness. Captain Stanley Lord probably persuaded himself that he was not to blame, that it was somehow some other ship that was involved. A third ship. The mysterious third ship that nobody can identify. But did he successfully blot out, for the rest of his long life, the knowledge that he had committed a profoundly evil act in leaving all those people to die in the cold waters of the North Atlantic? Did it ever occur to him in later years that if he had taken appropriate action, just taken his ship five or seven miles to the south, there would have been no *Titanic* disaster at all? Or was the responsibility too much to bear?